# Representing Australian Aboriginal Music and Dance 1930–1970

# Representing Australian Aboriginal Music and Dance 1930–1970

Amanda Harris

with contributions from Shannon Foster,
Tiriki Onus and Nardi Simpson

BLOOMSBURY ACADEMIC
NEW YORK • LONDON • OXFORD • NEW DELHI • SYDNEY

BLOOMSBURY ACADEMIC
Bloomsbury Publishing Inc
1385 Broadway, New York, NY 10018, USA
50 Bedford Square, London, WC1B 3DP, UK
29 Earlsfort Terrace, Dublin 2, Ireland

BLOOMSBURY, BLOOMSBURY ACADEMIC and the Diana logo are trademarks of Bloomsbury Publishing Plc

First published in the United States of America 2020
This paperback edition published in 2022

Copyright © Amanda Harris, 2020

Cover design: Louise Dugdale
Cover image: George Winunguj plays his didjeridu with David Cubbin, Jiri Tancibudek, Thomas Wightman, Patrick Brislan, Gabor Reeves of the Adelaide Wind Quintet, 1972. Photograph by Michael Jensen from collection of the Australian Information Service via the National Library of Australia, http://nla.gov.au/nla.obj-137007301. Reproduced with permission of Winunguj's descendants David, Rupert and Renfred Manmurulu.

All rights reserved. No part of this publication may be reproduced or transmitted in any form or by any means, electronic or mechanical, including photocopying, recording, or any information storage or retrieval system, without prior permission in writing from the publishers.

Bloomsbury Publishing Inc does not have any control over, or responsibility for, any third-party websites referred to or in this book. All internet addresses given in this book were correct at the time of going to press. The author and publisher regret any inconvenience caused if addresses have changed or sites have ceased to exist, but can accept no responsibility for any such changes.

Whilst every effort has been made to locate copyright holders the publishers would be grateful to hear from any person(s) not here acknowledged.

Library of Congress Cataloging-in-Publication Data
Names: Harris, Amanda, 1976- author. | Foster, Shannon, contributor. | Onus, Tiriki, contributor. | Simpson, Nardi, contributor.
Title: Representing Australian Aboriginal music and dance 1930–1970 / Amanda Harris, with contributions from Shannon Foster, Tiriki Onus and Nardi Simpson.
Description: New York : Bloomsbury Academic, 2020. | Includes bibliographical references and index. | Summary: "A new Australian music history seeking to understand disruption and continuation of Aboriginal music and dance and its representation in non-Indigenous performances." Provided by publisher.
Identifiers: LCCN 2020009264 | ISBN 9781501362934 (hardback) | ISBN 9781501362958 (pdf) | ISBN 9781501362941 (ebook)
Subjects: LCSH: Aboriginal Australians–Music–History and criticism. | Dance, Aboriginal Australian–History. | Music–Australia–20th century–History and criticism.
Classification: LCC ML3770 .H27 2020 | DDC 780.8999/15–dc23
LC record available at https://lccn.loc.gov/2020009264

| ISBN: | HB: | 978-1-5013-6293-4 |
|---|---|---|
| | PB: | 978-1-5013-7383-1 |
| | ePDF: | 978-1-5013-6295-8 |
| | eBook: | 978-1-5013-6294-1 |

Typeset by Integra Software Services Pvt. Ltd.

To find out more about our authors and books visit www.bloomsbury.com and sign up for our newsletters.

# Contents

| | |
|---|---|
| Warning | vi |
| List of Figures | vii |
| Notes on Contributors | ix |
| Acknowledgements | xi |
| List of Abbreviations | xiii |
| | |
| 1  Staging assimilation: Too many John Antills? | 1 |
|     *Prelude, Mungari Buldyan – Song for my grandfather* by Shannon Foster | 15 |
| 2  1930s – Performing cultures: Navigating protection, responding to assimilation | 25 |
| 3  1940s – Reclaiming an Indigenous identity | 45 |
| 4  1950s – Jubilee celebrations, protest and national cultural institutions | 63 |
|     *Interlude* by Tiriki Onus | 85 |
| 5  1960–1967 – Aboriginal performance takes the main stage | 93 |
| 6  1967–1970 – The end of assimilation? | 113 |
| 7  Disciplining music: Too many Peter Sculthorpes? | 131 |
|     *Coda* by Nardi Simpson | 149 |
| | |
| Notes | 154 |
| Bibliography | 202 |
| Index | 223 |

# Warning

Aboriginal and Torres Strait Islander people are warned that this book reproduces the names and photographs of people who have died.

# Figures

1.1 Fred Foster (left) and Tom Foster (right) with journalists, 1930, photo courtesy of John Foster — 17

2.1 'Aborigines' Gunyah at Bushland Exhibition', *The Sydney Morning Herald*, 12 September 1933, 12. http://nla.gov.au/nla.news-article17006273 — 26

2.2 Hood, Sam. *Aboriginals and Their Gum Leaf Band Pass the Dais*, 20 March 1932, Home and Away – 2136, 44240, State Library of NSW, Sydney — 28

2.3 Hood, Sam. *Float of First Garrison and Aborigines Pass the Dais*, 20 March 1932, Home and Away – 5294, 9994, State Library of NSW, Sydney — 29

2.4 Still from *In the Days of Captain Cook*, Rockdale Council, 1930. Title no. 45395, National Film and Sound Archive, Canberra. Tom Foster is pictured at centre looking directly at the camera — 31

2.5 'Aborigines Dance in Park', *The Sun*, 19 January 1938, 3 — 35

3.1 Ted Shawn dances for the natives at Delissaville native settlement, NT, 1947, John K. Ewers collection of photographs; BA1658/5/28,31, 428–9, 109612PD, State Library of Western Australia — 46

3.2 Mosek (centre) dances in tourist corroboree in Darwin Botanic Gardens, 1948, still from film *Doorway to Australia*, 1949, National Film Board, courtesy of NT Archives, NTRS 3543 — 47

3.3 Mt Margaret Mission Band in Melbourne, February 1947, photo taken by *The Herald Melbourne* and published 14 February 1947, BA1340/Era4/53A2, State Library of Western Australia. Back: Bundathunoo Fred Carey, gum leaf; Ningan Malcolm McDonald, drum; May Miller (O'Brien), tambourine; Ben Mason, banjo-mandolin. Centre: Bitha Joy Earle, tambourine; Stanley Evans, gum leaf; Front: Jessie Jones (Evans), ukulele; Laurel Nganyun Johnston (Cooper); ukulele; Dan Harris, kettledrum; Amy Waylee Arnold (Brownley), piano-accordion; Lois Thomas, banjo-mandolin; Sadie Corner (Canning), banjo-mandolin — 50

3.4 'Aborigines Seek to Regain Their Tribal Culture', *Examiner*, 12 August 1946, 1 — 51

3.5 'Aborigines Prepare for Corroboree', *Daily Advertiser*, 23 April 1948, 1 — 53

3.6　Photograph of Margaret Sutherland at the Piano with Harold Blair and a Number of Children, Records of the Australian Musical Association, 1952–95, 1940s, Envelope S, National Library of Australia, Canberra　55

5.1　Jimmy Little Snr and A. McLeod playing gum leaves accompanied by Margaret Williams at NADOC concert in Martin Place, Sydney, *Dawn*, July 1961, 3　96

5.2　Djoli Laiwanga, David Blanasi and a third man in programme: 'Pageant of Asia Spectacular', Sydney 1965, National Library of Australia　104

5.3　Still from *Pageant of Nationhood: Australia's 175th Anniversary: New South Wales Celebration*. From National Film and Sound Archive, Canberra. Title no. 56886　108

6.1　Bundjalung performers Herb Charles, Cecil Taylor and Rory Close performing in Casino, NSW in 1968. Photo printed in *Dawn*, January–March 1969, 12　120

6.2　Aboriginal Theatre Foundation Performers in Osaka, 1970. Dhambuljawa Burarrwanga, Rrikin Burarrwanga, Mulun Yunupingu, Wulurrk Manunggurr, Banambi Wunungmurra, Justin Puruntatameri, Max Kerinaiua, Henry Kerinaiua, David Gulpilil, Dick Budalil, Talbert Jalkarara, Djoli Laiwanga, David Blanasi, Felix Wambunyi, Lawrence Biellum. International Exhibition Expo 70 Osaka Japan – Aboriginal Dance Ensemble F1, 1968/3396, National Archives of Australia, Darwin　121

# Contributors

**Amanda Harris** is a Senior Research Fellow at Sydney Conservatorium of Music, University of Sydney, Australia, and Director of the Sydney Unit of digital archive PARADISEC (Pacific and Regional Archive for Digital Sources in Endangered Cultures). Amanda is interested in hearing the voices of those often excluded from conventional music histories through research focused on gender and intercultural musical cultures. She is editor of *Circulating Cultures: Exchanges of Australian Indigenous Music, Dance and Media* (2014) and co-editor of *Research, Records and Responsibility* (2015) and *Expeditionary Anthropology* (2018).

**Shannon Foster** is a Sydney D'harawal saltwater knowledge keeper, artist and interdisciplinary creative practitioner who has been teaching her people's stories for over twenty years to a range of audiences in prominent learning institutions. Throughout her career Shannon has noticed a large gap in site-specific, Sydney-based Aboriginal knowledge, not just in education but also in the wider Australian community. Shannon addresses this discrepancy through her doctoral research as she documents the stories and knowledges of her family – the D'harawal people of the Sydney region. Shannon comes from a long line of notable Sydney Aboriginal people including activists and performers Tom and Eliza Foster, La Perouse snake man and performer Fred Foster, and Aboriginal Liaison Officer and artist John Foster. It is on their shoulders that she stands as she shares her family's stories and knowledges for a continued connection to culture for future generations.

**Tiriki Onus** is a Yorta Yorta man and head of the Wilin Centre for Indigenous Arts and Cultural Development, University of Melbourne. He is a successful visual artist, curator, performance artist and opera singer. His first operatic role was in the premiere of Deborah Cheetham's *Pecan Summer* in October 2010, which he reprised in 2011 and 2012 for the Melbourne and Perth runs. He received the Dame Nellie Melba Opera Trust's Harold Blair Opera Scholarship in 2012 and 2013. In 2015 he was the inaugural Hutchinson Indigenous Fellow at the University of Melbourne.

**Nardi Simpson** is a Yuwaalaraay writer, musician and performer from NSW's north-west freshwater plains. As a member of Indigenous duo Stiff Gins, Nardi has travelled nationally and internationally for the past twenty years, performing in the United States, United Kingdom, Ireland, Canada, Vietnam and the Pacific Islands. Most recently she is a recipient of the 2018 Australia Council Signature Works Initiative where she will develop a series of sound works that explore 'The Sound of Contested Space' and is the recipient of the 2018 Black&Write! Indigenous Writers Fellowship with the State Library of Queensland where she is currently editing her debut novel, *Song of the Crocodile*. Nardi is also a Gamilaraay language teacher and cultural consultant heavily involved in the teaching and sharing of culture in both her Sydney and Yuwaalaraay communities and is the musical director of Barayagal, a cross-cultural choir of Indigenous and non-Indigenous singers to be run out of the Sydney Conservatorium of Music in 2019.

# Acknowledgements

I acknowledge that this book has been dreamt up, researched, written and reworked on Aboriginal land. I pay my respects to Elders past, present and future of the Eora, Dharawal, Gadigal, Dharug and Yuin peoples. I acknowledge the traditional owners of the Larrakia, Ngunnawal, Ngambri, Ngarigu, Wurundjeri lands on which research for this book has been carried out. My approaches to research and my growing understanding of the importance of listening closely to Indigenous perspectives, experiences and suggestions for ways forward has inflected the account given in this book. No scholarly (or any) work can be beyond reproach, nor should it. There may be ways in which I have interpreted the sources I have used that impose a white/European/non-Indigenous viewpoint on Aboriginal stories, even if I have tried to listen to those stories wherever I could find them. If I have done this, I hope someone will correct the record.

So many collaborators, advisors, friends and colleagues have enriched my thinking and practical endeavours, and given intellectual and emotional sustenance to the research and writing of this book. I am grateful to readers of earlier drafts of the chapters and the insights they have generously offered, many of which have been central to shaping the book's approach. Thank you to members of the Colonial and Settler Studies Network at the University of Wollongong, especially Claire Lowrie, Claire Wright, Frances Steel, Julia Martinez and Simon Ville, to members of the Sydney Conservatorium of Music work-in-progress group Chris Coady, Toby Martin, Isabel O'Keeffe and to readers Victoria Haskins, Linda Barwick, Joseph Toltz, Matt Poll, Jane Carey, Ben Silverstein, Louisa Smith, Nardi Simpson, as well as anonymous reviewers who offered their comments through Bloomsbury Publishing and on journal articles that have developed different aspects of this work. Thank you to Bloomsbury's responsive and expert editorial team, in particular Leah Babb-Rosenfeld, Amy Martin and Sarah McNamee, and to Andrew Devine for copy-editing. Linda Barwick has been such a generous, consistent and inspiring mentor throughout my career that most things I do have been influenced in some way by her mentorship. I'm also grateful to have been able to participate in Joy Damousi's mentoring programme during the writing of this book.

In development of the research, my thinking has benefited from rich and provocative conversations with Tiriki Onus, Shannon Foster, Nardi Simpson, Louisa Smith, Dorottya Fabian, Ian McLean, Chris Sainsbury, Reuben Brown, Georgine Clarsen, Rachel Fensham, Sally Treloyn, Lauren Booker, Jodie Kell, Georgia Curran, Allan Marett, Isobelle Barrett Meyering, Rachel Orzech, Jessica Hodgens, Lisa Slater, Amanda Card, Margaret Harris, Lee Wallace and Jo Harris. Thanks to a range of archivists, librarians and scholarly colleagues who have pointed me towards valuable sources. Robyn Holmes, Beth Mansfield, Margy Burn, Andrew Sergeant, Catriona Anderson, Damien Cole, Kate Boesen, Duncan Felton, Michael Herlihy and Shannon Sutton, all members of the exceptional staff of the National Library of Australia, contributed their expertise during my fellowship there. Thanks also to Mitchell Librarian Richard Neville, librarians of the Conservatorium Library Ludwig Sugiri, Marie Chellos and John Wu, Valerie Ng of the Sydney Opera House archives, Judith Paterson of the National Archives of Australia, Collette Hoeben of the ABC Archives, New Theatre archivist Lyn Collingwood, Charlotte Craw, Blake Singley and Grace Koch of AIATSIS, Mark Crocombe, Jordan Ashley and Colin Worumbu Ferguson of the Kanamkek Yile-Ngala Museum, Wadeye, Suzanne Young of the Northern Territory Library.

For permission to make copies of Warlpiri films for the community, for access to additional papers and audiovisual materials and for sharing memories about Beth Dean and Victor Carell, thanks to Kate Conti. For hints towards sources, thanks to Rachel Campbell, George Dreyfus and Vincent Plush. For research assistance, editing and tracking down of interesting images the wonderful Aurora interns Ash Johnstone and Zephyr Pavey, PARADISEC staff Prash Krishnan and colleagues Genevieve Campbell and Isabel O'Keeffe. Thank you to collaborators who are continuing to develop these ideas in new directions on the Australian Research Council project 'Reclaiming Performance Under Assimilation in Southeast Australia, 1935–75', Linda Barwick, Jakelin Troy, Matt Poll, Rachel Fensham, Tiriki Onus, Lyndon Ormond-Parker and Jacqueline Shea Murphy. Thanks also to participants in our community workshops and symposia who gave so generously of their creative talents, cultural and historical knowledge, Nerida Blair, Lou Bennett, Carole Johnson, Jacinta Tobin, Anna Haebich, Tim Bishop, Luke Forbes, Jonathon Potskin, Jo Paterson Kinniburgh, Lisa Haldane, Sharon Huebner, Peter Waples-Crowe, Cameron Davison, Adnan Bhatti and Kevin Hunt. For talking with me about events that they remember and that concern their families, thanks to Dorothy Blair, Lynne Thomas and Bill Gray.

To Payi Linda Ford, thank you for spending time watching old footage with relatives in Bagot, One-Mile and Palmerstone and for conversations about what it meant to see those old people dancing and singing and sharing culture with the wider public. And for hospitality and shared meals in Darwin to other members of Payi's family Emily, Chloe and Mark Ford, thank you. Thanks to the Tiwi Strong Women group members Francis Orsto, Frances Therese Portaminni, Augusta Puangatji, Regina Kantilla, Anthea Kerinaiua, Jacinta Tipungwuti and Gregoriana Parker, who watched footage and allowed me to experience how the room changes when dancing and singing ancestors appear on the screen. Thanks to Warlpiri men Harry Jagamara Nelson, Otto Jungarrayi Simms, Rex Japanangka Granites and Simon Japangardi Fisher for discussing with me Victor Carell's films of Warlpiri people. To Jane Horton, Raj Reddy, Maggie Sutcliffe and Rachel Tokley, thank you for many nights in your spare rooms in Canberra.

To deep friendships that support and balance me and for getting me out in the ocean, bush and fresh air now and then, thanks to Louisa Smith, Morag Mirankar, Vita Christie, Tanya Nash, Michael Malone, Georgie Pike and Evan Wills and the ever-thoughtful regular book group members Shooshi Dreyfus, Susan Collings and Sarah Hamylton. To the enduring support of my family Chris, Kathy, Nat and Roxy Harris and Myke McQuaid. To my little love Avril, thanks for keeping life joyful.

# Abbreviations

| | |
|---|---|
| AANSW | Aboriginal Affairs NSW |
| AAL | Australian Aborigines' League |
| ABC | Australian Broadcasting Commission |
| ACA | Arts Council of Australia |
| ACT | Australian Capital Territory |
| AETT | Australian Elizabethan Theatre Trust |
| AIAS | Australian Institute of Aboriginal Studies |
| AIATSIS | Australian Institute of Aboriginal and Torres Strait Islander Studies |
| AIDT | Aboriginal Islander Dance Theatre |
| APA | Aborigines Progressive Association |
| APB | Aborigines Protection Board (NSW) |
| APRA | Australian Performing Rights Association |
| ARA | Arafura Research Archive (Charles Darwin University) |
| ARC | Australian Research Council |
| ASIO | Australian Security Intelligence Organisation |
| ATF | Aboriginal Theatre Foundation |
| AWB | Aborigines Welfare Board |
| BPA | Board for the Protection of Aborigines (Victoria) |
| CEMA | Council for the Encouragement of Music and the Arts |
| CINAT | Cook Islands National Arts Theatre |
| FCAATSI | Federal Council for the Advancement of Aborigines and Torres Strait Islanders |
| MP | Member of Parliament |
| NAA | National Archives of Australia |
| NADOC | National Aborigines Day Observance Committee |
| NAIDOC | National Aborigines and Islanders Day Observance Committee |
| NAISDA | National Aboriginal Islander Skills Development Association |
| NAWU | North Australian Workers' Union |
| NBC | National Broadcasting Company (USA) |
| NFSA | National Film and Sound Archive |
| NIDA | National Institute for Dramatic Arts |
| NLA | National Library of Australia, Canberra |
| NMA | National Museum of Australia, Canberra |
| NSW | New South Wales |
| NT | Northern Territory |
| NTA | Northern Territory Archives |
| PARADISEC | Pacific and Regional Archive for Digital Sources in Endangered Cultures |

| | |
|---|---|
| PNG | Papua New Guinea |
| QLD | Queensland |
| RAS | Royal Agricultural Show |
| RL | Rangers' League (Sydney, NSW) |
| SLNSW | State Library of New South Wales |
| SLSA | State Library of South Australia |
| SLWA | State Library of Western Australia |
| SMH | Sydney Morning Herald |
| SRNSW | State Records of NSW |
| SSO | Sydney Symphony Orchestra |
| UK | United Kingdom |
| US/USA | United States of America |
| VCA | Victorian College of the Arts |
| WA | Western Australia |
| WWII | World War II |

1

# Staging assimilation: Too many John Antills?*

*It is naive, if not irresponsible, to assume that a meaningful confrontation of any culture can transcend the immediacies of its history.*

Rustom Bharucha, 2003[1]

At the height of the assimilation era, Australians were in the throes of planning celebrations of the 1951 Jubilee of Federation. How might we celebrate Australia's unification as a federated nation? How should we represent our identity? The Publicity Subcommittee for the event put forward an idea. A massed corroboree of Aboriginal people 'practically in their tribal state' could tour the nation. Performers would be accommodated on showgrounds in capital cities and regional centres across the country, they could build *gunyahs* and even some native animals could be introduced into the space for atmosphere and hunting demonstrations. This event, it was proposed, could 'be used to give the aboriginal [sic] people a new status in the eyes of the white inhabitants'.[2]

The proposal was not adopted, but a *Corroboree* did indeed tour the cities and towns of the nation, attracting large audiences, critical acclaim and prominent status in cultural histories of the assimilation era. The *Corroboree* was a symphonic ballet composed in 1944 by John Antill with new choreography by Rex Reid. Instead of the dozens of Aboriginal people proposed by the publicity subcommittee, *Corroboree* presented dozens of orchestral musicians from the symphony orchestras of each state and dancers from the National Theatre Ballet Company. No Aboriginal people were involved in the production. The show was acclaimed as a landmark Australian work.

How are we to disentangle Australian Aboriginal corroborees from Antill's *Corroboree*? Vernacularized words, like *corroboree* and *didjeridu*, to denote Aboriginal music and dance have long been recognizable to speakers of Australian English,

---

*My title references Rembarrnga artist Paddy Fordham Wainburranga's artwork *Too Many Captain Cooks*, http://collections.anmm.gov.au/en/objects/details/31547/too-many-captain-cooks; see also Chapter 7, and Ian McLean, *Rattling Spears: A History of Indigenous Australian Art* (London: Reaktion Books Ltd, 2016); Penny McDonald, *Too Many Captain Cooks* (Ronin Films, 1989).

while local Aboriginal words for song and dance practices have evaded audiences and practitioners. But more than that, non-Indigenous Australians have appropriated this language to stake a claim in Aboriginal culture and to represent Aboriginal music and dance to non-Indigenous audiences. Published in the 1930s, 'Aboriginal songs' composed by non-Indigenous composer Loam and collector Lethbridge and set to piano accompaniment were performed for decades afterwards. But what relationship do these songs bear to those that Aboriginal people were singing? These questions are at the heart of this book.

## Parameters of time and place

Geographically, this book is focused primarily on Australia's southeast region and the ways that representation of Aboriginal music and dance linked urban centres to Australia's Top End (centred on tropical Darwin and Arnhem Land) and its Red Centre (symbolized by 'the outback' and Uluru). The southeast was where cultural policy was birthed and took its first steps, but to enact this, its residents looked beyond the temperate Sydney, Melbourne or Canberra outskirts, and actively sought to tour the products of these new efforts well beyond urban centres.

There are many other studies to which this book is indebted, which have focused in detail on other regions, such as Anna Haebich's *Dancing in Shadows* on Western Australian Nyungar performance, and work on performance in Queensland by Malcolm Cole, Judith McKay and Paul Memmott. Distinct genres have also been explored in Clinton Walker's study of Aboriginal country music, and in considerable literature on Aboriginal and Torres Strait Islander theatre from Performance Studies scholars, especially Maryrose Casey.[3] This book is also influenced by similar approaches to understanding representation of Indigenous performance in other settler colonial nations especially in the United States by Philip Deloria and Jacqueline Shea Murphy and Canada by Dylan Robinson.[4]

In the four decades of the twentieth century that are explored here, the public representation of Aboriginal music and dance was contested. Each of the book's chapters is framed around a decade (with the 1960s divided between Chapters 5 and 6) and juxtaposes key events staged by Aboriginal people, with those staged by non-Indigenous people seeking to represent Aboriginal music and dance or grappling with it in their own practice. In a sense, this juxtaposition is artificial – in spite of a common interest in Aboriginal music and dance, the two groups of practitioners often had little to do with one another. On the other hand, this disconnect illuminates something crucial about Australian engagement with Aboriginal performing cultures in this period. Namely, that non-Indigenous Australians have engaged more readily with works of art that could be disembodied from the people who created them, than they have with living, singing, moving Aboriginal people. This practice echoes Philip J. Deloria's description of the practice of donning native dress in the United States:

playing Indian has been as much about reading books as it has been about meeting native people ... the ways in which white Americans have used Indianness in creative self-shaping have continued to be pried apart from questions about inequality, the uneven workings of power, and the social settings in which Indians and non-Indians might actually meet.[5]

This (dis)engagement was not apolitical and it impacted Aboriginal peoples' own engagement with their performing arts. As Linda Tuhiwai Smith reminds us, Indigenous peoples have long been appalled by the way 'the West can desire, extract and claim ownership of our ways of knowing, our imagery, the things we create and produce, and then simultaneously reject the people who created and developed those ideas and seek to deny them further opportunities to be creators of their own culture and own nations'.[6]

The performance events analysed here are those operating at what Martin Nakata defines as the 'cultural interface'.[7] In these events, non-Indigenous Australians aimed to define themselves as not-just-British but something else, as a people with a culture and history, even if that culture would build on events they commonly characterized as 'pre-history'. For Aboriginal performers, this representation took many and diverse forms, and acted as a means of continuing cultural practice within changing social and political frameworks. Some of these performances were necessarily reactive to the pressures placed upon them by oppressive or exclusionary government policies, others were opportunistic and display a willingness to share cultural riches with new audiences in efforts to educate, or to engage, or to protest.[8]

Commemorative events (always framed by the historical milestones of European-Australian settlement) were opportunities for engagement with mainstream audiences on a large scale – the memorialization of Cook's landing at the 150- and 200-year marks, and of the landing of the First Fleet, the celebration of fifty years since Australia was federated as a nation, and first and subsequent visits of the British monarch.[9] But other performance opportunities reflected more localized histories and politics – protests about land, freedom of movement and treatment by the administration of Aboriginal people, and events arising from the formation of new arts bodies determined to innovate and open dialogues between Australia's north and south, between the Indigenous and European, the Asian- and European-Australian.

## Listening to performance: Oral histories and the auditory

To think about Australian history through music and dance, this book traverses some disciplinary boundaries, in particular bringing together historical and musicological methods. The European mode of writing history has been more efficient at thinking about the visual than it has the auditory.[10] But while Aboriginal artists have famously worked across visual media, paintings and sculpture, visual representations of culture have always been tied closely to embodied expressions of that culture through dancing, singing and playing instruments. Indigenous histories have been recorded in cycles of song that have been passed from person to person through speaking, singing and listening, not only through writing, drawing and watching. In incorporating a range of auditory and visual primary sources and existing and new oral histories from those who remember the events of 1930–70 or how the stories of the events have been told since then, I aim to weave auditory histories into the fabric of how we can understand our historical entwinement. Australian Aboriginal people's rich oeuvres of song and dance point to the importance of embodied and auditory modes of knowledge transmission and continuance in the same way that the West's libraries of books and reams of paper archives reveal the dominance of the visual and the written in European epistemologies.

My own position as a non-Indigenous, Australian-born musicologist and historian must also be said to have driven the orientation of this book. The impetus for the book arises from my belief that it is incumbent upon non-Indigenous researchers like myself to interrogate our own histories of oppressing others, appropriating cultural materials that don't belong to us and failing to adequately engage with the creators of these cultural products. This kind of reckoning has been very slow to emerge in musicology and Australian art music history, and is still not as widely influential as it has been in other disciplines. However, to write a book that only documents histories of appropriation by non-Indigenous Australians would be to perform another kind of erasure.[11] The history of Aboriginal performers in the mid-twentieth century is one of the hidden histories that takes considerable digging in archives and living memories to document. But it is no less rich and influential than the considerably better documented histories of Western art music.

The methods of this research also require contending with certain disciplinary shifts. Historians have had a role to play (if not one that has always been welcomed) in shifts in anthropology, as part of that discipline's considerable reckoning with its past, its methods and its embeddedness in processes of colonization. But history too has started to adopt approaches long practised by anthropologists and ethnomusicologists, which privilege oral accounts and participation in communities, in order to overcome the limitations of relying on a written archive and its histories privileging the male, the white, the official, the literate viewpoint over histories kept through oral transmission, shared knowledge and repeated performance. Michel Naepels has explored the shifts in the practice of history writing that this rethinking has engendered, seeing this as a continuation of Marshall Sahlins' 'project of always counterbalancing the colonial history with its indigenous version, leaving space for conflicts of interpretation'.[12]

For at least the past thirty years, accounts of the Aboriginal history of NSW and Victoria written using textual archival sources, and those drawing on oral accounts and living memories of this history have existed alongside one another, sometimes in considerable tension with each other. For example, Gunditjmara elder John Lovett's foreword to the edited collection of oral histories *Living Aboriginal History of Victoria: Stories in the Oral Tradition* positions the approach of the book in direct contrast to non-Indigenous representations of local history: 'The memories and lifestyles of the narrators reflect what life means to be a Koori. You will, therefore, find no interpretation of facts, no "white-fella" history, within these pages. What you will find are revelations of lives, memories and lifestyles bared to the reader.'[13]

Similarly, Jessica Hodgens' recent PhD thesis on Dja Dja Wurrung history, written at the same time as a book by eminent historian Bain Attwood on the same history, makes significant interpretative distinctions between tellings of the story resulting from oral histories and from archival research. Hodgens' focus is on interrogating the survival of Dja Dja Wurrung people and their living cultural heritage and she therefore purposefully extends this history beyond the final chapter of Attwood's book, entitled 'Decline'.[14] In his earlier work, Attwood also grappled with oral histories, encumbered as they are with the burdens of memory, narrative and the teller's attempt to make meaning of events that happened in the past. In his *A Life Together, a Life Apart*, Attwood ultimately concluded that the oral accounts presented in the book may not be acceptable to a positivist view of history, but that the radical potential of history to contemplate the otherness of the past while reflecting on how this past is reconstructed in the present can be illuminated through just such oral narratives.[15]

John Lovett's assertion that oral histories show us 'what life means to be a Koori' hints at the way that history always attempts to make meaning of its sources, and that this meaning is always already bound up in the time and place from which it emerges. This means that in oral retellings (including performative ones), events of the past become imbued with meaning derived from the present. But nor can written sources be read without this meaning crowding in from all sides. A key foundational moment in the history of Indigenous–non-Indigenous relations in Australia, Captain James Cook's landing on Aboriginal lands in 1770 has featured repeatedly in performances in the twentieth century. Retellings of Cook's landing have also appeared in oral accounts of Australian settler colonial history by Aboriginal people. These oral histories have, in turn, been increasingly incorporated into and interpreted through scholarly work by Deborah Bird Rose, Tim Rowse, Maria Nugent and others, who have used these narratives to grapple with the question of 'what life means to be a Koori'.[16]

As Rose writes of Mudburra man Hobbles Danaiyarri's account of the Cook Saga, Cook 'is credited with initiating and establishing the conditions of the black-white relationship. The Saga is not so much about Captain Cook, per se, as it is about this relationship'.[17] In her interpretations, Nugent has been especially anxious to point out that Aboriginal narratives that suggest *Cook was here* have often been historically inaccurate in regard to geographic locations and timelines.[18] And yet as a means of making meaning of history, these oral accounts get to the essence of Cook's very consequential endeavours; if he did not actually captain the ships that brought the First Fleet of settlers planning to make a life in this place, his accounts of the lands he encountered set these events in chain with an inevitability (albeit 'a messy and complex process' in Nugent's framing)[19] that narratives like Danaiyarri's about Cook get straight to the heart of. The central role played by Cook in Aboriginal oral accounts of Australian settler colonization is also mimicked in twentieth-century memorializations of Australian history among non-Indigenous Australians. This narrative was repeatedly re-enacted (albeit chiefly in NSW, and in Queensland's Cooktown) throughout the twentieth century, enlisting Aboriginal people in representing their resistance and apparent concession to the visiting Europeans.[20]

Oral and performative narratives that make meaning of recent historical events can then illuminate the depersonalized commentary of paper archives. I take the lead from these approaches to history, which are innovative in combining oral narratives with documentary evidence (from the point of view of European methods of history writing) and simultaneously deeply situated in historical and traditional practice (from the point of view of Aboriginal traditions steeped in intergenerational transmission of knowledge through oral and performative accounts). This methodological approach means that audiovisual sources are regarded with as much seriousness as written ones, and oral accounts from those who remember our shared histories and have preserved these memories through retellings over time are given as much weight as the carefully preserved documents held in our national archives.

Narratives about how we should understand the course of history as it concerns Indigenous and non-Indigenous interaction and impact in Australia have been subject to regular shifts. In recent years, perhaps no shift has been more dramatic than that triggered by the increasingly persistent voices of Aboriginal activists calling for their land and citizenship rights to be recognized throughout the 1960s, combined with W. E. H. Stanner's challenge to anthropologists and historians that the romantic fascination with the rhetoric of a 'dying race' of Aboriginal people was not a truth to be worked around, but rather a notion requiring intervention.[21] In the years that followed, scholars increasingly interrogated a more truthful explanation for the decimation of Aboriginal populations than wistful social Darwinism that imagined Aboriginal people as a weak race that must inevitably succumb to the stronger.[22] In recent years, the focus on the violent acts of non-Indigenous perpetrators has shifted to one which not only acknowledges the harm done, but that also recognizes the resilience of Aboriginal people and their resistance of annihilation. Current efforts to contextualize histories of Aboriginal cultural expression increasingly attempt to hold both of these narratives in tension with one another, as evidenced in a recent exhibition at the National Gallery of Victoria in which colonial paintings were hung alongside works responding to those paintings produced by Aboriginal artists.[23] It is in the spirit of this effort at acknowledgement and recognition that this book aims to cast the resilience of Aboriginal performers alongside appropriative representation of Aboriginal music and dance.

Though the book aims to engage with these recent recuperative efforts in history more broadly, from a music history or musicology perspective the music and dance events that feature would commonly be perceived as peripheral to the main story. They are not the events that have contributed to the canon of important moments in Australia's music history, itself a minor player in the canon of (European) Western art music. In the histories of Western art music taught in Australia's conservatoria and high school music courses, the events which feature here are not even a blip on the radar of music history.[24] Indeed, Australian Aboriginal musics are almost never seriously considered in any of these contexts, though they feature in ethnomusicology (if 'traditional' or linking back to long-practised song and dance), or in popular music studies (if hybrid performances by Aboriginal people, and more often situated within sociology or cultural studies).[25] Even the performances staged by non-Indigenous performers that I focus on sit well outside of what might be thought of as serious musical milestones in Australia's formation of musical identity (with the significant exception of John Antill's *Corroboree*).[26] This research is therefore consciously marginal to musicology's focus on 'great works', and instead interrogates the ways that performance culture has operated in Australians' definition of a cultural identity in their adopted or inherited homeland, especially in reckoning with the nation's Indigenous history and ongoing Aboriginal presence.

It should also be said that the 'dance' in the title takes a secondary role to music in this book. This stands in contrast to many performative histories, which place the visual performing arts forms at the forefront and the auditory arts in a supporting role. For all of its prominence in Australian cultural history, ballets like Antill's *Corroboree* have chiefly been examined as choreographed ballets, rather than as free-standing musical works later realized in fully staged productions. However, *Corroboree* had a rich life as an orchestral work through live performance and radio broadcast for decades; and a far more extensive public profile than the two main versions of the choreographed ballet produced on stage. On the other hand, in Aboriginal cultural frameworks, music and dance can barely be separated, and it is highly appropriate to include dance in the frame of this book at the points at which it asserts itself as part of the public representation of Aboriginal performative cultures.

## Protection, assimilation, self-determination and the performing arts

The book is framed by the time period 1930–70 – a period characterized by aims to assimilate Aboriginal people into the mainstream population, enacted through government policy and Aboriginal 'protection' and 'welfare' administrations. As Anna Haebich and Russell McGregor have shown, policies of assimilation that placed pressure on the localized practices of Aboriginal people coincided with national reckonings with what it meant to be in that Australian mainstream.[27] The framing years 1930 and 1970 push at the boundaries of the operation of assimilation policy, especially because policies of 'protection', introduced in the southern states from 1869, were still very much in operation, not only until Commonwealth ministers adopted assimilation as official policy in 1937, but well beyond this date. The endurance of policies of protection and protectionist thinking are evident across Australian states and territories in the methods of government departments such as the Aborigines Protection Board (NSW) and Board for the Protection of Aborigines (Vic).[28] While these organizations had a change of branding to the Aborigines Welfare Board in 1940 (NSW) and 1957 (Vic), they still oversaw expulsions from Aboriginal reserves and exemption certificates – tools of assimilation that controlled Aboriginal peoples' movements, excluding them from Aboriginal reserves and thus from contact with family and community. In other parts of Australia, the shift from protection to assimilation was more gradual, or at least, is more difficult to observe in a clear-cut way. In the Northern Territory, though the 1939 'New Deal' had mapped out an assimilationist plan to raise the citizenship status of Aboriginal people, many remember the implementation of assimilation (rather than absorption) beginning with Paul Hasluck's appointment as the Minister for Territories in 1951. However, the status of Aboriginal residents of the NT remained 'wards of the state' until 1967 (with the exception of those granted full citizenship rights; the tragic operation of this right can be seen in the case of Western Arrernte painter Albert Namatjira).[29]

Indeed, assimilation thinking and even terminology was already in evidence during the protection era, before it entered legislative or policy discourse. Protection boards in the southeast differentiated between so-called 'full blood' Aboriginal people and those of 'mixed race'. NSW Member of Parliament Edmund Fosbery reported to Parliament in 1909 that 'the object of the Board, no doubt, is, and always has been, that these people who are living on the reserves that have been made for the Aborigines, who are half-castes, quadroons, or even octoroons, should merge as soon as possible into the general community'.[30]

Similarly, in the north, without using the term 'assimilation', Chief Medical Officer and Chief Protector of Aboriginals Dr C. E. Cook advocated in 1935 for the protection of Aboriginal people from the bad habits of mainstream society, while simultaneously advocating for governments' responsibility to equip 'the native ... to take his place in the white community with a proper realization of his obligations to it'.[31]

Music and dance performances, especially in relation to events of national or state significance, illuminate some of the complexities of protectionist/assimilationist thinking. Under protection/assimilation regimes, immense pressure was exerted upon Aboriginal people to abandon culture by banning the speaking of Indigenous languages and performance of ceremony and by rewarding actions that showed Aboriginal people were adopting mainstream behaviours like residing in a single house, in a nuclear family unit. These pressures were not just notional, but rather, punitively enforced – people who grew up under this regime remember mothers, aunts and grandmothers obsessively dusting and keeping a clean house, knowing that untidiness could lead to allegations of neglect of children, and that children were routinely removed from their families and placed in institutional care, sometimes indefinitely.[32]

Nevertheless, at moments of national nostalgia, events commemorating European settlement sought to memorialize and celebrate the lost arts that had been actively repressed. This desire for experiencing 'real' Aboriginal culture arose on anniversaries that evoked nostalgia for local history, and can also be seen in the stone tools and cultural objects stored in farmhouses around the country. However, these were rarely opportunities for self-representation by the local Aboriginal people, who had occupied the land and been forcibly moved off it in the recent past.[33] Instead of engaging with the Aboriginal people living on local reserves, for many commemoration and memorialization events, organizers sought to import this evidence of continuing cultural practice.[34] Aboriginal culture was, at those times, romanticized by bringing dark-skinned Aboriginal people from some distance to paint up and be on display, thereby performing the kind of imperialist nostalgia for culture Europeans had wilfully destroyed and continued to undermine, that Renato Rosaldo has described.[35]

The first such major re-enactment of Australian colonial history was the 1901 re-enactment of Cook's landing at Kurnell on the edge of Botany Bay, and around the headland from the Aboriginal reserve of La Perouse.[36] For the events of 7 January 1901, Queensland Protector of Aborigines, Archibald Meston coordinated a group of performers from across Queensland who charged the Sydney beach as the actors portraying Cook and his crew approached.[37] Aboriginal performers were brought from elsewhere to perform for a range of events in the 1930s, including the opening of the Sydney Harbour Bridge in 1932 when performers travelled to Sydney from the far south coast and northwest of NSW and Victoria, commemorations of Victoria's centenary in 1934, when performers were brought to Melbourne from Central Australia, and the 1938 150th year anniversary of the First Fleet's landing at Port Jackson, in which performers were brought to Sydney from Menindee in Western NSW, even while local Sydney Aboriginal people joined with campaigners from Victoria to stage a National Day of Mourning.

The protection/welfare boards in each state or territory were the overseeing bodies for requests, approvals and arrangements made for the participation of Aboriginal performers. The incomplete documentation that remains of these bodies shows their persistent blocking of the movements of Aboriginal people under their jurisdiction, especially of requests to travel outside of the country or state for performances not managed by the government or its boards.[38] The obstacles placed in the way of local Aboriginal people's mobility meant that Aboriginal people from other parts of the nation frequently stood in to represent 'Aboriginal culture' to NSW and Victorian audiences. As later chapters demonstrate, the machinations of the board could also be argued to have opened the door for non-Indigenous appropriations of Aboriginal culture that would increasingly emerge in the 1940s and 1950s.

Government bodies' oversight of Aboriginal people was also informed by the work of anthropologists, even if the latter did not always agree with the way their policy recommendations were implemented. The policy advice of anthropologists was highly influential throughout the period 1930–70. Australia's most prominent anthropologist, A. P. Elkin publicly advocated for assimilationist approaches, even if he later distanced himself from the ways in which these had been implemented. He also presided over the NSW Welfare Board from 1942 until 1969 as vice-chairman. In the performance arena too, anthropologists were an influential voice. Performances of 'Aboriginal' music and dance by non-Indigenous performers frequently cited anthropological work to imbue their performances with authenticity and authority. Non-Indigenous performers persistently attributed the origins of the stories used in their shows to anthropologists such as Elkin, C. P. Mountford and T. G. H. Strehlow, citing them in concert programmes.[39] Similarly, for Aboriginal people whose authority had been undermined in the public eye by disenfranchisement and assimilation pressures, they too referenced anthropologists. Aboriginal performers like Bill Onus quoted from anthropological work, as in the concert programme for the 1951 *Aboriginal Moomba* in Melbourne, which printed an excerpt from anthropologist Frederick McCarthy.[40]

In these shows, anthropologists' expertise confirmed the long traditional history drawn upon by the performances, and the need for recognition of their value by non-Indigenous Australia.

In 1933, the Australian Broadcasting Commission had articulated its aim to lay the foundations of an essentially 'national musical literature'.[41] This was consistent with a more generalized push emerging from fears of invasion of Australia during the Pacific war for a 'new set of sentiments relating to the nation's place in the empire … and the creation of a cultural voice that supplemented but did not and could not replace the British cultural inheritance', as Richard Waterhouse has argued.[42] This new conception of an Australian history and an Australian culture is in evidence in many and varied efforts by composers and choreographers and large-scale cultural institutions throughout the 1940s and 1950s. Australians increasingly saw themselves as Australian rather than British citizens and began to imagine their indigeneity to Australia. This involved a turn towards Australia's actual Indigenous people, as non-Indigenous citizens searched for a sense of distinctiveness and points of differentiation from Britain. Consistently across this period, the most enthusiastic adopters of the new Australian cultural identity were the newest arrivals. Repeatedly, recent immigrants from North America and continental Europe embraced the potential for Aboriginal culture to inform nascent Australian style and Australian identity.[43]

In seeking to make sense of these attempts to develop Australian cultural identity reliant on Aboriginal culture, I draw on a range of theorizations from Australian and international scholars. Non-Indigenous engagement with Aboriginal music in the 1950s was fundamentally self-referential. Non-Indigenous composers looked to the writings of non-Indigenous ethnographers, and to non-Indigenous choreography for ideas and inspiration. Their self-referring discourse explicitly excluded Aboriginal people, while simultaneously making a claim to authority to speak on Aboriginality and Australian identity. In looping back to anthropological discourse, performances of Aboriginal culture reproduced early Australian anthropological practices that Patrick Wolfe has characterized as a 'soliloquy – a Western discourse talking to itself'.[44]

Alternative theorizations from Indigenous scholars offer a more processual explanation of the repetitive practices of representation. In particular, Goenpul, Quandamooka scholar Aileen Moreton-Robinson's conceptualization of the Australian condition 'not as postcolonial but as postcolonizing with the associations of ongoing process, which that implies' creates space for the continuation of Aboriginal assertions of sovereignty.[45] Throughout the chapters of this book, the assertion of Aboriginal people's right to perform culture is as strongly in evidence as the repetition of attempts to marginalize this agency.

This book's end point, 1970, was an unofficial marker of the beginning of the era of self-determination. Though the Racial Discrimination Act was not introduced until 1975, the activism leading up to the 1967 referendum for constitutional reform and consequent redefining of Aboriginal people's rights and access to decision making saw dramatic changes in arts organizations. As in the Northern Territory, in 1967 the Victorian Aborigines' Welfare Board was abolished, in 1969 the NSW Welfare Board followed suit. Very quickly, new organizations like the Aboriginal/Islander

Dance Theatre (AIDT), the Aboriginal Theatre Foundation (1972) and the Aboriginal Arts Board (1973) went from their founding mix of Indigenous and non-Indigenous board members and staff, to being almost uniformly headed by and administered by Aboriginal people.[46] Though these changes were swift and dramatic in the domains of dance and narrative theatre, music performance contexts and institutions have been slower to follow suit (see Chapter 7).

## Overview of chapters

The book is structured chronologically, using key points in each decade to reflect on how performance responded to changes in policy for Aboriginal people from 1930 to 1970. This overarching chronological structure is disrupted by three essays contributed by D'harawal saltwater knowledge keeper and artist Shannon Foster; Yorta Yorta, Dja Dja Warrung cultural leader, visual and performance artist, curator, and opera singer Tiriki Onus; and Yuwaalaraay songwriter, storyteller and performer Nardi Simpson. Shannon (Prelude) weaves reflections on her great-grandfather Tom Foster's role in performing, communicating and maintaining culture around a song she has composed to a D'harawal text during the course of the writing of this book. Tiriki (Interlude) enlivens the historical account of his grandfather Bill Onus' performing, producing, crafting and nurturing of culture and of networks of community and kin with oral history that recalls the stories and memories that have kept his grandfather's actions alive across the decades. Nardi (Coda) reflects on the legacy of Aboriginal performers who came before her, but also the way that 'time folds in on itself', so that she continues to expand the possibilities for giving culture a voice in her musical life.

In the chronological sections of the book, the reader will notice that certain individuals appear again and again through this historical account. Cultural entrepreneurs and community organizers such as Yorta Yorta man Bill Onus and colleagues including Pastor Doug Nicholls produced an astonishing range of events throughout the 1940s, 1950s and 1960s that not only brought Aboriginal culture to the attention of wider publics, in spite of resistance from official bodies, but also connected and reconnected Aboriginal people with each other and their networks and communities all across the country, and well beyond Onus' immediate community. Onus appears repeatedly in Chapters 3, 4 and 5 as an influential and adaptive cultural leader, resisting the effacing pressures of assimilation and driving innovative community responses through cultural expression and political engagement.

Equally persistent and consistently underwritten by Australian cultural institutions were the collaborative creative team John Antill, Beth Dean and Victor Carell, whose numerous works appear repeatedly in Chapters 4, 5 and 6. Though any number of works were being created at this time by other non-Indigenous artists who referenced Aboriginal culture, Antill, Dean and Carell had adopted the role of self-appointed and officially supported spokespersons for the representation of Aboriginal music and dance in high culture. Their works were produced by the most influential arts companies, included in national commemorations and gala events for Royal visitors and aired through the national broadcaster, the ABC. Arguably their works had the widest reach to broad audiences, and thus could be thought of as having a strong impact on audiences' conceptions of Aboriginal culture through the last decades of the assimilation era.

Chapter 2 begins with the 1930s, the decade in which assimilation became official policy. It focuses on events in 1931–2 and 1937–8, when key shifts can be observed. In the early years of the decade, Australian identity was publicly performed at the Sydney Harbour Bridge opening in 1932. Yuin, Dharawal and Ngarigu people from the South Coast of New South Wales paraded across the bridge, representing their cultural distinctiveness by playing tunes on gum leaves, attired in loin cloths and body paint. Some of the participants in this event had been giving demonstrations of their culture in Sydney for some time – in 1931 Tom Foster and Wesley Simms – Dharawal men resident at La Perouse – exhibited themselves and their crafts in a Rangers' League Bushland show advocating for the preservation of Australian native bush. At 1938 commemorations, Ngiyampaa performers travelled to Sydney to perform the role of local Aboriginal people re-enacting the First Fleet's landing, while in direct protest against official events, Aboriginal activists from Sydney and Melbourne staged a National Day of Mourning by commemorating 150 years since the invasion of their lands. 1932 also saw the founding of the Australian Broadcasting Commission (ABC) and its fostering of a 'national creative style'. This preoccupation was evident in responses to the 1937 publication by Loam and Lethbridge of their set of six *Aboriginal Songs*, with reviews predicting that the songs might form the beginning of an Australian national folk tradition.[47]

Australian culture and practice in the 1940s (explored in Chapter 3) was heavily impacted by the war taking place on faraway continents but also, from 1941, in the very near Pacific. Chapter 3 focuses on 1940, 1946 and 1948–9, beginning with Aboriginal gumleaf musicians from Lake Tyers Mission Station who put their talents to work as part of WWII recruitment performances. The breadth of cultural activities during this period included those which tied Australian Aboriginal people's music and dance practice to fellow Indigenous peoples in the Pacific, with the performance of hula dances appearing alongside boomerang demonstrations. The pressure of war created a sense of urgency for Australians to define a sovereign identity through which to articulate their defence of their way of life. In 1944, John Antill composed his symphonic ballet *Corroboree*, premiered in 1946 by the newly rebranded Sydney Symphony Orchestra, a work that would come to be seen as momentous in Australian music history, and which features in Chapter 4's discussion of the 1951 Jubilee. It was no coincidence that this work took as its title an Australian Aboriginal (Dharug) word signifying a coming together in music and dance.[48] The Arts Council of Australia formed as a national body in 1948, bringing together Arts Councils across the states and territories as part of concerted efforts to build cultural infrastructure. A new generation of Aboriginal cultural entrepreneurs conversant in the economics of Australian cities in the southeast emerged after the war, leveraging their cultural products in a new way. The Australian

Aborigines' League, led by Pastor Doug Nicholls and Bill Onus, organized large-scale events, like the 1948 and 1949 *All Aboriginal Pageant* at Wirth's Olympia.

Chapter 4 traces the more thorough permeation of assimilation thinking in the 1950s, especially in the Northern Territory, after Paul Hasluck, the Minister for Territories decreed that all Aboriginal policy should now be guided by assimilationist aims.[49] Among Aboriginal musicians and dancers, the penetration of assimilation policy is evident in important cultural events seeking to intervene in public perceptions of Aboriginal culture, and also in a series of diplomatic exchanges that coincided with visits of the heads of state, particularly in 1951 and in the years 1953–4. In 1951 prominent Aboriginal entrepreneur and activist, Bill Onus brought talented and well-known performers from other parts of Australia to stage Melbourne's *Aboriginal Moomba – Out of the Dark*. Just two years later when Queen Elizabeth II visited Australia for the first time, considerably different performances of Aboriginal music and dance were mobilized for the Queen's entertainment, functioning as both cultural expression and diplomacy.[50] Beth Dean's touring shows played a significant role in disseminating ideas of how Aboriginal music and dance sounded and looked, popularizing the Loam 'Aboriginal songs' introduced in Chapter 2, which also appeared as accompaniment to new dance works such as choreographer Gertrud Bodenwieser's new work *The Kunkarunkara Woman* in 1955.[51]

The preconditions for a large-scale appropriative practice of Australian composition and choreography based on Aboriginal music and dance were established in the 1950s, and their realization in the early 1960s is explored in Chapter 5. The chapter begins by examining new public competitive events creating performing opportunities for Aboriginal musicians and dancers as part of NADOC talent quests and the North Australian Eisteddfod in 1961. In the 1950s and 1960s a range of Australian and international companies were supported by the Australian Elizabethan Theatre Trust (AETT) to tour Australia. These touring companies included prominent African American and Indian dance companies, and alongside these, the AETT also sought to expose southern audiences to Aboriginal performers from the Northern Territory. Chapter 5 details two particular events of 1963, which demonstrate the divide between music and dance produced by Aboriginal people but managed by welfare officers, and 'aboriginal ballets' produced by a non-Indigenous artistic team to coincide with another visit from Queen Elizabeth II. The two events – the *Aboriginal Theatre* presenting dancers and singers from northeast Arnhem Land, the Tiwi Islands and the Daly Region to Sydney and Melbourne audiences, and John Antill and Beth Dean's *Burragorang Dreamtime* each appeared on southeastern stages in 1963, but their approaches could not have been more different. In the 1965 Commonwealth Festival in London, non-Indigenous 'aboriginal ballets' were subsequently selected over performances by Aboriginal people to represent the state of Australian culture as distinct from other colonies of the British Commonwealth.[52]

Chapter 6 focuses on the closing years of the 1960s up until 1970 – a period that ushered in a new era of Aboriginal performing arts. As a decade, the 1970s became the cultural birthplace of performing arts organizations that remain important today. The 1967 referendum delivered new rights to Aboriginal people as they were brought under the legislative frameworks of the Commonwealth government, and as Aboriginal Welfare Boards were abolished. By 1970, Aboriginal performers had begun to build new frameworks for working within this changed political landscape. Well-established non-Indigenous performers now found themselves on unstable ground, and Beth Dean's proposal to revive her *Kukaitcha* 'aboriginal ballet' for the 1970 Cook bicentenary was quickly rebuffed in favour of Aboriginal and Pacific Islander performers representing the cultural practice of the islands Cook had visited 200 years earlier. 1970 also saw another celebration and re-enactment of James Cook's landing in Australia, this time featuring paid professional Aboriginal actors. In response, as in 1938, Aboriginal activists stood with Sydney Aboriginal people in asserting their presence in their Country, staging their own commemorations of the historical events.[53] Chapter 6 arrives at this point of 1970, when the assimilation era's end is evident in public policy and also in the performing arts.

The concluding chapter (7) considers the legacy of these crucial decades for current cultural practice in Australia. It examines the impact of self-determination policy in the performing arts, and the change that has been affected in arts bodies as a result. Though the early 1970s were transformative for a shift towards self-determination in Aboriginal theatre and dance ensembles, Australian art music has been very slow to follow trend. In contrast to changes in dance, the late 1960s and early 1970s saw the flourishing of a new Australian style of art music composition, led by composer Peter Sculthorpe, but also including composers such as Ross Edwards and Sculthorpe's students whose works would gain acclaim over the subsequent decades. Many of the most prominent of these composers' works drew on hybrid representations of Aboriginal music. These kinds of hybrid works had quickly fallen out of fashion in the dance field. While considerable scholarly literature (in performance studies in particular) has been devoted to Aboriginal and Torres Strait Islander theatre and dance in the period 1970 to now, similar attention to Australian art music and its continued engagement with Aboriginal cultural products and practices has been thin on the ground.[54] The last decades of the twentieth century were transformational for Australian art music composition in their own way, but were also increasingly disconnected from movements emerging out of Indigenous Australia. This final chapter examines how Aboriginal-influenced art music has continued to flourish up until the first decade of the new millennium, and examines the slow take-up of critical analysis of these movements in musicology or cultural history. Like the unhurried pace at which Aboriginal art has come to be regarded as modern and the categorical exclusion of 'tribal art from the contemporary scene' in Ian McLean's framing, 'Australianist' music has distanced itself from contemporary Aboriginal music performance.[55] The musicological analysis of 'Australianist' style has, until now, not been contextualized in the broader history of Australia's changing engagement with Aboriginal and Torres Strait Islander performance cultures, and in its reckoning with a distinct cultural identity.

## *Prelude*

I first met Shannon Foster in February 2018, at a little outdoor café on the edge of Sydney's Botanic Gardens, just up a walking path from the Conservatorium where I work. This is Gadigal Country, and Shannon also later told me about her D'harawal great-great-grandmother and how all that Country right down to Bennelong Point was home to her too. Linda Barwick and I sat down with Shannon that day over some lunch and Shannon showed us a series of photographs of her great-grandfather, Tom Foster. She told us how Tom spoke out at the 1938 Day of Mourning about Aboriginal rights. She showed us the musical score of songs he had composed to be sung in the church in La Perouse Aboriginal Reserve, now in the National Library of Australia. I too had come across Tom in my research – searches for traces of Aboriginal gumleaf bands and their travels across the southeast had led me to him.

Shannon and I have met regularly ever since. She's been an integral part of the events we've hosted for our Australian Research Council (ARC) project: 'Reclaiming Performance Under Assimilation in Southeast Australia, 1935–75'. Listening to Shannon reminds me again and again of the meaning a newspaper article, a photograph or an illustrated boomerang can hold for families who have had to struggle to continue cultural practice in the face of annihilating policies. It reminds me that history is in the present and that Aboriginal people in the past performed culture with future generations always in mind.

At our workshop on Ngarigu Country, Thredbo in the Snowy Mountains hosted by Jakelin Troy, Shannon sat down with some small, smooth stones she'd collected with Jaky's permission on our autumn walk along the river at the top of the mountain, and with her friend Jo. They sang a song Shannon had composed in D'harawal, the stones marking the beat. In this prelude, Shannon winds the history of her family, her relationship with archival records of her community, her grandfather and great-grandfather into the words of that song.

## Mungari Buldyan – Song for my grandfather

*Shannon Foster*
*D'harawal Saltwater Knowledge Keeper*

naway
ngalawah
ngara
wingara
bangaaaaa, bangaaaaa

Banga: to make or do. In the moment of now, wait, listen, understand, do, share.[1]

### Naway (now)

My earliest memories of my great-grandfather, Tom Foster, were regularly seeing a black and white photo of him that my father would reverently draw from a large envelope that he kept in the top of his wardrobe. In the photo, my father explained, was Tom and my grandfather Fred with two journalists (Figure 1.1). Fred was painted up and Tom was in his kangaroo skins, both kneeling down on the ground and showing the white journalists some details of the boomerangs they would make from the mangrove trees that lined the shorelines of Kamay (Botany Bay) near their Aboriginal mission home on Guriwal (whale) Country (La Perouse) south of what is now called Sydney.

These two men, my grandfathers, were what people would call 'real aborigines'.[2] With the scars of assimilation inflicted upon my body (my fair skin and green eyes), I live with the constant reminder from the white community around me that I am not 'real'.[3] I feel real, and I feel connected to these two 'real' men through my father's stories of them and the photos he shows me. Through these photos, I learnt about being a Sydney D'harawal saltwater person; we are the people who have survived over two hundred years of colonization here on the frontline of invasion on our Galumban (Spirit Country).[4]

My father always spoke with great pride about Tom and seemed exasperated by us not really understanding the magnitude of who he was. Growing up, I had no idea how 'real' my grandfathers would turn out to be, how valid was their existence, that they appeared in a considerable quantity of colonial archives and records. It wasn't until much later in my life, when catalogues were being digitized and Tom's name began appearing in internet searches that a fuller version of their public lives became clear. In online records, I found two hymns that Tom had written in 1930, 'Happy Today' and 'My Thoughts'.[5] Reading his thoughts and words, I could not comprehend what an incredible moment this was. I saw musical notes that I couldn't read, they were just marks on a page and it oddly never occurred to me that these marks on the page make

**Figure 1.1** Fred Foster (left) and Tom Foster (right) with journalists, 1930, photo courtesy of John Foster.

sound, that someone could pick this music up and play it and I could be immersed in another layer of this amazing man's spirit.

Finding Tom's music has brought many opportunities for us to discover even more about him. It is through his music that I have come to know Dr Amanda Harris, Dr Linda Barwick and the team of researchers working on a new project 'Reclaiming Performance Under Assimilation in Southeastern Australia, 1935–75'. They were beginning to research Tom and it was validating and strengthening to meet them and feel my awe for this man mirrored back to me. I was also relieved that they made contact with me to collaborate in the early stages of the project. More often than not, this does not happen in the research world and our stories are told by outsiders as if we do not exist.[6] At best, we are consulted with as an afterthought, at worst, we are erased out of the histories. This research was different; an important element factored into this project was that information was to be shared and that collaborations and acts of reciprocity for the community would be prioritized. I had always had a yearning to do more with music and song so I was looking forward to being a part of this work. Soon after, Amanda began sending me everything she could find about my great-grandfather, Tom.

## Ngalawah (wait)

It is easy to get swept away by the archival evidence of Tom's life as a cultural man and performer but this is not just about Tom's public life. For us, Tom is our grandfather, an Elder and a direct connection to our cultural heritage that deeply informs our cultural lives today as we work towards creating a future for our descendants. I feel compelled to find every skerrick and scrap of him, perhaps in a bid to find more of myself; the self that is mine alone but is questioned, judged and measured by every set of eyes that gaze upon my fair skin and green eyes as my mouth utters the words 'I am Aboriginal'. I feel sick as I feverishly pore over records, documents, pictures and archives, a kind of 'archive fever'.[7] I obsessively follow every trail down into the archival abyss, agitated by the prospect that there could potentially be more information out there that I do not know; that I have not found; that is not gathered and that, by losing any tiny morsel, we are losing him and, ultimately, a piece of ourselves.

The archival research space is full of contradictions for Aboriginal people.[8] I cannot help but feel a forging of my cultural identity when the archives unveil another piece of 'evidence' of who we are and who I come from. I do not need Western research to validate who I am, though it still performs this task, whether I want it to or not. I can use the archives to tell the stories of the destruction of colonization and the violence that has been inflicted on my family, and I need people to know that it is there and not deny it.[9] But I do not want others to misuse this information and to paint us as victims or use our damage to sell their research: to perversely and voyeuristically indulge in our pain and damage.[10]

The archives are full of lies, absences and at best half-truths. It is time for us to respond and to be included in the responses and examinations. I despise the archives when they are all we have. It shouldn't have to be that way. Every time I relish another crumb of information about my grandfathers, the joy is tinged with despair at not knowing or seeing this information until it is delivered to me through a white man's colonial archive, stained with the blood and pain of our ancestors.

But the reality that I always despairingly return to is that in the archives, I find so much of Tom. There are many astounding stories about our family out there in the records. I had always known that Tom was involved in an important event – a conference or a protest – I wasn't really sure. I know that I didn't always understand what it was and I don't remember when it became clear, but it is now a fixed and ever-present story in my life. In just simply searching Tom's name on the Internet, I was able to instantaneously find out that the conference Tom had been a part of was the 1938 Day of Mourning protest held here in Sydney, at Australia Hall, on 26 January.[11] This protest saw Aboriginal people from all over the country come together to ask, quite simply, for equal rights for Aboriginal people. This was one of the very first civil rights protests in the entire world and happened twenty years before Martin Luther King Jnr, Rosa Parks or Nelson Mandela hit the headlines, yet very few people know about it or have learnt about it in Australian history in schools, let alone in the mainstream media. No one knew that standing in the pictures with Aboriginal warriors Jack Patten,

Doug Nicholls and William Cooper is my great-grandfather, Tom Foster. Something changed in me at that moment, piecing it all together; I didn't just have a right to claim my Aboriginality, I had an obligation. I had to honour the work of these amazing people, the hardships they endured and tell their stories in an attempt to reawaken them from the erasure and oppression of Australia's 'silent apartheid'.[12]

I found the words that Tom spoke on that day in 1938 and they are powerful, concise and inspiring. 26 January 2018 saw the eightieth anniversary of the Day of Mourning protest and I was invited to deliver Tom's speech at an event held in Australia Hall to honour the day with other descendants. On that day, I walked up the same stairs that Tom had walked up eighty years earlier; I stood under the same roof that Tom had stood under and I read his words:

> The Aborigines have three enemies. The first is the Aborigines Protection board, which has meted out most callous treatment to our people, and has forced us to do as the white man wishes. The second enemy is the white missionary, who preaches to our people. Some of these are disgraceful. The third enemy is liquor. White men brought liquor for us, and it has helped to destroy our people. We should stand shoulder to shoulder to destroy these three enemies.[13]

There are no words to describe a moment like this. As I stood there in that moment I felt knowledge, connection and culture come full circle and I know exactly who I am, why I am here and what I have to do for the people who came before me, as well as for those who will come after me.

## Ngara (listen)

Every day spent looking for Tom brings surprises and magic, but I wasn't expecting what happened while I was getting ready to deliver Tom's speech on that morning in 2018, and it all started with another photo from my father's collection that we had seen regularly over the years. The photo pictures Tom with his daughter, my great Aunty Renee (senior). Tom is all dressed up in a good coat and holding something like a box or plaque – it's hard to tell from the old black and white picture. My father explained that it is a picture of Tom after he had performed a corroboree for the opening of the Sydney Harbour Bridge in 1932.

It was so hard to believe this story; surely if this had happened, we would have been taught this and heard about it outside our home?[14] It is such a sensational story and was hard to believe that Aboriginal people, my great-grandfather no less, would be allowed to do this at what would have been considered such an important, colonial event.

Dad would always go on to explain that my great-grandfather and the other Aboriginal men performing the corroboree were meant to be the first people to walk out onto the bridge at the official opening. The story in our family goes that just before they walked out a white man walked in front of the group and officially became the first person to walk out onto the bridge. Understandably, the Aboriginal men were incensed and my great-grandfather's anger and frustration is always the prominent subject whenever the story is told.

Hearing this story growing up, I had no idea if it was true. My father has been known to pull your leg on occasion and would tell tall tales to us kids. He is a great storyteller but he doesn't always let the truth stand in the way of a good story, so I was really sceptical. I became even more sceptical as the Internet opened up access to the world of archives and records and I relentlessly searched for colonial evidence of the corroboree but could never find anything about it. I don't know why I needed validation from outside our family's stories, or maybe I just wanted a picture to convince others. I searched for evidence of this corroborree for years even though I knew better than to dismiss my family's oral histories and question their truth; it had backfired before and I had learnt to trust what they knew, even if it isn't written down or in an archive somewhere.[15]

On the morning that I was about to deliver Tom's speech in Australia Hall, I was aimlessly scrolling through social media and there, out of the blue, was an old, black and white picture of a group of Aboriginal men in a procession. The photo credit said that it was taken in 1932 during the official opening of the Sydney Harbour Bridge. Years and years of searching records, archives, books and pages and pages of internet sites and here it is: the evidence that I had been looking for, randomly dumped into my newsfeed from a newspaper photo database, and on the day I was due to deliver his speech, no less.

I frantically scanned the photo and there he was. Tom was in his skins, playing the gum leaf and holding one of his Harbour Bridge boomerangs aloft and there, in the front of the procession, just as my father had always said in his story, was a white man (Figure 2.2). Through Amanda's research I have found out that the man represented the Aborigines Protection Board[16] who, after the event was organized by the Aboriginal men, swept in and claimed ownership over them and their presence there. No wonder they were angry and it is not surprising that the story carried through the generations to be here today.

## Wingara (understand)

In the digital archives, I continue to find an incredible array of information about Tom and I find ways to publish our counter-narratives. With each search, a breathtaking sea of references rises on the tide and washes through our worlds. The uncovering of this information has informed my cultural connections in ways I could never have known or understood until I looked into his eyes in the numerous images; until I heard the songs he wrote; until I saw his performances on film and until I heard the words he spoke in some of our most important moments as Aboriginal people.

As contemporary Aboriginal peoples, we now exercise a right of reply to the archives to not only correct information that has been wrongly recorded but to also open the opportunity for the expansion of knowledges through the inclusion of other information, from other voices. Worimi scholar and archivist, Kirsten Thorpe explains, 'The digital space provides us with opportunities to build counter narratives to colonial collections and to develop stories that give voice to Aboriginal worldviews and perspectives. It enables the material to be activated and animated in new and transformative ways'.[17]

In her travels through the archives, Amanda has unearthed images of an engraving that had been created during the events surrounding the opening of the Harbour Bridge in the early 1930s.[18] The engraving sits on a centrally located lot of land in La Perouse and has been anecdotally accredited to some of my uncles who were Tom's cousins and his constant companions during this period of time. It doesn't make sense, though, that Tom would not have also been involved in the creation of this commemorative engraving, yet he is not credited in the record of the work.

The sandstone engraving looks just like Tom's unique style and iconography and depicts a kangaroo that is facing forward with its head turned around looking at the hunter: an easily recognizable icon of my great-grandfather's artwork. This style of kangaroo appeared many times on the pokerwork boomerangs that my great-grandfather made to sell in the La Perouse tourist trade. I have seen these boomerangs, they are out there in the collections in museums and galleries and some of them have even found their way back to us, rematriating themselves back on to Country and into our families.[19]

So why isn't Tom's name in the archives with this engraving? I attribute this to the fact that he passed away very young in 1940 with heart disease; a common cause of early death amongst Aboriginal people living in deplorable mission conditions.[20] Until then, Tom had been a prominent and powerful figure and our oral histories and many colonial archival records substantiate this.[21] Once he passed away though, he wasn't there to carry on his presence in the stories and they were often written over by other voices. Through this work, I will continue Tom's presence and rewrite the stories that he has been written out of.

Tom's boomerangs are amazing pieces of culture and they always feature prominently when I speak about my research work documenting our Narinya (Living Dreaming). During a recent talk, I find myself addressing the audience, holding one of my great-grandfather's boomerangs in my hands. I tell the incredible story of how it came to be here with me over eighty years, and who knows how many owners, since it was created. I explain the transcendent feeling of placing the boomerang into my father's hands for the first time. I am lost for words. I try, but words don't capture the intensity and magnitude of the moment. I talk about how this brings us cultural strength and a sense of identity. How this wonderful man left us tangible culture to hold onto. This boomerang is evidence that not everything had been lost, stolen, erased, put behind glass, or worse still, held captive in a box somewhere in a basement on the other side of the world.[22]

Through a member of the audience though, I am brought back to our racist reality and I am reminded that non-Indigenous historians often see our cultural heritage very differently and through a deficit, colonial lens. Historians have made assumptions and drawn conclusions about the ways in which our cultural past and the visual evidence of this must be undermining to our cultural integrity because they do not consider it 'authentic' Aboriginal art.[23] I am told by a prominent historian in the audience that they had always seen boomerangs like Tom's as nothing more than kitsch, cultural denigration, humiliation and damage. They had never considered (nor thought to ask) how we feel about them. It had never occurred to them that what we see is physical evidence of our existence in a world where we have been consistently erased. Tom's boomerangs speak to us of survival, resistance, and cultural fortitude and strength. When we see what our Elders created we see staunch, courageous and innovative people who continued to create and promote culture under extreme and violent circumstances. They made sure they left behind vitally important links for us in this future and they left us a space to anchor to, to be able to speak out and tell these stories. We see evidence of who we are and how we have survived and resisted that which tried, and still contributes to, the destruction of who we are. But most importantly, we see our grandparents, our aunts and our uncles and how relentlessly their incredible stories have forged a way into a future that they had never even been considered a part of.

So how does an outsider feel that they have the authority to assume a position for us and speak about us as if we are not there? They need to ask themselves the question: are you researching with us or about us?[24] It is up to us to tell our stories, others do not do it well enough, accurately enough or thoroughly enough. Their knowledge of us is formed on colonial records: records that have been created to perpetuate lies; erase, diminish and oppress us in the pursuit of the colonial agenda. For every piece of us that I find in the archives, I find things that I wish I had never seen or heard.[25] The archives are the ruins of a battle, there are warriors and survivors but there are also bludgeoned lives and corpses. I do not want to rely on the bloodstained colonial records but our ghosts haunt them, pieces of us are left behind and need to be returned home to where they belong. They need to be with us and not lost forever or found by strangers wishing only to exploit them all over again.

## Banga (do)

To this day, I still appreciate the power in finding Tom's written music. To read his thoughts, to feel the trust in the words of his hymn in a world that was out to destroy him and everything about him. Late in 2018, I spoke about his songs and their impact on our lives at the Conservatorium of Music in Sydney in a symposium that was arranged through the research project.[26] The symposium brought together an amazing collection of people, descendants of the performers, researchers (both Indigenous and non-Indigenous), as well as contemporary performers. The symposium changed me in many ways: most importantly, it opened my eyes to the possibilities of actually creating music and song that could tell our stories and share our languages.

Sitting in the concert hall, I was entranced by the shiny grand piano sitting silent on the stage where the speakers had shared their stories and experiences. I imagined the smell and feel of its silken keyboard and the distinct beauty of its sound. An idea began to fill my head. I could feel the compulsion to speak as I had never felt it before. It was more than just a thought or an idea, it was a calling from aeons ago but as strong and as fresh as if someone was talking directly to me in this space and time. This was my opportunity to ask, for Tom, in this room of musicians, singers and performance professionals, could someone please play Tom's music on that beautiful shiny piano?

Everyone was keen to bring Tom's notes to life in one of the only places that could do justice to the sounds. Professional musician Kevin Hunt played the piano and Amanda offered her beautiful voice. Within moments, the Conservatorium filled with Tom's music played in perfect acoustic conditions. Every note swam through my heart and my mind, transcending all time and space, the music striking in a way that no sound has ever done before, or since. It was sublime. This had come from him, his mind, his heart; the spirit of the man that I revered filled the air. It was an incredible moment. With every note I understood with absolute clarity that from that moment on, I had to find a way to create music for our stories. And so, here in this space, generations after it was conceived, ceremony was enacted, culture was alive and I know, without a doubt, who I am.

## Banga (share)

It was a balmy afternoon in the season of the parradowee (eel spirit)[27] as my father and I sat in our backyard on D'harawal Country, on the songline of Kai'ee'magh (Georges River), a place that I had always known as my home. I was finally able to return some small part of the amazing array of gifts that I have received from being able to claim this astonishing heritage. On my phone is the recording of Amanda and Kevin performing my great-grandfather's music. Amongst the lili pili and the wattles, the delicate notes of Tom's music plays and strikes my father's heart. In every moment we hear Tom's pain, we feel his suffering but most of all, we know his resistance and survival in a world that was only there to wipe him and his people out.

Through his music we know that we are real, we are alive, we have lived on and we carry him with us, he is not forgotten. He is loved and valued and we will continue to speak about him and tell his stories and sing his songs. We will run our hands over the works he created and we will marvel at what he achieved, and what he still achieves, long after he is gone. His song and his spirit lives on in us, his footprints are embedded in this earth deeply enough to survive not only to this point in time, but long into the future.

Didjariguru guwanayio'miya (we thank you for remembering our Ancestors)

# 2

# 1930s – Performing cultures: Navigating protection, responding to assimilation

For two weeks each September between 1930 and 1937, the Rangers' League (a bushland conservation group) put on an annual exhibition at Sydney's David Jones and Farmers department stores, displaying the wonders of native bushland in Sydney's area. The aim was to convince the Sydney public that native bush was not just something that should be cleared to make way for the march of progress, but was a valuable and unique resource. As part of this public advocacy for the bush, rock art and items of Aboriginal cultural heritage were also documented, mapped and displayed to the public, and disseminated through brochures. In the exhibitions, Tom Foster and Wesley Sims – D'harawal men resident at Sydney's La Perouse Aboriginal Reserve – sat in exhibition, enacting living examples of this culture. Figure 2.1 shows Foster and Sims dressed in animal skins, holding objects that doubled as artwork and cultural practice (both in music making and hunting), and surrounded by a horde of the general public, straining to view their wares.

There are complex factors to disentangle in interpreting the image of Foster and Sims sitting in exhibit. Roslyn Poignant has written about how Aboriginal people were displayed as exhibits of savagery and Judith McKay and Paul Memmott have documented the touring Wild Australia shows where Aboriginal performers from Queensland were 'publicly paraded as "noble savages"'.[1] In the context of this particular exhibition, we could comment on a conflation of the bush and the people who lived there – Aboriginal people as part of the flora and fauna. But Tom Foster and Wesley Sims were not brought to the exhibits against their will, nor did they perform savagery in these exhibits. Rather, in letter exchanges, they negotiated to hold a stall as part of the exhibits during which they could sell items they had crafted that drew on their cultural heritage, learned from parents, grandparents and elders. They dressed in ways that reflected the culture from which these objects came, and they asserted their presence as people who had lived from and with the resources of the bush that the Rangers' League were advocating to protect, and who continued to hold knowledge about these practices.[2] Foster and Sims were being 'protected' too, under a regime that, in practice, limited their mobility and access to economic equality with other Australians. Indeed,

**Figure 2.1** 'Aborigines' Gunyah at Bushland Exhibition', *The Sydney Morning Herald*, 12 September 1933, 12. http://nla.gov.au/nla.news-article17006273.

at the last Australian Bushland Exhibition in 1937, Foster and Simms were unable to present their 'corroboree', having been sent by the state government on relief work, ironically, cutting roads through forests north of Sydney.[3] But wherever possible, Foster and Simms navigated a path through these 'protection' regimes, aiming to create an economically sustainable industry that simultaneously complied with the limitations imposed by the Aborigines Protection Board, and perpetuated cultural practice. Foster's great-granddaughter Shannon Foster still continues these artistic, artisan cultural practices in her artworks, in her scholarly work as a D'harawal knowledge keeper and in her political advocacy, in which she asserts, just as her great-grandfather did, that 'we are still here' (see Prelude).

In this chapter, I follow several of the activities of Tom Foster, as a cultural entrepreneur, composer, performer, community leader and activist. As a case study, Foster's career provides an opportunity to understand the performance of culture and resistance within changing policies of protection and assimilation in the 1930s.

Like Foster, a range of other Aboriginal people performed Aboriginal culture in ways that resisted assimilation pressures and engaged with settler colonial national representation in the 1930s.

The settler colony was actively grappling with how it should represent itself throughout this period, and some of these debates entered public policy through the newly established (1932) Australian Broadcasting Commission (ABC). The ABC quickly became a new vehicle for experimentation with a national style and the expression of that style through creative works drawing on Aboriginal music and dance, actively cultivating new works through its on-staff composers John Antill, Clive Douglas and Robert Hughes. I discuss the co-existence of these activities in the 1930s – Aboriginal people asserting their continual presence and ensuring they were included in public representation, and cultural bodies seeking to create new traditions that drew on Aboriginal culture, but that were disengaged from the ongoing presence of Aboriginal people.

## Exhibitions, openings, pageants and film: Entrepreneurial performances under protection

In the Rangers' League Australian Bushland Exhibition with which I opened this chapter, the NSW Aborigines Protection Board was listed among the exhibitors.[4] The naming of the stallholder as the board, when the exhibit featured living adult men, who also aimed to sell their craft and artworks as part of the exhibition, reveals the infrastructure imposed on the activities of Aboriginal people in NSW at this time. The NSW Aborigines Protection Board was formed in 1883. In Victoria, the Act for Protection and Management of Aborigines was introduced in 1869, bringing into being the Board for the Protection of Aborigines. Other Acts that clarified the powers of colonial governments to intervene in Aboriginal people's lives were passed in 1886 and 1890 (Vic) and 1909 (NSW). The boards, populated by government ministers, anthropologists and public servants including the Commissioner of Police and Director General of Public Health, initially oversaw tasks like the distribution of rations and blankets. However, the powers of the NSW board were increased from 1909, when it was given control of all Aboriginal reserves and stations. From 1915 the NSW board was able to remove children from families at any time, though policies of dispersal that had separated community members from one another had been in evidence since the earliest days of the colony.[5] The board's involvement in events like the Australian Bushland Exhibition was a bureaucratic intermediary between Aboriginal people and public organizations and spaces in which they were able to present art and crafts and to stage performances.

Tom Foster, however, was not just a participant in the exhibition as an unnamed Aborigine presented by the board, rather he actively negotiated with the organizers on the terms of his participation, and pursued this opportunity annually after initial participation in 1932. Correspondence in 1936 was addressed directly to Foster at no. 7 Aboriginal Reserve, La Perouse, and suggested that he might consider bringing along some Aboriginal children to make the exhibit more interesting and sell more wares.[6] Wesley Simms was listed among the stallholders requiring after-hours access to the gallery to arrange the exhibit.[7] Selling wares had been an ongoing part of tourist operations at La Perouse Aboriginal Reserve where Foster and Simms had lived since early in the century, when the tram line was extended to the La Perouse headland and tourist industries grew up around 'The Loop' where trams would turn to make the return trip into the city. Maria Nugent describes the tourists who travelled out to the end of the line expressly to see Aborigines in what quickly became a 'local amusement precinct'.[8]

Opportunities to perform Aboriginal culture in the Rangers' League public exhibitions may have followed on from public exhibits of Sydney Aboriginal culture that were part of the opening of the Sydney Harbour Bridge in March of 1932. The Bridge opening was marked by a massed parade in which thousands of Australians walked the length of the bridge to inaugurate the north-to-south journeys that would connect the two sides of Sydney harbour into the future. To represent this future, the pageant was led by 7,000 'young Australians'. The pageant was then designed to look backwards from this imagined future, depicting 'scenes from the history of NSW'. Leading the historical floats would be a band of Aboriginal gumleaf musicians 'dressed in war paint, with spears and boomerangs held aloft ready for a corroboree' (Figure 2.2).[9] This group of Aboriginal performers was followed by a float representing Captain James

**Figure 2.2** Hood, Sam. *Aboriginals and Their Gum Leaf Band Pass the Dais*, 20 March 1932, Home and Away – 2136, 44240, State Library of NSW, Sydney.

Cook and his ship the *Endeavour*, with two Aboriginal men with spears seated up front. On the float showing the landing of the First Fleet too, two Aboriginal men were seated holding spears, with another three men seated on one side (Figure 2.3). Tom Foster joined the gumleaf musicians along with performers who had travelled up from the south coast including Percy Mumbler, Guboo Ted Thomas and Eileen Pittman with others joining from the communities of Menindee and Brewarrina in Western NSW.[10] Shannon Foster recalls some disbelief when she was told the story that her great-grandfather performed a corroboree for the Harbour Bridge opening. As she was told, the Aboriginal performers were supposed to lead proceedings, 'but those two whitefellas led up front' (see Prelude).[11]

The contingent of Aboriginal musicians that marched across the bridge may have been intended to represent NSW's history, instead of its present, but the performers' very presence contradicted this representation. More than thirty Aboriginal performers walked the bridge that day, many were playing tunes on gumleaves held to their lips, one carried a drum, another clapsticks, most wore body paint and animal skin clothing with bare feet, some were suited and shod – at least one of these playing the gumleaf. At the parade end, the performers staged a corroboree while the remainder of the procession continued to make its way across the bridge.[12] To commemorate the opening events, rock carvings (still visible today) were created at La Perouse Aboriginal Reserve.[13]

**Figure 2.3** Hood, Sam. *Float of First Garrison and Aborigines Pass the Dais*, 20 March 1932, Home and Away – 5294, 9994, State Library of NSW, Sydney.

The performance of Aboriginal presence did not end at the south end of the bridge, but rather for two days an 'Aboriginal camp' was set up at Sydney's Vaucluse House. The camp coincided with a historical pageant. C. E. Pettitt from the Aborigines Protection Board and Keith Kennedy, an anthropologist acting at the Australian Museum, supervised the construction of an Aboriginal village on site. The performers, numbering around fifty, staged an afternoon corroboree, and the gumleaf band also 'enlivened the proceedings'. Instead of an opening act that would recede once the European actors took the stage, Aboriginal people sat in camp for the duration of the historical pageant. The performances were watched by around 300 people representing pioneer families (their names listed at great length in newspaper reports).[14] The living descendants of the Wentworth family of early European settlers and a descendant of the first white woman born in NSW also rubbed shoulders with the living descendants of the Aboriginal Mumbler, Timbery, Foster and Sims (among other) families who had witnessed these European incursions onto their Country, but who were not named in the printed programmes or media reports.[15] The Aboriginal performers were there when the arrival of the first settlers was re-enacted, and still there when the pageant brought events up to the present day. The performance of this continued presence reportedly disappointed some onlookers who had arrived under the impression that the main part of the pageant – the procession representing various important stages in Australia's history – was to take place. But that was listed for the night, and the crowd was entertained by about twenty 'aborigines who played upon gum leaves and initiated the onlookers into stages of a corroboree'.[16]

The organizers' intention to include Aboriginal people in the pageant as Australia's 'oldest families' seems to have fallen flat with the general public, who liked their history European. But to Mrs Norman Murray, Honorary Secretary of the Vaucluse Historical Celebrations Committee, the First Fleet families were among Australia's newest, not its oldest. As she told reporters, 'When Phillip landed 144 years ago the whole of New South Wales and of Australia had been occupied for long ages by a human population whose descendants, few and feeble folk now in these parts at the continent are still with us'. The *Queensland Times* reported that the Aboriginal performers 'fell in with it most heartily' when the idea of their participation was put to them.[17]

Performative events were often facilitated through anthropologists such as Keith Kennedy, who worked with the Aborigines Protection Board (APB) to ensure the authenticity of the 'picturesque shelter of Gibba-Gunya [that] formed a sacred cave in which the aborigines kept their churingas and other ceremonial outfit'.[18] While Aboriginal people embodied the continuance of culture for a public audience, this kind of academic stamp of authenticity was commonly bestowed on public displays of Aboriginal cultures by an authority in the traditions of the cultures (even when that authority mixed and matched words from languages of the east coast (*gunya*) with those from Central Australia (*churinga*)).

Keith Kennedy went on to draw on his career as a violinist in combination with his work in anthropology to stage lecture demonstrations of musical instruments from Aboriginal Australia and other Indigenous cultures. Pitching himself as 'violinist, scientist, world traveller', Kennedy performed his *Wandering in Many*

*Lands: a Lecture-Recital and exhibition of Barbaric Musical Instruments, Weapons and Implements of Sport etc.*[19] This popular representation of anthropology sat alongside Kennedy's performing career, and academic endeavours, in which he was president of the NSW Anthropological Society, honorary ethnologist at the Australian Museum and editor of the anthropological journal *Mankind*. During his career he amassed a considerable collection of musical instruments and other cultural heritage objects, which were displayed in a small museum in Townsville, where he later settled.

In addition to the mediation of anthropologists, performers needed to navigate the APB bureaucracy in order to access opportunities for paid performance in public. However, their participation seems to have had an entrepreneurial element as well – they were not just compelled to participate by the board. Indeed, the willingness of Aboriginal performers to participate in the frequently recurring re-enactments of settler history is remarkable. Performers such as Tom Foster repeatedly performed Aboriginal presence, and asserted their family and cultural ties to the Sydney region. These performances formed part of Foster's livelihood, but seem to have done more than just earning a living.

Footage of a commemoration in 1930 of Cook's landing at Kurnell saw Foster re-enact the presence of Aboriginal people on the Sydney shoreline after 150 years. In this film, the Mayor of Rockdale played the role of Captain Cook, while Foster and other family and community members from the La Perouse Aboriginal Reserve played the role of their ancestors who had confronted Cook and his fellow travellers in 1770. The silent film's narrative arc is troubling to current descendants of the communities who resided around Botany Bay at the time of Cook's landing, and whose ancestors

**Figure 2.4** Still from *In the Days of Captain Cook*, Rockdale Council, 1930. Title no. 45395, National Film and Sound Archive, Canberra. Tom Foster is pictured at centre looking directly at the camera.

both lived at La Perouse Aboriginal Reserve in the 1930s and performed in the film. Like many of the historical reconstructions in this period, the film sought to depict the (Aboriginal) past and (non-Indigenous) present in very direct ways by replicating scenes of Aboriginal women and children playing in the ocean at Kurnell and replacing them with white women and children in the same location with the caption 'The belles of 1770 and those of 1930'.[20] It is not possible to know whether Foster and the other performers knew that their performances would be edited in this way. Notwithstanding these narrative overlays, their performance asserted their presence in the Country in which Cook landed. It also asserted the continuation of this presence. They were not only still there, but they still crafted boomerangs and dwellings from the trees and foliage in the bay, their artworks were still produced on these boomerangs and they would be there to represent local Aboriginal culture to the Mayor of Rockdale, just as they had to the captain of the British ship in 1770 (Figure 2.4).

## From protection to assimilation

The performances of culture I've described so far were staged by Aboriginal people subject to the 'protection' of the board. However, significant shifts in Aboriginal policy occurred across the nation in the 1930s. One of the key proponents of change, and Australia's only university anthropologist, A. P. Elkin argued in 1944 that the transformations undergone by the protection regime in the late 1930s, shifting it towards an administration focused on 'welfare', were a shift from a negative, to a more forward-looking approach. Elkin noted that the name changes in Aboriginal administration between 1936 and 1939 were more than cosmetic.

Roles of 'Chief Protector' (WA, NT, Qld) were rebranded to 'Commissioner/Director of Native Affairs' and the NSW and Victorian Protection Boards became the Aborigines Welfare Board. Bodies formerly concerned only with 'protecting the Aborigines from injustice, cruelty and immorality' had not acknowledged the potential for a future for Aboriginal people. In Elkin's framing, the new focus on 'welfare' was 'based on the hypothesis and conviction that the Aborigines (even of full-blood) could eventually become worthy citizens of the Commonwealth, and not merely hangers-on to stations and townships'.[21] Though 'welfare' and 'citizenship' were the terms more freely used in Elkin's publication than 'assimilation', Elkin's vision, and that adopted by new policies approved at the 1937 Conference of Commonwealth and State Aboriginal Authorities and in the 1939 'New Deal', were assimilationist approaches that mapped out a gradual, but steady, progress towards economic and social conformism and the wider inclusion of Aboriginal people in mainstream society.[22]

At the 1937 Conference, a resolution had been arrived at on the 'Destiny of the Race'. Namely that: 'this Conference believes that the destiny of the natives of aboriginal origin, but not of the full blood, lies in their ultimate absorption by the people of the Commonwealth, and it therefore recommends that all efforts be directed to that end.'[23]

As Elkin's reflections suggested, this policy, alarming as the reference to 'absorption' may sound today, represented a shift towards thinking about the future of Aboriginal people in the Australian state, and a move away from assumptions that Aboriginal populations would not survive the process of colonization. The policy shift towards assimilation in a social and economic sense was consolidated in the years that followed. In 1939, John McEwan, Minister for the Interior announced a 'New Deal' for Aboriginal people. The deal aimed to raise the citizenship status of Aboriginal people, and to convert a nomadic life to a settled one. It was to be offered to those who underwent education/training and adopted a settled lifestyle. The Deal had been formulated by Elkin, J. A. Carrodus as Secretary to the Ministry for the Interior and McEwan.[24]

These shifts away from 'protection' and towards assimilation were momentous in one sense – they ushered in a possibility of thinking about an Australian future in which Aboriginal people would participate on the basis of equality. But the recommendations from advocates for assimilation policy, like Elkin, that community and cultural links were also to be regarded as central to the well-being of Aboriginal people were not realized in practice. Elkin may have advocated for the importance of communities remaining connected. But as vice-chairman of the Aborigines Welfare Board in NSW from 1942 to 1969, he also presided over decisions that routinely banished Aboriginal people from their communities through expulsions on the basis of non-conformance or reported transgression of settlement rules, as well as over the implementation of exemption certificates, which while bestowing citizenship rights, also prevented people from entering Aboriginal reserves, and therefore being able to maintain family and community relationships.

In the implementation of assimilation policies across the subsequent three decades, the shift towards a language of welfare retained the underlying paternalism of protectionist thinking. Though assimilation has been commonly characterized as a distinct era, the roots of policies that aimed at 'absorption' or 'assimilation' can be found in the earliest practices of administration of the colony. This fact, and historians' disagreement on when the start of the assimilation era can be located have prompted scholars (perhaps most notably Tim Rowse in *Contesting Assimilation*) to question the usefulness of periodizing assimilationist thinking at all.[25] While Elkin encouraged policies that gave Aboriginal people citizenship rights and enabled political engagement, he was also selective in his approval and disapproval of the take-up of these opportunities to advocate politically. Geoffrey Gray has pointed to Elkin's reluctance to recognize activists like William Ferguson and Jack Patten as Aboriginal, and to acknowledge their willingness to advocate for their own rights as the logical conclusion of citizenship.[26]

Tom Foster's performative representations of culture also took a more overtly politicized character at the time of this turn in policy. In 1938, he joined with activists from across NSW and Victoria including Pearl Gibbs, Jack and Selina Patten, Margaret Tucker, William Ferguson, Bill Onus, Doug Nicholls, William Cooper, Jack Kinchela, Helen Grosvenor and others to stage a Day of Mourning to coincide with nationwide celebrations, on 26 January 1938, of 150 years since the landing of the First Fleet, and with a re-enactment of this landing.

## Representing the national story: Aboriginal performance and re-enactment

The re-enactment that was part of official proceedings against which the Day of Mourning protested also involved Aboriginal people, some likely known to Tom Foster. In initial negotiations, the pageant committee had sought a group of performers from Palm Island and were in discussion with the Queensland Chief Protector's Office to arrange their travel. The committee had proposed film director Charles Chauvel as a suitable chaperone for the performers, who had already travelled to Sydney two years earlier for his film *Uncivilised* (filmed partly on Palm Island and partly in Sydney).[27] Aboriginal performers from Palm Island had participated in a range of public performance events including for the Duke of Gloucester in Brisbane in 1934. There is every reason to think that these kinds of performances for visiting royalty, as for major commercial films, were undertaken willingly. Indeed, in Western Australia, Nyungar performers had protested that their preparedness to perform a corroboree for the Duke had been overlooked. Quoted in the *Westaustralian Worker*, they asserted 'we ought to have been given a chance to show our respects to the Duke when he came to these shores. There was enough of us here who could have given H.R.H. a real corroboree … Instead of the mock corroboree given by the Boy Scouts'.[28]

Ultimately the NSW Protection Board's proposal to bring performers from Western NSW was less costly than the Palm Island idea, and negotiations with the NSW board more favourable.[29] The performers eventually brought in by the board came from Menindee Aboriginal Reserve in Western NSW. Descendants of these performers, like Aunty Beryl Philp Carmichael, who was a small child at the time, recall that the performers were coerced to travel to Sydney, and that fellow community members worried that they would not be back – were they to be massacred?[30] But some of these performers had also been brought to Sydney only six years earlier, and had paraded across the Sydney Harbour Bridge with Foster, and camped at Vaucluse House alongside locals resident in the Sydney area and from up and down the coast. Shannon Foster recalls that her great-grandparents Tom and Eliza Foster's house at La Perouse Aboriginal Reserve was a hub for Aboriginal visitors passing through Sydney.[31]

What then was different about the 1938 re-enactment? Like some of the earlier performances, it was a chance to perform Aboriginal culture and presence in a public event. It echoed Foster's own performances in the 1930 film *In the Days of Captain Cook*. Like the Sydney Harbour Bridge Pageant, it involved Aboriginal people in celebrations of national significance, in which Australians came together to mark a shared moment, even if the role of Aboriginal people was always framed as historical, rather than forward-looking. The performers from Menindee were photographed rehearsing for the official events on Sydney Harbour. Dressed in suits and shoes, the media reported that 'with their trousers tucked into their socks, the aborigines brought from Menindie to take part in the Birthday Pageant shuffled through a war dance … watched by the critical eye of Mr. Claude Flemming, Director of the Pageants', though the accompanying photograph showed an apparently humour-tinged scene with grinning dancers and onlookers alike (Figure 2.5).³² Directed by the pageant organizers' interpretation of Australian history, the performers' role was 'to express wonderment, and friendly curiosity in the white men landing from what seemed to them to be a great canoe'. This, the media claimed, was 'in accordance with historical records'.³³

Aunty Beryl recalls that the men's extraction from the reserve for the trip to Sydney was a traumatic one. A different attitude to travelling to perform in 1938, compared to 1932, may reflect changes in the communities of people around Menindee, and in the role of the Aborigines Protection Board (APB). Just as representations at a Sydney inquiry into conditions at Menindee were being reported in the Broken Hill papers, the all-male group of performers were travelling to Sydney for their performance in the re-enactment of Captain Phillip's landing. Menindee Aboriginal Reserve, situated outside of the township of Menindee on the Darling River, was only acquired by the APB in 1934. Almost 200 people were transferred there, including Ngiyampaa people

**Figure 2.5** 'Aborigines Dance in Park', *The Sun*, 19 January 1938, 3. https://trove.nla.gov.au/newspaper/article/231113349.

from their former APB residence at Carowra Tank Reserve, and Paakantji residents of the Darling River region, who had previously been camped in various locations around Pooncarie, Menindee and Wilcannia. By 1937, the appalling conditions at Menindee Aboriginal Reserve, in which tuberculosis was rife and residents were confined in tin huts in temperatures of 44°C, were a key trigger for an enquiry into the actions of the APB. Activist William Ferguson, whose brother Duncan Ferguson resided at Menindee, gave evidence to the enquiry, pointing out that the Menindee Reserve was located dangerously near to an old Aboriginal cemetery, a claim dismissed by the manager's wife Agnes May Park as 'superstition'.[34]

This coerced massed travel was by no means the men's first experience of public performance. The men brought down to Sydney included seasoned travellers and performers, such as Hero Black, a man well known in Western NSW who had been born on Marra Station, employed as an accordion player for boats on the Murray River, composer of tunes such as *The Menindee Waltz* and accustomed to travelling and performing up and down the eastern part of Australia from Queensland to Victoria.[35]

For the 1938 re-enactment, the performers, led by Black and including Archie Boney, Anzac Williams and Jimmy Wongrem,[36] were vocal about the unsatisfactory travel conditions, though it was the conditions, rather than their role in the pageant that seem to have been at the heart of their complaints. Black asserted they had been unable to go anywhere alone, received no pay for their performances, and were being accommodated in the yard of Redfern police station along with police dogs. In a response, John R. (Jock) Milne representing the APB noted that 'he had been instructed not to permit any persons access to them'. This may have been the reason for the APB rejecting the suggestion that the performers be accommodated in an Aboriginal camp at the showground, rather than in a police yard.[37] The APB claimed this was because 'persons with ulterior motives wished to get in touch with the aborigines', Chief Secretary Chaffey suggesting that 'steps had been taken to ensure the comfort and protection of the aborigines while in Sydney, and it would appear that mischief-makers were grieved that action had been taken to prevent the aborigines from being exploited.'[38]

However, activist and Aboriginal accounts of the Day of Mourning protests clarify these veiled references to the 'ulterior motives' from which the performers were being protected. Participants in the Day of Mourning were well aware of the presence of performers from Menindee in Sydney for the Pageant. Secretary to the Aborigines Progressive Association (APA), Helen Grosvenor, learnt from her father employed at Redfern police station that the Menindee performers were being billeted in huts in the courtyard. J. R. Milne, the APB manager, who had also overseen participants in the Harbour Bridge Parade, wielded the tools of the APB bureaucracy to ensure that William Ferguson and fellow activists were unable to make contact with the visitors, even though Sydney relatives of one of the Menindee performers, Peter Johnson, attempted to see him at the barracks.[39]

The concurrence of the enquiry into the APB and the 150-year anniversary of colonization, both involving residents of Menindee, highlights the intrinsically political nature of Aboriginal performances throughout this period. Performers came together in public performances of nationhood, and each time they asserted the connectedness of Aboriginal communities across the eastern region of Australia, and the commonality of their interests in performing to maintain culture, reinforce kinship and emphasize Aboriginal presence. Performing the role of Aboriginal people responding to Phillip's landing may have been a disturbing element of the Menindee performers' travels to Sydney, but recent issues in how control was exerted by the APB also likely influenced the performers' experience of being forced to perform. The board's deliberate intervention in separating Aboriginal people from each other, and the attempts of Sydney-based Aboriginal people to communicate with the visiting performers, made the Menindee performances a highly contested assertion of Aboriginal presence.

Though Paakantji and Ngiyampaa descendants attest to the duress under which performers were taken from Menindee to perform the re-enactment, the board, as a matter of course, was resistant to events that would take performers away from community or outside of the state of NSW, especially those driven by entrepreneurial initiative rather than state celebrations. Indeed, the APB persistently blocked the movements of Aboriginal people under their jurisdiction. In 1938, Mapotic Cinema Auckland wanted to tour three Aboriginal men around theatres in New Zealand, and wrote to the APB for permission – it was denied.[40] Also in that year, the board denied a request for six schoolchildren from the Aboriginal Reserve of Cumeroogunga (Cummeragunja) to participate in a concert tour in Victoria. They only reconsidered when the manager of the reserve intervened, setting conditions on the travel.[41] Similar requests for travel for sporting events were also denied by the board – including a ban on 'inter-station visits of Aboriginal teams', though football and cricket matches were to be permitted on Sundays at Aboriginal reserves, and a request to take the boxer Alby Roberts to the Philippines in 1933 – also denied.[42]

Limiting Aboriginal people's opportunities in this way was framed within the thinking of protectionism. When proposing an amendment to the Protection Act in 1934 that would make it unlawful for an Aboriginal person to be removed from NSW without the APB's written permission, the board cited a case 'of an aborigine taken to Perth as an entertainer, and left there destitute by his employer who went abroad to Singapore'.[43] But decisions on what Aboriginal people should be protected from were also in the hands of the board. The board's membership was constituted chiefly by elected government representatives, and therefore had a vested interest in how the state intended to control Aboriginal people. The treatment of the Menindee performers in 1938 was justified by claiming that there were those who wanted to exploit them. But the performers may well have welcomed the 'mischief-makers' from whom they were being protected, given that these activists were agitating for recognition of Aboriginal people's claims to citizenship and representation rights, were often directly campaigning against the actions of the APB, and some were even family members.

Commemorative re-enactments for official events are peppered through the history of performance in the 1930s and outside of the main capital city events I have discussed so far. In 1930, an 'all-Australia exhibition' was proposed at Sydney's defunct Maroubra speedway site to include a 'seven-acre tract depicting Early Australia, and the life and pastimes of the aborigines of the period'.[44] When the seventy-fifth year anniversary of European settlement of the Bellinger River region in NSW was celebrated in 1933, the 'Back to the Bellinger' commemoration included Aboriginal performers playing gumleaves and 'home-made guitars', as well as 'thirty-five full-blooded aborigines in the corroboree in full warpaint and ceremonial dress'. Ever the intermediaries for public representation of Aboriginality, the APB would contribute to the Bellingen corroboree and re-enactment of the landing of Captain Cook by providing ceremonial dress as well as a supervisor – Jock Milne, who had supervised Aboriginal performers' participation in the Harbour Bridge pageant, and would oversee the Menindee performers later in the decade.[45]

In 1934, Melbourne celebrated its centenary, and the inclusion of Aboriginal people in festivities provoked considerable discussion in the preparation years. Initially the proposal was that a group should be brought from Queensland for the celebrations. John Porter visited Queensland to plan the installation of an Aboriginal village which 'would be enclosed with an eight-feet iron fence and the whole enclosure will be restored to a completely primitive state. Visitors could purchase samples of native work such as boomerangs and spears. Every night different programmes would be provided in the central clearing. Realistic night attacks on prospectors would be staged by the aborigines'.[46]

But Porter's vision of a return to a primitive state (behind an iron fence) had failed to engage the Queensland Chief Protector of Aborigines, who immediately refused consent for the plan to 'exploit Aborigines', asserting the right to prosecute anyone removing Aboriginal people from the State.[47] The Victorian Board for the Protection of Aborigines (BPA) had also been approached to involve the Lake Tyers Concert Party to perform at the celebrations, but this request was denied.[48]

Ultimately the vision for representing Aboriginal culture was realized by the participation of the Aborigines' Inland Mission of Australia, who proposed quite a different display of Aboriginality – one that would demonstrate how Aborigines had 'embraced the white man's culture' – 'a unique opportunity for advertising the mission's work'.[49] The small group of performers who participated in the Centenary's Outback Australia Exhibition were Wangkangurru (Wonkonguru) people from Central Australia, who travelled accompanied by Protector of Aborigines and ethnologist George Aistone, and built *mia-mias* on the Melbourne Town Hall stage performing 'corroboree songs' and demonstrating weapons, bark paintings and ceremonial objects.[50] The exhibition at Melbourne Town Hall also featured well-known Aboriginal speakers Doug Nicholls and David Unaipon, who featured alongside Aistone and A. P. Elkin.[51]

In the lead-up to William Ferguson's founding of the Aborigines Progressive Association (APA) in 1937, he also participated in the Melbourne centenary celebrations, producing several floats for the parade – reportedly at the request of Kew City Council.[52] The group of Aboriginal performers who travelled with him from the north of NSW staged a depiction of historical scenes, and subsequently toured their gumleaf shows back in NSW.[53] Outside of commemorative events, public concerts of Aboriginal gumleaf bands were frequently advertised or reported on in papers, along with fundraising concerts serving a number of different causes, and performances for pure entertainment purposes, including rodeos and Wild West shows.[54]

## Representations for international visitors and on the popular stage

At urban Aboriginal reserves, tourism catered for both local day trippers, and also for international visitors. Sydney's La Perouse Aboriginal Reserve was frequented by passengers from cruise ships as well as visiting musicians and composers who wanted to meet Aboriginal people and know something of their musical traditions. In some cases, these visits were mediated through the Protection Board. Entertainment provided for passengers of the *S.S. Mariposa* in 1932 resulted in a payment of £10 from the American Express Company to the APB, who tabled a discussion at their meeting on how the funds should be distributed. (The outcome of the discussion was not documented).[55] Among the passengers was the composer Rudolf Friml, who was not only able to witness the corroboree staged by residents of La Perouse, but who was also treated to a rendition by the gumleaf band of his song 'Rose Marie' about the Métis (Aboriginal) Canadian lead role of Rose-Marie La Flamme of Friml's operetta by the same name.[56]

As with Friml's visit, visits with Aboriginal people by well-known performers were often reported in the papers with little more than a caption and a publicity photo. One early such report showed another connection to North American Indigenous cultures, publishing a photo of touring Sioux baritone Chief Eagle Horse in his meeting with 'an Aboriginal Queen' at La Perouse – Emma Timbery.[57] Chief Eagle Horse publicly commented on Australia's White Australia Policy, suggesting that had he travelled as John Jones, his skin colour would have posed no problems to Australia's immigration agents. Travelling under his actual name, he was detained on the boat until his employers signed a guarantee that he would be returned to the United States.[58] In many captions, visitors were reported to have fulfilled a life-long dream of meeting an Australian Aboriginal, as with the characterization of African American soprano Dorothy Maynor's meeting with Yankunytjatjara woman, Nancy Brumbie.[59] Maynor also offered to mentor Aboriginal soprano Nancy Ellis.[60] But some African American performers took a far more political approach to these meetings. Visits from African American dancers Katherine Dunham and Alvin Ailey and musician Paul Robeson in the 1950s and 1960s, and their public advocacy about Aboriginal rights are discussed in Chapters 4 and 5.

The 1930s also saw attempts to support the creation of new Australian work in the performing arts. In the genre of musical theatre, Nathalie Rosenwax created a prize in 1932 for a new work of light opera or revue. The second prize was awarded to Varney Monk's *Collits' Inn*, which subsequently premiered on 5 December 1932 at the Savoy Theatre in Sydney. *Collits' Inn* received around a hundred performances at major theatres in Melbourne and Sydney between 1932 and 1934 and was broadcast on ABC radio in June 1933.[61] As representation of Australian history, the show had it all. There were 'British soldiers in red coats, bushrangers with beards and revolvers, and blacks holding their corroborees in mountain fastnesses', as media commentators remarked when *Collits' Inn* was revived for Victoria's Centenary celebrations in 1934.[62]

The corroboree scene was a ballet interlude involving members of the cast in black-face with 'aboriginal costumes copied from photographs in the Melbourne Public Library'.[63] Inspiration for the corroboree had been derived from the singing of Queen Rosie, a senior woman from the Lake Illawarra (Wadi Wadi, Dharawal) tribe recognized by the wider community as a leader along with her husband King Mickie, also known for his knowledge of performance traditions.[64]

Drawing a direct comparison to Friml's evocation of Aboriginal Canadian performance in *Rose Marie*, Monk recalled that her corroboree scene 'was considered to be more spectacular than the Totem Dance in Rose Marie … and the wild abandon of the Snake and Kangaroo corroboree thrilled the audiences'.[65] Reviewers too drew parallels with *Rose Marie*, the Melbourne Argus suggesting that *Collits' Inn*: 'satisfies as no Rose Marie or Lilac Time can satisfy the long thirst for the symphony of the shaded road or the bushland barbarism of the corroboree in strains that owe nothing to the past.'[66]

This thirst for representation of bushland barbarism may be one reason the musical has not become part of the canon of Australian works, and in spite of its popularity in the 1930s, its iconic status was not retained into the later twentieth and twenty-first centuries. The same fate befell many of the productions emerging out of these efforts to foster an Australian style in the 1930s. No organization was more central to these efforts than the ABC.

## An Australian creative school: Composers, critics and the ABC

Non-Indigenous Australian art music composers in the 1930s were also turning to recordings of Aboriginal music (if not to living Aboriginal people) to inspire ideas for what might characterize an Australian creative school. Locally, renewed focus on building a national musical style emerged from the formation of the Australian Broadcasting Commission (ABC) in 1932. The advent of the ABC as a publicly driven cultural institution was foundational in the formation of an Australian musical culture. In 1967, Roger Covell suggested that 'Its federal directors of music have affected the whole movement of professional music-making'.[67] The Broadcasting Act of 1932 that established the ABC articulated a mission to form ensembles of musicians that would enable the rendition of high-quality performance.[68] Within a year of its establishment, small permanent orchestras had been established in Sydney and Melbourne, eventually moving towards professional orchestras in each state.[69] The ABC actively supported a range of Australian composers, including American-based composer Percy Grainger, who toured in 1934–5 combining hundreds of concerts with a series of twelve broadcast lectures about a broad range of musical topics.[70] Grainger later suggested that Australian audiences had been unreceptive to his 'more ambitious pieces'.[71] His 1934–5 lectures advocated for attention to non-Western musics, and in his opening lecture he pointed to the 'tunes that are lithe and graceful as snakes, and highly complex in their rhythmic irregularities' to be found in Australian Aboriginal music. The majority of the musical examples used to demonstrate his twelve lectures were drawn from Western art music, and Grainger was interested in how art music composers could use folk or 'primitive' melodies and rhythms in their compositions, but he also played examples from folk music and referred his audience to the recordings of Arrernte (Arunta) music recorded by E. Harold Davies.[72]

The ABC also explicitly encouraged the development of a national style both in its stated policy and support of composer/conductors like Clive Douglas and John Antill. In 1933, the Commission's first annual report stated its aim to 'lay the foundation of an essentially national musical literature'.[73] Composer Clive Douglas was appointed as conductor of the ABC's Tasmanian Symphony Orchestra in 1936 and remained in the Commission's employ as a conductor for thirty years. His Australianist works emerged from the first years of his employment by the ABC, during which he researched 'Aboriginal folklore in an attempt to find a means whereby an Australian expression could be injected into my music'.[74] In 1938 and 1939, he composed the opera *Bush Legend* (later reworked as *Kaditcha*), and orchestral tone poems *Corroboree* and *Carwoola*. Douglas' works were widely performed and he was awarded five national prizes for composition between 1933 and 1956.[75] However, Douglas never garnered the popular reception that John Antill's compositions of the 1940s would soon attract. A contemporary of Douglas, Antill too had joined the ABC in 1936, also working as a conductor of the Wireless Chorus, but offsetting this leadership with a range of administrative roles that saw him based in Sydney. After the premiere of Antill's *Corroboree* in 1946, the ABC would support Antill to study orchestration in London, promoting him to music supervisor for NSW on his return (see Chapter 3 for further discussion of Antill's works in the 1940s).[76]

A key public commentator who supported and pushed the ABC's national-style agenda was critic and editor of the *Australian Musical News*, Thorold Waters. Waters' reviews of many of the new works being performed in the 1930s were influential in setting an agenda focused on Australian national style. In commentary on performances of new works by Clive Douglas in 1937, Waters suggested that Douglas' works were early contributions to the kind of 'distinctive national creative school' that the ABC should be fostering.[77] Waters' encouragement of efforts towards a national style also extended to approval of (New Zealander) Alfred Hill's opera *Auster*.[78] Douglas recalled that he was strongly influenced by Waters' call for a national school, and immediately set his mind to the task.[79] Reception of his works would never hit the heights predicted by Waters' review, but Douglas remained engaged with the exploration of national creative style throughout his career.

The chief characteristic of this search for a national style was an investigation of the potential for Aboriginal music to offer something to Western art music composition. This approach was an attempt to ground an Australian tradition in a history more extensive than the 150 years Europeans had occupied the continent, and was consistent with European approaches to national musical styles that in the previous hundred years had increasingly sought to exploit folk music traditions in composers' homelands, bringing modal scale systems, extended metre and rhythmic figures into romantic and post-romantic classical music. In a theorization of this approach to folk musics published in 1956, Douglas referred directly to these European antecedents. He contrasted the materials of Aboriginal music to those available to European composers, suggesting that Aboriginal melodies were 'unmusical and undiatonic' and that the 'primitive rhythms give a monotonous regularity of the most elementary accent'.[80] To create an Australian symphonic style, Douglas suggested expressing these qualities through orchestration and proposed that a further challenge lay in attempting to evoke the diverse landscapes of the Australian continent. Using examples from his own works, he asserted that he knew of 'no other composer using the aboriginal idiom in symphonic music'.[81]

The characteristics of the turn towards Aboriginal music differentiated composers like Douglas and Antill from some of their predecessors. Percy Grainger (1882–1961) had also aimed to create a nationalist music that tied him to his home in Australia, even while most of his career was spent in the United States and Europe. But Grainger's peculiar brand of nationalism sought to explore the racial origins (as he imagined them) of white Australians, and so sought out Nordic music as a model for his theorization.[82] In some works, Grainger composed original tunes that mimicked the qualities of Anglo-Celtic folk song, while avoiding quoted material from existing song traditions.[83] Composer and writer Henry Tate advocated for the creation of a musical idiom that would imitate the sounds of nature and incorporate music in a treatise published in 1924.[84] Tate had specific advice about using Aboriginal music, though it has been followed by few composers:

> The music is surprisingly interesting. Wild and barbaric as much of it sounds, it is rich in rhythms and themes that, once annotated and fixed, will supply a copious reservoir of melodic germs and rhythmical fragments of the type that composers all over the world are continually seeking. Apart from the merely melodic and superficial aspects of this music, a deeper significance is not lacking in the novelties of musical architecture it suggests, and the extraordinary vivacity and vitality of utterance that are the outward evidence of a spirit within that might well inspire a composer who could respond to that mystic element which eludes description as effectually as it stimulates creative thought.[85]

Experiments in utilising Aboriginal melodies had also begun many years before. Naturalist John Lhotsky (1795?–1866?) had published the Australian colonies' first printed music in 1834 in collaboration with arrangers George Sippe, Joshua Josephson and James Pearson.[86] The arrangement for voice and piano was based on a song Lhotsky had heard Ngarigu women sing in his travels through the Monaro region, titled 'A Song of the Women of the Menero Tribe'.[87] In 1842, composer of Australia's first opera Isaac Nathan (1790–1864) had published settings of songs from Ngarigu and Wellington Wiradjuri song traditions.[88] An inference of Aboriginal rhythms has also been read into new compositions from the 1910s and 1920s by Percy Grainger (*The Warriors*) and Roy Agnew (*Dance of the Wild Men*).[89]

In 1937, another setting of Aboriginal folksongs was published based on songs sung in Queensland. Alfred S. Loam's arrangements were based on songs collected and notated by Dr H. O. Lethbridge in and around Maranoa, Queensland in his years of living there and touring the countryside as a regional doctor. Loam, conductor of the Maranoa orchestra, arranged the songs for voice and piano. They were published in 1937 and were received with claims that they might form the beginning of an Australian national folk tradition.[90] Published as the set *Aboriginal Songs*, they soon became well-known items of the Australian music repertoire.[91] Lethbridge and Loam also included the songs among other settings of Aboriginal melodies in performances by the Maranoa orchestra. In one concert in July 1938, the *Aboriginal Songs* were presented alongside a 'Narranyeri Dance' (presumably Ngarrindjeri) amongst a programme of works of Schubert, Mozart, Beethoven, Purcell, Brahms and Sibelius.[92]

These 1930s compositions were not the start of a tradition of 'aboriginal' parlour songs, but rather a vestige of the nineteenth century, when pianos became commonplace in bourgeois and upper-class households in Britain and continental Europe. Playing and singing parlour songs was one way that European women could demonstrate their breeding and social literacy. The possibility of songs with piano accompaniment was literally brought to Australia with the First Fleet in 1788, when assistant-surgeon George Worgan brought a Frederick Beck square piano to accompany his voyage on the *Sirius*, leaving it behind when he returned to England in 1791.[93] Currently being restored for return in 2020 to coincide with the 250th year anniversary since James Cook's visit, the piano is symbolic of the musical culture brought to Australia by the settler colonists, and which operated as a tool of cultural representation when Aboriginal songs were altered and curbed into the pitch and rhythmic conventions of European songs with piano accompaniment.

In recordings made by Alan Coad, the 'Aboriginal songs' featured alongside other Australiana, such as such as 'Swagman's Song' and 'Waltz with me Matilda' and Aboriginal tenor Harold Blair adopted them as part of his standard repertoire in the 1950s.[94] Margaret Walker's Unity Dance Group also took two of Loam and Lethbridge's songs on tour to communist nations to include 'aboriginal songs' alongside other Australian folk music (see Chapter 4) and choreographer Gertrud Bodenwieser utilized Loam's arrangements to accompany her new work *The Kunkarunkara Woman* in 1955.[95] Composer Peter Sculthorpe later used the song melodies in a range of his compositions, including *Two Aboriginal Songs* (1949), *Into the Dreaming/For Cello Alone* (1993, 1994, 1998), *Maranoa Lullaby* (1996, 2007, 2012), *Lullaby* (2003) and *Requiem* (2004).

The folkloric approaches to melody setting used by Loam, following in the stead of Lhotsky and Nathan, took a melody and set it to piano accompaniment. However, the composers of the 1930s and 1940s fostered by the ABC attempted an abstraction of the musical elements into large-scale orchestral compositions, in which the notion of musical drones (inspired by didjeridu), kernels of rhythm and melodic contour were placed alongside formulaic expressions of primitivism through driving rhythms, extensive use of percussion and short, repeated phrases. This was the kind of Western art music practice that would not only reach a wider public than the parlour song genre was able to approach, but would also address the expectations of music critics and music historians seeking to encourage an emerging national tradition of composition.

The criticism of Thorold Waters was crucial in this process, as was advocacy for Antill's *Corroboree* by English conductor Eugene Goossens, who would later exert considerable influence on Australian music as first permanent conductor of the Sydney Symphony Orchestra and director of the NSW Conservatorium of Music from 1947–56.[96]

Retrospectively, Antill's abstraction of an idea of Aboriginality into his orchestral work *Corroboree* would be assessed as a seminal moment for Australia finding its national voice (see Chapter 3). Roger Covell's influential 1967 music history *Australia's Music* reinforced the idea that Antill's *Corroboree* was the first work to make the public aware 'that music truly belonging to the twentieth century was being written in Australia', finding fault with Douglas' 1938 *Corroboree*.[97] But Covell also suggested that the true pioneer of naturalized Australian music was to be found in the 1930s, with Margaret Sutherland, a composer who, Covell asserted, had established a 'distinct personality in Australian composition'.[98]

Writing for chamber ensembles more prominently than orchestras, more than fifty of Sutherland's compositions were recorded by the ABC, even if she was never employed and supported as a member of staff in the manner of Douglas and Antill.[99] Arguably, this comparatively lesser institutional support also made Sutherland's contributions to the forming national school less publicly visible. Once orchestras had been established in each state by the 1950s, orchestral works started to feature among Sutherland's works, but chamber music remained dominant. Though Sutherland asserted her identity as a composer influenced by the Australian environment and culture, she never sought to create the kind of Australianist music favoured by Douglas and Antill. Her only works engaging with Aboriginal subjects were her 1950 tone poem *Haunted Hills* and her 1965 opera *The Young Kabbarli* (see Chapter 5). One patriotic work, *Land of Ours*, was performed during the 1934 Victorian centenary celebrations, and again in 1938 for the sesquicentenary.[100]

Aside from the institutional support from the ABC enjoyed by Douglas and Antill, both composers were also composers of film scores for the Department of Territories, the ABC and the Commonwealth Film Unit (later Film Australia). These government bodies would produce numerous films throughout the 1940s and 1950s in line with government policies of assimilation and administration of colonial territories (like PNG). In combination with Antill's role as the composer of music for state and royal visits, Antill and Douglas were the musical mouthpieces of the state in Australia's mid-century.

The institutionalization of musical culture marked by the advent of the ABC, not just as national broadcaster, but as driver of cultural agendas, founder of orchestras and employer of emerging composers, delineates the 1930s as a starting point for development of Australianist music. In Chapters 3 and 4, we will see how Antill emerged as a key creative voice in Australia's efforts to define a cultural identity. In the decades of the 1940s and 1950s, alongside, but unconnected to the ascendance of Antill, Aboriginal performers continued to represent themselves in public cultural spheres and to use performance as a political tool in the fight for civil rights.

# 3

# 1940s – Reclaiming an Indigenous identity

In 1947, Ted Shawn arrived in Australia for a three-month stay. Internationally renowned and widely credited as co-founder of the American modern dance movement, Shawn was to teach courses in the technique and philosophy of dancing hosted by Perth's Patch Theatre, and deliver lecture recitals supported by the Adult Education Board.[1] Shawn's tour of his lecture recitals featured American folk dances, including his famous 'Invocation of a Thunderbird' dance, presented in Native American feathered headdress and moccasins, as well as an Osage-Pawnee pow wow dance, and African American and Cuban spiritual dances. The American dances were juxtaposed with his interpretations of dances from the Syrian Sufi dervish tradition, Japanese, Spanish and Indian dances.[2] The highlight of Shawn's visit, widely reported in the media, was a stay of five days at the Aboriginal community of Delissaville (now Belyuen), south of Darwin, where Shawn watched performances by thirty dancers.[3] Building on his established repertoire, Shawn wished to recreate some of the Australian Aboriginal dances on his return to the United States. At the close of the first night's performance, Shawn reportedly addressed the performers, saying: 'I have come half-way round the world to see you dance ... I have seen some of the greatest dancers in the world and this night I have seen them equalled.'[4]

Accompanied by journalists John Ewers (on his first visit to an Aboriginal reserve) and Douglas Lockwood, guided and advised by Native Affairs Officer Bill Harney, and hosted by Superintendent Tom Wake, Shawn exchanged dance practices with Delissaville dancers (Figure 3.1), many of whom had been recalled to the community from elsewhere; as one article reported, 'Many Darwin housewives as a consequence find themselves without domestic labour'.[5] Though the dancers were recalled from work, they were compensated only in rations for the performances for Shawn. He had capitalized on the cheapness of Australian sugar, bringing a quantity for payment of the dancers, 'The rest of the payment will be in flour, tobacco and tea'.[6]

Ewers, who had expected 'the dancing of an illiterate and primitive' people, was astonished to find: 'The whole thing was so like a theatrical performance, so rich in choreographic detail, such a curious blending of drama and comedy, that I could not think of them as ritual dances.'[7]

**Figure 3.1** Ted Shawn dances for the natives at Delissaville native settlement, NT, 1947, John K. Ewers collection of photographs; BA1658/5/28,31, 428–9, 109612PD, SLWA.

In subsequent interviews, Shawn hailed the dancing of *wangga* dance leader Mosik (Mosec) as 'a mature artist, combining intensity with emotional ebullience' (Figure 3.2). Shawn had observed the dances of many 'primitive peoples', but never anything 'so highly evolved'.[8] Another standout artist was Beeanamu (Bianomu), who 'would be a sensation in London or New York'.[9] Though Shawn had found his way to Delissaville, his visit had begun by hearing John Antill's music for *Corroboree*, an indication of the sway (as representation of Aboriginal music) that Antill's new musical work already held just one year after its premiere.

In this chapter, I look first at the performances of Aboriginal people in patriotic efforts during the war and then post-war events that saw Aboriginal performers asserting their presence on public stages through organizations like the New Theatre, leading to all Aboriginal productions in 1948 and 1949. I then discuss Aboriginal

*1940s – Reclaiming an Indigenous Identity*  47

**Figure 3.2** Mosek (centre) dances in tourist corroboree in Darwin Botanic Gardens, 1948, still from film *Doorway to Australia*, 1949, National Film Board, courtesy of NT Archives, NTRS 3543.

tenor Harold Blair's entry into the world of classical music and the role of composer Margaret Sutherland in this. Blair's travels to the United States mark him as unusual among Aboriginal performers, who as a rule were blocked from travelling outside of Australia. However, his tour is also an example of new exchanges of culture between Australia and the United States evidencing a shift in orientation away from the British motherland and towards a fellow settler colony. Finally, I show that while Aboriginal people were opening up new spaces for representing their performing arts in Australia and abroad and attracting acclaim for their artistry, the ABC was supporting non-Indigenous composers in their continuing exploration of representationist music.

## War-time participation and new public venues for Aboriginal performance

The war years (1939–45) saw a relative hiatus in cultural activity in Australia. However, the necessity for full participation in the war effort opened up entry points for Aboriginal people to become part of the national narrative. Many young Aboriginal men quickly sought to enlist in the armed forces, though many were discharged through discriminatory policies before they were sent overseas to serve.[10] The tools of Aboriginal performance were also wielded in aid of the war effort as performers were rallied to the recruitment of young men. Victoria's Lake Tyers community (who had been excluded from national commemorations of colonial history in Victoria's centenary celebrations in 1934 – see Chapter 2) was involved in these recruitment drives to an extraordinary extent. Gumleaf bands from Lake Tyers Mission Station performed in recruitment drives for WWII after a mass enlistment of twenty-six men from the community in 1940. As Alick Jackomos recalled, 'They performed regularly at recruitment rallies outside the Melbourne Town Hall, playing in their Gum Leaf Band on the tray of a military truck'.[11] Gumleaf bands had been a key medium for ensemble performance for Aboriginal musicians since around 1900.[12] In the 1920s and 1930s established groups associated with Wallaga Lakes Aboriginal Station toured all around NSW, becoming involved in a mixed bag of events, from fundraisers to parades, sporting events and community concerts.[13] The repertoire of gumleaf bands included minstrel songs like those by Stephen Foster, 'Swanee River' and 'Old folks at home', Australian folk songs like 'Jacky Jacky' and Christian hymns.[14]

In Melbourne, the Aboriginal community around Fitzroy included members who had lived on Lake Tyers, Wallaga Lakes and Cummeragunga stations and reserves. During the war, members of the community organized dances at local halls as well as public concerts that rallied public support for the soldiers serving overseas. These concerts also publicly demonstrated the contributions of Aboriginal Melbourne residents to the war effort. Margaret Tucker was the organizer of one of these, in aid of Red Cross Prisoner of War Funds in March 1944. Melbourne's *Argus* suggested that audiences would experience something new in this display of Aboriginal talent. In the article, which promised hula hula girls trained by Tucker herself, teenage contralto Lucy Green and firemaking and gumleaf performances, Tucker's contributions to the war effort were emphasized. Not only was she employed full-time at a munitions factory along with three other 'Aboriginal girls' also involved in the concert, but her daughter was employed at the Department of Aircraft Production and her husband was a gunner in the 9th Division.[15] In later life after a career of advocacy for Aboriginal rights, Tucker described her experience as a soprano singing in concerts at dances and in high-class homes, only to return to the daily grind of work as a maid.[16]

The potential for Aboriginal performers to contribute their performance expertise to patriotic efforts was also recognized elsewhere. Queensland Aboriginal, Torres Strait Islander and South Sea Islander Dulcie Pitt (later Georgia Lee) with her sisters Heather and Sophie formed the Harmony sisters during WWII, and with brother Walter performed jazz and blues popular with African American soldiers stationed in the Cairns area of north Queensland.[17] In shows at the Trocadero during the war, Dulcie Pitt sang and performed hula and performed in fundraising for the Red Cross, continuing the performance of Hawaiian traditions when she moved to Sydney in 1944 (soon adopting her stage name Georgia Lee and relocating to Melbourne in 1949).[18] In NSW after performers from the Purfleet Aboriginal Station staged a 'Corroboree and Vaudeville', promoted by the station's Superintendent J. R. Milne (who had also coordinated performers at the Sydney Harbour Bridge opening and 1938 re-enactment events – see Chapter 2), the *Manning River Times* suggested the performers could be deployed for 'patriotic purposes'. The entertainment had been excellent, and the performers were 'ready and willing to help'.[19] The format for this show also foreshadowed large-scale performances that would be staged in Melbourne in the later 1940s, combining contemporary popular song items, dances (Charleston and hula), comedy and a gumleaf band in one half of the programme, with performances of corroboree dances, in body paint in the second half.

At least some of these performers seem to have staged the same show again, much further south, in Kincumber, north of Sydney. The *Gosford Times* reported that many of the performers travelled down for seasonal bean-picking work, and had staged the show at Kincumber School of Arts.[20] The travel between Aboriginal stations and reserves and sites for bean picking and other seasonal work has featured prominently in oral histories of Aboriginal lives in the 1930s and 1940s.[21] These travels also meant that performers separated by hundreds of kilometres in their places of residences met for parts of each year and shared music and dance. This may explain the quick and wide proliferation of practices such as gumleaf bands playing popular tunes and of hula dancing.[22] Author Anna Vroland commented in 1951 that a gumleaf band appeared at almost any entertainment she attended in Aboriginal Victoria.[23]

The migration of performance traditions also mimicked seasonal movement that had been practised by people on the east coast for thousands of years. Dharawal elder Queen Rosie reported that all tribes from Wollongong to Jervis Bay could speak one language, but south of that they could not.[24] These families in turn were related to many residents of La Perouse Aboriginal Reserve in Sydney, who (like the Timberys) traced their lineage back to those who had met Captain Cook at Kurnell. People up and down the NSW coast often resided at a number of different Aboriginal reserves over time ranging over a couple of hundred kilometres.[25]

Gumleaf playing also showed up in some mission-organized bands, where European instruments such as accordions, tambourines and string instruments dominated. One such touring group in the 1940s visited the eastern states from the West Australian Mt Margaret Mission. The Mt Margaret Native Minstrels featured fifteen Aboriginal children from the Mission, accompanied by the Mission's director (Rod Shenk) and his children and a musical director (Lindsay Lovick). A photograph from the Shenk family's collection shows the musicians, two of whom played gumleaves (Figure 3.3). The group's repertoire featured African American spirituals, and even Aboriginal composer and gumleaf player Tom Foster's Aboriginal spiritual 'I'm happy today'.[26] Reviews of the performances attested to the fine instrumental playing and singing.

In local communities, occasions for music and dance were a way for Aboriginal people to gather together in wartime. In Sydney's Redfern, Bill Onus had organized weekly dances at the Railway Institute Hall. Candy Williams continued these when Onus returned to Melbourne, Onus then organising community dances in the Aboriginal community of Fitzroy.[27] By the late 1940s, public, commercial shows with a distinct political component appeared alongside the localized concerts and dances. The credentials of participation in the war effort were still used to promote these post-war concerts. The New Theatre's August 1946 production *Coming our Way* and the

**Figure 3.3** Mt Margaret Mission Band in Melbourne, February 1947, photo taken by *The Herald Melbourne* and published 14 February 1947, BA1340/Era4/53A2, SLWA. Back: Bundathunoo Fred Carey, gum leaf; Ningan Malcolm McDonald, drum; May Miller (O'Brien), tambourine; Ben Mason, banjo-mandolin. Centre: Bitha Joy Earle, tambourine; Stanley Evans, gum leaf; Front: Jessie Jones (Evans), ukulele; Laurel Nganyun Johnston (Cooper); ukulele; Dan Harris, kettledrum; Amy Waylee Arnold (Brownley), piano-accordion; Lois Thomas, banjo-mandolin; Sadie Corner (Canning), banjo-mandolin.

ballet *White Justice* depicted ongoing Nazi occupation of Spain, and advertised the contributions of Aboriginal dancers by noting concerts they had given in army camps and hospitals and fundraising for prisoners of war; one dancer had even served in the Middle East and New Guinea.[28]

Capitalizing on this stage for sharing performance cultures, acclaimed dancer Eric Onus emphasized the potential for Aboriginal dance to be part of European dance traditions:

> Even in art forms, such as ballet, aboriginal and European culture could be brought harmoniously together, Eric Onus, member of the Aborigines' League in Melbourne stated during the week. He was referring to the aborigine ballet which is a feature of the revue Coming Our Way, now at the New Theatre, Flinders St. It represented an important step in the fuller development of his people. The ballet is based largely on corroboree movements, and depicts the struggle of the aborigines against exploiting squatters, and their final reconciliation with the white man.[29]

1940s – Reclaiming an Indigenous Identity        51

The event featuring the Aboriginal performers dancing to the music of Finnish composer Sibelius dealt with a strike of Aboriginal station workers in Port Hedland in northwest Australia (see Interlude). Dancer Margaret Walker recalled that the journalist Jim Crawford had visited Port Hedland and told the group about it on his return; the dancers, led by Eric Onus, used the story as the basis of their ballet.[30] Importantly, in the same month as the public-facing show was staged, members of the Melbourne Aboriginal community also staged a cultural revival event, reported in the media as 'an attempt to counter the effects of the white man's civilization' – language markedly different from Onus' description of the potential for bringing together of traditions.[31] In this event the Australian Aborigines' League on the land of a 'white sympathiser' in Heidelberg came together in a tribal dance (Figure 3.4). Footage of this event was taken by Bill Onus, and appears in Alec Morgan and Tiriki Onus' new film *Ablaze*.[32]

Figure 3.4 'Aborigines Seek to Regain Their Tribal Culture', *Examiner*, 12 August 1946, 1. http://nla.gov.au/nla.news-article96488537.

In another follow-on event, Jim Crawford wrote a play, *Rocket Range*, about Aboriginal people being moved off their lands in Central Australia to make way for a defence facility, and featuring a cast of Aboriginal characters (performed by non-Indigenous actors in full body make-up, with the action performed in silhouette) at Sydney's New Theatre in 1947.[33] Aboriginal presence in this production was mediated through contributions from non-Indigenous artists and researchers. Music for the production was composed by John Antill, who had quickly shot to prominence as a public commentator on Aboriginal culture, following the premiere of his ballet *Corroboree* in 1946.[34] Weapons for the production were borrowed from photographer Axel Poignant. Staged again in 1948 at Melbourne's New Theatre, the theatre introduced the film with a screening of C. P. Mountford's film *Walkabout* showing Central Australian Pitjantjatjara people explaining rock art galleries at Uluru and dancing the associated stories.[35]

Eric Onus' appearance in the New Theatre's production of *White Justice* was significant for several reasons. Firstly, it is evidence of emerging ties between Aboriginal performers and radical theatre closely associated with left-wing politics and the Communist party in Melbourne and Sydney. The New Theatre was not synonymous with the party, but frequently staged plays characterized by the media as propaganda plays. It also presented amateur theatre in a public setting, and its theatres, established in the 1930s in Sydney and Melbourne created an outlet for creation of and public engagement with new works, which continues today (albeit in Sydney only). For Aboriginal performers like Eric Onus, this was just one stage on which presentations of culture were appearing, but it would continue to be a forum for advocacy for workers' rights as well as Aboriginal rights into the 1950s (as I discuss in Chapter 4).[36] On these stages, Aboriginal performance was presented to a majority non-Indigenous audience, complementing the performance contexts created by Aboriginal people for each other.

Other shows in this public performance genre would soon follow, and it seems that *White Justice* may have been a springboard for further shows. Echoing Eric Onus' sentiments in his 1946 performances at the New Theatre, the 1948 corroboree season at Wirth's Olympia in Melbourne aimed to show that 'the Aborigine is quite capable of development along cultural lines'.[37] A permanent circus between 1907 and the 1950s on the site of the present-day Melbourne Arts Centre, Wirth's included large-scale Aboriginal displays in 1948 and 1949. These corroboree seasons featured performers from all states, some of whom had appeared in the New Theatre's 1946 *White Justice*: Princess Lilardia (Margaret Tucker), Tom Foster (fire-stick manipulator from Lake Tyers), Bill Onus (boomerang expert), Eric Onus, Jamesy Scath (comedian and dancer), Edgar Bux (versatile baritone), Bill Bargo (whipcracker, guitarist and bushcraft expert), Ted (Chook) Mullett, May Lovett, Joyce McKinnon, gumleaf bandsmen and ritual dancers. Harold Blair (tenor) provided the commentary.[38] The Aboriginal performers invited 100 Repatriation Hospital Diggers to a show as an 'anzac gesture' in 1949.[39]

One reviewer thought the show was disappointing in being 'straight vaudeville', including hula dancing, singing cowboys and comedians, when the crowd had booked to see 'their first Aboriginal corroboree'.⁴⁰ The potential for this corroboree to emphasize traditional performance had been reinforced by media leading up to the event, showing painted-up performers holding boomerangs, with a bush backdrop (see Figure 3.5).⁴¹ Eric Onus was appraised by reviewers as the standout performer, in his role as a dancer and in several other acts.⁴² Following his performance in *White Justice*, Onus had featured in another 1946 play *Fountains Beyond* that told the story of Aboriginal people living on the outskirts of white society who were sporadically offered employment to turn ancestral sites into urban landscapes. In the original 1942 production, half of the cast blacked up with body make-up.⁴³ In the 1946 production, Sydney actor Charles Stanley played the 'half-caste' lead role of Vic, while Eric Onus played the lead role of Henry, an 'old aboriginal, who clings to tribal standards'. Displays of 'native instruments' and photographs from the Northern Territory adorned the foyer at the shows.⁴⁴ Onus' theatre work complemented his activism for Aboriginal rights, from protests about seasonal workers' conditions in 1942, to his participation in the forming of the Australian Aborigines' League (AAL) in 1946, his role in this organization was also remarked upon in media reports about the production *Fountains Beyond*.⁴⁵ The branding of the 'corroboree season' at Wirth's Olympia as a production of the League was also reported as an effort to 'encourage interest in aborigines' claims for citizen rights'.⁴⁶

Figure 3.5 'Aborigines Prepare for Corroboree', *Daily Advertiser*, 23 April 1948, 1. http://nla.gov.au/nla.news-article144755228.

Audiences' disappointment, as reported in the media, on finding that the 'corroboree season' was 'straight' vaudeville, expresses the tension of assimilation-era politics. Public statements by Eric Onus and the AAL indicate that the show attempted to demonstrate inter-cultural literacy – the ability of Aboriginal people to both display the uniqueness of their performance culture, and simultaneously to demonstrate mastery of popular performance genres common to European vaudeville shows. While in daily life Aboriginal people were expected to display mastery of European social mores in order for their claims to citizenship rights to be seriously considered, on stage audiences wanted a different kind of authenticity, one which marked the performers out as unblemished by European influences.

Similarly, contradictory expectations came from Aboriginal Welfare Boards, who did not embrace the claim to citizenship rights that was a natural conclusion of Aboriginal people's adoption of settler approaches to life. While A. P. Elkin publicly argued for assimilation as a strategy to gradually prepare Aboriginal people for taking their place as full citizens, he also denied political agency to those Aboriginal people who actively advocated for these rights in their own manner. As member of the NSW Aborigines Welfare Board throughout the 1940s, Elkin oversaw denials of permission for requests from Bill Onus to enter Cummeragunja Reserve in 1941 accompanied by a photographer from *Pix* magazine (Onus had been among those to walk off in protest in 1939 – see Interlude), and William Ferguson's request for a rail pass to visit all Aboriginal stations and reserves also in 1941.[47] Ferguson and Onus might have been held up as examples of successful assimilation, being men who were articulate, stably employed and upstanding members of their communities, but their outspoken advocacy for the rights of other Aboriginal people was greeted with suspicion by those same groups ostensibly working for the assimilation of Aboriginal people.

The performance events of the 1940s were a platform used by the AAL to appeal for public recognition of Aboriginal culture. Fighting the same battle from another front, Harold Blair an Aboriginal tenor studying at the time at Melba Conservatorium of Music, acted as narrator for the corroboree seasons at Wirth's Olympia. Blair would soon become well-known across the nation for his tenor voice, presenting recitals of European art song nationally and travelling to the United States for training and concerts.

Until 1944, Blair had been an agricultural worker in Queensland. Born on Wakka Wakka Country on Cherbourg mission and being later moved to Purga Mission, Blair had worked on farms after obtaining an exemption certificate releasing him from the control of Queensland's Native Affairs. Blair subsequently met unionist Harry Green at Ipswich, who invited him to a Communist Party event at Ipswich Town Hall. Green enthusiastically advocated for Blair, setting up an audition with famous Wagnerian soprano Marjorie Lawrence at the Lennon's Hotel in Brisbane.[48] Lawrence immediately contacted the media to publicize the raw talent she had heard in twenty-year-old Blair's voice, the discovery echoing her own astronomical trajectory from rural Victorian farmer's daughter to principal soprano of the Paris opera.[49] Interested in the potential for Blair to stand as a public representation of Aboriginality, Lawrence was quoted in widely syndicated media reports to tell Blair: 'You have a fine voice. If you work hard you will be one of the greatest ambassadors for your race it is possible to imagine ... You can do more than politicians or fine speeches.'[50]

With continuing support from Harry Green and his networks of unionists, Blair soon found his way to the Melbourne Council for the Encouragement of Music and the Arts (CEMA), where composer Margaret Sutherland was acting secretary and would continue to mentor and promote Blair in the years that followed (Figure 3.6).

**Figure 3.6** Photograph of Margaret Sutherland at the Piano with Harold Blair and a Number of Children, Records of the Australian Musical Association, 1952–95, 1940s, Envelope S, NLA.

Sutherland rallied CEMA to support Blair's application to the Melba Conservatorium, where he began to study music in July 1945.[51] Australia's first CEMA had been formed in 1943 by Dorothy Helmrich after her return from touring Europe as a mezzo-soprano and observation of the UK organization by the same name. Like its UK model, CEMA's objective was 'to take the arts to the people – the country people – to encourage amateur groups – to provide a field in which artists could support themselves by their art'.[52] Given these aims, it is perhaps unsurprising that Melbourne's CEMA seems to have had strong representation from members of the Communist party and sympathizers.[53] These networks shared common political interests with Harry Green's unionist networks.

While Blair's years of study at the Melba Conservatorium were a crash course in European art music education, his residence in Melbourne also provided opportunities to build networks of Aboriginal performers and activists like fellow Aboriginal student and contralto Lucy Green, and leaders Bill Onus and Pastor Doug Nicholls, whose public performance activities were just getting started in the mid-1940s. Blair also met touring African American singer Todd Duncan in June 1946, an event which precipitated his tour of the United States in the early 1950s.[54] Enduring collaborations were formed in these years between Blair and many members of the Melbourne Aboriginal community, and would extend into the Sydney Aboriginal community – La Perouse Aboriginal people giving him a farewell luncheon before his US tour.[55] Blair and Doug Nicholls would repeatedly collaborate in public performance, and a number of regional shows in the 1940s and 1950s featured Blair as singer and Nicholls as speaker. In 1947, Blair appeared in an 'All Australian Aborigine Variety Show' organized by Nicholls. The show also featured Lucy Green, Margaret Tucker (Lilardia) and numerous performers from the Melbourne Aboriginal community in demonstrations of hula, 'corroboree dance', tap dancing, guitar playing and singing, with musical arrangements by the participants.[56]

Blair's participation in the Olympia's corroboree season and later in the *Aboriginal Moomba* 'Out of the Dark' (see Chapter 4) is evidence of his embeddedness within circles of Aboriginal activism and cultural expression that were finding voice in the 1940s. But he also successfully bridged the separation between these cultural events and those officially supported by arts bodies and the ABC. Before departing Australia, he toured as a soloist with the Queensland Symphony Orchestra, sponsored by the ABC, and then embarked on a farewell tour in 1949 singing around twenty-five benefit concerts; on the opening night he was accompanied by Margaret Sutherland on piano.[57] The tour raised the necessary funds for his travel to the United States. At one Adelaide concert, Blair also premiered one of Sutherland's new works, *The Bush*, to a large audience including a considerable number of Aboriginal people, who packed out the town hall.[58] Blair's performance as alternate cast for the National Theatre production of Smetana's opera *The Bartered Bride* was evaluated as 'first-rate'.[59] While there was some confusion over the lack of birth records when obtaining a passport, Blair was not blocked from travelling to the United States as some of his Aboriginal colleagues would be a few years later (see Chapter 4 and Interlude). In the United States, he studied with Todd Duncan's own teacher, Sara Lee, and with Lola Wilson Hayes.

In spite of accounts suggesting that Blair only began to speak about Aboriginal rights late in his career, his participation in performances staged by the Australian Aborigines' League coincided with his classical music training in Melbourne.[60] He performed in these public demonstrations of culture, and increasingly began to use the platform of his fame to advocate for Aboriginal citizenship rights, especially access to an education equivalent to that of other Australians.[61] In performance too, Blair sought to keep his Aboriginality in frame even as he demonstrated his mastery of European performing traditions. At early performances, he habitually presented his hosts with boomerangs from home as a gift of thanks, and as his solo career developed, Blair performed settings of Aboriginal songs from Maranoa in Queensland and from Central Australia as part of his repertoire (discussed further in Chapter 4).[62]

## Representing an Aboriginal idyll: Non-Indigenous composers and the ABC in the 1940s

Margaret Sutherland's close association with Harold Blair occurred in a period when some of her works evoking the Australian bush and Aboriginal culture were first performed. *The Bush*, performed by Blair, had been composed in 1934 and her major work *Haunted Hills* was composed in 1950 (see also Chapter 4). In the timing of this, Sutherland was in step with her contemporaries, though 'Australianist' work was not the main business of her compositional practice. Her style is often considered exemplary of innovative Australian composition in the mid-century, though she did not receive the widespread public accolades of many of her male colleagues.[63] Many of Sutherland's contemporaries (especially Clive Douglas and John Antill, introduced in Chapter 2) also sought to pioneer an Australian style that evoked Australia's natural environs and the presence of Aboriginal people, but these did not involve any active engagement with Aboriginal performers or musicians. The music created by some of these colleagues also drew on musical motifs and primitivist characterizations in a way that Sutherland's music did not. The work composed in 1946 that would eclipse all others was John Antill's *Corroboree*.

As Jennifer Hill has suggested, *Corroboree*'s rise to fame is 'almost mythic in Australian music history'.[64] Its discovery was precipitated by conductor Eugene Goossens, who recounted in 1948 that he had asked to be shown some Australian works during his first Australian tour. Of the forty orchestral scores delivered to his hotel room, almost all were deemed unworthy. The rose among the thorns was Antill's *Corroboree*.[65] Goossens subsequently partially premiered the work in Sydney in July 1946, performing the full score in London in October (with an Australian 2BL broadcast arranged to coincide with the performance) and in Cincinnati in November of the same year.

Antill attended the London performance in person, his fare having been raised over a four-day period by public subscriptions through the *Daily Telegraph*, supplemented by donations from the NSW Minister for Tourist Activities and Immigration (Clive

Evatt), Sydney Savage Club, the Musical Association of NSW, Actors Equity and musical families.[66] The mythology of this Australian music origin story was made all the more powerful by Goossens' subsequent influence on classical music culture in Sydney as first permanent conductor of the Sydney Symphony Orchestra and director of the NSW Conservatorium of Music, and as member of various cultural boards and committees hosted by the ABC.

*Corroboree's* presentation to a visiting British conductor also foreshadowed the trajectory of Antill's career with his repeated commissions for visiting British royalty (see Chapter 5). Until this point, John Antill had enjoyed a career as conductor of the Wireless Chorus, alongside other roles at the ABC, but this one orchestral work launched his reputation as a composer. The formula of ballet based on Aboriginal themes was one which Antill continued to explore to considerable financial and professional (if not lasting artistic) success throughout his career, as we will see in Chapter 4.

Some scholars describing the key protagonists of this Australianist style have likened composers' approach to the Jindyworobak literary movement headed by poet Rex Ingamells, which attempted to incorporate words from Aboriginal languages into English-language poetry.[67] Composers including James Penberthy, Douglas and Antill, working in parallel through the late 1930s to incorporate Aboriginal themes into their compositions, cherry-picked Aboriginal elements in much the same way as the Jindyworobak poets.

For Penberthy, the first Aboriginal-themed work was *Euroka*, a ballet based on an Aboriginal myth of a 'sun goddess', while Douglas and Antill each independently titled their work *Corroboree* – a word deriving from the Sydney Dharug language, but which had been vernacularized in Australian English and used across the country by Aboriginal and non-Indigenous people alike.[68] Douglas and Antill harvested musical elements from what they understood of Aboriginal music – especially using or mimicking Aboriginal instruments – to imbue symphonic works composed for large orchestral forces with an Indigenous flavour. Douglas and Antill were also building on a longer history of Australian composers using Aboriginal music in this way to inspire new works (as discussed in Chapter 2). When Roger Covell published his account of Australia's music in 1967, he assessed these attempts to create a national style drawing on Aboriginal music as deserving of 'sympathy rather than ridicule'. Holding up Margaret Sutherland as a truly unique Australian voice and believing in the promise of Peter Sculthorpe, Covell appraised 'the Jindyworobak idea' as 'basically ... a kind of longed-for "short cut" to cultural maturity and national identity; an impatience with the slow process by which a literature truly naturalizes itself in a newly settled country and a desire to, as it were, take advantage of the experience of the Aboriginal inhabitants of Australia and their uniquely close relationship with the country'.[69]

But for all the reassessments that hindsight produced, the impact of Antill's *Corroboree* after its first performance in 1946 and its centrality for several decades afterwards as a key work in Australia's musical literature should not be underestimated.[70] In 1972, James Murdoch reported that it was still the best-known work in the repertoire, and that alongside Douglas' *Namatjira* (1956) and Robert Hughes' *Sinfonietta* (1957), it was broadcast at least once a fortnight on the ABC, 'though Sculthorpe's *Sun Music* must be rapidly replacing it'.[71] In 1982, *Corroboree* received an award for 'Most performed Australasian serious work' from the Australian Performing Rights Association (APRA), with further awards in 1985 and 1989.[72]

The post-war years also saw new organizations formed that would complement the cultural work of the ABC. In 1945, Richard Goldner founded Musica Viva, a chamber music organization that would create further contexts for performance of Australian art music (see discussion of Musica Viva festivals in Chapters 6 and 7). And in 1948, the Arts Council of Australia became a national body. The new national institution brought together Arts Councils across the states and territories as part of concerted efforts to build cultural infrastructure. The state bodies had grown out of state CEMA organizations, modelled on organizations of the same name in the United Kingdom and supporting art for the people (their support of the New Theatre and of Harold Blair has already been discussed). Mimicking the 1947 name change of the UK branches, the new president of the national Arts Council was Dorothy Helmrich, who had established CEMA in 1943.[73] While the ABC retained its focus on orchestras and promoting large-scale works, the Arts Council toured a range of smaller ensembles alongside orchestral productions, ensuring that music and dance reached regional towns and communities. In the 1950s, the Arts Council would become a key organization for sponsorship of touring shows (as I discuss in Chapter 4). The genesis of *Corroboree*'s shift from popular orchestral work to national ballet spectacle can be found in Helmrich's efforts with the Arts Council in the late 1940s. As Helmrich later recounted, in conversations with Antill in 1949, 'we decided it could be made into a very interesting ballet ... Artistically and financially it was one of the biggest theatrical "hits" in Australia'.[74] In fact attempts had been made to commission a ballet production of *Corroboree* at Sadler's Wells in 1947, but this did not go ahead when proposed choreographer Robert Helpmann reportedly decided he would need more background knowledge about the complexities of the ballet before attempting it.[75] Nor were Helmrich's offers of a commission to Australian-based choreographers Eduard Borovansky and Gertrude Bodenwieser taken up.[76] Ultimately it was Rex Reid who produced the first choreography for the 1950 production.

## Taking Aboriginal music to the world: US–Australian exchange in the 1940s

The immediate post-war era not only saw a flourishing of attempts to define Australian cultural identity in new ways, but also the redrafting of international diplomatic relationships. US soldiers had been stationed in Australia during the war, and Aboriginal and Torres Strait Islander performers' role in entertaining the troops has already been mentioned. Harold Blair travelled to the United States for a national tour and to receive further singing tuition from celebrated African American singer and campaigner against segregation Todd Duncan in 1949. This seems to have been the first time a performer openly identifying as Aboriginal was permitted to travel to the United States as an independent artist. Another well-known performing artist, circus high-wire performer Con Colleano already enjoyed a high-profile international touring career by this stage. But Colleano adopted the public persona of a Spanish performer, the obscuring of his Aboriginal identity allowing a freedom of movement that otherwise would have been impossible.[77]

Attempts by other Aboriginal performers to tour to the United States in subsequent years, like that of Bill Onus in 1952, were quickly quashed by ASIO (Australian Security Intelligence Organization).[78] It is possible that Blair's outspoken engagement with civil rights in the United States and the comparisons he drew in public speeches to segregation of Aboriginal people on reserves in Australia may have increased the wariness of the Australian government about allowing Aboriginal people to represent themselves to a wider Australian public.[79] Certainly, any agitation or union activity by Aboriginal people was routinely linked to the Communist Party and thus flagged as a potential security risk (see further discussion in Chapter 4).

Formal collaborations between Australia and the United States also emerged in the last years of the 1940s. One large-scale collaboration was the Australian-American Scientific Expedition to Arnhem Land that travelled across the Far North over nine months in 1948, with a team of American and Australian scientists. Leader of the expedition C. P. Mountford had already toured his films depicting Central Australian Aboriginal rock art in the United States, and his collecting efforts would bring into circulation recordings of Aboriginal music and dance performance from the north that would influence new musical and choreographic works for a number of years afterwards. Always with an eye to building his reputation as an ethnographer, Mountford formed reciprocal relationships with composers and choreographers, disseminating his recordings of Aboriginal song to composers such as Mirrie and Alfred Hill and encouraging them to use them as the basis of new compositions. Mountford also introduced the composers to those who could stage performances of these new works, each composer and choreographer crediting Mountford as the point of origin of the stories, and song materials that formed the basis of their works.

During one of his American tours preceding the Arnhem Land expedition, Mountford met American dancer Beth Dean and her Australian baritone husband Victor Carell. Inspired by Mountford's films, and his extensive knowledge of Aboriginal art and performance practices, Dean and Carell began to investigate the potential for creating new performance works based on Aboriginal dance and music. In 1953 Victor Carell recounted that the idea to 'exploit Australian song' came to him while working on NBC radio programmes in New York in 1945.[80] After hearing a programme of South African folk songs, Carell put together his own programme of songs, a path that led him to arrange to meet Mountford, who was touring his films about Aboriginal art in the United States at that time.[81] Dean and Carell would arrive in Australia in 1947 as part of the cast of the touring Irving

Berlin musical, *Annie Get Your Gun*. During the three years of touring with *Annie*, they pored over books by anthropologists T. G. H. Strehlow and A. P. Elkin and in particular Spencer and Gillen's 1899 *The Native Tribes of Central Australia* and films made by Mountford at the Department of Information film studio, described in a publicity article about Dean as 'sacred male dances no woman is allowed to witness'.[82]

By 1950 Dean and Carell had channelled these resources into a new show 'Dance and Song around the World' toured by arts councils and adult education boards across Australia (see Chapter 4). Mountford had also shared recordings of songs from Groote Eylandt and Oenpelli (now Gunbalanya) collected on the expedition with the married New Zealander/Australian composers Alfred and Mirrie Hill.[83] Mirrie Hill used these recordings as the basis for several piano compositions in 1949, while Alfred sourced Australian content for his songs from Aboriginal poems recorded, reworked and published by Bill Harney and A. P. Elkin.[84] Mountford not only encouraged others to use songs collected by him in their creative works, but closely followed the works, maintaining friendships with both the Hills, and Dean and Carell, and preserving copies of their outputs and the press surrounding them among his papers.[85]

As suggested by these interactions, the reciprocal sharing of Aboriginal cultural materials between anthropologists and creative artists was self-referential, like many non-Indigenous conceptualizations of Aboriginality, including the dying race discourse.[86] Non-Indigenous choreographers looked to the writings of non-Indigenous ethnographers, and to the compositions of non-Indigenous composers for ideas and inspiration. Their self-referring discourse explicitly excluded Aboriginal people, while simultaneously making a claim to authority to speak on Aboriginality and Australian identity. In looping back to anthropological discourse, performances of Aboriginal culture reproduced early Australian anthropological practices that Patrick Wolfe has characterized as a 'soliloquy – a Western discourse talking to itself'.[87]

The materials collected through ethnographic research circulated among Australian creators of new work, but visiting artists frequently sought to meet directly with Aboriginal performers. Ted Shawn, whose engagement with Aboriginal dancers in Delissaville opened this chapter, was just one such visitor. Shortly after Shawn's visit, another American would mimic his approach to combining European dance traditions with Indigenous ones from around the world. Like Shawn, Beth Dean would praise the genius of Mosek, and share her dance practices with Aboriginal dancers in remote communities. Dean's efforts to perform Aboriginal dances may have been inspired directly by meeting Shawn in Melbourne shortly after he had seen Mosek perform, an experience she and her husband recalled decades later.[88] Dean credited Shawn as the father of 'ethnic dance' (with co-founder Ruth St Denis) and soon became a local expert in a range of world dances. Within six years of this meeting, Dean would be recognized as an Aboriginal dance expert, choreographing the second, and most famous, staging of Antill's *Corroboree* and performing it for the gala performance for Queen Elizabeth II in 1954.

## From wartime to national identity: looking to the 1950s

The evidence of cultural exchange between the United States and Australia in these immediate post-war years was not just the result of new ties forged through the presence of the US military during the Pacific war, but also coincided with Australia's weakening ties to Britain.[89] The post-war era coincided with reconceptualization of Australian citizenship, as distinct from British citizenship, and a push for a dramatic programme of immigration that would bolster Australia's population in light of fears about the security of the nation's borders. James Curran and Stuart Ward describe the 'new nationalism' characterized by the disorientating effects of the separation from Britain. This disorientation reflected not only Australia's weakening ties to its imperial parent but also the downgrading of the racial ties of empire.[90]

The 1950s would see renewed political agendas in which a new uniquely Australian national identity would be defined. This identity was necessitated by the impetus to impress upon waves of new immigrants the expectation to assimilate. In the realm of Aboriginal policy, the ideas underpinning assimilation had been in circulation since 1937 (discussed in Chapter 2), but assimilation began to dominate public policy with renewed force from 1951. Following the 1951 national native welfare conference, Paul Hasluck would tell the media: 'it was expected all persons of aboriginal blood or mixed blood in Australia would live like white Australians. The acceptance of that policy governed all other aspects of native affairs administration'.[91]

As the Aboriginal administration impressed upon Aboriginal people the need to integrate more closely into mainstream Australian culture, increasing pressure was placed on the maintenance of specific regional Aboriginal traditions. Just as Aboriginal people were increasingly steered away from maintaining their own cultural practice, non-Indigenous people turned new attention towards it. The desire for a uniquely Australian identity, rather than one defined by Australia's links to Britain and greater Europe captured the attention of non-Indigenous creative practitioners for decades to come. A crucial element of this more inward-looking attempt to define Australian culture was the turn towards cultural practices that were uniquely Australian; those of Australia's First People, especially those of the Centre and Far North.[92] Resistance to these overarching agendas of cultural replacement would characterize Aboriginal music and dance performance in the early years of the 1950s.

4

# 1950s – Jubilee celebrations, protest and national cultural institutions

In March 1951, the North Australian Workers' Union (NAWU) newspaper, the *Northern Standard*, printed extracts of a letter from Sydney's New Theatre. A group representing the New Theatre had leafleted performances of John Antill and Rex Reid's ballet *Corroboree* at the Tivoli Theatre. The leaflet told audience members that in Darwin Aboriginal people were refusing to stage a different kind of corroboree, in solidarity with a leader of workers' strikes Fred (Nadpur) Waters:

> the proud people who danced their Corroborees in the freedom of their tribal life had changed ... no one who tonight has seen the great cultural debt we owe to the original Australians can ignore these things. The integral idea of human rights, which is the very corner stone of all culture, demands that we do something more than admire aborigines from the safe distance of the Tivoli auditorium.[1]

Fred (Nadpur) Waters had been banished for a period of six months from Bagot Aboriginal Reserve in Darwin to the remote Central Australian community of Haasts Bluff (Ikuntji) some 1,700 km distant, after leading a strike of Aboriginal workers.[2] In solidarity with Waters and the previous strike leader Lawrence Wurrpen (Urban) who had been gaoled, Daly River and Tiwi performers had staged a corroboree strike in February 1951, refusing to perform for American visitors disembarking from the Stella Polaris and disrupting the Darwin Botanic Gardens' regular entertainment for cruise ships.[3]

In Melbourne, the Australian Aborigines' League passed a resolution 'condemning the intimidation of the Northern Territory aborigines by the Native Affairs Branch' and sent protests to Prime Minister Menzies.[4] New Theatre member and founder of the Unity Dance Group, Margaret Walker also published a review of Antill and Reid's *Corroboree* ballet linking it to the current state of political, economic and social exclusion suffered by the Aboriginal owners of the cultures that had inspired it:

Corroboree was interesting for the first 15 minutes ... after that, the lack of story or explanation of the symbolism makes the ballet, in spite of very good theatrical effects, somewhat tedious ...

At the same time as Aboriginal Fred Waters is being sent to certain death at Haast's Bluff for leading a strike of Aborigines in the Northern Territory for better conditions, we cannot watch the ballet without considering the other side of the picture of the life of the original inhabitants of Australia – and what the white invasion has meant to their tribal life. LET US REGISTER OUR PROTEST AGAINST THE INHUMANE TREATMENT OF THE ABORIGINES BY THE DEPARTMENT OF NATIVE AFFAIRS BACKED BY THE BIG BUSINESS INTERESTS OF THE NORTHERN TERRITORY.[5]

Walker then went on to discuss her own planned dance productions. Her work would depict 'Scenes of Aboriginal Life – showing tribal life, the invasion of the white man – leading up to the recent Fred Waters case'. This show would be toured to East Berlin in June 1951. Among the performers would be Wiradjuri man Ray Peckham and Aboriginal rights campaigner and South Sea Islander activist Faith Bandler.

The leafleted March 1951 performances of Antill and Reid's *Corroboree* at the Tivoli were part of a nationwide tour of the ballet, funded by the Arts Council of Australia and the ABC as part of the celebrations of Jubilee year – fifty years since the Federation of Australia as a nation. The early 1950s saw a proliferation of music, dance and theatre performances after the relative quiet of wartime and recovery in the 1940s.

In scholarly accounts of the wild success of Antill's ballet, and its quick adoption as symbol of an emerging national culture, the political entanglements with Aboriginal and workers' rights reported by the NAWU are wholly absent. Yet, this was by no means the only time politics would encroach on national celebrations and their expression in the arts. To contextualize these developments, I start by introducing the arts institutions that began to play an active role in supporting Australian music events in the 1950s. These organizations led discussions about the kind of performances that should be presented to the Australian public during the Jubilee celebrations, engaging with emerging concepts of post-war cultural identity and the impression of its national culture that Australia should seek to project.

## Cultural renewal – arts bodies in the 1950s

Cultural policy that had drawn the focus of governments of the late 1940s generated a range of new initiatives for cultural renewal in the early 1950s. In 1954 the Australian Elizabethan Theatre Trust (AETT) was established 'to provide a theatre of Australians by Australians for Australians'. Named to commemorate the first visit of Queen Elizabeth II to Australia, 'the hope in 1954 was that there would occur in the arts in Australia a new Elizabethan age, as productive and inspiring as the first Elizabethan age in England in the sixteenth century'.[6]

The trust was a visionary influence on local arts. Though triggered by a visit from the British Queen, the trust's efforts marked a turn towards continental European performance genres and support for home-grown institutions for local cultural production. It established national opera (1956) and ballet companies (1962) and their associated orchestras (1969), and would found the National Institute for Dramatic Arts (NIDA, 1958), the Australian Chamber Orchestra (1975) and other important national companies. Supplementing these nascent national companies, the trust also toured an astonishing range of Australian and international companies throughout Australia in the 1950s and 1960s.

Important African American dance companies, and those from non-European dance traditions, especially India, were toured by the AETT. Companies such as Katherine Dunham's and Alvin Ailey's (in 1956 and 1962/5 tours respectively) exposed Australian audiences to established African American modern dance, even at the same time as paranoid national politics continued to discriminate against applications from non-white potential immigrants.[7] Touring artists also brought their politics with them, engaging with local social issues in direct ways. During her 1956 tour, Dunham used the stage of the Tivoli Theatre to open a fundraising campaign for Aboriginal girls in Melbourne, handing a cheque to Aboriginal leader Pastor Doug Nicholls.[8] African American dance traditions would also go on to be highly influential in the creation of Aboriginal dance companies in the 1960s and 1970s. Ailey and Dunham were succeeded by the Eleo Pomare company who performed at the Adelaide Festival of Arts in 1972. A core dancer from this group, Carole Johnson would remain in Australia playing a pivotal role in training Aboriginal dancers and establishing the Aboriginal Islander Dancer Theatre (AIDT) (see Chapter 7). The Trust also directly intervened in the representation of Aboriginal music and dance on Australian stages in its efforts of 1963, as we shall see in Chapter 5.

Alongside the Trust, performing arts were also supported by Arts Councils and Adult Education Boards. As discussed in Chapter 3, the Arts Council of Australia formed as a national body in 1948, bringing together Arts Councils across the states and territories (now called Regional Arts councils). The 1943-founded NSW Division (formerly Council for the Encouragement of Music and the Arts (CEMA)) was led by Dorothy Helmrich, and was a key organization in one of the milestone events of the 1950s – the two productions of John Antill's ballet *Corroboree* staged to considerable fanfare in Sydney and toured nationwide in 1951 and 1954.[9]

The Adult Education Boards' touring programmes discussed in this chapter included the extensive tours of Beth Dean and Victor Carell.[10] The Tasmanian Adult Education Board placed particular emphasis on bringing performers to small towns in Tasmania, since the island was not on the touring schedule of most performing companies, and therefore had little access to music, dance and theatre.[11] The Tasmania Adult Education Board supported Dean and Carell's shows in the early 1950s within the scope of their aims for the 'popularisation of science through simple practical research' and 'Discussion group courses on subjects in demand: literature, appreciation of music ... understanding painting, drama, economics, world affairs, etc.'[12] Dean and Carell's shows, in which they depicted song and dance from all over the world, including Aboriginal Australia, were billed alongside dancers performing their own cultural traditions, such as Shivaram from India, through evening concerts that ended the day's classes and toured a selection of small towns.

The Arts Council also toured local and international groups including Gertrud Bodenwieser's dance company (1951–7), Latvian dancer Vija Vētra performing Indian and other dances (1962), the Kalakshetra Dancers of Madras (1966) and the Ronne Arnold Modern Dance Company (1968). African American dancer Ronne Arnold would collaborate with Beth Dean over the subsequent decade (including on productions of *Corroboree*), eventually becoming involved in the Aboriginal and Torres Strait Islander dance training institution NAISDA.

It would be more than a decade after the end of WWII before most of these arts bodies and new performing companies would become established institutions. The directions in which they would develop were in evidence in the first major national display of culture in the new decade – the Jubilee Festival. The ABC continued to have a hand in the curation of performance events, and was heavily involved in the organizing committees for major public events for the Jubilee Festival. Marking fifty years since Federation of Australia as a nation, the Jubilee saw a wide variety of performances staged around Australia, but especially in Sydney and Melbourne.

## 1951 – Representing Australian culture for the Jubilee

For the most part, Jubilee celebration events did not differ greatly from the kinds of community gatherings familiar to most residents of Australian towns and cities – presented in this year on a grander scale than annual events might have been – including agricultural shows, race meetings, fireworks displays, football matches, parades and military tattoos.[13] But from their earliest meetings, the Federal Arts Sub-committee for the Commonwealth Jubilee Celebrations 1951 also debated what large-scale performances might be included that would attract more than the usual amount of attention, especially internationally, from overseas newspapers, radio reporters or newsreel organizations. One proposal put to them to address this was to hold a massed Aboriginal corroboree in all states (see Chapter 1).

This proposal never came to fruition, but the justifications offered by those advocating for it reveal a growing preoccupation with how Australia might represent itself culturally on the world stage. As member of the NSW Publicity Sub-committee Ken Hall (producer-director of Cinesound Productions) wrote in his minute proposing the corroboree:

> This Jubilee Year should be used, as far as humanly possible, to achieve world-wide publicity for this great and rapidly growing Democracy IN ADDITION to its other most important function – that of inculcating into the Australian mind a sense of National pride …

The American people have made wide use of the American Indian in National publicity.

We, in Australia, have not made use of the Aboriginal race at all. The average Australian himself knows little, or nothing, of the Aboriginal people and inbred in many Australians is a feeling that approximates contempt for them – born no doubt of the attitude of many of the earlier settlers towards them. They were called a 'degraded race' and many other derogatory remarks were and are still being thrown at them.

The Australian Aboriginal, out of contact with the white man, is anything but a degraded person, has real dignity, undoubted intelligence and bush-craft which is equalled by few other Native peoples. Fair minded men will agree that the Aboriginals have not always had complete justice at the hands of the white man who took their hunting grounds from them.

THIS JUBILEE CELEBRATION COULD BE USED TO GIVE THE ABORIGINAL PEOPLE A NEW STATUS IN THE EYES OF THE WHITE INHABITANTS.

As an even bigger thought [sic] – put forward by another member of the Committee, Mr MacAlpine of Consolidated Press – was that the occasion might be used for the Commonwealth Government to make some gesture towards the Aboriginal people in this Jubilee Year.[14]

Hall proposed that the government work with the Aborigines Protection Board to produce the corroboree, by bringing 75 to 100 Aboriginal men, women and children 'practically in their tribal state', 'to become the highlight of Celebrations in each State'. These people could camp on showgrounds, living 'at least somewhat as they do in the wilds'. The recruits could 'perform Corroborees, indulge in spear and boomerang throwing, fire-making, give examples of tracking, and many other interesting occupations', or be part of a larger bushman's carnival involving both Aboriginal and white stockmen. Hall's conclusion returned to the theme of political recognition implicit in this proposal: 'The Aborigines should eventually – or at least a representative section of them – arrive at Canberra for the Commonwealth Celebrations in May and it is then that some gesture on the part of the Commonwealth Government towards the Aboriginal people could be made'.[15]

Hall was a member of the publicity sub-committee, not the arts sub-committee. The latter, to whom the idea was referred, quickly sought ways to quash the massed corroboree proposal, even though it had been forwarded for advice to the Department of the Interior and to chair of the committee, Charles Moses (also long-term general manager of the ABC). The department had thought it difficult, but not impracticable, however, Moses declared that there was no money for such an event. A. P. Elkin weighed in to assert a protectionist agenda, advising that bringing Arnhem Land Aboriginal people south (Arnhem Land not being an explicit stipulation of the proposal, but presumably implied in the reference to Aborigines 'practically in their tribal state') would pose the 'grave risk that they would suffer in health, even a likelihood that one or two would catch bronchitis or pneumonia and die. This would have a very bad effect upon the tribe'. He also expressed doubts about the possibility of reproducing a 'true corroboree atmosphere' in a showground.[16]

The event did not go ahead. Moses and his ABC assistant Betty Cook were efficient in finding a solution as a 'good way of getting rid of it' – the committee should be referred to 'Commerce and Industry' as an attraction for the various royal agricultural shows.[17] The message here was clear: a corroboree might fit with the crafts and animal displays of the agricultural show, but it was not to detract from the performing arts budget. Instead, another massed production was proposed (in addition to the range of opera, ballet, choral and music theatre events).[18] Samuel Coleridge-Taylor's *Hiawatha* had been staged to critical and popular acclaim in Melbourne in 1938, and the arts committee set about arranging touring performances as part of the Jubilee celebrations.

*Hiawatha* (c. 1900) – a song cycle set to poems by Anglo-American Henry Wadsworth Longfellow to a North American Indian (First Nations) theme, composed by an English composer of Anglo- and African- (Sierra Leone) parentage – was a clear fit with notions of Western art music and conventional theatre. In spite of its exoticized theme and the mixed cultural heritage of its composer, the work was a cantata, composed in three movements for orchestral instruments with vocal soloists and a massed choir and a performance time of around two hours. The work had been important to the civil rights movement in the early twentieth century, but this was not raised in Australian discussions about the proposed performances.[19]

The proposal to feature *Hiawatha* in Australia's Jubilee celebrations met with considerable controversy in the popular media, leading to questions being asked in parliament about the soundness of the committees' decisions. MP Parkes, addressing Prime Minister Menzies, made a theatrical protest in the House of Representatives, mimicking Longfellow's poetry to ask whether an Australian theme involving Aboriginal corroboree might not be more appropriate for the celebration of fifty years since federation:

> Have we not a local Antill,
> Of the famed Arunta tribesmen,
> Who will dance among the shadows
> A corroboree of passion.[20]

In February 1951 it was decided that, due to a failure to secure the rights, *Hiawatha* would not go ahead, though funds had already been expended on costumes and the composer Coleridge-Taylor's high fee.[21] With the collapse of *Hiawatha* plans, John Antill's *Corroboree* ballet which had premiered in 1946 in its orchestral version (see Chapter 3) became the focus for a nationwide tour as part of the Jubilee celebrations. Antill had been an invited arts sub-committee member alongside his role as director of music at the ABC, though he appears to have stepped down from the committee.[22] In contrast to discussions of the financial constraints around other works, *Corroboree* soon became 'first financial priority on both music and drama sub-committees' and the ABC made their orchestras in all capital cities available for presentation of the ballet.²³ *Corroboree* was not only unique in its successful navigation of modernist trends and Australian themes, but it captured something of the *zeitgeist*; Antill's contemporaries were also working on symphonic works with Aboriginal themes and submitting them for consideration for the ABC Jubilee festival. In particular Mirrie and Alfred Hill were working with recordings provided by ethnographer C. P. Mountford to derive tunes which would imbue their symphonic writing with an Aboriginal flavour.²⁴

All plans for corroborees performed by Aboriginal people were scrapped from the Jubilee celebrations schedule, with the exception of what one journalist described as the arrangement of 'a few [Aboriginal people] to "waylay" a whaleboat now making its way, to the boredom of most Australians, down the River Murray in the wake of Captain Sturt'.²⁵ Beginning their journey on 1 January 1951 a group of actors were tracing the exploratory journey of Sturt along the Murray River. For the film documenting the re-enactment made by the Department of the Interior, a group of Paakantji and Ngiyampaa performers had been arranged to approach the travelling party. The musical score for the film was composed by Malcolm Williamson (later to become Master of the Queen's Music 1975–2003). Appearing only on screen, the participation of Aboriginal performers in this official event fell well short of the original vision for a massed corroboree.

But as Stephen Gapps has shown, the general public took the depiction of Aboriginal presence during these foundational journeys into their own hands. Though not depicted in the official film, as the actors progressed on their three-week journey, 'hundreds of local people "blacked up" as Aborigines in what proved to be at times a quite bizarre series of events'.²⁶ This public response to the call to 'dress historically' and greet the group travelling Sturt's route suggests that the appetite for representing Aboriginal culture was not confined only to officially supported productions like Antill's *Corroboree* ballet. The general public had no hesitation in inserting Aboriginal presence into the national story, even if in place of representation by Aboriginal people themselves.

Though public events featuring Aboriginal performers were few, space was made in the Jubilee celebrations for displays of Aboriginal material culture. In a tour of the Commonwealth showing the arts of Australia, images of Aboriginal paintings and in some cases the paintings themselves were included.²⁷ Paintings and images of rock art were mobile, static and unencumbered by the problems of organizing people, protecting them from outside influences and health hazards, and regulating their behaviour in public shows. The organizers were spared the necessity of negotiating the terms of this representation with the Aboriginal artists, as paintings were loaned by anthropologists Elkin and Mountford and by the Melbourne Museum. The inclusion of visual artworks suggests that official committees were indeed receptive to Aboriginal art forming part of how Australia should be represented to the world. But Aboriginal paintings and photographs that could be hung on walls conformed to expectations of visual art in ways that the Aboriginal performing arts did not. Representatives of music institutions represented on the arts subcommittee such as the ABC, Musica Viva, the Arts Council and NSW Conservatorium could conceive of *Hiawatha* and

Antill's *Corroboree* as 'music', but Aboriginal musicians performing a corroboree in their own manner jarred with the vision for touring orchestras and singers in formal concert hall settings.

## Aboriginal self-representation in the Jubilee and beyond

The Jubilee Celebrations Arts Subcommittee did include one Aboriginal performance event in the festival programme – one that fit more comfortably with the committee's conception of the arts – a national tour by Aboriginal tenor Harold Blair. As discussed in Chapter 3, Blair had catapulted to fame in 1945, studying at Melbourne's Melba Conservatorium and embarking on national tours on completion of his degree in 1949. On his return from training and concerts in the United States, the Arts Council arranged another national tour. In an account of his home-town concert in Ipswich, the reporter suggested that the audience had been thinking little about the Federation of Australia but instead their attention was fully concerned 'with the discovery that Blair, an aboriginal, can perform feats of "culture" heretofore exhibited only by white Australians who usually assume that white civilisation is inaccessible to Australians of the wrong pigment'.[28]

Thrust into this role as cultural interlocutor, Blair soon appeared in new productions by non-Indigenous composers and playwrights in the role of the Indigenous protagonist, or in some cases, alongside white performers in blackface (e.g., in the 1962 production of 'Uncle Tom's Cabin').[29] In 1952, Rex Ingamells, the poet closely associated with the Jindyworobak literary movement that emerged out of the late 1930s, staged his play 'Mirrabee – The Story of the First Kangaroo' at a Music for the People Concert in Adelaide. Ingamells' 1938 pamphlet had called for 'an understanding of Australia's history and traditions, primeval, colonial, and modern', and like other Jindyworobak poets, he sought to incorporate words from Aboriginal languages into his poetry.[30] In preparation for 'Mirrabee', Harold and Dorothy Blair worked with Ingamells to craft a 'native mat', or so the papers reported.[31] To a background of music by Elford Mack, Blair narrated the musical action. Blair was also reported as showing the orchestra how to use boomerangs as percussion instruments, while the resident oboist experimented with playing didjeridu.[32] In August 1955, Blair appeared in the TV production *'Play-About' Art: An Aboriginal Picture Story in Black and White*. Appearing as an actor alongside Pastor Doug Nicholls, the music for the production opened not with songs performed by Blair but instead with a recording of John Antill's ballet *Corroboree*. The backdrop was described in the script for the production as 'Namatjira-like', in front of which Blair described the traditions of Aboriginal storytelling through painting.[33]

In the 1951 ABC tour, Blair displayed his proficiency performing core works of the German, Italian, English and French operatic and art song traditions (including recitatives and arias by Purcell, Handel, Mozart and Verdi and art songs by Debussy, Fauré, Britten and Quilter). In most programmes, Blair also included several songs representing Aboriginal culture. The songs he chose were the Loam and Lethbridge 'Aboriginal songs' *Maranoa Lullaby*, and *Jabbin Jabbin* (discussed in Chapter 2) and a setting of a Central Australian Pitjantjatjara hymn by Ronald M. Trudinger *Nananala Kututja*. Enamoured of this song and its sensitive arrangement, Blair asserted in interviews that he planned to commission further songs from Trudinger, though there's no indication that this ever transpired (possibly because of Trudinger's reluctance to 'interfere with the spirit of tribal corroborees').[34] The Ernabella Choir directed by Trudinger performed publicly for carol services in Alice Springs (1953) for Queen Elizabeth II in Adelaide (1954) for the Duke of Edinburgh (1956), and it continues as an ensemble today.[35] Blair collaborated with Pastor Doug Nicholls on an Aboriginal choir of their own, including renowned singers like sopranos Margaret Tucker and Lorna Beulah (see more on Beulah in Chapter 5) and members of Melbourne's Fitzroy Aboriginal community, including Green and Briggs family members, publicly performing for the 1957 opening of new TV station GTV-9.[36]

As this ongoing engagement with the Melbourne Aboriginal community indicates, Blair not only toured art music with the ABC and Arts Council, his performances also continually engaged with Aboriginal politics. This advocacy was continued in the United States, where Blair had commented on segregation and American civil rights and the comparative restriction of movement of Aboriginal people in Australia and their segregation on Aboriginal reserves.[37] Alongside his 1951 Jubilee tour, Blair also performed in the Melbourne production *Out of the Dark: an Aboriginal Moomba*.

The *Aboriginal Moomba*, though ultimately part of the Jubilee year celebrations, had not been proposed by any of the official celebration organizing committees, but rather only came about as a result of direct advocacy by the Australian Aborigines' League. In an article published in October 1950, the *Herald* reported that though the first fully staged ballet performance of John Antill's *Corroboree* was planned, Aboriginal Victorians themselves had been excluded, with little regard for the Australian Aborigines' League's active record of staging public performances (see Chapter 3 for some of these).[38] By January 1951, Pastor Doug Nicholls began speaking out about the neglect of Aboriginal Victorians in the planning of the Victorian Centenary and Jubilee celebrations.[39] At a meeting of the Australian Aborigines' League in the following weeks, reported on by Melbourne's *The Argus* newspaper, Nicholls suggested that among other things a large corroboree could be included in the Jubilee festival. Other delegates at the meeting provocatively proposed a series of floats preceding a Day of Mourning rally on the banks of the Yarra river:

> The first, carrying full-blooded aborigines, would represent the aborigine before the coming of the white man.
>
> The second, with a chained aborigine guarded by a white man with a whip, would represent the introduction of Western "civilisation".
>
> The third, with aborigines in European dress, would represent the present day.[40]

Bill Onus' grandson Tiriki Onus recalls from his family's stories that reversal of the decision to exclude Aboriginal Victorians swiftly followed this proposal of a float with Aborigines in chains (see Interlude).[41] Within days, Nicholls was invited to join the Melbourne Centenary celebrations committee.[42] Antill's *Corroboree*, with choreography by Rex Reid, was still performed on the festival's opening night, though reviews of the *Aboriginal Moomba* favourably contrasted it with Antill and Reid's collaboration.[43] One reviewer sought to unsettle characterizations of Aboriginal music as monotonous and European music as novel:

> It is rather a chastening reflection that the original proprietors of this country, who were forgotten in the initial plans for the Jubilee celebrations, ended up by providing one of the most artistic contributions … It was all done with the utmost simplicity, with a rhythm and a naturalness of acting and a quality of miming which put it in an entirely different class from the Australian ballet on the same subject done recently on the same stage. There was a variety in the monotony of the chanting and the dancing of these primitive folk, instead of the monotony which their European imitators get into the variety of theirs.[44]

The resulting *Aboriginal Moomba*, produced by prominent Aboriginal entrepreneur, activist and president of the Australian Aborigines' League, Bill Onus and the League's secretary, Pastor Doug Nicholls combined traditional and contemporary music and dance, bringing together talented and well-known performers from other parts of Australia and an experienced non-Indigenous producer and script writer. The headline performers were Harold Blair and Georgia Lee (Dulcie Pitt), a Cairns-based Torres Strait Islander jazz singer. Blair and Lee also took two of the lead roles in the first half of the programme, entitled 'The Past', alongside Nicholls, Onus and Queenslander Jacob Chirnside. In part two, 'The Present', the programme highlighted Aboriginal people's resilience: 'The Aborigines, while maintaining their inherent characteristics of courage, endurance and imagination, have adapted themselves to the new customs and culture of the white people'.[45] This half was arranged in a series of 'tableaus of progress' that included a diverse range of performances from Blair's art songs, Lee's songs from the Torres Strait Islands, and an 'Out of the Dark' cabaret by Lee, along with Dharawal (La Perouse) snake man Fred Foster, Picanniny Pete, the Williams Brothers, Joan and Allan Saunders and Joyce McKinnon.[46]

The public shows of the 1940s associated with the New Theatre and staged at Wirth's Olympia (discussed in Chapter 3) had provided a model for how traditional dance and music could be publicly performed and privately cultivated in gatherings outside of Melbourne. Bringing performers together for a commercial show was an opportunity to corroboree – to come together and share culture, strengthening ongoing ties between people up and down the east coast, after decades of displacement, dislocation and disruption of community networks.

Traditional music and dance had also made a one-off appearance in a mainstream theatre production, in Edmond Samuels' 1950 *The Highway Man*. Lake Tyers man Ted Mullett had sung and danced 'a corroboree' in this live musical comedy after Samuels had encountered Mullett on the banks of Melbourne's Yarra river.[47] Reviews praised the effectiveness of Mullett's performance and his deep baritone voice, one review favourably comparing it to Antill and Reid's *Corroboree* and suggesting more performance by Aboriginal people (rather than non-Indigenous representation) would be welcome: 'This dance was absolutely first-rate; as good as Corroboree though of course without the interest of Antill's barbaric orchestrations; authentic to aboriginal forms and movements; dramatic and exciting – a dance that should be preserved and introduced into another less second-hand framework of entertainment.'[48]

La Perouse resident Fred Foster who appeared in the 1951 *Aboriginal Moomba* had not been involved in the Melbourne events of 1946–9, but in 1950 he had been associated with boomerang-throwing competitions organized by Bill Onus as part of the Yulunga festival in Sydney's Bondi. The festival opened with a corroboree performance led by 'Old Chief Ned', included Aboriginal performers in a gumleaf band and a girls' choir singing traditional songs. Onus' niece Cissy Onus was pictured leading a hula dance.[49]

When the Yulunga festival's first night's activities were cancelled, the visiting Aboriginal people decamped to the nearby La Perouse Aboriginal Reserve, the papers reporting that they 'went bush'.[50] People had travelled from as far away as White Cliffs Aboriginal Settlement in Western NSW for the event, once again demonstrating the connections between Aboriginal people across the state that were cultivated through such public performance events. The boomerang competition was won by Joe Timbery, descendant of the Timbery family resident at La Perouse whose lineage is traced back to those who met Captain James Cook on his 1770 visit. Joe Timbery's renown as a boomerang expert continued, he went on to win the following year's competition at Yulunga and his throwing left Queen Elizabeth II 'excited' after he travelled to Wagga Wagga to give a display in 1954.[51] Fred Foster had reportedly missed out on competing because he was away looking for snakes for his snake show, which would also feature in the 1951 *Aboriginal Moomba*. In an interview related to the Yulunga festival, Onus pointed out the close relationship between his cultural activities and advocacy for Aboriginal rights. Onus asserted that he aimed 'to contribute the best their race has to offer in return for good education, and high standard of living from white fellow-countrymen'. This was the motivation for Onus to strain 'his time and finances to put native corroborees on a "ballet" basis'.[52]

The involvement of performers from the wider Victorian Aboriginal community, Sydney (especially La Perouse) Aboriginal community and Aboriginal performers travelling from Western New South Wales and Queensland (especially Palm Island) in events from the late 1940s into the 1950s evidences a continuing reclamation of performance cultures and the right to present these cultures in public spaces on the performers' terms. Though performances by musicians and dancers from Palm Island were being orchestrated by Welfare Boards, activists like Onus and Nicholls also cultivated the networks that these touring shows provided, integrating them into wider performance practices.[53] The responsibility of representing their performing culture to a wide public was ever present in the minds of the organizers of the *Aboriginal Moomba*. According to one report, as the performers from Central Queensland, Sydney, and Victoria camped together at the showground: 'Aboriginal Pastor Doug Nicholls warned the cast of the tremendous responsibility they carried. "Never before have we had the chance to show the public what we can do. This is it," he said.'[54]

Director of Melbourne's Princess Theatre Garnet Carroll advocated for the significance of the kinds of performances presented in the *Aboriginal Moomba*, noting that it was entertainment for a 'sophisticated audience'. Not only did Carroll suggest that all state governments should include a show like it in their Jubilee programmes, but it 'should be shown to the Royal family next year'.[55]

When the newly crowned Queen Elizabeth II did visit in 1954, the *Aboriginal Moomba* was not on the programme, although she was presented with local corroborees in several locations along her journey, mostly from Aboriginal performers brought long distances to perform away from their own Country. A group of performers based at Darwin's Bagot Aboriginal Reserve travelled over 3,000 kilometres to perform music and dance for the Queen at Toowoomba in Queensland, boomerang champion Joe Timbery demonstrated his prowess 500 kilometres from home at Wagga Wagga, Pitjantjatjara performers from Yalata Mission in South Australia made the 1,000-kilometre trip to Adelaide and Torres Strait Islanders travelled 1,000 kilometres to perform at Cairns.[56]

In Sydney, the Queen was also presented with a gala performance that included Antill's *Corroboree* with new choreography by Beth Dean. Though all the dancers and musicians performing this were non-Indigenous, Dean had sought permission to bring Warlpiri man Nosepeg Junkata Tjupurrula to Sydney from Central Australia so that he might sit 'before the curtain with one spotlight on him while the orchestra have a beating sticks effect', and leave the stage before the dancing began.[57] Her request was denied by the Administrator of the Northern Territory after Dean and Carell's publication of secret-sacred photos in the popular magazine *Pix* came to the department's attention.[58] The ways in which the welfare administration arbitrated on Aboriginal performers' participation in public representations makes the productions of Bill Onus and Doug Nicholls in Melbourne all the more remarkable.

## The left and political performances of Aboriginal culture

Public shows like the *Aboriginal Moomba* asserted the Aboriginal performers' right to represent their own culture on stage, but also continued their engagement with wider questions of Aboriginal rights. Equal pay for Aboriginal workers was one of these, and became an issue when the Queensland Director of Native Affairs refused the Actors' Equity rates of pay intended by the *Aboriginal Moomba*'s producers, insisting that payments to the Queensland performers would be held in an 'aboriginal trust fund'. The producers had been forced to agree to these conditions, without which the Palm Islanders' participation would have been disallowed (as it had in a number of other events – see Chapter 2). But Doug Nicholls stated publicly after their departure that the seizing of wages into government-administered trust funds 'robs him [the aborigine] of his common rights'.[59]

By July 1951 when Nicholls had commented on the stolen wages of Aboriginal Queenslanders performing in the *Aboriginal Moomba*, he and other members of the Australian Aborigines' League had been engaged in campaigns for workers' rights for some time. 1951 had seen worldwide dockside strikes by workers, who often linked their activities directly to the communist movements gaining widespread political power across Asia and eastern Europe. In the United Kingdom, wave after wave of strikes brought dock operations to a standstill, and Australian workers were similarly engaged with these international politics.[60] One of the most highly publicized strikes, discussed in syndicated news across the nation, saw Northern Territory unionists side with Aboriginal workers Fred (Nadpur) Waters and Lawrence Wurrpen (Urban), and in turn Aboriginal performers refuse to stage a corroboree, as discussed at the opening of this chapter. According to the *West Australian*, the NAWU had published claims in their bulletin that 'the aborigines had put on many splendid corroborees for Territory residents and visitors but had never been paid'. Instead they had been given 'a few rags or packets of cheap and nasty tobacco'.[61] In a statement in response to the actions, the Minister for the Interior, Mr Anthony, lamented that the strikes were inspired by communism, and that the state had a duty to protect Aboriginal people as 'wards of the state' from communist influences.[62]

In the southeast too, dockside strikes and Aboriginal performance were part of the same story. In 1951, the Unity Dance Group developed a new work 'Aboriginal Girl', performed in Australian events including an *International Moomba* alongside dance troupes from Indonesia, Thailand, India, China, the Ukraine, Israel and Switzerland.[63] The production was also toured to East Berlin, featuring Australian South Sea Islander activist Faith Bandler (then Mussing) who danced the role of the Aboriginal girl and sang 'Aboriginal songs' (by Loam and Lethbridge – see Chapter 2), and Wiradjuri man Ray Peckham. In the volatile environment of the Cold War, the tour of East Berlin sparked a flurry of investigation within ASIO (Australian Security Intelligence Organisation) and other Australian government departments, who moved to restrict the passports of those who had travelled to Soviet countries.[64] But while the passports of all delegates were seized on their return, Ray Peckham's passport was withheld before departure. The involvement of an Aboriginal delegate had been met with 'tremendous applause everywhere' according to the Communist Party newspaper the *Tribune*, but the government did not concur. The ship, ready to depart for East Berlin, was stranded on the docks while Peckham waited for his passport. In language echoing the Minister for the Interior's rationale for condemning the Darwin corroboree strike, Peckham recalled: 'they reckon they were protecting me from going to Europe, cause they knew that we was heading for the GDR'. But after action from Bill Onus, employed at that time on the docks, the department was quick to acquiesce to threatened strikes, Peckham vividly recounted: 'the might of the trade union movement was moving into em, "if Peckham doesn't go on this ship, then this ship doesn't leave this harbour", and we'll tie up every ship that's in port and round the shores of Australia. Down comes the passport eh, four hours later! Yeh, that's true.'[65]

The Unity Dance Group that had produced 'Aboriginal Girl' had been formed from the Melbourne New Theatre movement and founded by Margaret Walker in the 1950s. Walker (née Frey) was a dancer and left-wing activist, who had studied classical ballet at the Borovansky Ballet Academy in Melbourne and founded the Unity

Dance Group supported by the Council of the Encouragement of Music and the Arts (CEMA). She had shifted her focus to folk dances after realizing the impracticalities and inaccessibility of ballet for the wider population. On the initiative of Rob Taylor from CEMA, the Unity Dance Group performed at lunchtimes for factory workers, later performing to entertain striking workers.[66] Walker continued to be involved in Aboriginal dance circles well into the new era of self-determination that saw the establishment of the AIDT, later NAISDA and Bangarra. Her son, Kim Walker, remains a key driver of Aboriginal dance in Australia, as CEO of the NAISDA training programme for emerging Aboriginal dancers.

The Unity Dance Group engaged in a range of political performance activities in the early 1950s, frequently including Aboriginal performers. In 1947 the group appeared in performances for *Rocket Range*, a production by journalist Jim Crawford, performed at the New Theatre in Sydney's Newtown.[67] *Rocket Range* was a response to Aboriginal people being moved off their lands in Central Australia to make way for a defence facility, though it was performed only by non-Indigenous actors in full body make-up, with the action performed in silhouette. The members of the dance group for this performance are not known, but the play included actors Don Monro and John Paton who would later be involved in Black Theatre and Nindethana Theatre productions of the 1970s produced by Bob Maza and Jack Charles.[68] In April 1951 *Rocket Range* was staged again as a workshop to highlight the case of Waters and Wurrpen in the Northern Territory (see opening of this chapter).

In Margaret Walker's papers are histories of dance in which Walker traced dance through stages from 'primitive communism' through the middle ages, and onto ballet. In positioning Aboriginal dance, Walker used an example from Melville Island (Tiwi) Pukamuni burial ceremonies to demonstrate her thinking, suggesting that Tiwi tribes' technological advances were evidenced by the intricate links between religious frameworks and the performance of ritual through dance. She also contrasted the disconnected traditions of professionalized dance created by the ruling classes and folk dance:

> When one studies the dances of these periods it can be seen that the folk dance forms survived and persisted because of their close connections with the life of the people.
>
> It is apparent then that our Association must study the democratic cultural traditions of our country if it is going to produce dances that reflect the struggles and aspirations of the Australian people.[69]

In the framing of Walker's communist politics, modern Western capitalist societies were, in Marxist terms, a necessary stage before socialism could be achieved.[70] This political framing was able to incorporate Aboriginal people as one of the oppressed groups (also exemplified as a 'primitive communist' society) who would be liberated through socialism from the current oppression. In the same year as the Berlin tour, Walker's group also participated in a workers' art festival, in which participants scripted, rehearsed and performed a 'pageant of Australian history'. The bulletin reporting on these events emphasized that the British settlers 'saw convicts and aborigines alike as slaves'.[71]

In 1958, another Aboriginal musician toured communist China – soprano Nancy Ellis. Ellis had been offered mentoring opportunities with visiting African American soprano Dorothy Maynor in 1952, was then supported in 1953 by Paul Hasluck's assimilation funding to study at NSW Conservatorium of Music, and a few years later was part of Communist Party celebrations for International Women's Day, travelling to China with a group of artists the following year.[72] In practice, philosophies based on equality meant that communist and labour movements sought to include Aboriginal people in their representation of Australian culture. Though mainstream performing arts institutions cast themselves as apolitical, their representation of culture valued only European performance genres, thereby setting an agenda for the support of non-Indigenous composers and closing doors on Aboriginal performers seeking to represent their own performance cultures.

## Popular representation of Aboriginal music and dance: Touring ethnographic shows

What then was being supported by these mainstream performing arts bodies, beyond the Jubilee Festival? One key touring show that represented Aboriginal culture was a production by Beth Dean and Victor Carell. Funded in large part by Adult Education Boards, the didactic component aimed to educate audiences on 'authentic' Aboriginal dance and music traditions. In 1950 Beth Dean and Victor Carell staged a series of concerts through the Adult Education network that would lead on to national tours.[73] The shows included Dean's solo renditions of sacred Aboriginal men's initiation dances as well as 'Aboriginal songs' composed by Alfred and Mirrie Hill, Arthur S. Loam and Victor Carell. Dean, the recently arrived choreographer and dancer from Denver, and Carell, her Australian baritone husband, just returned from Italy and the United States, toured their show entitled 'Dance and Song around the World' to all Australian states in hundreds of performances between 1950 and 1954. The show situated the performances of Aboriginal culture within a tradition of 'ethnic dance' and music, and programmed them alongside music and dance originating in the Americas, Spain, the Pacific and Asia, as well as with classical ballet.[74] But it was the performances of Australian traditions on Australian soil that attracted the most interest.

Though Australian Aboriginal music and dance formed a small part of the early programmes, the songs performed were explained in disproportionate detail in the programme notes, with attributions to ethnographer C. P. Mountford and several paragraphs outlining the stories behind the dances and songs. In 1952, when the show had been touring for two years, the programme increasingly focused on demonstrations of Australian Aboriginal songs, dances, musical instruments and sacred objects alongside 'authentic Maori dances'. By now, the Aboriginal material occupied the full second half of the programmes, while the first half took a pan-Indigenous sweep across the dances and music of Native Americans, Maori and Mexican traditions. This shift away from traditional ballet and music of the Western art music tradition may have been a response to reviews which consistently praised Dean's Indigenous dances and dismissed her uninspired renditions of European traditions.⁷⁵

In the show's programmes, the sacred origins of Dean and Carell's performances were emphasized, sometimes explicitly as men's sacred dances. Dean asserted that she was probably the only woman in the world to perform these. Dean and Carell also insisted on the authenticity of their costuming and musical instruments, noting, 'all costumes are authentic'. In a 1952 article about their show, Dean was quoted as saying 'The audience expected a third rate vaudeville show and were inclined to resent our act at first. However the spirit and fire of the genuine tribal ritual won them over'.⁷⁶ The shows toured across the nation from 1950 to 1953, and were also staged at the American Museum of Natural History, Denver Museum of Natural History and several anthropological societies, universities and major theatres in the United States and Europe. Dean received invitations to talk from benevolent organizations such as Quota International and Rotary, prestigious Sydney private schools, public libraries, and women's organizations like the Sydney University women's union and Women's International Zionist Organization.⁷⁷

Dean's claims for authenticity were based on her familiarity with the work of anthropologists rather than any acquaintance with Aboriginal people and their performance traditions. While on tour with *Annie Get Your Gun*, Dean and Carell spent time with Charles and Bessie Mountford as well as T. G. H. Strehlow. They viewed films provided by Mountford and read Spencer and Gillen's weighty 1899 account of Central Australian Aboriginal performance.⁷⁸ Mountford and anthropologist A. P. Elkin were also the sources of recordings that inspired the songs and piano works by Alfred and Mirrie Hill used by Dean and Carell in their shows, and kept up an active correspondence with the composers about their use of the materials.⁷⁹

Both Alfred's songs and Mirrie's piano works (dedicated to Beth Dean) formed standard parts of Dean and Carell's repertoire in their touring shows, with the piano works performed by a range of different pianists who joined their tours for shorter periods of months. In subsequent years other singers would widely perform Alfred Hill's songs alongside Alfred S. Loam's collection *Aboriginal Songs* (Chapter 2), so that the songs became well-known items of the Australian music repertoire, though Mirrie Hill's piano works enjoyed a less active performance life.⁸⁰ In recordings, such as those made by Alan Coad, the 'Aboriginal songs' featured alongside other Australiana, and the songs took on a weightier significance as representations of Aboriginal culture when Aboriginal tenor Harold Blair adopted them as part of his standard repertoire in the 1950s.⁸¹

After three years of touring 'Dance and Song around the World', Dean's reputation as an expert on Aboriginal dance was sufficiently established to attract an invitation from the President of the Arts Council Dorothy Helmrich to choreograph Antill's *Corroboree*. Only then did Dean and Carell make their first 'expedition' into remote Aboriginal communities in the dry season of 1953. Over an eight-month period, they travelled through parts of Arnhem Land and Central Australia, staying mainly at station homesteads as the guests of white station owners, or at missions as the guests of missionaries or local native settlement superintendents. They observed as many dance performances as they could gain access to, ranging from short demonstrations by individual dancers, to week-long boys' initiation ceremonies, attended only by Carell, but also filmed by him and later released commercially.[82] This subsequent fieldwork equipped Dean and Carell with a rich store of memories and sketches of Aboriginal dances along with the stories, legends and cultural context used to inspire performances for the remainder of their decades-long careers.

In her substantial reading about Aboriginal cultures, Dean had learnt about gender restrictions on certain kinds of ceremonies and the taboos that existed on women observing male sacred ceremonies (she does not seem to have read work by Phyllis Kaberry and others who discussed women's ceremonies). On the basis of this knowledge, she boasted that since men's sacred ceremonies were taboo to women, she was possibly the only woman in the world who could (or would) dance the material. As one journalist sensationally paraphrased:

> When the men of Australia's few remaining aboriginal tribes perform their sacred dances, no woman is permitted to watch. At one time death was the penalty for disobedience of this age-old tribal law. But one woman – a white woman and an American – not only knows many of the secrets of the aborigines' dance ceremonies, but performs passages from them herself.[83]

It is likely that Dean exaggerated the extent to which her dances replicated sacred men's dances. Though she had viewed some of C. P. Mountford's films containing secret/sacred material, the dances from the Yuendumu initiation ceremony that she later wrote about were seen only by her husband in 1953, as she was absent during the restricted parts of the ceremony along with the other women. Well before the 1953 trip, Dean and Carell had acquired a range of cultural objects and musical instruments (likely from their friend Mountford's extensive collection). The objects were demonstrated as part of Dean's concert programmes. A running order for one lecture indicates that Dean demonstrated a wooden *tjurunga*, with the accompany text noting that she had been excluded from the group collecting the object she would hold and describe: 'This sacred board was given to my husband at the time he visited the Snake rock but I ... a woman, was not allowed to join them.'[84] A scene in which Dean handled and examined a stone *tjurunga* was also included in Carell's 1953 film *Carrumbo*.

Like Margaret Walker, Dean also aimed to include Aboriginal dance practices into a larger narrative about the historical evolution of dance. In the lectures accompanying her performances, she sketched a lineage of dance practices that had led to modern dance and ballet of the twentieth century, a theoretical framework that she realized more fully in her 1966 book *The Many Worlds of Dance*. Unlike Walker, the narrative did not reference the politics of Aboriginal experience in the 1950s, despite the links to workers' politics that Adult Education movements represented. Rather, Dean's narrative of 'ethnic dance' was structured around concepts of social Darwinism, and the idea that so-called 'primitive' dance might show us the origins of western dance traditions:

'To understand the sophisticated forms with which we are familiar in our own theatre, we have here sought out some of the roots of dance among the few so called primitive people left on our globe. Through observing the primitive we can see the path of our own artistic development.'[85]

Dean's exploration of the origins of dance was ambitiously conceived as an exploration of the history of humanity, as she indicated in her frequently reiterated phrase 'Dance is thought made manifest in movement and rhythm'. She cited the dance innovations and styles of Aboriginal and other so-called primitive dancers as the origins of modern (Euro/American) dance. This juxtaposition of modern interpretations of traditional dance practices with theorization of the evolution of dance provoked comment from reviewers of her shows: 'It was difficult to decide where anthropology left off and art began in Beth Dean's recital'.[86]

Unlike Margaret Walker's activities in left-wing theatre contexts that included Aboriginal actors, musicians and dancers in performances both locally and overseas, Dean and Carell's programming avoided presenting specific cultural products back to the people to whom they belonged. In North America, Dean performed no Native American dances, in New Zealand, no Maori dances (though these were routinely included in programmes performed elsewhere), and yet her reputation in Australia was founded on her performance of Australian Aboriginal dances (especially those derived from men's initiation ceremonies). Revealingly, however, when Dean staged performances in the Northern Territory's Alice Springs and Darwin in 1953, she omitted the Aboriginal dance and music numbers that were otherwise standard on her Australian touring programmes. Bringing Aboriginal dance to Darwin, asserted Carell, would be like 'bringing coals [sic] to Newcastle'.[87] Their avoidance of performing dances based on recordings made in Central Australia while in the region suggests some sensitivity to their transgression of cultural protocols. It also points to pervasive notions of Aboriginal culture as being absent from the populated centres on the east and southern coast of Australia, and discoverable only in the centre – a kind of territory apart, which, from the perspective of many coastal dwellers, might as well have been a foreign country.[88] Australia's Indigenous character was to be found in its vast centre, as far away as possible from its Europeanized urban centres.

Perhaps as a result of Margaret Walker's engagement with working-class politics, she was more able to reconcile the Aboriginal past and present of the southeast with conceptions of Aboriginal dance cultures and her relationships with Aboriginal people in her home town. By contrast, Dean subscribed to social Darwinist ideas about remote Aboriginal people representing the remnants of a passing culture. By bringing the culture of Australia's authentic Indigenous centre to the coastal settlements, Dean's demonstrations aimed to promote the recognition of Aboriginal people as rich in cultural, historical and ecological knowledge. She conceptualized these efforts as attempts to counteract the apparent indifference of the non-Indigenous Australian populace to the traditions of the land that they and their ancestors had settled. Dean's insistence that Aboriginal music, dance and legend were noble, worthwhile, intelligent and worthy of serious artistic attention was a counterpoint to the cultural cringe of Australians who looked beyond Australia's borders for artistic inspiration. But at the same time, her performances were not grounded in serious engagement with Aboriginal cultures. Although in New Zealand she took trouble to learn Maori dance through the proper channels, and retained lifelong relationships with her dance mentors there, her representation of Australian Aboriginal dance techniques and traditions did not engage with living Aboriginal people.

## 'Just some sort of pastiche': High art and Aboriginal representation[89]

Though Dean and Carell's performances between 1950 and 1953 were closer to vaudeville than modern American or European dance, Dean ultimately sought to bring reimaginings of Indigenous dance traditions into modern ballet choreography. This goal came to fruition in 1954, when Dean choreographed a new version of *Corroboree* – Antill's 1946 ballet that had already toured the nation for the Jubilee Festival, with choreography by Rex Reid. The new version would feature in a gala performance for Queen Elizabeth II's first visit to Australia, an event that would initiate another national tour.[90] Accounts from Aboriginal people who remember the tours of Aboriginal-themed shows in the 1950s and 1960s suggest that while the performances' representation of putatively authentic dances and songs brought the idea of Aboriginal music to the stage, they also highlighted disparities between the valuation of Aboriginal cultural products as central to Australian distinctiveness, and the social, economic and political realities of Aboriginal people's access to the cultural marketplace. Debra Bennet McLean recounted in 2005 her memories of reactions to the touring performances of John Antill's symphonic ballet *Corroboree* in Queensland:

> As a *Goorie* child born in the late 50s and growing up in the 60s, I recall how Antill's music, and the National Ballet performance, caused quite a stir in *Murri* circles.[91] Being pre-referendum days, some saw it as official recognition of our existence in this country, even a backhanded compliment to Aboriginal people. Others considered it an 'experiment', and though the term was not then used in my community, others saw it as 'appropriation' without our consent by the 'Other'. In reality, we asked ourselves how many Aboriginal people could ever really contemplate, let alone afford, to attend the ballet in the era of the 'colour bar'; most Aborigines could not walk freely into an Australian town without an exemption form or 'dog tag'[92] at the time of Antill's composing *Corroboree*, nor could they even sit in the same milk bar or use public toilets at the time of the premiere of the ballet *Corroboree*.
>
> In some ways, the *Corroboree* phenomenon was comparable to the '*Black and White Minstrel*' shows popularized in American culture. *Corroboree* was in fact white people painted as black people, telling a black story.[93]

Though *Corroboree* has occupied the historical limelight, there were other composers and choreographers seeking to stage orchestral and ballet performances on Aboriginal themes in the 1950s as well. Some of these did attempt to engage Aboriginal performers in the event. Margaret Sutherland's *The Haunted Hills*, composed in 1950, 'was about the original people', although, as she explained in an oral history interview in 1972, she deliberately avoided branding it as such. The orchestral tone poem evoked a place in the Dandenong Ranges known as 'Haunted Hills', but Sutherland was anxious to avoid the 'pastiche' that Antill's *Corroboree* represented. Critical of Antill's superficial approach and of the way he was publicly promoted before he was ready to enter the limelight as a composer, Sutherland distanced her work from popular enthusiasm for Antill's *Corroboree*.[94] She also emphasized that in her time living in Adelaide, she had known local Aboriginal people well, and the work was composed in the years following her active support of and collaboration with Aboriginal tenor Harold Blair.

Another composer focusing on Aboriginal themes and supported by major arts bodies including the AETT was James Penberthy, a West Australian composer working in the same genres as Antill on the east coast (and aware of the competition from Antill and Sculthorpe in securing commissions for major new works).[95] Penberthy worked closely for much of his career with Russian-Australian (*Ballets Russes*) dancer Kira Bousloff, with whom he co-founded the West Australian Ballet in 1953. The two later married. His ballet and opera works built on literary explorations of tensions between Aboriginal people and settlers and the entwinement of their lives, in operatic collaborations with Katharine Susannah Prichard on *Brolga*, and in *Dalgerie* based on Mary Durack's 1955 novel *Keep Him my Country*.

In the earliest discussions with the AETT about this production, Penberthy raised the possibility of having 'coloured principals' in the opera representing Aboriginal characters, after Durack had suggested this course of action. Penberthy immediately proposed Harold Blair and sought to find an Aboriginal woman to play the supporting role of Noala.[96] For the lead role of Dalgerie, African American soprano Leontyne Price was proposed in conjunction with a planned ABC tour. Like Antill and Dean, Penberthy also sought to promote his work as suitable for international representations of Australian culture – in particular he hoped it might be performed as part of Olympic or Commonwealth Games celebrations.[97]

Correspondence with the opera wing of the AETT reveals that they were actively guiding Australian composers towards topics that represented Aboriginal themes. In one letter general manager of the Elizabethan Opera, Robert Quentin, attempted to steer Penberthy towards using a title drawing on Aboriginal concepts: 'I do not think that your new title "Australian Son" is worth a pin at the Box Office, on the Bills or in anybody's head … Please do think again on the lines of an Anglicised aboriginal expression. You know "Dream Time", but much better than that.'[98]

Penberthy's collaboration with Stefan Haag on the production of *Dalgerie* was also pitched as an opportunity for Haag to build expertise on Aboriginal-themed music and dance. Penberthy suggested that Haag read Phyllis Kaberry's work on Aboriginal women and indicated that working closely with Elizabeth and Mary Durack and

Donald Stuart would position him strategically: 'When you get him back he will be certainly the blackfeller authority as far as the theatre is concerned'.[99]

Other West Australians also showed interest in developing stages for Aboriginal performance rather than non-Indigenous representations of it. The Perth Festival programme's lack of local flavour provoked some to call not just for new Australian musical works to be supported, but for experts in 'corroboree dancing' to feature in the ballet programming. Writer Henrietta Drake Brockman published an article suggesting this kind of programming and criticizing the 1953 festival programme.[100] Continuing his interest in Aboriginal culture (see Chapter 3), dancer Ted Shawn wrote with disgust to his journalist collaborator Keith Ewers on being sent the article, about the Festival's 'English-rooted consciousness'. Shawn would have liked to see the festival use 'only Indigenous themes'.[101]

## Conclusions

Though arts bodies repeatedly funded touring shows of high-art productions by Antill and Dean between 1951 and 1954, such funding was not accessible to groups like the Australian Aborigines' League, who sought unsuccessfully to found their own touring theatrical association in 1953 to be led by 'professional boomerang thrower and fire-eater' Bill Onus.[102] Their proposal built on the success of the *Aboriginal Moomba*, but also on the *Corroboree Seasons* that had featured in Wirth's Olympia in the years leading up to this, and more recent cabaret shows in St Kilda featuring noted dancers Eric Onus, James Scott and Charlie Williams and singer-dancers Margaret Tucker, Geraldine and Evelyn Briggs and Win Onus.

The stark contrast between growing interest in Aboriginal paintings and its representation on the world stage in the 1950s and the exclusion of living Aboriginal music and dance performers from public stages was not lost on the performers themselves. In a 1957 speech, Harold Blair made a direct comparison between the use of Aboriginal designs in the 1956 Melbourne Olympics and the lack of recognition of the artists who created these designs:

> During the Olympic Games Aboriginal designs were extensively used on souvenirs and decorations, and this should lead to an interest in the people who created the designs used. During Moomba you will see many of the particular dances and skills of our ancestors, and this should rouse your interest in our ancient arts. Aborigines can bring an old and fascinating culture to enrich the Australian way of life in many ways. The old legends of this ancient race are as picturesque and as full of meaning as those of other lands.[103]

Harold Blair had identified the inherent hypocrisy of assimilationist thinking that valued the arts of Aboriginal culture, but denied Aboriginal people the right to publicly represent them. This sentiment was echoed in Debra Bennet McLean's comparison of the tours of *Corroboree* with the denial of rights to Aboriginal people to even attend theatres that I have already quoted. In the subsequent decade to 1967, support for exhibitions of disembodied artworks but denial of opportunities for Aboriginal performers to represent their cultures on stage would continue, prefacing major shifts in representation after the 1967 referendum, as we will see in Chapters 5 and 6.

# *Interlude*

In June 2019 I travelled down to Wurundjeri Country, Melbourne, to work with Tiriki Onus on a paper we were planning to write together. We spent the day at the Wilin Centre for Indigenous Arts and Cultural Development, at the Victorian College of the Arts (VCA), University of Melbourne. Each time I visit the Wilin Centre, we sit around a big table in the open space, right there as you walk through the door. Tiriki and I started the day with just the two of us sitting there, but as the day went on more people joined. Students studying dance, theatre or music at the VCA dropped in to chat with Tiriki, or to encourage everyone to come along to a showing of their current work. Most stopped a moment for a cup of tea or a yarn. Staff working at the centre joined us for a while, needing Tiriki's input on something. Tiriki ordered in lunch for everyone.

Tiriki's mum, Jo, brought in the suitcase of his grandfather Bill's photos and clippings, and 'the Moomba book' – a weighty, bound book where photographs and media about the 1951 *Aboriginal Moomba* trace the journey that production took through the activities of the Australian Aborigines' League, the protests of solidarity and inclusion, culminating in a hit show for the Jubilee festival in Melbourne. Jo stayed for the day, reminiscing about her late husband and Tiriki's father Lin and other people who appear in the photos. At about 3 pm, I suggested we get a voice recorder to capture Tiriki telling the stories of Bill's legacy. Listening to Tiriki describe his grandfather's production of musical events, exchanges of dance, boomerang-throwing performances, crafting of functional homewares adorned with Aboriginal art, I think about Tiriki's own career, his talents as an artist, a singer, a theatre-maker, a cultural leader. I think about continuities, about how culture lives on and is carried through the lives of Yorta Yorta people like Bill and Tiriki. I think about how both Bill and Tiriki weave together culture and political advocacy for Aboriginal rights. This is an edited transcript of the conversation we recorded.

## Tiriki Onus, 20 June 2019

*The only way people were legitimately able to practice and perform culture is to do it publicly – it becomes hiding in plain sight – it's the only place you're allowed to do it.*

I think every art form for Bill is powerful but, significantly, that idea of performance. Even though Bill's probably best known for the material cultural practice that he's engaged with – the souvenirs and the artwork – it's his work as a performer, which came from those early vaudeville troupes, and then the performances of corroborees up here at Wirth's Olympia where the arts centre is now, and then the *Aboriginal Moomba* in 1951. This idea of performance is really powerful. Then there are the films. Film makes performance that much more portable, and you can reach larger audiences. Bill has been in a few films already by this point – quite big films, films that were getting theatrical releases and I think he started to be quite taken with the technology, and with the ability to reach audiences of that size. At about the same time as Bill has just finished working on *The Overlanders* (1946), he starts making more of his own films, pulling together material from all over the place and eventually producing this film (that has been unearthed in the National Film & Sound Archive), which is just labelled *Aborigines in the Community*. It was due to have a proper theatrical release, but it gets close to its final editing stages before ASIO (Australian Security Intelligence Organisation) steps in and quashes the whole thing. But even before that, Bill had been recording meetings of early meetings of the Aborigines Progressive Association (APA), the Australian Aborigines' League (AAL) and filming community stuff with just small hand-held cameras. Over the subsequent years, even if it's just filming things that are happening at Aboriginal Enterprises or getting involved in other people's films, he stays really significantly involved with film as a medium even up to the point where he was making films for the AAL just months before his death. So, his last film is *Forgotten People*, which he brought together for the AAL in 1968 just after the referendum, and just before he died.

Throughout this whole period and in relation to the AAL, the issue of visibility is being so hotly contested and has become a major challenge for anyone trying to even have a voice in the first place, let alone deciding how and where one will apply said voice. I think we now have a tendency to view with our 2019 eyes, whether it be corroborees in Wirth's Olympia or *Alcheringa* or *Moomba* or whatever. We can view that notion now of having to perform one's aboriginality as being highly distasteful, and in many ways it can be distasteful, it's certainly not something I do. But I think that's very distinct from what's going on in these early works – the notion of asserting your aboriginality and claiming that publicly. Because even though a corroboree and Wirth's Olympia or *Alcheringa* documentaries might be seen as being somewhat twee, or distasteful nowadays I think we have to kind of view those with early- to mid-twentieth-century eyes and realize that just the very notion of putting an Aboriginal person on the television in *Alcheringa* is a massive shift, to not show Aboriginal people in a deficit model, which it didn't. It talked about the technologies and the knowledges which had persisted for so long. We had Bill introducing these pieces, which is hugely significant at the time to have an Aboriginal person hosting a programme as an authoritative voice. I mean there's words like 'primitive', words at which we cringe nowadays, but I think one also has to speak to the audience that one is holding.

I don't think it's just out of my own kind of family pride that I defend these positions, because I think it happens with a lot of artists of the time. I mean you even look at

Albert Namatjira painting his country. He's not painting in dots or something else that we would expect to see coming out of Alice Springs now, but it's quite an authoritative power to say: this is my Country and I'm showing it to you. And in that same manner, when Bill's able to stand up and take a degree of control over that narrative, I think it's a really powerful and significant step. We tend to lose sight of the privileges that we enjoy now, when we analyse the world that those people lived in and will never understand it, but the very fact that these stories are still here to be told I think it's pretty damn important. And if it was painting up and dancing around Wirth's Olympia, well that's ok. This is about being visible and being present and at the same time taking the form and then subverting people's understanding of it, which I think it's really important and powerful. Because otherwise you'll just have people like John Antill and Rex Reid telling people what a corroboree is, and hideous, grim, grotesque masks and black full body suits. Rex Reid's decision that he couldn't have Aboriginal dancers in *Corroboree* because they wouldn't be able to dance to the standard required, and then you see footage of *Corroboree* and you're like oh my god! The chicken dance is my favourite part!

## The Melbourne docks, Wirth's Olympia, the New Theatre

What you can see is that most of the people there who have jobs or trades are working as labourers en masse down at the wharves because you could, even though it was still illegal for a lot of these people to be working. I think that post-war era, certainly for the unions, changed a lot for people too, for those people who had come back from the war and had been fighting alongside others. It helped to humanize people in that space. There's a story that's always gone back and forth and been shared and told back to me by others – in '51 when Ray [Peckham] and Faith [Bandler] are just about to leave with the dance group to go to East Berlin and their passports are seized, they're denied exit. Bill, in his capacity with both the unions and the Australian Aborigines' League, really stirred up this groundswell of resistance to the point where the unions say: well if you don't give Ray his passport then we're not letting this ship out of the harbour, and more to the fact, we are going to tie up all the other ports in Australia until this basic human right is afforded him.

Eric [Onus] was always the big performer of the family while Bill had the ability to perform and did it quite well certainly, with the fire-eating and boomerang throwing, it was Eric who was actually more at home on the stage than Bill was and so was able to really take advantage of that. You'll see him dancing in works like *White Justice* in the New Theatre, you see him singing, apparently, he sang quite beautifully – he used to sing *Old Man River* his daughter (Aunty Judy) said. From what I can gather from his dancing as well, he moved incredibly easily between different styles and techniques and was quite proficient as a dancer and as performer in general. So whilst Bill was, for want of a better word, more profiled than Eric, Eric had, maybe because of that, more freedom to try things out and get more creative with things. Bill was the orator and the organizer and had to be up front talking about things whereas Eric got to be up front performing in things. I mean the two of them just do everything together for their entire lives right up until Bill dies, they're inseparable, but at the same time it's, I don't know, you lose one, you kind of lose aspects of the other.

You see this in the *Moomba* book, where any mention of Aboriginal people in the press is being recorded by Bill or Eric or someone like that. For the League, it's trying to always position the visibility of Aboriginal people right up there in front – whether it's arguing about stockmen's wages or whether it's acknowledging civil rights actions. '46 is only a few years really after the Cummeragunja walk off, which was such a significant moment for Bill and Jack [Patten] and Eric and all the other Yorta Yorta people and others who were living there on Cummera at the time. There was a great parallel between the Cummera walk off and the Pilbara strike as well, then the Yandi mine. That strike has never really ended, but there are these great parallels, so when they find out about the Pilbara strike then they move incredibly quickly to try and create some sort of acknowledgement of it, some other response here in Melbourne in the southeast.

It's extraordinary to look at this *White Justice* which is performed in September of '46, only a handful of months after the strike actually begins all the way out in the Pilbara. They bring back, they write, produce and then put on this show with the New Theatre. And it's this socialist workers' theatre and communist organizations who are stepping up and working alongside Aboriginal artists. Margaret Walker goes on and has such a huge history of working with Aboriginal people and communities. It is an incredibly galvanizing moment and, to my mind, bringing something like that together in that amount of time is incredible. I don't know if the Sibelius [musical accompaniment] was brought in from something else or if it was a specific piece that then dance was created around. It's part of a bigger review called *Coming Our Way*. In the New Theatre then, this is one of their early connections with Aboriginal performers and then, Jack Charles gets his start at the New Theatre some years later, and of course Jack goes on to start Nindethana down here in Melbourne, just before the National Black Theatre get started up in Redfern.

It's a hugely successful time for this kind of production, and it goes hand in hand with all of that production of material cultural objects. You see in that 1946 film this revival of dance and performance in a very practical, lived way that hasn't really happened outside of the public performance space for some time. It's in that performance space, and that's what I think is really strong, where people are being objectified and turned into curios. But it's also that performance space, in which people are able to maintain culture and identity and a sense of self whether it's in Wirth's Olympia up here, performing these big public corroborees throughout the '40s and '50s, or whether it's *Moomba* and even before that. If you go back you can see that there are records of these public corroborees going back a hell of a long way. I mean, John Antill writes *Corroboree* based on a performance he saw out near La Perouse when he was a kid and then writes *Corroboree* itself thirty or forty years later. There's this tradition of performance which is just kind of lost that we don't acknowledge in that space. The role of that public *nadgee* or corroboree, or whatever you want to call it, is big.

At something like Wirth's Olympia, these corroborees were a regular occurrence or certainly the displays of boomerang throwing were worked into these largest shows. Those early Wirth's performances really lead up to the birth of *Moomba* as a show – that was a vaudeville show, for want of a better word, a variety show. I think the content of the first half would have been similar to the whole of the Wirth's show from what I've been told. It was very much cultural practice, life as it was, without many of the innovations that *Moomba* had – the first half being more traditional and the second half being much more contemporary, even though I hate those words. It was big exhibition piece of this kind of corroboree-type performance.

This is that ability to reach the masses. You have *Moomba*, which is done in the Princess Theatre – flash and fancy and at a very high level. But I think it bears out in Bill's artwork as well as his whole approach to Aboriginal art and the souvenir industry – it needs to be accessible. If you're going to try and win people's hearts and minds, then you want to get to as many people and places as you possibly can. That's a big influence behind his adoption of film as a medium, that it is kind of a great leveller, and that people are going to access this on all sorts of different levels. I mean there's only the cinema for people to go to back in these days or something like Wirth's. You're going to fit thousands more people into Wirth's Olympia than you are in the Princess Theatre or somewhere like that, so you can make a huge impact on these large, large numbers of people.

That bears out with things like the performances that were being done for the Red Cross and other organizations like that through the war, those fundraising efforts. I mean those performances being more exclusively mainstream performance, even though they were performed by Aboriginal troupes and performers. But the performers weren't necessarily embracing Indigenous identities and were seen by some I think as being tools of assimilation. But then that kind of performing and enacting cultural practice also becomes this incredibly powerful tool to reaffirm and maintain cultural practices. That's certainly the way in which you see Bill and Eric really kind of challenging that. I mean you look at the New Theatre production: on paper what would be quite a ground-breaking work for anyone to put on in those days in '46, made all the more so by the fact that you've got this strong political alliance between the New Theatre and the Australian Aborigines' League, with all the Indigenous parts being played by Aboriginal performers. I mean that's pretty novel and ground-breaking for its time.

## *Aboriginal Moomba* in 1951 Jubilee Festival, Melbourne

The Melbourne City Fathers came out and announced that there would be no Aboriginal presence in the Jubilee celebrations, you'd think that you just kind of do that on the quiet somewhere and just silently exclude people, but because they did, it meant that Bill and Doug Nicholls and others are able to come out and put out a statement saying: look that's fine if you're going to exclude us then we'll just enter the parade ourselves. We will hire a truck, we'll put it in the parade and we'll have Aboriginal people in chains on the back being whipped by white overseers. Understandably the Melbourne City Fathers got a bit worried about that because it's a big event and they wanted to show the world and so although there was no opportunity for something to then be created and put into those Jubilee celebrations. I think they thought that they were just going to buy off the Australian Aborigines' League with a large sum of money and let them go and do something, it'll be a flop and everything will be alright.

So, they gave them some £2,000, huge money for the day. Predominantly Bill, but also Eric and Doug and others, then were very shrewd with it down to every last penny. They scoured the countryside for performers – lots of people coming from Lake Tyers and other areas, but right up the east coast as well. That connection with Harold Blair was very important, and Georgia Lee from the Torres Straits. Bill had his connections back into Sydney through his Koala Park, Redfern days and then Harold had all of his Queensland connections as well to bring everyone together for this review show in two halves of traditional and contemporary. But the thing I love about Bill is that it doesn't just end with the performance, he goes and commissions artwork. Paula Carey, who was his designer at the time, created this fabric, which then they use to create costumes for twelve Aboriginal usherettes. The set designer takes inspiration from Albert Namatjira's work and they have all these people attached to it all doing this under the direction of Aboriginal artists.

You have this entirely Aboriginal-controlled show – at least it has non-Indigenous people involved with it, but largely everyone on stage is Aboriginal, all the management, the direction of the production is Aboriginal, apart from some of the production staff – it leads to this insane blockbuster of a show that then gets talked about, has to go to the King, has to go everywhere. Then they fall into the same problem that they have with Ray Peckham and Faith Bandler – we would love to send it to the King and to the United States, into other places, but if we do that then people are going to know what's going on here and they start cancelling. They start not allowing people to travel. I mean, they stopped Bill from going to the United States. The year when Bill gets stopped going to the United States, that's the year after Ray Peckham and Faith Bandler incident [1952], so I think it's highly likely that this has something to play in it too. I mean, in Bill's ASIO file there are copies of letters that ASIO sent to the US consulate.

This idea of allowing Aboriginal people out, not just to tell their story, but allowing Aboriginal people out to see the way that things were in the rest of the world, and to start coming back and telling people it's different elsewhere. Especially people in that kind of volume, ok Ray Peckham and Faith Bandler may sneak their way out, that's one thing, but if you're taking forty people away to let them see stuff and come back that's a whole other thing altogether. It becomes highly problematic. It's interesting to think what more may have happened with *Moomba* had it grown and gone on, because *Moomba* is Bill's big moment in that impresario space, and then after that he becomes much more involved again in film and certainly in the souvenir trade. And then he's also becoming much more focused on politics – he's president of the Australian Aborigines' League and he stays president of the AAL for years and years after the war right up until his death in 1968.

In the film *Aborigines in the Community*, you can see a message: we'll be here, together we stand. It's one which we could do a bit more of these days really. But I think the idea – we are one people, and this is what we achieve when we stand together, indeed, this is what we can achieve if given our own self-determination – I think that idea of self-determination is where Bill starts to move away from people who want to do good for Aboriginal people, as opposed to supporting and helping Aboriginal people to do good for themselves, and that's when he starts running afoul of more and more people.

Things start to move from being seen and having a voice to then being able to normalize other people to Aboriginal cultures. Once Bill has found a voice, then he's trying to find other ways to use it and becoming more adept at that. All of these art forms are kind of different tools for Bill to get his message as a kind of cultural ambassadorship. Souvenirs especially being really powerful: that if you could just get into the front room of someone's house then it's only a short step into their hearts and minds.

# 5

# 1960–1967 – Aboriginal performance takes the main stage

Between 14 November and 21 December 1963, the *Aboriginal Theatre* produced by the Australian Elizabethan Theatre Trust performed to capacity audiences in a two-week run at Newtown's Elizabethan Theatre in Sydney with one-week at St Kilda's Palais Theatre, Melbourne. The performers had travelled down from Bathurst Island, Yirrkala (northeast Arnhem Land) and the Daly River region for the performance, which presented a series of songs and dances, from traditional stories about the moon, thunder, spears and a Tiwi Pukamuni burial ceremony, to newly composed and created work, depicting topical themes of the era, like aeroplanes and cowboys. Each night's show began with a fire-making performance, in which the audience saw a darkened stage gradually illuminate with sparks and fire and the smell of burning leaves, created by Frank Artu Dumoo, Skipper Anggilidji and Barney Munggin. The performers then presented a series of works devised by each group – bringing a variety of public performance genres from the Tiwi Islands, Arnhem Land and Daly Region into dialogue with one another. The danced performances were alternated with solo didjeridu performances, though publicity materials depicted a quartet of didjeridus.

The programme cover for the *Aboriginal Theatre* featured a bark painting 'specially done' by Narritjin Maymuru from Yirrkala of 'Bolngnor' and 'Wirradilaku' – Thunder and Spear legends also performed during the shows.[1] During the performances, screens were also erected above the performers' heads on which images of bark paintings and carvings from an associated exhibition were projected.[2] The artworks on display had been collected by Dorothy Bennett, who exhibited a total of 260 bark paintings, 200 pieces of sculpture and 30 baskets and straw mats from her travels through Tiwi country, the Daly Region and Arnhem Land, including some created by artists who also appeared as performers in the show.[3]

Co-located on the 1963 tour, the two representations of Aboriginal culture – the performance and the exhibition – also played an important role in music, dance and visual art movements that would emerge after 1970. Music and dance performances from these same communities later featured in the Aboriginal Theatre Foundation (see Chapter 6) that would merge into the Aboriginal Cultural Foundation in 1975.

The artworks of the Bennett-Campbell Trust contributed to creating a commercial market for Aboriginal painting and sculpture, while channelling payments back to artists. But the realization of these two kinds of representation also differed in important ways, especially in their degrees of entanglement with Aboriginal welfare structures. The *Aboriginal Theatre* was intensively managed by welfare officers in the lead-up to the performances, stage management of the shows themselves and in discussions about the potential for subsequent performances. Whereas, after permission to collect the artworks was granted by the Welfare Office, their management, exhibition and sale was a private matter for Bennett's enterprise. In their potential to represent Australian culture, the afterlives of the two types of cultural production also differed. While the Bennett collection of bark paintings went overseas to represent Australian culture less than one year after the 1963 shows, it took more than seven years before Aboriginal musicians and dancers would be included in an international tour.

Thus, while performance opportunities for Aboriginal people that had been developed in the 1950s continued apace in the subsequent decade, Harold Blair's vision (with which I ended Chapter 4) was still a work in progress throughout the 1960s. That is, interest in Aboriginal art had not yet led to interest in Aboriginal people and their living embodiment of culture on a national scale. As Blair's analysis suggests, music and dance performance created a forum in which Aboriginal people could represent themselves and their cultural products, unmediated, to live audiences. The performances could only be transmitted by the performers *in situ*, and this generated opportunities for exchanges of cultural understanding that are difficult for static objects to replicate. While material culture could hang on gallery or museum walls independent of the artists who created them, the necessarily embodied character of performance saw Aboriginal musicians and dancers excluded from official representations of Australian culture in more enduring ways.

In this chapter, I introduce some of the new opportunities through which Aboriginal musicians and dancers were able to publicly perform, before exploring some of the ongoing limitations imposed on these opportunities by the state. I begin with two public competitive events that provided new stages for Aboriginal performance – the NADOC talent quests in Sydney, and North Australian Eisteddfod in Darwin, both bringing Aboriginal talent to the public from 1961.[4] The NADOC event encouraged Aboriginal people to perform as soloists or in ensembles, using the instruments of folk and popular music – guitars, accordions and voices – while the North Australian Eisteddfod introduced categories facilitating 'traditional' song and dance (including didjeridu and clapsticks) that co-existed with folk singing and classical ballet and music.

I then examine in detail the major touring production that arose from performances in the North Australian Eisteddfod – the 1963 *Aboriginal Theatre*. Those music, dance and theatre critics who reviewed it also reviewed or were directly involved with a second production in 1963 in which Aboriginal culture was represented by non-Indigenous performers – *Burragorang Dreamtime*. Examined alongside one another, the two productions reveal shifts in how Aboriginal and Torres Strait Islander performing arts were received, and presage reactions to non-Indigenous representations that would soon come, after the momentous referendum of 1967.

## NADOC: New opportunities for performance

In 1956, the National Aborigines' Day Observance Committee (NADOC) was formed by Anglican organization the National Missionary Council of Australia in cooperation with the Commonwealth government.[5] The annual Aborigines' Day featured church services and participation in national activities by school children, and the Federal government released a booklet about Aboriginal people in each of the initial years' observance. These booklets advocated explicitly for the assimilation of Aboriginal people into the wider community, positioning this as a remedy to previous misguided beliefs that Aboriginal people would die out over time.[6] Films were also distributed, the first in 1958 entitled *The End of the Walkabout*, and 'Aboriginal concerts' performed.[7] From 1959 onwards an annual demonstration was staged in Sydney's Martin Place, with a talent quest introduced in 1961, giving NSW Aboriginal people opportunities for public performance and to compete for prizes, the organizers hoping that participants would be encouraged 'by the opportunity of being brought to Sydney'.[8] Many Aboriginal musicians participated in these events, initially just focused on NSW, but later broadened to have a national focus. The committee that had been formed to 'foster any real Talent found', included composer John Antill as well as ethnomusicologist Alice Moyle, with Antill acting as examiner, just as Moyle would adjudicate the North Australian Eisteddfod around the same time.[9]

The terms of the commemorative day were strongly framed around assimilation, so that there was little opportunity for performance within traditional Aboriginal song and dance genres. Nevertheless, the concerts featured gumleaf players, along with other instrumentalists playing guitars (Figure 5.1), piano accordions and Peter Doolan's instrument consisting of an 'oil drum, broom handle and two strings', and especially singers, including the choir of the Singleton Bible Training College, run by the Aborigines' Inland Mission.[10] Subsequently some performers appeared in television broadcasts, including Peter Doolan from Walgett, Max Cutmore, Arch Walford, Steve Duke and Clive Cutmore of Moree.[11] Mrs L. H. Cocks assembled all of the recorded entries for the event, arranged the TV appearances and set off through northern NSW immediately after the event's conclusion to scout for further talent. In the course of the 1960s, regional concerts were staged outside of Sydney, such as the Moree Talent Quest in July 1966.

These events lacked the large-scale support from government and the ABC that many non-Indigenous arts events had been able to secure, though Antill as an ABC employee was permitted to act as judge. As the committee's secretary reported, the group's approaches to the ABC for this to be a public concert had been declined: 'It had been earlier decided, on Mr. Antill's advice, not to try to organise a large concert this year. It was realised that a great deal more experience would be necessary before this could be done successfully.'[12]

Mr. A. McLeod and Mr. Jimmy Little senior, accompanied by Miss Margaret Williams, all of Nowra, play a gum-leaf duet during the National Aborigines' Day ceremonies in Martin Place, Sydney. The Chief Secretary, Mr. C. A. Kelly, is seated on the right of the picture. (By courtesy, Sydney Morning Herald)

**Figure 5.1** Jimmy Little Snr and A. McLeod playing gum leaves accompanied by Margaret Williams at NADOC concert in Martin Place, Sydney, *Dawn,* July 1961, 3.

Though Antill had advised that more experience would be necessary, a number of experienced Aboriginal performers with established public profiles performed at the concerts. Even before the talent quests had begun in 1961, country singers Jimmy Little (already famous as recording artist and actor by this time) and Candy Williams performed at the Martin Place demonstration in July 1960.[13] Their participation continued, reports indicating they were the highlight of the 1962 event. By 1963, Jimmy Little was acting as judge of the talent quests.[14] As in many of the events of the

1940s and 1950s, Aboriginal performers made the most of these state-organized events to build networks and connect with other Aboriginal musicians across the east coast. Feature entertainers and talent quest participants alike in the 1962 event formed an ensemble for a self-produced 'All Coloured Show' the following year.[15] On the eve of Aborigines' Day the following year, Jimmy Little led an ensemble in a Revue at Sydney's Anzac House, including Candy Williams, Lorna Beulah, Harold Blair, Freddie Little, Doug Peters (Jimmy Little's brother and brother-in-law respectively), Col Hardy and Betty Fisher.[16]

The members of this ensemble were either already well established as touring performers or had local performing profiles. Talent quest winner Lorna Beulah not only received a scholarship to the NSW State Conservatorium in 1962, but went on to perform in professional touring shows such as the 1965 tour of George Gershwin's *Porgy and Bess*. Cast with African American principals and Maori performers trained for the show, Beulah joined *Porgy and Bess* when one Maori performer became ill during the tour.[17] Eva Mumbler, Col Hardy, Candy Williams, from distant parts of NSW, had all been part of the music culture of Sydney's Redfern Aboriginal community, and Mumbler (then Eva Bell) had released a 1956 commercial recording with her cousin Olive McGuiness under the name of their duo Olive & Eva.[18] Joe Timbery already enjoyed a high profile as a champion boomerang thrower (having performed for Queen Elizabeth II in 1954 – see Chapter 4), and was another winner of the 1962 talent quest, with his 'didjeridoo band'.[19] Harold Blair's touring career has already been discussed in Chapters 3 and 4, and Jimmy Little was described by *Dawn* magazine at the time of his performance for Aborigines' Day as a 'teenage idol'.[20] In the face of this wealth of touring, recording and public performance experience, Antill's dismissal of the potential for a large-scale concert on the basis of lack of experience seems to suggest alternate agendas, or at least a narrow definition of what was suitable content for concerts.

The participation of Aboriginal activists such as Charles Perkins in the Aborigines' Day demonstrations and the speeches given (often drawing attention to the injustices perpetrated against Aboriginal people) show that this event was not excessively censored by the Welfare Board, even if architect of the government's assimilation agenda, Paul Hasluck, was a regular speaker. Many of the Aboriginal performers framed the sharing of their musical talents as advocacy for Aboriginal causes. Lorna Beulah, who *Dawn* quoted with the disclaimer 'Not that she is a very militant crusader for Aboriginal rights', asserted that it was important to her that she sing in Australia 'so that the community can see what aborigines can do'.[21]

Though performing artists Little, Hardy, Williams and Beulah built touring careers within Australia, they faced obstacles in being included in representations of Australian culture overseas. One proposal from the NADOC committee suggested sending Aboriginal performers to the Expo in Montreal in 1967, but this was not supported by the national committee. Aboriginal bark paintings were sent, however, along with a non-Aboriginal boomerang thrower, Frank Donnellan, who had reportedly outcompeted Aboriginal throwers for the honour.[22] The NADOC committee proposer, R. P. Greenish, responded to this lack of support with a cutting satirical song:

There'll be a ball held in old Montreal
Some Australians will be there – but not all ...
Not only the folk of the ACT
But aborigines too are not free ...
We have here a colour bar
Quite as black as any tar
But let's not blazon this afar
Second-class citizenship can jar.[23]

In 1969 (following the 1967 referendum – see Chapter 6), the constitution of NADOC was redrawn to provide for significant Aboriginal participation, moving the organization towards the Indigenous-led NAIDOC organization more familiar today.[24]

## North Australian Eisteddfod: New public performance opportunities for Aboriginal music and dance

In 1957, a Darwin committee established a new forum for Northern Territory residents to perform publicly and to cultivate the performing arts. The North Australian Eisteddfod, held in Darwin Town Hall and featuring categories much like any eisteddfod from other parts of Australia and beyond, quickly transformed into an event more representative of the demographics of the territory. By the 1960s, the categories included didjeridu solo with singing sticks accompaniment, Aboriginal interpretative group and solo dance, and didjeridu and songmen duet. Both adult and primary children's sections existed for each category, except for Aboriginal camp fire group singing (eight to twenty participants).[25] These new categories attracted a wide range of performers who travelled into Darwin from locations as distant as Lajamanu (870 km southwest), Maningrida (510 km east) and elsewhere. The eisteddfod also played a role in the founding of the Darwin Festival. By 1971, organizers discussed the possibility of a change of name of the event to reflect the format the eisteddfod had begun to assume, adult sections were no longer competitive and eisteddfod council president, Grant Tambling, proposed naming the event 'Eisteddfod and Festival of Arts'.[26]

Throughout the 1960s, the Aboriginal performance sections of the North Australian Eisteddfod not only became a prominent feature of the event, but were valued in equal standing to the events originating in European traditions – classical singing (lieder), ballet, choral singing, piano performance etc. Indeed, the Aboriginal music and dance performances were often singled out as raising the standard of the overall show.[27] A film made in 1963 documenting the eisteddfod highlighted the multicultural flavour of the event to an extent that was uncharacteristic of Australian media at the time. The film's narrative and editing of footage strongly emphasized the side-by-side inclusion of European and Aboriginal performance traditions, as well as the potential for crossover between them. In one scene, the narration pointed to the way that Aboriginal performers had quickly moved into all categories of the eisteddfod in the few years that Aboriginal performance categories had been incorporated. This narration played over footage of a piano-accompanied song recital by Delissaville (Belyuen) man Rusty Moreen. Moreen had also featured in the opening of the film, meandering through Darwin's streets and wandering into the local church to listen to the rehearsals of a white choir singing 'Waltzing Matilda'.[28]

The film also highlighted the inclusion of Darwin residents of Asian heritage, not just in participatory roles in the event, but also showing Mayor of Darwin Harry Chan on the eisteddfod organizing committee. Though the film featured numerous clips of 'traditional' music and dance performance, rather than adaptive performances in European genres, it was showcased in Sydney at the 1966 NADOC celebrations.[29] This demonstration of continuing practice from afar was accompanied by a display of didjeridu playing by visiting Yolngu musicians Michel Baluka and Larry Bilayna alongside the more hybrid local performance acts presented during the NSW NADOC show.[30]

Because of the wide dispersal and rich cultural diversity of Aboriginal performance traditions across the Northern Territory, welfare officers in each Aboriginal reserve assisted local communities to send representatives of performance traditions to the eisteddfod in small groups. But once combined, these small groups made for an increasingly large contingent of performers from remote communities, and from major towns as far south as Alice Springs. The logistics of transporting the performers (including groups of up to thirty school children from each community) and of accommodating and rationing them while away became a major logistical undertaking each year.[31] It also prompted protests from some welfare officers, who called upon the eisteddfod council to assist in managing this burden by curtailing the permitted participant numbers, as a 1968 letter attests:

> I must support Mr Allom in his request that the numbers be reduced as I feel that the Eisteddfod has now got out of all proportion and is not an Eisteddfod in the true sense of the word but is developing into an experiment by Welfare Branch. As indicated in the report following the last eisteddfod, we should be more selective and curtail the numbers attending to approximately 200.[32]

Tensions that arose between the Welfare Office and eisteddfod council suggest a conflict between policies of assimilation that saw aspects of Aboriginal cultural practice suppressed and the Australian public's broader interest in Aboriginal performing arts during this period. The NT welfare officers were foot soldiers of assimilation policy, but had often been drawn to their profession because of an interest in Aboriginal culture. When performing arts representatives like the eisteddfod council sought performers, welfare officers were well equipped to make recommendations based on knowledge of performance practices that were informed by years living within Aboriginal communities, or in the case of Ted Evans, extensive travels throughout the Northern Territory and acquaintance with the songmen and dancers responsible for performance and maintenance of particular song cycles and their associated dances, ceremonies, stories and Country.[33]

Like 'corroborees' that had long brought people together in cultural exchange, the eisteddfod played an important role in supporting ongoing performance practices.

The weeks of preparation each year of high-quality performances in a competitive forum helped give validity to ongoing performance of traditions that might otherwise have been under pressure to fall away in favour of church hymns in language, or communication and teaching in English.[34] Children who travelled to the eisteddfod were trained to sing standard English-language repertoire. Tiwi woman Jacinta Tipungwuti recalls learning these songs for the eisteddfod and remembers that it was only after people completed their schooling that they were able to develop knowledge in Tiwi song practice. Now children are able to learn Tiwi songs from their elders as part of everyday life.[35]

The cultivation of public performing opportunities for highly skilled and knowledgeable local talent led towards the professionalization of Aboriginal performing arts that emerged in the 1970s, and that is discussed in more detail in Chapter 6. After the first couple of years of Aboriginal music and dance in the eisteddfod, AETT chairman H. C. Coombs arranged for new executive director of the trust, Stefan Haag, to visit Darwin to watch entrants in the eisteddfod.[36] On his return Haag recommended to the board of the AETT that a full theatrical performance be staged in Sydney and Melbourne the same year.[37]

## 1963: Touring northern performance to the south

From the range of performances Haag had watched in July that year, groups of dancers were chosen from three Aboriginal communities – Yirrkala, Bathurst Island and a small group from the Daly Region (the Daly performers were chosen in particular to include fire-makers and women).[38] Logistics and planning for the new *Aboriginal Theatre* were managed through a series of negotiations between Haag for the AETT, and Harry Giese and Evans for the NT Administration. This managerial oversight is indicative of the reach of the welfare regime in managing the lives of Aboriginal people. This was particularly evident in the AETT's rebuffing of approaches that circumvented the established framework. At least one direct approach was made to Stefan Haag by Sam Passi, chairman of council, Murray Island (Mer), Torres Strait, who sought to promote the dances of his own community as suitable for the *Aboriginal Theatre*.[39] Haag seems to have been unreceptive to the direct line to the performers that Passi offered, preferring his established relationship with NT welfare officers.[40] It is certain that unsolicited offers were often rejected by the AETT, but these particular rejections also seem to indicate the structural confines within which Aboriginal dance and music was supported by the AETT in the 1960s.

The performers of the *Aboriginal Theatre* ranged in age from teenagers to men in their sixties, though the programme asserted that it would present the 'oldest Australians', simultaneously suggesting that the opportunity to experience 'the fantasy and nobility of the age-old aboriginal spirit, places it among the greater innovations in world theatre in 1963'. Of the hundreds of ensembles and productions being supported by the AETT and overseen by Haag, the *Aboriginal Theatre* seems to have been one of his pet projects, and Haag would attempt to revive the idea to tour the *Aboriginal Theatre* in Australia and abroad again and again in subsequent years. The minutes of the board meeting in 1964 show that members discussed whether the show should be altered to be more theatrical and less 'anthropological'. Stefan Haag argued that the theatricality of the work could be enhanced without compromising the 'authenticity' of the performances.[41]

The shows aimed simultaneously to engage those interested in Aboriginal performance from an ethnographic and/or historical perspective and those creating and producing new works of modern dance, music and visual art on Australian stages. In the 1940s, 1950s and 1960s, anthropologists frequently acted as cultural brokers between performers, the arts sector and the media. The list of invited VIPs for the Sydney performances of the *Aboriginal Theatre* included a range of university and museum anthropologists and academics, including Frederick McCarthy from the Australian Museum, A. P. Elkin, Alice Moyle, Arthur Capell and William Geddes from the University of Sydney, among a shorter list of prominent individuals from the arts sector including dance critic and choreographer Beth Dean, New South Wales Conservatorium of Music's director Sir Bernard Heinze, president, Arts Council of Australia, Dorothy Helmrich, visual artist, Russell Drysdale, and government ministers including the Chief Secretary and Minister for Tourism (also responsible for Aboriginal welfare in NSW) the Honourable C. A. Kelly. Several of the invited anthropologists, including Australia's most prominent anthropologist and expert on Aboriginal cultures at this time, A. P. Elkin, not only attended, but wrote to Stefan Haag in praise of the performance in the days afterwards.

Artistically, most agreed that the show was a great success, even if it posed financial challenges for the AETT.[42] Haag had championed the project, not only as an early initiative in his role as executive director of the AETT, but also as artistic director of the show itself (though he was criticized in some quarters for trying to juggle both roles).[43] For the performers sharing their culture, the potential for the performances to be forward-looking and future-facing seems also to have been a key motivator. Looking at footage and listening to recordings of the *Aboriginal Theatre* today, family and community relatives of some of the performers agree that the dances and songs performed were being demonstrated so they could be seen in the future, and they were done properly – even if the Tiwi mourning songs were being publicly demonstrated instead of ritually performed for a particular recently deceased person. As senior Tiwi woman Jacinta Tipungwuti told me while listening to a recording of the Tiwi songs in the 1963 shows, 'they had that strong culture! And they left that for us ... generation to generation'.[44]

Though the AETT board's characterization of the performances as 'anthropological' suggests a reluctance to regard Aboriginal performing arts as 'modern', this was not necessarily how the work was received by Sydney and Melbourne audiences, and by critics embedded in the music and dance scene. The *Sydney Morning Herald*'s music critic Roger Covell, who, a few years later, wrote the field-defining book for contemporary Australian western art music, *Australia's Music*, reviewed the 1963 shows:

> The unique entertainment that brought authentic music, dancing and mime from the great artistic traditions of the Australian aborigines to the stage of the Elizabethan, Newtown ... and brought them in the person of the inheritors of these traditions: the aborigines themselves ...
>
> It is hard to know which to admire more: the untroubled assurance, the truly professional aplomb, with which these 45 artists have transplanted their ceremonies from the bare earth arenas of their tribal grounds to a spotlit city theatre, or the sympathetic integrity with which Stefan Haag has put the resources of Western stagecraft at their disposal ...
>
> There is no need to pretend that this is an equivalent of any other kind of theatre. This is an experience to tell your grandchildren about.[45]

Covell's reaction to the *Aboriginal Theatre*, which contained a certain revelatory sense of having discovered something that one didn't know was there, is replicated in some of the correspondence sent to Australian Elizabethan Theatre Trust director, Stefan Haag, congratulating him on the production. Like Covell, audiences seemed suddenly to recognize the *Aboriginal Theatre* as in fact, not old Australians at all, but rather, vital, living and continually transforming culture.

Choreographer and *Sydney Morning Herald* dance reviewer Beth Dean also praised the professionalism and intensity of the performers in her review of the event, adding that the show was 'strong, exciting and intensely interesting fare. Everyone should see it'. Dean claimed that the performance did not live up to some of those she and her husband had witnessed on Country. Though she had built a career on performing Aboriginal dances in the theatre of the 'white man', she characterized the Aboriginal dancers' efforts to do so as lacking the authenticity of a fireside performance. 'If the performance lost anything last night, and it did, it was that the Aborigine could not be stimulated by his own environment, challenged by his own competition as he dances around the fire at night ... The Aborigine last night could not be free to give his best in the narrow, tradition-bound, proscenium-arched theatre of the white man.'[46]

Philosopher, public intellectual and sometime theatre reviewer Alan Ker Stout found himself surprised by the show, which he had approached with low expectations.[47] The critic was impressed enough to recommend that the *Aboriginal Theatre* would be an appropriate touring show to represent Australia overseas:

> The success of this whole presentation suggests that in it the Trust may have discovered a dramatic experience that is both uniquely Australian and exportable. It speaks a universal language and has a universal appeal. Since it survived unharmed the drastic move from the scrub of Arnhem Land to the theatre stage of Melbourne and Sydney, what is to prevent its further transplantation to London, Vienna or Paris.[48]

Indeed, Stout was not the only one to imagine that the *Aboriginal Theatre* could represent Australian culture internationally, though each time an international tour was proposed, representatives of the government were quick to impose obstacles. Only a few further performances of the *Aboriginal Theatre* resulted in the 1960s, in the Sydney Trade Fair in 1965 (more on this below), in the Darwin Festival in 1966 and Perth Festival in 1967 (performers from Yirrkala and Bathurst Island in both cases, the Daly region performers only joining in Perth).[49] The ensemble was not fixed for each show, rather it was constituted by different groups of Aboriginal dancers and musicians each time, with the groups determined largely by the NT Administration.[50] Haag had also proposed taking the 1965 *Aboriginal Theatre* group on a four-week tour of Canberra and Melbourne. This idea was quickly quashed by the NT Welfare Administration, Evans indicating 'The boss is not very keen about the tour of Canberra/Melbourne, & possibly New Zealand, mainly because of the time welfare officers would be away from duty.'[51] A US tour by American promoter Sol Hurok proposed for November–December 1965 did not go ahead out of concern for how the Aboriginal performers would cope with winters in the United States, as Ted Evans wrote to Stefan Haag: 'Permission for this company to leave Australia must be obtained from the Department of Native Affairs... As you know they are one of the most primitive people on earth added to which they are used to a year round temperature of 90°F therefore there may be some opposition to their leaving the country for the colder northern climate.'[52]

Discussions among members of the AETT board noted that the reaction of the welfare people should be sought before mounting another tour for a couple of years.[53] Similar suggestions of an overseas tour that would bring together the *Aboriginal Theatre* performers and a group of performers from New Guinea was presented to Paul Hasluck, but 'Administration officers would not have a bar of such an arrangement'.[54] This state oversight of professional opportunities for Aboriginal people marks out the 1960s as distinct from the self-determined performances that would emerge from policy and constitutional change after 1967, but that really took effect in the 1970s. The initial 1963 event sparked discussion that would later lead to the establishment of the Aboriginal Theatre Foundation in 1969, an organization that became fully run by Aboriginal people by 1972 (discussed in Chapter 6).[55]

Two other proposed events in 1965 highlight the perceived potential for Aboriginal music and dance to represent Australian culture to international audiences. In 1965 Rembarrnga, Gunwinggu and Ngalkbun dancers from Beswick settlement were supported by the AETT to perform as the *Aboriginal Theatre* in the *Pageant of Asia* during the Sydney Trade Fair in 1965. The show was a financial failure, in part because bad weather washed out the fair, but the concept was ambitious and prescient of large-scale national events in the 1970s that situated Australian performance traditions within the wider neighbourhood of the Asia-Pacific (see Chapter 6). In the pageant, a map of the world was painted onto twenty-thousand square feet of canvas laid out on the Sydney Showground, and dancers brought from fourteen countries performed within the section of the map representing their homelands. The inclusion of Australian Aboriginal dance in this show put these performance traditions in dialogue with those of Australia's near neighbours, though the idea had been criticized in some government quarters. H. Neil Truscott wrote for the Department of External Affairs: 'there is a vast gap between the sophisticated songs and dances of the Asian peoples and those of the aborigines and Papuans, which, though of some merit and considerable interest, are primitive by comparison.'[56]

The kinds of Aboriginal dances selected for the show reflected the scale of its production space, and Haag wrote to Evans: 'the decorations of the desert tribes with stuck on feathers and high-peaked head dresses would, in my opinion, stand much more chance of getting across at such a distance' (Figure 5.2).[57] Though some government representatives were dismissive, the show featured several performers who would go on to prominent performing careers in Australia and overseas, including David Blanasi and Djoli Laiwanga.[58]

The financial implications of the Pageant of Asia venture opened Haag to considerable criticism. Not only did this come from the AETT itself, but also from outside. Beth Dean would later cite the 'disastrous' pageant in arguing (possibly out of professional jealousy) that Haag should not be 'allowed to work towards' the

**Figure 5.2** Djoli Laiwanga, David Blanasi and a third man in programme: 'Pageant of Asia Spectacular', Sydney 1965, NLA.

new Aboriginal Theatre Foundation.[59] The Federal Council for the Advancement of Aborigines and Torres Strait Islanders (FCAATSI), who had supported the AETT's efforts to tour the *Aboriginal Theatre* also compared the pageant with the AETT's *Porgy and Bess* production, questioning whether these were good strategies for giving Aboriginal performers experience of European theatre. In response, Haag articulated the aims of the pageant and of the *Aboriginal Theatre* more generally:

1. To draw attention of Australian audiences to the fact that these people have a culture of their own to be highly regarded, commanding respect on all levels – and
2. To develop, in the Aborigines, a pride in their heritage thus contributing towards their feeling of self respect as well as giving them a practical demonstration of the Australian society into which the latest laws are aiming to integrate them. It is my belief that in these aims and hopes we have succeeded unquestioningly, particularly in the Aboriginal Theatre venture.

I would like to note that at no time was our aim the integration between a western culture and ethnic culture – in fact, the contrary. In other words the project of PORGY AND BESS, using Maoris and American Negroes was totally different in aim and therefore, not to be associated or confused with our intentions concerning the Aborigines.[60]

The AETT proposed a further major performance for the *Aboriginal Theatre*, to represent Australian culture on the programme of the Commonwealth Festival in London in 1965. To Stefan Haag's disappointment, the *Aboriginal Theatre* was rejected. In this case the 'welfare' of the performers was not the key motivator for this decision, rather this was a question of Australia's national identity on an international stage. Specifically, the decision was about showing the Commonwealth how Australia had developed its own voice in European genres. As Stefan Haag related to Evans:

government circles have expressed the doubtful wisdom of the aborigines being the major contribution to the Commonwealth Festival in that it would tend to suggest that there is no cultural achievement in Australia other than the indigenous one of the aborigines. Hence it was felt that initially at least preference should be given to orchestras and theatrical companies. A defensible point of view I think even though you and I and many others will be disappointed.[61]

The AETT and welfare officers were not the only ones to lament this decision, Frank Hutchens, head of the NSW Conservatorium of Music, had acted as judge at the North Australian Eisteddfod in 1964, and expressed amazement at the artistic ability of the Aboriginal performers, reportedly telling Evans the decision was 'very short sighted'.[62]

The government's position reveals their eagerness to present a unified Australian identity, one that mapped onto a European performance medium. Other settler colonies shared these preoccupations. New Zealand would send to the Commonwealth Festival the Christchurch harmonic choir of fifty voices who would sing in Westminster Cathedral, while Canada would send French-speaking theatre companies and English-language ballet. Like Australian composers, Canadians had also developed representations of their First Nations traditions that appropriated culture while excluding Indigenous people. Radhika Natarajan suggests that Canada's Commonwealth Festival offering 'affirmed the availability of First Nations and Inuit artistic production for white appropriation and excluded Canada's European immigrants and "visible minorities", Asian and African ancestors, from the performance of Canadian nationalism'.[63]

By contrast, colonies from which British colonizers had withdrawn, but which still remained part of the Commonwealth took the opportunity to demonstrate the individuality of their creative talents at the festival – Pakistan would send the Khattak Dancers, India its finest classical musicians led by Ravi Shankar as well as Kathakali dancers. Kenya would send the Embu Drummers, Ghana an orchestra of xylophones, flutes and drums.[64] In total, 1,200 performers travelled to England and the event ran for three weeks in a festival of multiculturalism that Natarajan has characterized as 'postimperial reengagement ... that promised aesthetic equality through the acceptance of difference'.[65] Natarajan notes that in Britain, this embrace of cultural diversity sat uneasily alongside imperial nostalgia, but in Australia and in its representations at the festival, the possibility of multiculturalism was unrealized amidst anxiety about its cultural achievements.

Australia was, however, well positioned to present the work of Australian composers actively producing a body of new work that displayed the kind of cultural achievement the government was anxious to showcase. The symphony orchestras established by the ABC in the 1940s were now mature companies, and the AETT had recently established the Australian Ballet (1962). Representatives of Australian art music had gathered in Hobart in 1963 for a composers' seminar supported by the ABC and Tasmania's Adult Education Board, an event remembered as a landmark in cultivating a culture of compositional activity.[66]

Government concern about allowing Aboriginal performance to stand for Australian culture also demonstrates that resources to promote and support Aboriginal cultural practice were directly in competition with resources to exhibit European performance genres by non-Indigenous people.[67] The 1965 London Commonwealth Festival programming highlights this opposition poignantly in its selection of a representation of Australian culture that drew on notions of Aboriginality in Antill's *Corroboree*, and in the championing of Sculthorpe who would later go on to capitalize on this appetite for representation of Aboriginality devoid of Aboriginal people.[68]

The Sydney Symphony Orchestra (SSO) opened the festival at the Royal Festival Hall with a performance of a new violin concerto by Malcolm Williamson featuring Yehudi Menuhin as soloist. Each of the SSO's concerts featured at least one work by an Australian (non-Indigenous) composer conducted by Dean Dixon, Sir Bernard Heinze and Joseph Post. By presenting orchestral compositions by non-Indigenous composers, including some that represented a notion of Aboriginality in 1965, Australia could demonstrate its cultural achievement as distinct from Britain, but also as not only 'the indigenous one', differentiating itself from other British colonies in the Commonwealth whose native traditions had not been successfully replaced by hybridized European ones.[69] The directness of this replacement is highlighted by how Antill's *Corroboree* was represented in England. Expatriate Australian Dudley Glass had addressed the Royal Society of Arts in 1963, writing that though Aboriginal people had given little to music with their monotonous music and crude instruments, the 'ingenious' John Antill has given a ballet suite 'the flavour of aborigine music', portraying native dance ceremony and using different totems for different parts of the ballet.[70]

This contradictory sentiment, in which Aboriginal music was deemed to have little value and yet non-Indigenous composers were praised as innovative for evoking it in their music, permeated decisions about how Australia should be represented overseas. While performers of the *Aboriginal Theatre* were not deemed sufficiently representative of Australian culture for the Commonwealth Festival, their artworks (discussed at the opening of this chapter) were considered exportable. Dorothy Bennett took what Harry Giese described as 'a comprehensive exhibition of Aboriginal bark paintings and artifacts to the Festival'.[71] In representing itself to international audiences, the Australian government sought to maintain a narrative of Aboriginal people as something old and static, not modern and constantly transforming. Tangible artworks were sent overseas – works standing in for the artists who had created them, but live performers were excluded from events like the Commonwealth Festival in favour of non-Indigenous composers and performers who would represent Australia as a culture in dialogue with European modernity.

## Performing replacement: Antill and Dean's 'Aboriginal ballets', and Peter Sculthorpe

As the repeated appearance of John Antill and Beth Dean in this book suggests, the choice of Antill's *Corroboree* for the Commonwealth Festival was consistent with how settler colonial replacement of Aboriginal people had been performed to the nation throughout the assimilation period.[72] As a counterpoint to the *Aboriginal Theatre's* eye-opening production, Sydney audiences in 1963 had attended a major production by Antill and Dean – *Burragorang Dreamtime* – a set of two ballets composed in 1959, staged by the Arts Council of NSW in 1963 and then filmed for television broadcast on 22 January 1965 on ABC TV as *Dreaming Time Legends*, following the Governor General's Australia Day speech.[73]

A major public production during Queen Elizabeth II's visit, the 1963 performance was staged at the Sydney Showground as part of the *Pageant of Nationhood*. *Burragorang Dreamtime* was intended to depict life before the invasion of settlers by using 'an Aboriginal concept about how the world began' and preceded a re-enactment of the landing of Captain Arthur Phillip and the First Fleet onto the Country of the Gweagal clan, and his greeting by 'aborigines'.[74] The ballet was danced by an all non-Indigenous cast dressed in brown body stockings adorned with white decorative paint. Beth Dean performed the lead role. Captain Phillip's landing scene was prefaced by the following narration: 'The Dreamtime of the aborigines is about to come to an end. The great Spirit heroes fade into the dim past. The everyday poetry of the aborigine is soon to become in fact – only a Dreamtime… Out from the endless sea – out from the mists of the world appeared a new Spirit image – the white man …'[75]

As the ballet concluded, the actor (Peter Potok) playing Governor Phillip emerged. Unlike re-enactments in previous decades of the twentieth century, already discussed in Chapters 1, 2 and 4, the 'aborigines' in this extravaganza were not brought in from another part of NSW or beyond. They were not 'aborigines' at all, but rather non-Indigenous dancers from the ensemble who had just completed the ballet, who played the role of Aboriginal people confronting, and ultimately retreating from, the invading British (Figure 5.3).

Not only did the placement of *Burragorang Dreamtime* in the *Pageant of Nationhood*'s narrative enact an attempt at replacement, so too were the residents of the Burragorang Valley being displaced through the march of nationhood. The ballet's narrative was drawn from a Gundungurra story about the birth of the first waratah flower – a symbol appropriated as the official state flower for New South Wales. In 1960 the Burragorang Valley, west of Sydney, where the ballet's legends of the Waratah and Boomerang originated, was flooded to create the Warragamba Dam – the major drinking water supply for the Sydney region. As the NSW Aboriginal Welfare Board's magazine *Dawn* exclaimed: 'There is no help for it. The Valley's fate was written on the day when Phillip founded his city on Sydney Cove. Burragorang is only 60 miles away from Sydney's heart; its vast catchment area (3,383 square miles) makes it the most eminently suitable permanent storage for the city's water supply. It now must die.'[76]

**Figure 5.3** Still from *Pageant of Nationhood: Australia's 175th Anniversary: New South Wales Celebration*. From National Film and Sound Archive, Canberra. Title no. 56886.

By the mid-1950s, all residents, both Aboriginal and non-Indigenous, had been relocated out of the area that the Gundungurra people had populated for thousands of years.[77] Dean and Antill's *Burragorang* ballets had first been performed for Princess Alexandra of Kent on 11 September 1959, before the valley was flooded, but after people had been ejected.[78]

Rather than engaging with the displacement of Aboriginal people, artists like Dean and Carell responded to these events by romanticizing stories of erasure into representative performances, in which the replacement of Aboriginal people by the settler colony was re-enacted, and in which performing cultures were also literally replaced. Instead of Aboriginal and Torres Strait Islander dancers performing a corroboree for the Queen, as occurred in towns as varied as Wagga Wagga, Toowoomba, Townsville, Cairns and Whyalla during both the 1954 (see Chapter 4) and 1963 visits, Dean and the dancers and Antill and the orchestral musicians performed Aboriginality with little regard for the continuing existence of Aboriginal performers attempting to find new contexts for representing their own music and dance at home and overseas.[79]

Like the *Aboriginal Theatre* later the same year, this production received a review from the *Sydney Morning Herald*'s music critic Roger Covell with a lukewarm assessment of the *Pageant of Nationhood* as successful overall, even if it 'went on a little too long', if the aboriginal ballet scenes were 'inevitably disjointed' and if on the whole it was 'diffuse and often pointless'.[80] The *Aboriginal Theatre* may have struggled to find opportunities for further performances, especially those that represented Australia on an international stage, but ultimately it was the precursor to the Aboriginal Theatre Foundation of 1969 that would usher in a highly influential movement in Indigenous Theatre, discussed further in Chapter 6.[81] For the 'Aboriginal ballet' collaborations of John Antill and Beth Dean, the trajectory has been the inverse. That is though rarely performed since, in the 1950s and 1960s, the possibilities for staging of their collaborations were almost unlimited. Covell commented that Antill was 'at times a kind of musician-laureate for state occasions'.[82]

The ballets staged for the *Pageant of Nationhood* that seemed so disjointed to Covell, stood as representations of Australian culture that imagined the key legends of Australia's nationhood – an Aboriginal past, and a modern non-Indigenous present. Unlike other commemorative events that brought Aboriginal people into the nation's capitals from elsewhere (sometimes under duress), Dean and Antill represented this Aboriginal past without any involvement of Aboriginal people, a practice they had each repeated since 1946 (Antill) and 1950 (Dean) in numerous productions. Aboriginal-themed ballet was central to Dean's professional profile and had built on her 1950 'Dance and Song around the World' productions, discussed in Chapter 4. For Antill, the focus on Aboriginal ballet seems to have been more reactive, encouraged perhaps by Dean and Carell, but also driven by the commissions he received, an indication of the enthusiasm of cultural institutions, including the ABC, for non-Indigenous representations of Aboriginal performance. In Dean and Carell's biography, Antill recalled that: 'after Corroboree everybody thought of me as a ballet writer. Many stories and commissions came my way. Ballet seemed to be the thing expected of me and it kept pushing the symphonic works into the background. I had been a symphonic man all my life.'[83]

In David Symons' musical biography of Antill, he notes that the 1961 *Black Opal* marked the end of Antill's association with Aboriginal themes. The choreographer of the work, Dawn Swane reportedly asserted that Antill was reluctant about this project for fear of being typecast as 'Aborigiana'.[84] Indeed, though Dean continued to pursue opportunities to choreograph 'Aboriginal ballets' (discussed in Chapter 6), these were no longer collaborations with Antill.

Beth Dean also reported that in 1963, Antill attended the performances of the *Aboriginal Theatre*. According to Dean (whose review of the shows has already been quoted), the impact of this on Antill was profound:

> This was far different from anything Antill had seen before. It was not the rather impromptu 'tourist version' by Aborigines who had not been living a tribal life for many years, sometimes generations, as they survived on the outskirts of towns. John was thrilled. One may wonder what Antill might have done if he had experienced this kind of Aboriginal music in his early days, rather than on his 60th birthday.[85]

It was two years after the *Pageant of Nationhood* that Antill's *Corroboree* featured among the works performed by the Sydney Symphony Orchestra in the 1965 London Commonwealth Festival. The chosen works remain significant in conceptions of Australia's art music history and retain a symbolic power as formative compositions. It was then almost twenty years since *Corroboree*'s premiere and Peter Sculthorpe would go on to be Australia's most prominent national composer, a reputation based on his creation of what some listeners think of as a uniquely Australian style. This evocative Australian style was characterized by development of melodic material derived from Elkin's recordings of Aboriginal song from Central Arnhem Land, and the use of string instruments to imitate Australian birdsong. The Commonwealth Festival's *Sun Music I* precedes this turn in Sculthorpe's style and draws on Japanese Noh theatre traditions, rather than Australian ones, but in its integration of Japanese music into a European classical format, its use of experimental notation and repetitive rhythms, the work was deemed to represent an emergent Australian cultural identity in a way that the *Aboriginal Theatre*'s performances did not.

Though *Sun Music I* does not draw on Aboriginal music, in the early 1960s Sculthorpe was exploring ways to incorporate the sounds of Aboriginal Australia into his music. Correspondence between Sculthorpe and ethnomusicologist Alice Moyle in 1963 indicates his attempts to procure a 'recorded didjeridu and bullroarer sounds as "background" to some film music' he had recently composed (*The Fifth Continent*). Moyle pointed out to Sculthorpe that the Australian bullroarer would be unsuitable given it was only used in 'rare and secret ceremonies', and so had seldom been recorded; she suggested he source commercial recordings of bullroarers from PNG. Moyle then described a range of different didjeridu styles that could be relevant, depending on the musical context.

In a revealing sign off, Moyle offered to discuss Aboriginal music further with Sculthorpe:

Whenever you come to Sydney I shall be glad to demonstrate to you the stylistic differences in Aboriginal music. And speaking for the few – very few – who are now engaged in probing into this strange and complex music I can only say that it is time Australian musicians themselves began to treat it with more knowledge and discrimination. Unless they do, the ABC will not.[86]

## Conclusions: New stages for Aboriginal music and dance

A defining feature of new contexts for Aboriginal music and dance in the 1960s was the way in which performers from different traditions were brought together into a scratch ensemble (in the several instances of the *Aboriginal Theatre*), or into competition with one another (in the North Australian Eisteddfod and NADOC talent quests). These new contexts might be thought of as reimagined 'corroboree' spaces. In its use in Dharug and Dharawal languages *corroboree* signifies large groups of people coming together and performing music and dance, and is often linked to ceremonial practice.[87] However, in its appropriation into the Australian English vernacular, 'corroboree' has taken on a multitude of meanings and associations. In Paul Carter's framing of 'corroboree' in Australia's colonial history, performative cross-cultural interactions have acted as an attempt to articulate the 'disputed spaces occupied by Aborigines and Europeans'. As Carter suggests, the corroboree came to operate as a 'transitional object, a specially manufactured symbolic event' whose cross-cultural communication articulated a response to white invasion. Some European Australians embraced the symbolic currency of this performative response, manipulating it to their own political ends.[88]

But Aboriginal people have moved with these changing significations of 'corroboree', and the years following the 1967 referendum would see opportunities for performers to come together in Aboriginal music and dance taking the public stage and touring overseas like never before. Groups like the Aboriginal Theatre Foundation would be momentous in localizing the performance of Aboriginal culture internationally, bringing a regional focus to owned and self-represented cultural practice, in dialogue with global contexts for performance.

6

# 1967–1970 – The end of assimilation?

The events interrogated in this chapter are bounded by two markers of national significance: the 1967 referendum on constitutional change and the 1970 Cook Bicentenary. Many of those lobbying for the Yes vote in the referendum would also rally for Aboriginal recognition in the Bicentennial protests. The landing of Captain Cook at Kamay (Botany Bay) had been regularly re-enacted since 1901. However, the bicentenary of this event in April 1970 was contentious as never before, and protests by Aboriginal people were just as visible as official commemorations organized by government bodies.[1] Around Kamay on the anniversary, a re-enactment of Cook's landing went ahead for the entertainment of Queen Elizabeth II and the Sydney public, with Aboriginal actors paid equity rates to perform the presence of Gweagal people confronting the disembarking party. On the other side of the bay, at Guriwal (La Perouse), protesters threw wreaths into the sea and staged a Day of Mourning.

The protesters may not have succeeded in derailing the main commemorations, but their actions had shifted discussions between the Memorial Bi-Centenary Committee and arts bodies including the Arts Council, Australian Ballet and various individuals in the lead-up to the events. In this chapter, I contrast a series of performative events between 1967 and 1970, revealing the shifting ground on which questions of who should represent Aboriginal performance culture were contested. The shift following the referendum from non-Indigenous representations of Aboriginal culture dominating mainstream, high-culture contexts (such as gala ballets and orchestral concerts) towards self-representation by Aboriginal performers was swift and dramatic. The chapter ends with consideration of the official programme for Cook Bicentenary commemorations, a programme that brought together performers from across the regions touched by Cook's travels, and that became a testing ground for new directions in staging representation.

## 'Right wrongs write yes for Aborigines': The 1967 referendum[2]

The 1967 referendum is popularly remembered, especially among many Aboriginal people, as the event that shifted the classification of Aborigines from 'part of the flora and fauna' to citizens of Australia. As Gumbaynggirr man Gary Williams puts it, it meant 'we were recognized as people'.[3] This memorialization attests to the widespread experience of being treated as less than human that so many Aboriginal people recall. More widely, the referendum is remembered as the moment Aboriginal people got the right to vote (though Aboriginal people had had at least a theoretical right to vote, if they were able to comply with the conditions of the individual state or territory that governed their lands). More than 90 per cent of the Australian population voted 'Yes' to the constitutional changes proposed in the referendum, which removed the power of states to exercise discriminatory powers applying only to Aboriginal and Torres Strait Islander people, and counted Aboriginal and Torres Strait Islander people in the total population. The Yes result, indicating that such a vast majority of Australians thought that Aboriginal people should be regarded as citizens of the nation, had effects far more profound than just the constitutional ones. Rodney Hall, involved with the Queensland Council for the Advancement of Aborigines and Torres Strait Islanders, recalled Aboriginal families dressing up and going into parts of the city they would never normally visit, imbued with a new sense of entitlement: 'There were black people on the streets in a way that we had never seen them … It was so touching. People were up … and walked out in the streets of Brisbane, down Queen Street where they never went.'[4]

This sense of liberation was mimicked also in performance arenas, where new possibilities emerged for theatre and dance companies and the stages available to them. Performers were released from the arbitration of government intermediaries and worked towards self-determination in Aboriginal-run companies over the five years following the referendum, resulting in an explosion of new performing arts organizations and productions in the 1970s. Most prominent among these in music and dance were the Aboriginal Islander Dance Theatre (AIDT, formed in 1976 – later NAISDA), and the Aboriginal Theatre Foundation (founded in 1969). These two organizations would have a momentous impact on the Aboriginal performance landscape, and their actions arguably continue to shape it today. Theatre companies working in the sphere of narrative theatre also proliferated in this period, especially in the activities of Sydney's Black Theatre and Melbourne's Nindethana Theatre.[5]

However, it would be several years before these shifts were universally felt across the performing arts, and staged representations of Aboriginal culture without Aboriginal people continued in the late 1960s, especially in high art forms.

## Art music and Aboriginal master musicians: A shake-up for Australian composition?

In the domain of Australian art music, Australia's cultural life was also being evaluated. In 1967, as conceptions of the place of Aboriginal people in the nation state were being reimagined, Australian art music had been catapulted into shape by the publication of a field-defining book by Roger Covell. Covell's *Australia's Music* was not the only study of Australian composition in production at this time; Donald Peart had published a pioneering article on the subject a year earlier, as had composer Larry Sitsky, and Andrew McCredie's *Musical Composition in Australia* and James Murdoch's book *Australia's Contemporary Composers* would appear two and five years later respectively.[6] But it was Covell's monograph that gave contour to a school or tradition of Australian composition, even if the dominance of his interpretations have been contested in some recent scholarship.[7]

Covell's inclusive title *Australia's Music* differentiates it from the composer-centred approaches of Peart and Murdoch. The contents of Covell's book conceived of Australian musical practice as broadly historicized and inclusive of Aboriginal musics (to which seventeen pages were devoted) and folk musics (thirty pages), even if these inclusions were a small percentage of the whole (290 pages).[8] A broad-minded and erudite scholar, critic, poet and composer, Covell's conception of the music of Australia ranged beyond the boundaries of Western art music, though obituaries to Covell appearing during the writing of the current book emphasized his contribution to Western art music only, reflecting the narrow scope of Australian institutional musicology in recent decades.[9] Covell's approach was reminiscent of Percy Grainger's broad conceptualization of music articulated in broadcasts over ABC radio in 1934 (see Chapter 2). Critical of Euro-centric conceptions of art music, while acknowledging it as his own preferred artistic framework, Grainger had written:

> What would we think of a Professor of Literature who knew nothing of Homer, the Icelandic sagas, the Japanese Heiki Monogatori [sic], Chaucer, Dante and Edgar Lee Masters? We would think him a joke. Yet we see nothing strange in a Professor of Music who knows nothing of primitive music and folk-music, and music of mediaeval Europe, and the great art-musics of Asia, and who knows next to nothing of contemporary music.[10]

Nevertheless, a key feature of *Australia's Music* was the judgement Covell passed on a range of works and contemporary composers featuring in the performance landscape in the twenty years leading to the book's publication. Showing the most potential, in Covell's view, were George Dreyfus, a German-born composer whose family had fled the Nazi regime when Dreyfus was a child, Tasmanian-born Peter Sculthorpe, for whom Covell would go on to write libretti, building on a close personal association, and Sydney-born Malcolm Williamson who resided in the United Kingdom from the 1950s onwards, and was made Master of the Queen's music in 1975, continuing in this role until his 2003 death.[11] Covell characterized Dreyfus as a 'serious composer' and author of 'one of the most accomplished scores to be produced in Australia'. And in Covell's assessment, 'of all the younger contemporary composers in Australia Sculthorpe speaks with the most personal voice'.[12]

Covell also documented his views on the potential for Australian music to draw on elements of Aboriginal music. Though dismissive of the 'jindyworobak' approach (see Chapter 3), Covell saw potential 'in the assimilation of those elements of it – notably of rhythm, scale structure and microtonal intervals – which seem to explore territories of music relatively untouched by the standard varieties of European music'.[13]

Covell reserved judgement on whether Aboriginal music would have a positive impact on Australian composition, but emphasized the importance of universities and conservatoria providing opportunity for detailed study of Aboriginal musics alongside other non-European musics.

Though Covell praised Dreyfus and Sculthorpe side by side, their approaches to Australian national identity through music could not have been more different. While Dreyfus seems to have agreed with Covell's assessment of the importance of direct experience of Aboriginal musical practice, Sculthorpe went on to make 'Australianist' music his chief stylistic feature, expanding the 'flirtation with musical jindyworobakism' that Covell had identified into an approach to Aboriginal music that was atmospheric rather than explorative.[14] A few key melodies derived from transcriptions or audio recordings of Aboriginal song were used as the basis of numerous compositions across Sculthorpe's career. Most frequently featured were two melodies, *djilili* (whistling duck) recorded by Elkin in Arnhem Land in 1949[15] and used (in some cases repeatedly in new arrangements for different instrumental combinations) in Sculthorpe's *Port Essington* (1974, 1977), *Dua Chant* (1978), *Djilile* (1986, 1990, 1995, 1996, 2000, 2001, 2003, 2008) and *Kakadu* (1988), and the 'Maranoa Lullaby' from the 1937 *Australian Aboriginal Songs* published by Loam and Lethbridge, used by Sculthorpe in *Two Aboriginal Songs* (1949), *Into the Dreaming/For Cello Alone* (1993, 1994, 1998), *Maranoa Lullaby* (1996, 2007, 2012), *Lullaby* (2003) and *Requiem* (2004).

By contrast, Dreyfus' approach engaged directly with live performances of Aboriginal music, rather than atmospheric effects, causing considerable stir at his work's premier at a Musica Viva festival. Dreyfus' collaboration with George Winunguj (see cover photograph) on *Sextet for didjeridu and wind instruments* was commissioned for Musica Viva's 1971 Spring Festival. The work showed 'two composers from two distinct cultures working together within an expressive framework', as Dreyfus explained at the premiere. Dreyfus' introduction had not only provided this context but also 'had side-swipes at university musicologists, Australian composers who write "Aboriginal" music, and other foibles of our musical life', according to *The Canberra Times*. In the music critic William Laurence Hoffmann's opinion, the collaboration with Winunguj could not be evaluated along conventional lines, but he nevertheless approved of Dreyfus' approach: 'Very sensibly he did not attempt any synthesis of such diverse cultures as Aboriginal and European music; rather he composed three movements for wind quintet, each expressing a different mood, and then against this predetermined background Mr George Winunguj improvised his didjeridoo part to express from his own experience the same moods.'[16]

George Winunguj was not only performer/composer in the collaboration with Dreyfus, but stood as a candidate for the Legislative Council in 1968 elections, and worked as the Methodist Overseas Mission Christian Education Regional Supervisor.[17] He was a cultural leader in his home community on Goulburn Island and led a cultural restoration project for the Aboriginal Theatre Foundation (ATF), along with Albert Barunga.[18] In 1973, Winunguj toured with the Adelaide Wind Quintet to the United States, Europe and Nigeria. Winunguj's son, daughter-in-law and grandson – David, Jenny and Rupert Manmurulu – remain cultural leaders in their community of

Warruwi (Goulburn Island) today, continuing to bring Mawng performance practice to audiences in other parts of Australia and overseas.[19]

The final paragraph of Covell's *Australia's Music* almost resembles a script for the collaboration between Dreyfus and Winunguj:

> the exhilarating prospect of a genuine interaction between eastern and western traditions includes the fruitful encounter of western-trained musicians who have become excited by the properties of non-western music and of musicians from non-European races who have eagerly chosen to adopt many of the techniques of the European tradition. Australia's chances of making itself understood among its neighbours and of understanding them may well be helped materially by an advance guard of musical interchange; and the multi-racial nature of music as it will certainly develop in the Pacific and Asian regions will be – though its dilution of many individual traditions will be regretted sincerely by musicians from all races – of an almost incredible richness. If the opportunity is not ruined by other factors, these areas could see the growth of the most fecund musical culture that has ever existed on earth.[20]

## Representing Australian culture overseas – 1968 Olympics

While post-referendum changes were on the way in 1967, and art music was beginning to define its boundaries, a new 'Australianist' ballet was also in preparation, programmed to represent Australia in the upcoming Mexican Cultural Olympics. Choreographer for this event, Beth Dean, had initially offered a section of her *Corroboree* ballet to John Antill's musical score for the Olympic festival since she considered it to be 'the best example of Australian Folkloric theatre'.[21] When the Mexican Ambassador raised some problems with performing Antill's music, the director of Mexico's Ballet Folklorica who would be performing the work suggested that their ensemble members could learn Aboriginal songs and to play the didjeridu to accompany Dean's choreography. Dean's efforts to act as gatekeeper for Aboriginal cultural representation are evident in her response:

> For your information, members of the Sydney Symphony orchestra and other musicians here, have tried for years to learn to play the didjeridu, the aboriginal drone tube. They have not succeeded. Therefore, it is impossible for musicians from Mexico to play it, especially without a skilled teacher and at least a year's practise [sic]. *There are no teachers*. Aborigines have not been able to explain clearly their techniques. And those who do play this instrument live thousands of miles from Sydney as wards of the government in their tribal state. Detribalised aborigines neither play nor dance. Nor can the quality of the sound, the intent of their chants be duplicated by a people whose ear is more accustomed to Western scale music sounds [emphasis added].[22]

Though Dean claimed there were no teachers of didjeridu, Mayali man David Blanasi (Bulanatji) had, just earlier that year (and before the referendum), made headlines when he travelled to London to perform as didjeridu virtuoso on *The Rolf Harris Show*, instructing Harris in playing the instrument while on tour with him, in the beginning of an ongoing professional association.[23] Group workshops in didjeridu playing would later become a mainstay of Blanasi's international career and reputation as a master of the instrument. In her own review of the AETT's 1963 *Aboriginal Theatre* a few years earlier, Dean had also praised the 'star of his instrument' Dhalwangu, Yolngu man, Joe Yangarin from Yirrkala, whom she would later involve in the *Ballet of the South Pacific*.[24]

Instead of proposing to bring a *yidaki* (didjeridu) master like Yangarin and singer with her to Mexico, Dean ultimately negotiated with ethnomusicologist Alice Moyle (on recommendation from Stefan Haag at the AETT) to use a recorded song cycle from Arnhem Land as the taped soundtrack for the new ballet she would choreograph – *Kukaitcha*.[25] Perhaps the immediate post-referendum months could have been the right time to suggest engaging Aboriginal performers in the representation of Australian culture abroad, though it is not clear whether this would have helped Dean's case for government support for the venture. In spite of persistent lobbying, she was unable to overcome the government's reported resistance to sending anything 'of a cultural nature' to Mexico during the Olympics year.[26]

Though Dean publicly asserted that her decades-long promotion of Aboriginal dance was a reflection of her respect for its artistic value, she not only repeatedly performed these dances without the direct involvement of Aboriginal people, but also focused on themes of transgression of the culture she claimed to hold in such high esteem. The story on which the ballet was based came from a book of stories published by Dean's husband Victor Carell.[27] Kukaitcha, an account of Aranda (Arrente) traditions from Central Australia originally recorded in Spencer and Gillen's *The Native Tribes of Central Australia*, was a tale of transgression, one that Dean seemed to find particularly tantalizing, if the frequency with which it was mentioned is any indication.[28] In the programme note for the ballet, Dean indicated that:

> Kukaitcha is the story of a ritual spearing, told by the old songman. Accompanied by the Didjeridu musician. Aboriginal tribal sanctions are invoked by Kukaitcha, the wiseman, against Wura, the woman who witnessed forbidden sacred ceremonies ... The focal object in the ballet is a Tjuringa. The spirit of life is believed to reside in these sacred boards or stones. These sacred totemic symbols may be handled only by those disciplined people who through trial by ordeal i.e. stringent self denial and initiation, have proven their integrity. By long prepared study, the men demonstrate their integrity, proving that they are capable to receive into their hands this spirit of life as signified by the Tjurunga, they preserve them and pass them with the knowledge they represent onto succeeding generations. *No woman or uninitiated boys may look upon these sacred symbols*. Death is the penalty for those who dare [emphasis added].[29]

Performing the role of the woman who had transgressed cultural law by witnessing ceremonies forbidden to her in *Kukaitcha*, while publicly proclaiming her ability to dance men's dances that women should not even see (see Chapter 4), Dean seemed more enamoured of the sensationalism of these transgressive actions than of the richness and complexity of the cultures she aimed to represent.

## Internationalizing Aboriginal performance: New stages for the *Aboriginal Theatre*

While the Mexican Cultural Olympics propagated non-Indigenous representation of Aboriginal culture abroad, the emerging post-referendum era also saw new possibilities for international touring of Aboriginal performing artists, though protectionist interference persisted. The Australian Elizabethan Theatre Trust's highly successful 1963 performances by the *Aboriginal Theatre* had led to several more performances in 1965 and 1967, as discussed in Chapter 5. However, though local Australian productions had been realized, Stefan Haag's attempts to support an overseas tour had not yet come to fruition. In the late 1960s, NT welfare officer Ted Evans began negotiations with Stefan Haag about another instance of the *Aboriginal Theatre* that would perform at the 1970 Expo in Japan. Approached for advice about what to include in the Expo in 1968, Haag had immediately recommended the *Aboriginal Theatre*.[30] As in earlier unsuccessful international tour proposals, this suggestion required some lobbying, since the Department of Aboriginal Affairs had taken the position of not recommending an Aboriginal dance group be part of the Expo in case they 'merely be regarded by spectators as curios'.[31] Eventually Aboriginal Affairs agreed on the participation of an Aboriginal dance group, on the condition that they were directed by Stefan Haag. They also expressed a concern that assimilationist aims be kept in view in the process of including Aboriginal people in the exhibits:

> The point should be made in treating the exhibits that Australian human history did not start in 1788, but some 30,000 years ago. (At the same time it is important also that the various presentations should not portray Aboriginal persons, culture and structures as being merely supplemented by the modern Australian counterparts, but as being gradually integrated into them.)[32]

Post-referendum efforts that focused on Aboriginal people living in remote communities, distant from the centres of political and economic power, saw non-Indigenous government representatives and arts administrators work closely with Aboriginal people to effect a transition from government-led enterprises to Aboriginal-led ones (as discussed below). But the communities of the southeast were often excluded from these kinds of supports. The Aboriginal Theatre Foundation's focus on performers from remote Top End communities for the 1970 Expo demonstrates this.

After the plans for the shows had been publicized in the media, Lismore (NSW) teacher and local historian Marjorie Oakes attempted to advocate for the inclusion of performers from the southeast in these representations of Aboriginal performance. Writing to the Australian Commissioner-General of the Osaka Expo, Oakes proposed he consider the 'superb artists from Wooderbong Aboriginal Reserve NSW. They are: Herbert Charles, Rory Close (dancers) Cecil Taylor (songman)' (Figure 6.1).[33] Oakes compared their dancing to the Russian ballet, applauded the singing of 'consummate artist' Cecil Taylor, and included press reports about their recent corroboree performances and public displays. The men had accepted an invitation to perform in Sydney, but Oakes asserted they would not put themselves forward 'into the white man's world'. The stark realities of life under the southeastern states' assimilation regime in the mid-century, and especially the constant threat of child removal and fracturing of family groups, meant that those who did continue traditional practice likely did not put themselves forward, as Oakes' appeal suggests. Though NADOC events provided a public forum for NSW performers (see Chapter 5), this was focused on performances consistent with assimilation agendas, rather than efforts to sustain traditional practice. A reply to Oakes is not on record, but the Osaka Expo proceeded with the proposed group of Northern Territory performers (Figure 6.2).

**Figure 6.1** Bundjalung performers Herb Charles, Cecil Taylor and Rory Close performing in Casino, NSW in 1968. Photo printed in *Dawn*, January–March 1969, 12, courtesy AIATSIS.

**Figure 6.2** Aboriginal Theatre Foundation Performers in Osaka, 1970. Dhambuljawa Burarrwanga, Rrikin Burarrwanga, Mulun Yunupingu, Wulurrk Mununggurr, Banambi Wunungmurra, Justin Puruntatameri, Max Kerinaiua, Henry Kerinaiua, David Gulpilil, Dick Budalil, Talbert Jalkarara, Djoli Laiwanga, David Blanasi, Felix Wambunyi, Lawrence Biellum. International Exhibition Expo 70 Osaka Japan – Aboriginal Dance Ensemble F1, 1968/3396, NAA, Darwin.

Replicating the mediation of the welfare administration in earlier versions of the *Aboriginal Theatre*, Ted Evans coordinated the choice of performers for Osaka in his role as chief welfare projects officer for the NT. Though in earlier shows he had emphasized engaging the right people to sing the required songs, for the 1970 Osaka shows Evans aimed to shift the presentation into a new realm. In this show, expert dancers were engaged for each dance, but each dancer would teach the others his dance, so that all would perform as an ensemble throughout. This plan was not only a departure from previous productions of the *Aboriginal Theatre*, but also a departure from song and dance practices across traditions in Aboriginal Australia in which songs are owned and are able to be performed only by their owners or those given permission to perform them. However, there is also historical precedent for songs and dances to be shared and even traded among Aboriginal people of different language groups, likely through more formalized processes than those operating in the shows.[34]

These complexities of song ownership and performance were argued about among non-Indigenous officers in these 1969 negotiations. In correspondence between Evans and Father M. Sims of Port Keats Mission (where Daly region performers resided, now known as Wadeye), Sims argued that it would be 'farcical to exchange their different characteristic styles. This can only lead to a breakdown in their basic styles'.[35] In retort, Evans suggested:

> This is only an extension, or perhaps rather a revival of something that has been going on for thousands of years and was brought to a halt by European settlement and intrusion. Dance themes and styles, both secular and sacred, were as much a medium of exchange and trade between neighbouring tribes as were material goods.[36]

Sims' and Evans' contrasting positions suggest the complexity of navigating a post-assimilation era in which the continuation of performance practices was valued in ways that could now be separated from government objectives to integrate Aboriginal people into the mainstream.

The performance opportunities of the post-referendum era were important to the future of Aboriginal music and dance performance. Many of the performers engaged in the international tour to Osaka built on existing performance experience, or would continue to pursue ongoing careers. Perhaps most famous among these were David Gulpilil, Djoli Laiwanga and David Blanasi.[37] Blanasi had already established a performance relationship with the Osaka show's principal artist – Rolf Harris – and even while the Expo shows were taking place, plans were being made for ongoing professional opportunities for the show's performers. As a newspaper article reported, the Osaka dancers were expected to form the 'nucleus of a full-time Aboriginal Theatre'.[38]

Indeed, the first meeting of the Aboriginal Theatre Foundation (the organization alluded to in these comments) had taken place on 22 October 1969. The ATF was incorporated in 1970 and boasted a full programme of activities in 1971. The membership of the ATF's board is a study in the changes taking place in the transition into a new age of self-determination in the early years of the 1970s. The original 1969 board was led by some of the same Welfare and Arts Administrators behind so many of the events discussed in earlier chapters in this book (in particular Chapters 4 and 5) – Harry Giese, Ted Evans, Stefan Haag and Mary Durack were original members, with Bill Gray joining in 1971 and Lance Bennett appointed as director. Giese, Evans, Gray and Haag had collaborated on the 1963 *Aboriginal Theatre*, Durack had worked with Haag and James Penberthy on his 1958 opera *Dalgerie*, and Bennett's mother Dorothy Bennett had staged the art exhibitions associated with the 1963 shows. But by 1972, members of the executive committee now included emerging and established leaders of Aboriginal performance, who would continue to play a leading role in international touring and performance opportunities of the future. Albert Burunga (Mowanjum, WA), George Winunguj (Warruwi, Goulburn Island), Horace Wikmunea (Weipa South, Qld), Harry Kolumboort (Wadeye, NT) all became members of the executive in 1971 or 1972, with Johnny Short (Lockhart River, Qld) joining in 1974. In the report on activities up until the end of 1971, membership of the foundation was reported as 248 Aboriginal and sixty-six non-Aboriginal.[39] The membership reflected the representation of the northern states and territories, in which regional committees were also formed (Western Australia, Queensland and Northern Territory). When the executive of the newly rebranded Aboriginal Cultural Foundation was elected in 1975, all were Aboriginal.[40]

The scope of activities of the ATF included not just touring concerts like one in 1971 in which Northern Territory performers toured the southern state of NSW (reminiscent of the 1963 *Aboriginal Theatre* tour), but also international tours, and inter-community exchange, in which for example Northern Territory dancers visited communities in the Kimberley, Western Australia. This approach to cultural exchange mimicked the sharing of dances in the 1970 Osaka performances, but also brought together music and dance traditions separated by great distances, yet linked by historical trade practices.[41] Contemporary dance festivals throughout the region also built on these practices of cultural exchange established in historical practice, but supported through official channels in new ways from 1970 onwards. The Laura dance festival in Cape York began in 1972 after a regional festival sponsored by the ATF and has continued with the kind of cultural exchange and competition established by the ATF's links to the North Australian Eisteddfod.[42] A similar approach to cultural exchange has also been part of the Barunga Festival begun in 1985, that combined performing arts with political engagement, most famously with Prime Minister Bob Hawke's promises of a treaty during his visit in 1988.[43]

The public display of Aboriginal dance forms was also articulated by the ATF as an explicit strategy in ensuring the continuation of cultural practice. In summaries of the first years of activities, the foundation reported that in areas where few young people were learning the dances, such as Kununurra, public performances at the North Australian Eisteddfod were fostered in order to 'boost local Aboriginal interest in the traditional culture'.[44] Committee member Mary Durack confirmed that these public performances were not conceived as 'promotion of tourism but that of Aboriginal confidence and sense of identity'.[45] The North Australian Eisteddfod that had been the genesis of the 1963 *Aboriginal Theatre* (see Chapter 5) now featured as a meeting place for senior custodians of cultural knowledge, negotiating the terms of performance. In 1972, elders from across the north had held a non-competitive festival at Winnellie Showground. Participation was only for Aboriginal people, though a non-Indigenous audience was allowed.[46]

The professionalization of Aboriginal music and dance performance that the ATF represented greatly expanded the possibilities for international touring that had been so actively quashed and overridden by the government prior to the referendum (see Chapter 5). In the first fifteen years of its operation, performers from the communities of Yirrkala, Bamyili (Beswick/Barunga), Groote Eylandt, Aurukun, Gapuwiyak, and Lajamanu were part of international tours to Fiji, New Guinea, Samoa, Hawaii, Malaysia, Mexico, Nigeria, Hong Kong, the United States, Italy and France.[47]

## Staging representation for the Cook Bicentenary

The growing profile of the ATF and their associated professional performance contexts had a significant impact upon the viability of the kind of appropriative shows that

Beth Dean, John Antill and Victor Carell had been staging for close to two decades. In 1969, the two threads of performance collided in negotiations with the Minister for Social Services and Aboriginal Affairs about how the Cook Bicentenary should be commemorated. Carell had proposed that 'our recommended dance expert (who is best qualified in this country for this job outside of my wife)' Ronne Arnold should be sent by the department to remote Aboriginal communities in order to select dancers to be brought to Sydney for a month of training with Beth Dean in preparation for a *Ballet of the South Pacific*. Carell and Dean also asserted that their involvement was central to producing a high-quality performance, though they expected no payment: 'We need to develop our culture in a way that will bring us into the internationally accepted art forms and as we will be presenting aboriginal culture we want it performed in a manner that will bring pride to our Aboriginal people and pride and interest and more knowledge for the rest of Australians.'[48]

The proposal, which would include the Aboriginal performers in a *Ballet of the South Pacific* alongside dancers from New Zealand and the Cook Islands, was greeted with a mixed reception by the Minister for Social Services and Aboriginal Affairs, and Northern Territory administrators, as well as by H. C. Coombs in his role as chair of the advisory body of the Council for Aboriginal Affairs and of the new Australian Council for the Arts. Coombs agreed with the minister that the inclusion of Aboriginal dancers was an interesting proposal, but emphasized that the Council's first priority was to support the new performance troupe assembled for the Expo in Osaka. Establishment of the Aboriginal Theatre Foundation was already in progress 'with the aboriginal communities themselves', reported Coombs, underpinned by support from the Australia Council for the Arts for the move to professionalization.[49]

Dean continued to push for the superiority of her skills in coordinating the proposed ensemble of dancers, in one letter describing the rumour that Stefan Haag would be 'allowed to work towards such an aboriginal theatre' as 'a crime against a wonderful culture'.[50] In response Coombs suggested she be directed to Aboriginal communities in Sydney or in other states and territories 'from which it might be possible for dancers to be chosen and trained'.[51] Dean and Carell's lobbying of government and arts bodies was extensive throughout the remainder of 1969, and was met with equally persistent resistance to their approach. The concerns expressed by others over the course of their career had now reached a critical mass, but Dean and Carell remained tone deaf to the changing sentiment, which prioritized opportunities for Aboriginal people to represent their own practices on stage. In one letter, responding to anthropologist Frederick McCarthy's concern about their depiction of sacred ceremony and questions about the assertion of copyright, they declared:

> In case you are concerned with Corroboree, the ballet it is a modern, highly sophisticated choreographed ballet. The music has nothing to do with the aborigines. It is a complex symphonic work requiring a full symphony to play it. The ballet to this music, although I used the psychological quality of a youth going through initiation, has no bearing to an actual ceremony ... Not at any time

would we, or should anyone else, try to depict on the stage an actual Aboriginal sacred ceremony ... it must be protected.⁵²

In response to Dean and Carell's ongoing pursuit of their interests and their direct and indirect lobbying of government, arts bodies and anthropologists, H. C. Coombs was blunt: 'Frankly, I would be reluctant to recommend expenditure of this magnitude on a project with no promise of continued benefit to cultural life in Australia'.⁵³

Ultimately, Carell was given permission to self-fund a tour of the Northern Territory recruiting Aboriginal dancers. He and Dean hoped that chief welfare officer Ted Evans might consult with them on the production. But Evans, as a board member of the newly established ATF, would have been in no position to do so. The Aboriginal members of the ATF's executive had shut down any possibility of the ATF being involved with 'Cook Celebrations'. As the *Northern Territory News* reported, 'there were divided views on the celebrations among the Aboriginals of Australia' and the Foundation had felt it 'unwise to take sides on the matter'.⁵⁴ The message that not all Indigenous people would welcome a celebration of Cook was reinforced to Dean and Carell by their friend and associate Leslie Greener who wrote to them, 'I could wish that the occasion for this co-operation of three Governments was something other than Capt. Cook's arrival. What the Cook Islanders, the Maoris and the Aborigines have to celebrate about that I don't know'.⁵⁵ In spite of the withdrawal of the ATF and media reporting of the planned protests, Dean and Carell's enthusiasm for the celebrations proceeded unabated.⁵⁶

The *Ballet of the South Pacific* opened at Her Majesty's Theatre on 6 April 1970, bringing together twenty Aboriginal performers from the north with dancers from the Cook Islands.⁵⁷ Dean and Carell had helped to set up the Cook Islands National Arts Theatre (CINAT) in 1969, as well as the Dance Theatre of Fiji, and would mount the first South Pacific Festival of Arts in Suva, Fiji in 1972 (in which the ATF would participate).⁵⁸ Dean and Carell also sought further international performance opportunities for the Aboriginal dancers involved, who had come from the Tiwi Islands, Yirrkala, Milingimbi, Mornington Island and Daly River region.⁵⁹ Carell wrote to Ted Shawn, who had publicly applauded the talent of dancers Mosik (Mosec) and Beeanamu (Bianomu) in the Delissaville community he visited in 1947 (see Chapter 3), suggesting an international tour of Aboriginal dancers to Shawn's Jacob's Pillow.⁶⁰

Though Dean and Carell had been unable to secure the participation of the AETT's Stefan Haag and the NT Administration's Ted Evans, the format of the *Ballet of the South Pacific* very closely mimicked the format of the 1963 *Aboriginal Theatre* that Haag had produced, even to the extent of including some of the same musicians/dancers and many members of the same communities. Yolngu didjeridu virtuoso Yangarin, whom Dean had wholeheartedly praised in her 1963 reviews, was a feature performer, and members of the Bathurst Island Tipungwuti, Puruntatameri and Portaminni families were involved in both the 1963 *Aboriginal Theatre* and 1970 *Ballet of the South Pacific*. The shows also followed the same format of sets of dances and songs from each distinct cultural group. As in 1963, two women had been included in the group, but this time they (Regina Portaminni (now Kantilla) and Irene Babui) presented a set of dances without the men.⁶¹

In the 1970 shows, however, Australian Aboriginal performers only made up the first half of the programme, while part two was performed by the recently formed Cook Islands National Arts Theatre. The juxtaposition of these culturally distinct music and dance traditions received high praise in the press, Frank Harris admiring the 'enticing illustration of cultures'.[62] The *Ballet of the South Pacific* ran for two weeks in Sydney with a subsequent tour to Canberra, Brisbane and Melbourne, and many of the performers would later return to Sydney as part of the Festival Fortnight throughout Sydney's suburbs and region to celebrate the opening of the Sydney Opera House in 1973. John Antill's fanfare *Jubugalee* also featured in the Opera House opening night concert.[63]

Concerts and festival programmes to commemorate 200 years since Cook's voyage along the east coast of Australia also featured the music of non-Indigenous Australian composers, including newly composed works. A Royal Concert at Sydney Town Hall on 2 May 1970 featured an orchestral work by Nigel Butterley commissioned by the Sydney Symphony Orchestra, alongside European works. Musica Viva commissioned new chamber works from Ian Cugley, Barry Conyngham and Ross Edwards, and two other John Antill works were heard alongside *Corroboree* in Sutherland in southern Sydney.[64] In London, the Australian Musical Association staged a Cook Bicentenary concert, opening with a new work by resident composer Don Banks.[65]

In addition to lobbying for the *Ballet of the South Pacific*, Dean and Carell had also pitched *Corroboree* to the artistic directors of the Australian Ballet, Peggy van Praagh and Robert Helpmann. In a terse exchange, van Praagh expressed her doubt about the wisdom of attempting to represent Aboriginal dance through European ballet: 'As was discussed in Canberra, when you are transferring an aboriginal rite to a westernised form of theatre it needs extremely sensitive handling, and I believe Sir Robert [Helpmann] feels as I do, that we would like to see how you intend to do this before finally committing ourselves to the production of "Corroboree".'[66] Van Praagh's response was evidently taken by Dean and Carell as the slight it was intended to be, and Carell responded: 'We were told later that he [Helpmann] informed the Trust that he had "got rid of that problem" [staging *Corroboree*]. It will now be performed as part of the Arts Council and Cook's Memorial Bi-Centenary Committee's event in March 1970.'[67]

Though head of the Arts Council, Dorothy Helmrich, had also been made aware of the potential sensitivities by A. P. Elkin, she did not let the changing times get in the way of another *Corroboree* production. Elkin, who had largely supported Dean and Carell's performance endeavours of the 1950s and 1960s, had cautiously recommended the production, though his response could equally be read as a diplomatic reproach:

> I thought quite highly of it. I thought Miss Dean had made great use of her studies of the literature and the field, and had presented a highly commendable work of art ...

Apart from the Jubilee of the Arts Council, this is a good year for bringing Aboriginal art and ideas into prominence because of the new emphasis being laid on Aboriginal affairs by Commonwealth and State Governments. I personally would like to see Aborigines from the north come down again to Sydney, to show what they themselves can really do in forms of artistic expression.[68]

Helmrich and the Arts Council proceeded with the new *Corroboree* production, though it was altered (whether in response to these concerns is unknown) by casting Australian-based African American dancer Ronne Arnold in the lead role of the 'boy Initiate' instead of Beth Dean herself who had performed the lead for the Queen in 1954. But instead of *Corroboree* featuring in the key celebrations of the bicentenary, it was produced in the suburban Gunnamatta Park in Cronulla featuring Arnold's Australian Contemporary Dance Company (1967–72) alongside two other Antill ballets with choreography by Dean and Arnold.[69] Unlike in 1951, or in the Royal performances in 1954, 1959 and 1963 (which they referenced extensively while lobbying for a role in the 1970 programmes), *Corroboree* was not the headline event of the official celebrations.[70]

## Re-enactment and protest at the Cook Bicentenary

While Dean and Carell's ballets had featured in the royal itineraries of 1954, 1959 and 1963, the Queen does not seem to have attended the Antill ballets or the *Ballet of the South Pacific* in 1970.[71] Instead, she played her role as head of state at the re-enactment of Cook's April 1770 landing. This time, instead of the choreographed ballet at the Showground in 1963, the re-enactment was staged at Kurnell involving a replica *Endeavour II*, visiting three-mast sailing ships and a large group of Aboriginal performers positioned on the beach. The Queen arrived by sea, just as Cook had done, disembarking from a yacht onto the royal barge to approach the shore. She was greeted by the NSW Premier, the Governor and their party on the docks, rather than by members of the Gweagal tribe who had met Cook and his crew. Prime Minister Gorton sat in the crowd gathered behind the landing spot. In total, 20,000 members of the public were in attendance, while thousands more watched on television.[72]

Footage from the event shows the Aboriginal performers positioned in the immediate foreground of the Queen's vantage point, seated in a straight line on the beach alongside *gunyahs* built for the event. They remained in place while the Queen disembarked and moved to the royal dais, rising only when the actors performing the role of Cook's party approached the beach. But as the Queen's barge approached, clapstick beats were heard in the background, accompanying the official commentary and reminding the viewers that Aboriginal people were still there, just as they had been when that other boat approached 200 years earlier. As the engines of the barge slowed and the boat approached, canoes could be seen in the foreground, piloted by Aboriginal men, paddling and watching, spears aloft. As the national anthem ('God

Save the Queen') concluded, the clapsticks again resumed, even as the Royal Navy band marched away.[73]

The Aboriginal performers were all named in the programme for the event, and were led by Noongar performer Ken Colbung (Nundjan Djiridjarkan), who also acted as Aboriginal adviser on the production, and whose wife Betty Colbung also performed.[74] Other performers included Gadigal men Jim Madden and Ken Gordon, and Bundjalung performers Stan Roach, Vera Roach and Ben Blakeney.[75] Blakeney would perform the role of Bendalong from the sails of the Sydney Opera House at its opening three years later.[76] The official speeches alluded to ongoing Aboriginal presence in ways that previous re-enactments had not done. The NSW Premier acknowledged that Cook's ship had been unwelcome in 1770, and that destruction of Aboriginal culture had ensued: 'The Aborigines who made, as we have seen this afternoon, some resistance, have suffered from their contact with European culture. We are now trying to restore something of what they inevitably lost in moving out of the stone age into the age of machinery.'[77]

This nod to the suffering of Aboriginal communities had not featured in previous re-enactment ceremonies, and some sensitivity to Aboriginal people is in evidence in the editing of the re-enactment production, even if the overarching agenda was an unabashed celebration of Cook. In one draft of the re-enactment narration, an initial sentence was struck out, suggesting that efforts for a faithful re-enactment (according to Cook's and others' journals) was to be balanced with consideration for the sensibilities of Aboriginal people participating in and observing the scene: 'Musket shots will be fired at the Aboriginals who opposed the landing and there will be, on arrival on the beach, a faithful re-enactment of events which took place, including the first contact with the Aboriginals of East Coast.'[78]

In the re-enactment staged in north Queensland's Cooktown, shots were fired at the Aboriginal actors. A group of forty Torres Strait Islanders then performed a dance that the papers reported was the highlight of the Queen's visit. Aboriginal onlookers reportedly outnumbered white onlookers by two to one, in what one report described as the 'tiny ghost town' of Cooktown.[79] Across the nationwide events, other minor attempts to include Aboriginal culture in a concept of Australian nationhood were made. A massed display by over 10,000 school children from the Sydney area included not just folk songs in the European folk tradition like *Waltzing Matilda* and *Click go the Shears*, but also 'Aboriginal songs' – the Maranoa region songs set to piano accompaniment by Loam and Lethbridge in the 1930s (see Chapter 2). Weekend visits to the Aboriginal community at La Perouse were advertised, complete with boomerang demonstrations by world champion Joe Timbery. A production of Varney Monk's *Collits' Inn* was staged with its corroboree ballet, and Saturday night entertainment at Campbelltown on Sydney's outskirts included 'Whip cracking, Didgeridoo playing, Gum leaf playing', with Jimmy Little as the headline performer.[80]

Though minor adjustments had been made in 1970, the reinforcement of Cook as a colonizing figurehead was also enacted through the bizarre recruitment of new British immigrants bearing the surname Cook or Cooks, sixteen of whom arrived in Sydney on a flight landing at Mascot airport (very close to Cook's landing spot on the day of the re-enactment, as a spokesman for the Immigration Department pointed out).[81] This ongoing colonization by British Cooks does not seem to have been the focus of any of the Aboriginal protests, which were just as vocal as they had been in 1938 (see Chapter 2). Across the Bay at (Guriwal) La Perouse, Aboriginal protestors threw wreaths in the water to commemorate the invasion.[82] They were joined in protests across the nation. Aboriginal people donned funeral dress to greet the Queen at Sydney Airport, staged a torchlight procession to Canberra's Parliament House, a costumed silent vigil in Brisbane, a March through Melbourne, a mourning demonstration on the coast of South Australia and a funerary procession in Perth.[83]

## Conclusions

If the 1967 Referendum occasioned a shift in thinking about the possibility for Aboriginal people to take a new place in the Australian state, significant changes would not be enshrined into Australian law for a number of years. Important legislation was passed with the 1975 Racial Discrimination Act and 1976 Aboriginal Land Rights Act, though many assert that the Australian legal regime continues to block Indigenous land sovereignty.[84] Cultural institutions saw dramatic shifts in the 1970s. NAISDA, founded by African American Carole Johnson, increasingly became an Indigenous-run organization and was formative in the birth of the acclaimed Bangarra Dance Theatre. In dance and theatre, Aboriginal performance has permeated high art forms, as it has done in visual art mediums, in productions performed and managed by Aboriginal people. This flourishing of Aboriginal and Torres Strait Islander arts organizations after 1970 has been documented by a substantial scholarly literature, especially in dance and performance studies.[85]

However, in music, non-Indigenous art music composers continued to represent Aboriginal music in their compositions throughout the twentieth century and into the twenty-first. Only very recently have these begun to involve Aboriginal people. Performances by Aboriginal musicians after 1967 sustained and grew a profile in folk, popular or 'world music' realms that remain at a remove from 'art music'. In the final chapter, I examine some of the reasons for Australian art music's failure to engage with Indigenous cultures in the ways seen in other high art forms, and examine new developments, which may point to a way forward.

# 7

# Disciplining music: Too many Peter Sculthorpes?

*The Captain Cook from a million years ago. We've got his song, we're dancing for him, we're dancing culture for him ... When he died, other people were thinking they could make Captain Cook another way. New people, all his sons, new Captain Cooks. The first Captain Cook never made war. These new Captain Cooks started shooting people down in Sydney. All their families followed. They took over. They made war, to shoot and kill Aboriginal people. That happened all over Australia from the new Captain Cooks, 100 years ago, 200 years ago. Too many Captain Cooks. We the Rembarrnga tribe, we know only one Captain Cook. This story is for all time. Nobody can change our law. Nobody can change our culture because we have ceremony from Captain Cook.*

Paddy Fordham Wainburranga, 1988[1]

The 1963 Australian Elizabethan Theatre Trust's *Aboriginal Theatre* opened with the sound of clapstick beats. As the lights went up, the narrator told the audience: 'This sound has been going on for thousands of years'. As his narration ceased, the audience heard a delicate and expertly phrased rendition of the Diver Duck song from Barney Munggin, a Nankiwumirri (Nangomeri) man resident at Daly River (b. 1910).[2] Audiences and critics alike were captivated by this demonstration of performative cultures rarely glimpsed on the stages of capital cities in Australia's southeast. Far more familiar to these audiences had been the representations of Aboriginal culture that had been so consistently supported by Australian musical institutions, and had enjoyed repeat performances, international tours, frequent radio broadcasts and publicly funded salaries for the composers.

The persistent clapstick beat was also the key device opening John Antill's iconic symphonic ballet *Corroboree* (1946). Antill captured the beat's unsettling regularity and continuity in the opening movement of the orchestral score of *Corroboree*, where its repetition takes a syncopated rhythm. Throughout the opening movement of *Corroboree* the clapstick beat persists in the background. The orchestra attempts periodically to drown it out. But as the dynamic levels recede, it becomes apparent to the listener that the clapstick beat is still there. It has always been there. But more than that, it continues in spite of the industry of a large number of orchestral players and their modernist antics.

The persistent clapstick beat of *Corroboree*'s opening evoked a century and a half of settler experience of Aboriginal soundscapes. Quoted Aboriginal melodies or rhythms were not needed to evoke this soundscape, reiterated so hauntingly under the layers of modernist primitivism in Antill's orchestral writing. Antill captured something that had long preoccupied non-Indigenous people – the sounds of Aboriginal presence. Appearing in literature and increasingly in musical composition the sound was a haunting reminder that Aboriginal people are still here, and that the settler colony must remain vigilant in asserting itself to remain dominant. Aboriginal music has long been embedded in the psyche of non-Indigenous Australians.[3]

Tributes to the haunting presence of Aboriginal music have often been countered by dismissive evaluations of its value – in Clive Douglas' 1956 positioning paper, Aboriginal song was described using words like 'undeveloped', 'unmusical', 'monotonous' and 'crude'.[4] In the works of most non-Indigenous composers, Aboriginal song is represented by melodic and rhythmic kernels, devoid of engagement with the specifics of regional practices. In *Corroboree*, a work whose presence has troubled the performance of Australian music and dance culture in the history documented in this book, Antill did not appropriate Aboriginal musical culture. He successfully represented it in a way that settler Australians continued to experience it – as a background presence, a remembered soundscape from childhood, one that was not well understood, was constant, but which would always be subject to inundation by the productivity of nation building. In evoking Aboriginal soundscapes, *Corroboree* may have appeared to celebrate Aboriginal culture, but the action it performed did the opposite, replacing Aboriginal performance cultures on public stages.

Most chapters in this book have focused on the diverse ways in which Aboriginal performers sought to recuperate and maintain culture through public music and dance, however, in this concluding essay, I seek to grapple with the ongoing representationist practices of Australian art music and responses to it. Though cross-cultural musical collaborations have been attempted throughout the twentieth century, a clear role for Aboriginal and Torres Strait Islander composer/musicians has not yet crystallized as it has in the other 'high' art forms of dance, visual art and theatre.

I begin by showing the persistent influence of nineteenth-century conjectures about Aboriginal cultures and their take-up in representationist music and dance. I then consider the usefulness of settler colonial theory for understanding the repetitive nature of colonizing dynamics and their iterations in the remarkably insular domain of art music. As a counterpoint to this, I consider the disruptive potential of Indigenous interventions offered by recent theorizations of the process of 'postcolonizing'. I end by presenting examples of collaborations or interventions that might point to ways forward.

## A *tjurunga* by any other name: Settler colonial theory, representation and the nation state

*Tjurunga*, an Arrernte word denoting the sacred stones, or wooden objects used in secret ceremonial contexts by initiated men, has had a currency among those interested in Aboriginal cultural practice throughout Australia during the twentieth century. The word entered the Australian vernacular through Spencer and Gillen's 1899 book *The Native Tribes of Central Australia*, along with a raft of other Arrernte words. Alongside *tjurunga/churinga* (*tywerenge*), most prominent in the national imagination was *Alcheringa* (*Altyerrenge or Altyerr*), a term translated by Spencer and Gillen, and widely adopted thereafter as the Dreamtime, or Dreaming (the western desert word *Tjukurrpa* is also widely known).

In his field-defining 1999 book, *Settler Colonialism and the Transformation of Anthropology*, Patrick Wolfe critiqued Baldwin Spencer and Francis Gillen for the violence their work inflicts on cultural relativism in their representation of Arrernte knowledge and practice.[5] Wolfe's focus was on Spencer and Gillen's 1899 claim that Arrernte people did not understand the cause of human pregnancies. Wolfe showed that Spencer and Gillen projected theories about European history onto Aboriginal people 'independent of empirical Indigenous data' and that this reinforced imperial thinking about Aboriginal people as a race so alien to white Europeans as to be less-than-human.[6] Wolfe traced the implications for Aboriginal policy and legislation of this popular thinking, including the implementation of policies of removing children from their families, one feature of what would eventually become known as assimilation policy with its aim of diluting the influence of Aboriginal world views on subsequent generations of children.

Though these European world views insisted on excluding Aboriginal people from known epistemologies, Ian McLean suggests that Aboriginal responses to European colonizers performed the opposite function – incorporating Europeans into known worlds:

> There are many accounts of Aborigines first perceiving the colonists not as aliens or even culturally foreign, but as dead relatives returning from the spirit world. And while it didn't take long for Aborigines to be dissuaded of this, they nevertheless incorporated these strangers into their kin systems as if they were indeed relatives. Where colonists saw a gulf, Aborigines saw bridges.[7]

McLean's interpretation echoes evidence presented by Indigenous scholars and artists in varied forms throughout Australia's recent cultural history. Leading Rak Mak Mak Marranunggu scholar Payi Linda Ford articulates the ways that connecting with people across difference is fundamental to her humanity. Co-writing with researchers Linda Barwick and Allan Marett of their collaboration, she notes:

> In our experiences collaboration in ceremony is founded on longstanding relationships (things that people share) rather than on any attempt to cover differing social categories (things that separate people by highlighting differences) … Working together is a fundamental value that underlies human ways of being in the world. Without working together, we would be lost to each other and from the world.[8]

The choice of Spencer and Gillen as objects of Wolfe's critique of settler colonial epistemic violence was not an arbitrary one, but rather reflects the pervasive influence of their theorizations.⁹ Spencer and Gillen's profuse writings on Central Australian Aboriginal cultural, religious and domestic practice influenced anthropological thought, public policy and popular notions of Aboriginality. Their work also captured the imagination of creative artists seeking to depict the mysticism and power of little-understood Aboriginal cultures. The original manuscript of John Antill's *Corroboree* reproduces complete stories and extensive drawings of totems derived from Spencer's books on Arrernte (Arunta) culture from 1927 and 1928.[10] The costume designs by Robin Lovejoy and William Constable for the staged ballet also drew on these designs among other sources depicting totems and ceremonial wear.[11] Antill's long-term collaborator Beth Dean would base her education about Aboriginal dance in the late 1940s on Spencer and Gillen's books. Captivated by the power of sacred knowledge forbidden to women, she fixated on *tjurungas* acquired during travels through Central Australia in 1953.

Two *tjurungas* gifted to Beth Dean by Haasts Bluff settlement manager Les (L. G.) Wilson, who had himself acquired them by unknown means, were used repeatedly in her touring shows.[12] Handling the sacred objects after having danced what she claimed were secret men's dances, Dean would recount stories of how those transgressing the rules of handling such sacred objects could be dealt with in Arrernte, Warlpiri, Pitjantjatjara and Pintubi societies. Dean's notes for public lectures show that while holding a *tjurunga*, she would say 'Even to-day should a native woman see one of these or even be told about it and the accompanying blood letting ceremonials, she could be killed. There was one such tribal murder near Arayonga while we were in the area a few years ago'.[13] The sentencing to eighteen months' hard labour for Pitjantjatjara-man Charlie, the protagonist of the tribal revenge killing of another man (Selly), to which Dean referred, hit the Sydney papers the day after a full pictorial article by Dean and her husband Victor Carell was published in *Pix* magazine. Dean and Carell's accompanying photographs showed bloodletting of the kind shown by Selly to a woman who had condemned him to death in Areyonga.[14] Dean and Carell opened their book *Dust for the Dancers* with a related story, and narrativized these transgressions in their 1968 ballet *Kukaitcha* (see Chapter 6).

The fascination with these most sacred and treasured of spiritual terms brought into circulation by Spencer and Gillen was not just alive in the assimilation era, but rather it continues, even very recently featuring in Australian settler performance cultures.[15] Prominent non-Indigenous composer Ross Edwards named his 2009 choral mass *Missa Alchera* denoting his bringing together of sacred non-Indigenous (Latin) and Aboriginal (Arrernte) religious concepts. Edwards opens his mass with bass voices performing an almost unsingable low drone, an ostinato figure that persists for the entirety of opening *Kyrie* movement. Evoking the didjeridu (or *yidaki*) an instrument essential to musical practice in the far north of Australia, some 4,000 kilometres distant from Arrernte Country, the drone in *Missa Alchera* evokes an unspecific but continuing presence of Aboriginal people and their music in the psyches of non-Indigenous Australian composers. Composed only ten years ago, *Missa Alchera* demonstrates that the representational approach of evoking the haunting ongoing presence of Aboriginal people – in their absence from any part of the creative work – is alive and well.

Non-Indigenous composers and their representations of Aboriginal presence have been co-opted into the wider nationhood project, which aimed to tame Aboriginal Country and define its value in economic terms. John Antill's position as composer of a work that would found a national creative school was not just produced out of his own creative industry and good fortune, rather, it capitalized on the state agenda for representing Aboriginal culture without the messiness of engaging with Aboriginal people and their political demands and physical needs. In addition to the commissions for commemorative events that have been discussed at length in previous chapters, Antill also composed music for films produced by Film Australia, the Department of the Interior and the ABC. The film titles are evocative of the broader national story-making project: *Port Jackson* (1948), *Turn the Soil* (1948), *The Inlanders/Mantle of Safety* (1949), *Australia Now* (1957), *Dark Rain* (1958), *New Guinea Patrol* (1958), *The Land that Waited* (1963). In a ballet collaboration with choreographer Margaret Barr on *Snowy* (1961) that became the first ballet performed for television, Antill's music accompanied a narrative characterizing the colonization of the Australian landscape (through damming the rivers into hydro-electric energy production) as relieving the country of its suffering: 'From the Snowy Mountains in the Great Dividing Range, three mighty rivers run: the Murray, the Murrumbidgee and the Snowy. Once, not long ago, they flowed unchecked, unchained, to waste their waters in the far-off seas. And the land suffered.'[16]

Antill's music backgrounded the message that through taming the land (and the people who had cared for it for so many millennia), the settler colony was rediverting the wastefulness of the continent's prehistory.

## Replacement and 'postcolonizing'

A range of scholars have sought to theorize the structures determining Australian engagement with Indigenous cultures. Perhaps most influential among historians has been settler colonial theory as formulated by Patrick Wolfe and championed by Lorenzo Veracini, but also building on earlier work in American Native Studies.[17] Wolfe suggests that in settler colonial nations where the colonizing forces have come to stay with no plans for withdrawal, the ongoing influence of Indigenous cultures is framed within an overall 'logic of elimination'.[18] Veracini adds that settler colonies actively seek to replace Indigenous cultures and settlers seek 'acquisition of entitlement as indigenous', corresponding to an 'indigenous loss of entitlement as such'.[19] But as Veracini's reference to replacement implies – not all elements of the Indigenous disappear in this process. The creative commodification of secret and sacred knowledge disseminated by Spencer and Gillen across the twentieth century is one manifestation of the ways in which 'the native repressed continues to structure settler-colonial society'.[20]

Though counter-formulations (especially by Indigenous scholars – more on these below) contest the inevitability suggested by Wolfe and Veracini's theories, the structural aspects of the settler colonial theory of replacement are useful in making sense of the repetitive qualities of settler representations of Aboriginal culture over the period 1930–70 examined in this book. This is especially the case in understanding art music, a field characterized by the persistence of its ties to established European traditions, by its aloofness from popular culture and mass appeal, and in this period, by an adherence to the central tenets of European modernism – especially the high value placed on complexity, novelty, difference and suspicion of the traditional and conventional.[21]

As the examples of representationist art music throughout this book suggest, non-Indigenous composers routinely looked to the parts of Australia most remote from their daily lives for inspiration about Aboriginal cultural practices, insisting on the absence of connection with living people, even while Aboriginal people in nearby urban centres sought to maintain and perform culture.[22] In Chapter 5, we saw how the *Aboriginal Theatre*, whose show so surprised Sydney and Melbourne audiences in 1963, was reported to be unlike anything city dwellers had experienced. At commemorative events throughout the assimilation era, Aboriginal people were brought in from elsewhere to perform Aboriginal culture considered to have been lost from the urban landscape (examples in all preceding chapters).

Not only has Aboriginal culture been characterized as something remote from the experience of non-Indigenous Australians, encounters with it have been framed as moments of chance rather than opportunities for further engagement. In many of the appropriative productions in the 1930s, 1940s and 1950s, creative producers claimed to have been inspired by one-off encounters with living, performed Aboriginal culture. Most familiar among these stories is Antill's recollections of the corroboree witnessed at La Perouse Aboriginal Reserve as a child, when he noted down melodies and rhythms that he would later score into *Corroboree*.[23] In a similar vein, when working on *Collits' Inn* in the 1930s, Varney Monk wrote about having encountered Dharawal singer Queen Rosie by chance on the street in Kiama, inspiring the corroboree scene featured in the musical. And when Edmond Samuels needed an Aboriginal man to play the tracker in *The Highwayman* in 1951, he recalled wandering along the Yarra River and happening upon a man there, Ted Mullett, who sang him a song in language.

Though framed as chance encounters, these stories point to the continuing presence of Aboriginal people with considerable cultural knowledge living in urban spaces, to the extent that it was possible to stumble upon them while seeking new creative ideas (or indeed to know that a walk along the banks of the local river might make such an encounter likely). Queen Rosie and her husband King Mickey (Johnson) were involved in celebrations of the Wollongong centenary in 1896 and in 1923, the Kiama and Bombo communities along with the Aborigines Protection Board had fundraised to provide Queen Rosie with a house after her husband's death.[24] Ted Mullett was a frequent performer in Melbourne. Mullett was resident at nearby Lake Tyers Mission Station and a member of the Lake Tyers Concert Party. Some suggested he was 'known as Australia's Paul Robeson'. In discussions about concerts for the Old Pioneers' Memorial Committee's annual concert on Pioneers' Day 1937, Mullet was requested as a potential performer.[25] Almost fifteen years later, he was still to be found on the banks of the Yarra, able to summon up a song for a stranger looking for authentic material for a new theatre production.

These narratives of opportunistic encounter counteract the claim that non-Indigenous creative artists were representing cultural practices that no longer existed, or were unaware of continuing Aboriginal presence; a presence that could nonetheless be happened upon on city streets and riverbanks. Expert singers like Queen Rosie and Ted Mullett were characterized as remnants of an otherwise lost tradition, opening up the space for representation of Aboriginal cultures by others. The perpetuation of the idea that Aboriginal culture was not alive and well in one's own neighbourhood, but rather was an exotic commodity of far-off places, provided a convenient premise for these narratives of replacement.

In 1938 while local Sydney Aboriginal people protested the commemorative celebrations, performers from far western NSW were brought to Sydney and expected to perform a corroboree to re-enact Aboriginal presence at the First Fleet's arrival (Chapter 2). In 1951, John Antill's *Corroboree* celebrated Australian culture at Melbourne's opening Jubilee concert, though Aboriginal performers had staged their own 'Corroboree Season' at one of Melbourne's most popular performance venues in 1948 and 1949 (Chapters 3 and 4). Events like the 'Corroboree Season' have until now been written about by historians seeking to uncover ongoing negotiations of Aboriginality in urban spaces.[26] Representations of Aboriginal culture in Antill's *Corroboree* have been examined in musicology, performance studies and history as evidence of the search for an Australian cultural identity. However, juxtaposing the two as I have done in this book reveals that support for Australianist creative work cannot be disentangled from the deliberate replacement of those Aboriginal performance cultures that the new non-Indigenous productions aimed to represent.

While settler colonial theory provides an apposite explanation of how this narrative of replacement has been performed so persistently, some Indigenous scholars have resisted the apparent inescapability of settler colonial theory, and its tendency to occlude the possibility of Indigenous worlds continuing in spite of the settler colony's impositions. One alternative theorization of settler and Indigenous relationships in Australia is offered by Goenpul, Quandamooka scholar Aileen Moreton-Robinson, who suggests we might 'conceptualize the current condition not as postcolonial but as postcolonizing with the associations of ongoing process, which that implies'.[27]

As Moreton-Robinson's framing suggests, Aboriginal people have often seen their public performance as a process of 'postcolonizing', or as ongoing resistance to state agendas that aimed to erase their cultural practice. Reflecting on the many public performances staged by his grandfather Bill Onus in vaudeville shows, theatre productions, festivals, film, television and through production of material culture, Tiriki Onus suggests that Aboriginal people realized that one way to maintain cultural practice was to hide it in plain sight. If people were prevented from continuing ritual, spiritual and ceremonial practice on their home Country and from teaching their children culture through language, song, art and story-telling, then they would work within the officially approved channels for cultural production. Restrictions on practice of culture did not apply to stages where a representation of Aboriginality in national events was wanted. Performers and cultural entrepreneurs like Bill Onus quickly realized the potential of these stages for maintaining cultural practice:

> the only way people were legitimately able to practice and perform culture is to do it publicly – it becomes hiding in plain sight – it's the only place you're allowed to do it ... the notion of asserting your aboriginality and claiming that publicly ... it's quite an authoritative power to say: this is my Country and I'm showing it to you ... the very fact that these stories are still here to be told I think it's pretty damn important. And if it was painting up and dancing around Wirth's Olympia, well that's ok.[28]

In a similar analysis, Anne (Wirrimah) Thomas, along with her husband Ted (Guboo) Thomas, well known for their tours as gumleaf musicians and multi-instrumentalists, framed public performance as a substitute for exercising political agency. As Anne Thomas recalled in 1987, public dances and performances of folk musics that had been so active in the assimilation era fell away once Aboriginal people were able to advocate for their rights in explicit ways:

> They got rid of the managers in 1969, the white managers, from all the reserves, so that made a change. People didn't have a set way of life after that. They used to play the local gumleaf and all that, and used to have dances, and used to get together and all that, but after that they began to stand on their own two feet. They got rid of the managers ... and they began to set up structures and committees and have conferences on politics and land rights ... Aboriginal people then had to prove themselves, that they did have a lasting culture and that they meant to retain that culture. And so that's what's happening today, whereas the tribal culture, the white managers stopped the men activating their culture, because they couldn't come and go any more. But it didn't stop the women teaching their children about the Aboriginal culture, so they reinforced that culture and that area and that totem wherever they were.[29]

Onus' and Thomas' analyses describe the function of public music and dance making, in the form of folk, vaudeville or hybrid performances by Aboriginal people, as assertions of culture and political presence. They suggest that the need for people to come together in this kind of collaboration receded once a different kind of political voice was attained. Popular vaudeville shows, and touring folk bands, especially those with a uniquely Australian flavour like gumleaf bands, were avenues for adaptive 'postcolonizing', where pathways to other forms of high art were largely closed.

Those who did succeed in accessing the rarefied realm of high art making were few. In the immediate post-war era, the problem of reintegrating returned servicemen saw a period of access to the arts, during which the separation between high and popular arts was minimized. Tenor Harold Blair's relationships with unionists enabled him to access classical musical training through the people's music organization Council for the Encouragement of Music and the Arts (CEMA) in the late 1940s (Chapter 3).

Solidarity between non-Indigenous workers and people of oppressed cultural groups made this a logical alliance. Ballerina Mary Miller's training also occurred during what might be characterized as the 'high assimilation' era of the decade after WWII, in which the possibilities for integration with the mainstream, including high culture, were relatively open. Mary Pearson (formerly Miller) recounts that she was supported to train at the West Australian ballet founded by Kira Bousloff through the 'cottage home' institution in which she was raised, after being removed from her family at age seven. This was part of a larger agenda that Pearson understood as originating in the assimilation project: 'we were lighter in skin and would probably be assimilated more easily'.[30]

Indeed, a key architect of assimilation policy – Paul Hasluck – would directly link the training of Aboriginal people in the fine arts to the goals of assimilation. Funds raised from Hasluck's 1953 booklet *Native Welfare in Australia*, in which a 'new deal' for Aboriginal assimilation was promoted, were donated to a fund to bring West Australian Aboriginal singer Nancy Ellis to NSW Conservatorium to further her studies.[31] Blair's, Miller's and Ellis' careers are examples of entanglement with settler colonial impositions on Aboriginal people. But theirs and many of the stories told in this book also present narratives of resilience – the resilience of Aboriginal people/performers, but also the resilience of cultural practice and its adaptation to ensure its continuation.

Yawuru scholar Shino Konishi suggests that one alternative to settler colonial theory's frameworks for understanding such histories is the potential for 'extra-colonial histories'.[32] The events in this book may have been set in a scene of historical entanglement, but the performances by Aboriginal people could equally be extracted from this to show their 'extra-colonial' potential. In particular, the activities of Bill and Eric Onus and Doug Nicholls in the 1940s and 1950s, though embedded in resistance to colonial priorities, also created extra-colonial narratives in coming together on Country to exchange dance, boomerang throwing and other cultural practice. In newspaper reports, the location of these events was characterized as on the land of a 'white sympathiser', a term evoking a sense of a world beyond the reach of colonial society, in which white Australians could be allies, but where their agendas were not the force against which Aboriginal people were reacting.[33] Their work also evokes the regenerative and 'transformative alternatives' profiled by North American Indigenous scholars such as Leanne Betasamosake Simpson as 'Indigenous resurgence' and the refusal to 'centre whiteness'.[34]

## Challenges to the hegemony of representationist Australian music

In the remainder of this chapter, I describe several musical projects in which art music and Aboriginal music have played a role, while seeming to resist narratives of replacement of Aboriginal people and culture through non-Indigenous representation. Some of these are collaborative projects between non-Indigenous composers and

Aboriginal composer/performers that have suggested a possibility for alternative approaches to dialogue. Collaborative efforts have been persistent, if not central to mainstream approaches. Key music institutions for Western art music supported some of these experiments in collaboration, though by and large these have not been representative of the dominant tradition in Australian art music practice. In exploring these approaches, I set the stage for a consideration of how the insularity of classical music has isolated it from other creative disciplines, and of the potential for changes to be wrought within music institutions.

In 1966, English composer Peter Maxwell Davies was composer-in-residence at Adelaide University. During this time, he was introduced to Aboriginal music by Catherine Ellis. In a foreword to James Murdoch's 1972 book, Maxwell Davies wrote that since meeting ethnomusicologist Ellis, Aboriginal music had 'influenced my formal design greatly in the orchestral work I was then writing'.[35] In particular, the through-composed extended structure of works like *Worldes Blis* (1966–9) and Maxwell Davies' symphonies were influenced by the structural insights of understanding Aboriginal song cycles, Indian raga structures and plainsong. For the composer, these musics were 'something beyond entertainment: it really goes into the very core of one's own existence'.[36] But unlike works with a notional atmospheric nod to Aboriginal music, Maxwell Davies' hearing of the recordings shared with him by Ellis led him to understand 'processes of transformation of contour to finely tuned modal filters in a way that could generate harmonic tension over a large time-span'. Through his career, Maxwell Davies acknowledged the debt to Aboriginal music in his thinking about musical and harmonic structure though he did not overtly refer to Aboriginal cultures in his works, nor claim to represent them.[37]

James Penberthy, whose unpublished autobiography acknowledged the likelihood that his grandmother was Aboriginal, engaged with Aboriginal music and dance subjects throughout his career.[38] Opera, ballet and a cantata were influenced by recordings of Aboriginal song from Arnhem Land made by Colin Simpson in 1948, and were composed to libretti and stories that depicted Aboriginal protagonists in the works *Earth Mother*, *Brolga*, *Dalgerie* and *Swan of the Bibbulman*, the last three drawing on texts by Katharine Susannah Prichard and Mary Durack.[39] In oral history interviews, Penberthy emphasized the pervasive influence on his creative practice of Aboriginal culture and its 'unequalled' social system and of the tragedy of Aboriginal people being dispossessed of land.[40] Penberthy suggested that his self-expression was aimed not only at people, but at 'nature and country and so on, in being with it and being related to it'.[41]

Penberthy's framework for conceiving of music as just one way of existing in relation to people and Country is reminiscent of Indigenous frameworks articulated by scholars such as Leanne Betasamosake Simpson: 'Indigenous worlds aren't institutions or states, they are relationships, movement, processes – life itself. I came to understand that the theories or stories or philosophies of resurgence inherent in Indigenous thought were the ways my ancestors had always lived.'[42]

Penberthy's approach to using stories highlighting dispossession and relationship to Country differed from most contemporaneous art music composers, as did his experimentation with the engagement of Indigenous performers in key roles. In 1954, the West Australian ballet (probably represented by Penberthy and Kira Bousloff) attended a corroboree demonstration at Wiluna to get ideas for new ballet works.[43] They also exchanged dance demonstrations with members of the AETT's *Aboriginal Theatre* while on a tour in Darwin in 1964.[44] The 1959 performance of the opera *Dalgerie* at Perth Festival included a corroboree performed by Aboriginal people from the area.[45] The West Australian Ballet Company's first Aboriginal ballerina, Mary Miller, performed the lead role in the ballet *Kooree and the Mists* and the solo work *Brolga* in the 1960s.[46] Harold Blair was cast in a singing role in *Dalgerie* at the opening of the Sydney Opera House in 1973.[47] All of these works had premiered with non-Indigenous performers in body-paint costumes and blackface before featuring Aboriginal performers in later versions.[48]

Performances of works composed earlier in the century also began to include Aboriginal performers after 1970. Margaret Sutherland's opera *The Young Kabbarli* depicting a story from the life of Daisy Bates featured dancer and singer David Gulpilil and didjeridu player Dick Bundilil in 1972 performances by South Australia's Intimate Opera Group in Adelaide and Melbourne to celebrate Margaret Sutherland's seventy-fifth birthday, with other members of the cast in blackface.[49] The work was recorded the following year at Flinders University in South Australia with the same cast.[50] Also in 1973, a variety of Aboriginal performers participated in concerts for the opening of the Sydney Opera House, including David Blanasi, while Aboriginal actor Ben Blakeney delivered a speech as the spirit of Bennelong from the tip of one of the sails of the building.[51]

For its 1971 Spring Festival, Musica Viva commissioned three new works, Peter Sculthorpe's *The Stars Turn*, Ian Cugley's *Work for Double Wind Quintet* and George Dreyfus' *Sextet for Didjeridu and Wind Instruments* (see Chapter 6). The sextet commission had come after the Adelaide Wind Quintet had heard Mawng didjeridu musician George Winunguj perform during a visit to Yirrkala in northeast Arnhem Land.[52] Dreyfus collaborated with Winunguj in composing the sextet; Winunguj also performed in the premiere concert.[53] In attributing the co-composer credit to Winunguj ('two composers from two distinct cultures working together within an expressive framework'), Dreyfus broke with common practice in Australian music.[54] In 1973, Dreyfus' sextet was toured by Winunguj and the Adelaide Wind Quintet to Fiji, ten US cities and London, with Winunguj proceeding on to Nigeria to preach, while his quintet colleagues continued the tour in Switzerland.[55] The work was also recorded by the initial ensemble, and toured with an SBS film crew to Germany in 1989 with Richard Walley the didjeridu soloist with members of the East Berlin Philharmonic Orchestra, but has had only one further Australian performance, in 2011 by William Barton with musicians of the National Academy of Music.[56] It is unclear whether a review of the recording by the influential Roger Covell may have had an impact on Australian performances. Though Covell's review mostly enthused about both the work and the performance of it, he also mused:

> The two worlds do not meet: they co-exist. That, perhaps, is the lesson. Now that it has been done, I do not see how anyone can usefully do it again.[57]

By contrast, Sculthorpe's *The Stars Turn*, in a variety of arrangements, has enjoyed at least fifteen further Australian performances.[58]

Another composer supported by Musica Viva's chamber music festivals was Malcolm Williamson. After moving to London in 1950, Williamson was brought to Australia for the 1967 Musica Viva Spring Festival, occasioning some controversy about his claim to Australian music funding while a resident of Great Britain.[59] Later, as the bicentenary of European settlement of Australia approached, Williamson turned his attention to politically engaged work relating to Aboriginal Australia (though he was still resident in the United Kingdom). For 1988 he composed a symphonic statement to text by historian Manning Clark, and also set some of Oodgeroo Noonuccal's (Kath Walker's) poems in the works *The True Endeavour* (1988) and *Bicentennial Anthem* (1988).[60]

The examples of Peter Maxwell Davies, James Penberthy and Malcolm Williamson do not demonstrate collaborative approaches to Aboriginal music. However, like George Dreyfus' collaboration with George Winunguj, they do stand apart from the main representationist practices in Australian art music, in which composers have engaged little with Aboriginal musics, even in recorded form, working instead with an excerpt of notated melody, a rhythmic motif, or a concept or word (e.g., *Alcheringa* or *corroboree*) as a vehicle for accessing a claim for indigeneity in Australia. Many prominent composers' representation of Aboriginality has tended towards the atmospheric (including Alfred Hill, Peter Sculthorpe and Ross Edwards), rather than the specific or the attentive to regional difference or formal structure. In 1991, ethnomusicologist Catherine Ellis suggested that 'very few composers have taken the trouble to examine the structural intricacies of Aboriginal music. They have preferred to look at the superficialities: a descending melody, a regularly repeated stick beat, a didjeridu-like sound.'[61]

The distinction I make here (following Ellis) between atmospheric representations of Indigeneity on one hand and engagements with the intellectual premise, structural complexity, or political agendas of Aboriginal music on the other may seem subtle, but the narrative implications are significant. When John Antill named his work *Burragorang Dreamtime*, or Ross Edwards underpinned his *Missa Alchera* with a constant bass drone, or Peter Sculthorpe riffed on the *djilili* melody in works as diverse as *Port Essington*, *Kakadu* and *Dua Chant*, they drew on the rhetorical capital of Aboriginal cultures to make a claim for *their own indigeneity* as the voices of Australia. Though the public rhetoric around these works claimed that they aimed to persuade listeners of the value of Aboriginal culture, value (through public recognition, commissions for new works, performances and recordings) was attributed to the composers and their works rather than to the cultures that ostensibly inspired them.

We might think about this in the terms of Sara Ahmed's analysis of whiteness studies and anti-racism. Ahmed suggests some anti-racist actions could be described as 'unhappy performatives': utterances that would 'do something' if the right conditions had been met, but which do not do that thing, as the conditions have not been met.[62] While works like the collaboration between Dreyfus and Winunguj might point listeners to the possibilities of further investigating the musical world of Mawng didjeridu music, works like Sculthorpe's *Djilile* or *Kakadu* refer only back to themselves (in Wolfe's terms 'soliloquy – a Western discourse talking to itself'), especially when the melodies used appear repeatedly in dozens of works composed decades apart (Chapter 6), and thus begin to constitute a voice so uniquely Sculthorpe's own that they no longer resemble the Aboriginal music on which their performative capital is dependent.[63]

Arguably, a different kind of performativity was enacted when Penberthy centralized Durack's heroine *Dalgerie* in his opera and sought out Aboriginal singers and actors to play the lead roles.[64] Through engagement with the national story, these actions make space for the humanity of Aboriginal people, arguably as tragic figures, but also as complex and nuanced characters in a shared story. When Maxwell Davies attributed the influences on his conceptual thinking about how music can operate to Aboriginal song cycles, how they draw out philosophical realizations through structural complexity and ties to spirituality, he made a claim for the humanity of Aboriginal people and of the potential for their contribution to expanding the currents of artistic practices and the thinking that underlies them. When Williamson revoiced Oodgeroo Noonuccal's poetry in song, he acknowledged the contribution to major shifts in thinking about Australian sovereignty that resulted from the persistent and vocal activism of creative artists such as Noonuccal, whose creative practice could not be separated from her public advocacy and activism. This engagement with intellectual and philosophical features of Aboriginal worldviews is performative in its disruptive and recuperative potential for the otherwise pervasive views inherited from Spencer and Gillen's characterizations of Aboriginal culture as primitive and low on the evolutionary scale.

If Dreyfus, Maxwell Davies and Williamson found ways of working with Aboriginal music that avoided the representationist mode of more popularly celebrated composers, in many other spheres, the rise of Aboriginal self-representation and self-determination in the 1970s and 1980s also saw an exclusion of Aboriginal performance cultures from large-scale public events, as though new terms of engagement had not yet been determined after the cultural shifts of the post-referendum era. As I have shown in previous chapters, Aboriginal people and their allies advocated strongly for Aboriginal arts to be included in public celebrations of local and national culture. This was evident in 1934 anniversary celebrations in Melbourne (Chapter 2), the Australian Aborigines' League's advocacy for inclusion in 1951 Jubilee celebrations (Chapter 4), and debates in the West Australian media about inclusion of Aboriginal performance culture in Perth's 1953 festival.[65]

The Australia Council for the Arts, founded in 1967, funded development of Aboriginal arts in separate allocations from the outset, a practice which supported the widescale development of Aboriginal theatre and dance companies.[66] However, while so many Aboriginal-run performing organizations were driving a whole new agenda in the early 1970s, mainstream festivals and events went quiet on Aboriginal representation through the 1970s and 1980s. An example is the Perth Festival, which had only begun to feature Aboriginal music and dance in a significant way due to the AETT's efforts in the 1960s. After 1967, Aboriginal performance again disappeared from view until an Aboriginal Arts in Perth festival in 1983.[67] Similarly, Darwin Festival was an event that built on the cultural work of the North Australian Eisteddfod, and which in the 1960s featured a nightly 'Aboriginal Theatre' that seems to have continued the performances developed for the AETT's 1963 shows. As Micky Dewar shows, when the Festival regrouped after the destructive Cyclone Tracy in 1974, the practice of featuring 'Aboriginal Territorians as cultural protagonists in the festivals' was strangely absent.[68] This omission of any identifiably Aboriginal performers continued until 1989, after which an explicit Aboriginal component was reintroduced.[69] As the self-determination era separated Aboriginal performing arts from hybridized expressions of national culture, did the non-Indigenous public also withdraw from including Aboriginal people in their sense of cultural identity? The protests with which national celebrations in 1988 were greeted reset possibilities for national representation of Aboriginality once again, after the major rethinking of 1967.

While Australian festivals were continuing through the 1970s and 1980s without presenting Aboriginal performing arts, innovative new collaborations were founded by Aboriginal-led organizations across the country. After an almost total ban on Aboriginal people touring overseas to represent their own culture (with few exceptions – see Chapter 3 for discussion of Harold Blair's tour), this period also saw considerable opportunities for performance of Aboriginal music and dance internationally (performances by George Winunguj with the Adelaide Wind Quintet and David Blanasi's didjeridu tours are two examples that have been discussed). Significant new organizations were formed, including the Aboriginal Theatre Foundation and its extensive international touring (see Chapter 6) that built on shows staged by the AETT in the 1960s, but also theatre and dance companies that would open up whole new Australian performance contexts.

In 1971 Yorta Yorta actor Jack Charles founded the Nindethana Theatre Company in Melbourne along with Torres Strait Islander and Yidindji man Bob Maza, receiving a grant from the Australia Council for the Arts the following year.[70] Charles had got a start with acting through the Melbourne New Theatre's production of *A Raisin in the Sun* in 1958, just as some of his predecessors such as Eric Onus had built on associations with the New Theatre (Chapter 3).[71] In Sydney, Bob Maza also led the Black Theatre. After touring Australia with the Eleo Pomare Company, African American choreographer Carole Johnson received funding in the 1972 Australia Council round to take dance training out of the major cities and to Aboriginal people in communities all over the country.[72] Johnson became founding director of the Aboriginal Islander Dance Theatre (AIDT) that would later form the Indigenous dance training organization NAISDA, and would lead to formation of the Bangarra Dance Theatre.[73]

The AIDT had links back into dance movements of the 1950s, with the continuation of Margaret Walker's engagement with Aboriginal dancers and her presentation of dance for the people. Margaret's son, Kim Walker, is now CEO of NAISDA, and his oral history in the National Library of Australia's collection gives a rich picture of the early days of those Indigenous dance organizations in formation, and the Aboriginal dancers including Wayne Nicol, Cheryl Stone, Richard Talonga, Michael Leslie and Dorothea Randall who collaborated with Johnson and fellow African American Ronne Arnold to build the AIDT in the early days. As Kim Walker makes clear, the founding of the

AIDT, and its influences from black American dancers (such as Alvin Ailey, teaching Lester Horton's method), with whose dance styles Aboriginal dancers found quick affinities, was not just about creating new art: 'it was a cultural ... it was political'.[74] Like Margaret Walker's Unity Dance Group and their performances for factory workers and striking labourers in the 1950s, in the early 1970s, activists associated with AIDT like Gary Foley, Chicka Dixon and Bob Randall led the group in explicitly political forms of dance, Dixon arranging a tour of every gaol in NSW.[75]

## Conclusions: Genres for Aboriginal music and dance

These radically self-determined, new performance movements were chiefly oriented within disciplines of dance and theatre, rather than in music. Whereas Aboriginal and Torres Strait Islander dance and theatre quickly moved from the folk domain onto the main stage, music remained in the realm of the popular, and only very recently (in the 2000s) has made significant inroads into 'high art'. These most recent incursions have come in the form of collaborative work between non-Indigenous and Aboriginal composers and musicians, as well as leadership by Aboriginal composers. George Dreyfus' collaboration with George Winunguj in 1971 may have pointed to a potential shake-up, but this was apparently not widely influential. Though reviews trumpeted the collaboration as something potentially field-opening and path-breaking, it was Peter Sculthorpe's approach to representationist composition and his embeddedness within the institution of the University of Sydney that proved the dominant approach throughout the 1970s and up until at least 2000.

In 2005, ethnomusicologist Stephen Knopoff reviewed two new works featured in the Adelaide Festival. One, a collaboration between Jardine Kiwat, Grayson Rotumah, Jensen Warusam and Kerry McKenzie and Chester Schultz was 'unprecedented to the extent that it is a large-scale, mixed-genre work for orchestra and contemporary instruments composed primarily by (and about) Indigenous artists'. The second Sculthorpe's *Requiem*, performed with new parts by composer and virtuoso didjeridu soloist William Barton, Knopoff characterized as 'not a collaboration, but a more traditional exchange ... but there is an extraordinary rapport between the two'.[76] Gordon Kalton Williams has also pointed to collaborations between Richard Mills and Galpu Wilderness and Elcho Island Dancers on the work *Earth Poem/Sky Poem* commissioned in 1994 by Darwin Symphony Orchestra, and between Iain Grandage and the elders of the Spinifex Lands and West Australian Symphony Orchestra on the 2005 *Ooldea*.[77]

Didjeridu player and composer William Barton has become a sought-after collaborator on new compositions, recently working with Liza Lim on the 2006 orchestral work *The Compass*, and on the 2007 concerto *Kalkadungu* with Matthew Hindson. Both works have enjoyed multiple Australian and national performances and recordings. In a discussion of the collaborative process of composing *Kalkadungu*, which involved agreeing on a structure, using a central melodic motif composed by Barton and Barton and Hindson composing different sections of the work independently before bringing them together, Barton reflected on his engagement with classical music genres: 'It was an active, conscious thought to pursue the classical world. I know that the majority of the audiences in the concert hall have never had the opportunity to meet an Aboriginal person before, let alone see them on stage with a full orchestra.'[78]

Thematically related to the subject of *Kalkadungu* (which deals with Aboriginal warriors who engaged in guerrilla resistance to the colonists) is the collaboration between Paul Stanhope, Steve Hawke and the Yilimbirri Ensemble from Bunuba community in the Kimberley of Western Australia *Jandamarra* (2014).[79] The plot of the choral and orchestral cantata follows resistance leader Jandamarra after his involvement in a gun battle with police at Windjana Gorge on 16 November 1894. In the work, Stanhope and the *junba* musicians invoke the impossibility of drowning out the presence of Aboriginal song, whether through violent repression, words or oblivion. Richardson, the white trooper, drinks and attempts to drown out the *junba* song being repeated over and over again. In a reinvention of the persistent background of Aboriginal presence articulated by a number of earlier Australian composers (see opening of this chapter), Hawke's text chimes the English words 'the song went on and on' as the *junba* singers led by Kristin Andrews (in both the 2014 and 2019 performances) eloquently perform this continuity – the *junba* and its accompanying beat (produced by clapping and body percussion) repeating again and again, pushing at the limits of melodic quotation in the oratorio's structure.[80]

The musical works discussed so far fit securely into the conventional mode of Australian art music, defined by a tangible musical score as primary object, and where live performance is a secondary product. However, Bangarra Dance Theatre, a major company in the high-art realm of contemporary dance, has also pioneered a new kind of ballet music, especially through its prolific director of music and composer Nunukul and Munaldjali, Yugambeh man David Page. Though Page's oeuvre of compositions created for Bangarra's shows is substantial, in the absence of published musical scores, his works are rarely conceptualized as part of the Australian art music tradition. For example, though an obituary on the Australian Music Centre's site acknowledges Page's twenty-seven compositions for Bangarra among his extensive other musical works and collaborations, none of these are listed in the generally comprehensive and inclusive Australian Music Centre online database of works.[81]

Works that cross the boundaries of art music and other genres have seen collaborative projects blurring lines between jazz, *manikay* song, chamber music and historical and contemporary Tiwi songs. Some recent work in this area staged in major performance venues includes the collaboration *Crossing Roper Bar* (2010) between Paul Grabowsky, Benjamin Wilfred, the Australian Art Orchestra and Young Wagilak group. The eventual work recorded was the product of collaborative music making over a period of five years. As Aaron Corn describes, in this collaboration's combining of musical elements, the musicians 'marry the aleatory of Manikay with the indeterminacy of jazz', producing a musical work not easily rendered in notation and where the work changes with each performance.[82] Taking a similar approach to musical collaboration and over an extended time period, and combining musical approaches based on improvisation is Ngarukuruwala, a collaboration started in 2007 between the Tiwi Strong Women's Group and Sydney musicians led by Genevieve Campbell. Combining improvised instrumental music, recently composed songs in modern Tiwi language with guitar accompaniment, archival recordings of song in old Tiwi language as well as effects from historical audio tapes, Ngarukuruwala creates a contemporary performance practice in dialogue with traditional practice and current revitalization of song.[83]

The teaching of art music and Aboriginal or other non-western musics in music conservatoria have remained segregated into musicology and ethnomusicology domains respectively, in spite of considerable work in both disciplines that blurs the boundaries between them, as well as ground-shifting analyses of this work by Nicholas Cook and others.[84] Addressing the Australian art music world's adherence to modernist aesthetics, Dharug composer Christopher Sainsbury's recent platform paper suggests some possibilities for decentring the musical score and making way for art music to benefit from the possibilities of Indigenous composers' creative contributions. Early in his career as a composer, Sainsbury came to the conclusion that the 'dominant European tradition in music composition emphasized far too weightily its own aesthetics', but he also saw that in choosing to cease pursuing this aesthetic, he 'quickly became an unknown'.[85] Sainsbury's scholarly writing is just one part of his advocacy in this area. Along with his own work as a composer, Sainsbury has founded the 'Ngarra Burria: First Peoples Composers Initiative' in partnership with the Australian Music Centre, mentoring emerging Indigenous composers. Recent participants such as Elizabeth Sheppard, Brenda Gifford, Tim Gray, Nardi Simpson and Eric Avery have brought to the programme a wealth of experience as composing and performing musicians in genres outside of the classical music sphere.

Deborah Cheetham, Yorta Yorta composer and operatic soprano, has not only had commissions for new works and multiple performances of her operas, but like Sainsbury, has coupled her creative work with mentorship of other Aboriginal musicians. Like Sainsbury, Cheetham identifies the exclusion of Aboriginal artists from the operatic world:

> I guess this is one of the last frontiers for Aboriginal experience. Maybe I'm being unrealistic, maybe there are many more frontiers. I think that opera is a rarefied world; I think that Opera Australia [the national company] has a lot to answer to. They have no Indigenous talent development program at all – on or off stage. Forgive me, but I think that most of the big companies that are federally funded to a degree have to [offer such a programme].[86]

Since Sainsbury published his Platform Paper on the Ngarra Burria composers programme, he reports that it is making an impact, with new commissions for Aboriginal composers featuring in a recent exhibition *The Songs of Home* at the Museum of Sydney, and cultural organizations following suit.[87]

Nardi Simpson is a Yuwaalaraay singer/songwriter, composer, playwright and novelist. In 2019 she was a participating composer in Ngarra Burria. In a final Coda to this book, she offers a rethinking of how creativity and cultural knowledge function. Just as significant moments of activism and assertion of the right to represent one's own culture – in 1938, in 1951, in 1963, in 1967, in 1988 – have shifted the cultural landscape, 2020 – the 250th anniversary of Cook's landing on Gweagal shores – is a moment in which non-Indigenous Australian institutions, academics, composers have the opportunity to listen to Aboriginal people. We can listen to what they have to say, we can listen to the musical voices that are emerging, not just from the past, but from the present, right around us.

## *Coda*

On a Thursday afternoon, Nardi Simpson came to my office at the Sydney Conservatorium of Music, on Gadigal Country, Eora Nation. We had arranged to meet to record a conversation that might go in the book. We had chatted/yarned about these things a number of times already standing out the front of the building looking in, and talking about how this space, this building, this institution could be a place where Aboriginal musicians could take up space, could come together and learn new skills, but also contribute the kind of knowledge that they hold and that the institution lacks. I'd listened closely to Nardi teaching Yuwaalaraay and Gamilaraay words to a group of us assembled to sing with the Barayagal choir that she and Kevin Hunt direct. These words were as much taught through movements of Nardi's body, the shapes she makes with her hands, and pictures of the things they described, as through the sounds the words made.

I'd learnt to sing some of the songs Nardi composes and had them resounding in my ears as I went through the week. I'd been inspired by her presentation at our symposium of her new creative work, *The Sound of Contested Space*, in which she captured the melody of her Country, recording sounds of the river and the land and weaving them together. She described the dilemma of complying with Australia Council funding that expected a public showing of the new creative work she would create, and yet knowing that this work was being written to be heard on Country, to sing back to Country. I realized from how she looked at me when I said that it would be an amazing installation in the city somewhere, that I had missed the point. Each time I came away from listening to her, something Nardi said would stick with me.

We recorded the conversation from which this text is excerpted over a cup of tea and a shared brownie. I fretted about the sounds of the clarinet lesson coming through the wall that would be picked up on the recording, and that I thought might get in the way of the conversation. She reminded me that the clarinet sounds would just remind us where we were when we recorded this conversation. They were part of the place where this conversation was taking place. The place had its own role in the way our conversation would flow, and what we would say. While she talked, her palm struck the wall each time the place inserted itself into her train of thought.

This is an edited transcript of that conversation. It is written down as a yarn that emerged from our interactions, from the place where we sat, from the prompts that arose from the book manuscript I had already drafted and from matters important to me and important to Nardi. These events, they are not just historical facts after all. They are things that matter to people, that matter to us.

## Nardi Simpson, 29 August 2019

I'm Yuwaalaraay, far northwest New South Wales – Lightning Ridge, Walgett, Angeldool, both my grandparents are from that tiny little town, I was born in Sydney and I grew up in Sydney, always going up and back school holidays, and I think that had a big effect on how I understand place, always not being where you're from has played out in very interesting ways for me musically, in education and how I talk about the world now. I'm a songwriter, I like to say storyteller now. I play guitar and sing I'm doing some composing. I don't think I can say I'm one thing, I've just signed a publishing deal for my first ever novel that's going to be released next year. Sound and words are important to me and they find their way in and around me through different ways.

In that time you're looking at, blackfellas couldn't go anywhere! They weren't allowed to move. Think about that long line, songs everywhere in every leaf of every tree and then the language for your songs and the reason why you sing them restricted and you can't go anywhere. How did it survive? Up at Angledool, where my old grandparents were born, they had a Warlpiri man there, at the mission. Think about that fella, poor man! You know and then they moved all them down to Bre [Brewarinna] and there was Angledool people, Brewarrina people and Tibooburra people. How did song survive that? They must have been very strong people! And actually not just song, that's got to come from a bed of sound that people still practice. Amazing old people, what they all went through!

Going back to where we started, when our families lived in the bush and they came down to Sydney, everyone was an Aborigine, because no one saw black, so everyone was an Aborigine. You put that gaze over what we were just talking about – 1930 to 1970 – where people were saying 'Look at us we're black!' Now, people have moved on to know that, actually we're not all black, we are all completely different. We do acknowledgements to country about Gadigal and Cameraygal and you are Yuwaalaraay, Gamilaraay. Now we're saying actually that's great we're going to do this in ways that are specific to us.

When I was reading your thing and thinking about the dates, I think about Jimmy Little a lot and how he was at the mercy, in a contemporary sense, of the industry and he navigated his own way successfully through that. That had to happen so I can say they're commissioning me for a thing and I'll do what I want. I've got this great idea that's not just on the page and I want you to do that. That had to happen so I have the luxury of saying that. Hey?

You look at it from the other side of the coin everything they struggled for, people like me are sort of shitting on, saying we don't need that! Stuff the industry we'll do it our own way! All that hard stuff they had to do just so we can say we're not interested in that anymore. So then when I think how do I relate to what you're talking about, I think, I'm a product of it. 1930 to 1970 is exactly the same stage, when the classical music world is using Aboriginal stuff, and so then you could say it's not about disregarding those old fellas, it's doing the same thing that those old fellas, trying to force your way in but with a conversation that's relevant to today.

But time's folded in on itself and we're doing the same thing now, we're lucky we've got those fellas to show us they've got the plan. In fifty years' time maybe the same thing will be happening again in another way and that is a beautiful thing to think of. It doesn't matter if no one ever knows a thing that I wrote, somehow, I've been part of a continuation of something. People don't need to know anything about me, but that road has been laid, and I've been some little pebble in it.

I'm interested to see that people or organizations or institutions are actually aware that they are deficient in an Indigenous voice in what they do. I don't know how that's happened and for whatever reason, they are searching for blackfellas to write music for them. That realization is actually the thing that, as blackfellas, we hardly ever see happen. That is the leap. How to remedy that is a tiny little step, but that awareness is the thing that educators strive to get people to see.

How can you approach music from a cultural lens? All of these institutions are asking: how can we look at this a different way? They're not radical things because people are looking for that anyway. It always happens with culture. If you pulled out three of these fellas down the road [composers] and said here's a story (I'm making this up), here's a story: it's got to have a pelican, a mullet, a grass seed and a river in it how do you translate that into jazz? How do you translate that into composition? It's just using culture as a way to be creative, it's not using culture to say you should be singing the dreaming story of the eel here, it's not saying you should or shouldn't be doing something, it's using culture for everyone to pull their talent, that's what I'm talking about. What if this was a resource?

I mean there are big questions: how do we get blackfellas to come in here anyway, how do we do that? Well, it comes back to space, environment. Where is the Con? Is it in the mind or in the building? How can we disrupt this building, the constraints of this, make the knowledge and the people and the relationships available? That is what I think is most valuable, 'cause I couldn't talk to you about composition, but I can talk to you about culture and you could translate it and we could have a yarn and we could find where we meet. The universities are asking themselves how can they better engage? It's about doing something completely differently. Then the other problem that arises is that you can plan it to a certain extent, but you can't control it. It's about process, not about outcome and our lives are too geared for that in institutions. They need to know what it will look like at the end.

We're so disconnected from what being creative is, that doing things differently seems like a ridiculous ask! Isn't that what artists do? Isn't that what we're supposed to do? I understand that the institution as well as constricting, it also uplifts people's practice in certain ways so the question I would ask is – what's your relationship to this institution? What's your relationship with the learning and the teaching that you do here with your own deeper practice not as a teacher or a lecturer but your creativity? This thing is connected to that and you need to learn all those different things so you can move within them. So then you're engaging with a kind of framework of relationship, rather than a community, rather than a town or the components of a town. I think whitefellas are encouraged to think about being in all those different cells 'cause we say

Yuwaalaraay,
> sand goanna,
>> live in Gadigal

You've got to know all your little parts so that then you can work it out!

The other thing is that there are different rules, you know, so in theatre and dance, you need the bodies, but with music you don't need a blackfella. I could write it, but I want to have a say on where and how and why this is going to be performed, because if it's got cultural business inside of it, even if it's a representative of me and where I'm from and who I'm from, with cultural work comes an A4 sheet of dos and don'ts. It's really great that institutions have realized they don't have anything in a place they should. The next leap is not having control over what can be performed there because that's not appropriate. In theatre when blackfellas needed to have control over their cultural work, they formed a theatre company. In music, we're at the mercy of an audience. Where does that put us as musicmakers? We're trying to get this New South Wales First Nations Musicians Co-op off the ground, as a way of saying: we're all scattered. We need to be getting together and talking about being creative in the way that musicians do, for each other, forget about industry stuff we can go on about that later. In New South Wales, we lack a formalized relationship.

Ngarra Burria [First Peoples Composers Initiative] is not about your personal practice and how that intersects with others' personal practice. It's about extending your knowledge, thinking about music in different ways, and being exposed to different people and opportunities. Stiff Gins is not challenging for us. I think I would have put that to bed and done my writing and then that would have been it for me, but the push of all these new sounds and different ways to think, and the challenge. Chris Sainsbury said, 'well I think the discussion we're trying to have here is about decolonising instruments'. Everywhere we have people telling us what to do. I know how people go around culture, whitefellas, I know what non-Indigenous people want and I know how to make culture drive it, not me. Then it comes from the right place.

I want to do something that hasn't been done before with the tools and knowledge that I have and who I am and where I'm from and that's what I want to do. And it's completely related to you – *The Sound of Contested Space* – remember I was yarning about that at the symposium we had here? The topography and the shape of rivers and field recordings and maps and making speech into melody and all that, totally related to you. How do we play with past, present, future in a musical sense in a performance, in place? The seed of our knowledge is in our ear – Yawularaay, Gamilaraay – when the boys have initiation, all the knowledge is about *bina* (your ear). The more knowledgeable you get the more you listen. Our word for listen, know and understand is all the same word. I'm like the translator and there's an institution there, and there's a mob there, and I'm the one right in the middle of it. That's what I want to do, so you know, I'll do it! The first thing is to do it and then you can call it what you want! Because also if it's themed by culture, it will be about country. One person will think it's about place, one person will think it's about the shape of the river, one person will think it's about a cello with an emu sinew in it. There are levels of different knowledge for people.

And then so if we had our little group of First Nations yarn ups, then we would say you know that mob will want to see a score, good, well how can we translate a score? What is the score to us? Then you're starting to go somewhere really interesting. Sometimes some people will need to read that language. But if I know that language, then I can say well hang on a second could we talk about the flexibility in that thing because I've got a really great idea. I can justify it musically and culturally and whatever, they will be part of it! That's exciting for artists and people and practitioners and if a uni can foster that, then you are extending those conversations. All the little mes running around who are doing Ngarra Burria and other things, we need to be together and to back each other up and support each other to ask that question.

Even though the time frame 1930–70 has nothing to do with me it's got everything to do with me and that perspective and also what happened. When we talk culture-way, we say what's the environment of that? What's the surroundings of that? In culture-way, everything's connected. When I read your book's title, I thought what good can I be? Of course, I am a product of that, it's not in isolation, you know? We're always going to have these yarns about institutions that never seem to change, maybe not in this time, maybe not in that forty years, maybe not in this forty years. Ask a different question, we've just got to keep asking.

History, the past, is always right up there close to us. We're always bringing forth the past because we can't go anywhere if we don't have that.

# Notes

## Chapter 1

1 Rustom Bharucha, *Theatre and the World: Performance and the Politics of Culture* (London: Routledge, 2003), 1.
2 Material collected by the General Manager of ABC, as Chairman of the Federal Arts Sub-Committee for the Commonwealth Jubilee Celebrations 1951, Proposed Native Corroboree [box 13], SP497/1, 74, NAA, Sydney.
3 See for example: Anna Haebich, *Dancing in Shadows: Histories of Nyungar Performance* (Crawley, Western Australia: UWA Publishing, 2018); Clinton Walker, *Buried Country: The Story of Aboriginal Country Music* (Sydney: Pluto Press, 2000); Maryrose Casey, *Creating Frames: Contemporary Indigenous Theatre 1967–1990* (St. Lucia: University of Queensland Press, 2004); Malcolm Cole, 'Tropical Sounds: A Cultural History of Music Education in Cairns and Yarrabah: 1930–1970' (James Cook University, 2014); Judith McKay and Paul Memmott, 'Staged Savagery: Archibald Meston and His Indigenous Exhibits', *Aboriginal History* 40 (2016).
4 Philip J. Deloria, *Playing Indian* (New Haven: Yale University Press, 1999); Jacqueline Shea Murphy, *The People Have Never Stopped Dancing: Native American Modern Dance Histories* (Minneapolis: University of Minnesota Press, 2007); Dylan Robinson, 'Listening to the Politics of Aesthetics: Contemporary Encounters between First Nations/Inuit and Early Music Traditions', in *Aboriginal Music in Contemporary Canada*, ed. Anna Hoefnagels and Beverley Diamond (Montreal & Kingston: McGill's-Queen's University Press, 2012). In a New Zealand context, see also Marianne Schultz, *Performing Indigenous Culture on Stage and Screen* (Basingstoke: Palgrave Macmillan, 2016).
5 Deloria, *Playing Indian*, 189–90.
6 Linda Tuhiwai Smith, *Decolonizing Methodologies: Research and Indigenous Peoples* (London: Zed Books, 2013), 30.
7 Martin Nakata, 'Australian Indigenous Studies: A Question of Discipline', *The Australian Journal of Anthropology* 17, no. 3, Delimiting Indigenous Cultures: Conceptual and Spatial Boundaries (2006): 27.
8 Peter Phipps also suggests that 'Cross-cultural performances have long been a part of the repertoire of strategies of indigenous cultural survival and assertion, sometimes even in contexts where those performances are part of the colonial exploitation of culture' in 'Globalization, Indigeneity and Performing Culture', *Local-Global: Identity, Security, Community* 6 (2009): 44.
9 Before Queen Elizabeth II's first visit in 1954, Aboriginal people had performed for other royals. John Maynard discusses performances for the Duke and Duchess of York in 1927 (just outside of the dates included in this book): John Maynard, *Fight for Liberty and Freedom: The Origins of Australian Aboriginal Activism* (Canberra: Aboriginal Studies Press, 2007), 91.
10 Some notable exceptions are Samia Khatun, *Australianama: The South Asian Odyssey in Australia* (London: C. Hurst & Co., Publishers Ltd, 2018); Martin Thomas, 'The

Rush to Record: Transmitting the Sound of Aboriginal Culture', *Journal of Australian Studies* 31, no. 90 (2007); Joy Damousi and Desley Deacon, eds., *Talking and Listening in the Age of Modernity: Essays on the History of Sound* (Canberra: ANU E Press, 2007).

11  In particular, Kauanui evokes this in her criticism of work centring on Patrick Wolfe's formulation of settler colonial theory: 'to exclusively focus on the settler colonial without any meaningful engagement with the indigenous – as has been the case in how Wolfe's work has been cited – can (re)produce another form of "elimination of the native"'. J. Kēhaulani Kauanui, '"A Structure, Not an Event": Settler Colonialism and Enduring Indigeneity', *Lateral* 5, no. 1 (2016).

12  Michel Naepels, 'Introduction – Anthropology and History: Through the Disciplinary Looking Glass', *Annales. Histoire, Sciences Sociales* 4 (2010): 879. See also Inge Clendinnen on combining the methods of history and anthropology in *Dancing with Strangers* (Melbourne: Text Pub, 2003).

13  Alick Jackomos and Derek Fowell, *Living Aboriginal History of Victoria: Stories in the Oral Tradition* (Cambridge; New York, Melbourne: Cambridge University Press, 1991), 5. See also Lee Chittick and Terry Fox, *Travelling with Percy: A South Coast Journey* (Canberra: Aboriginal Studies Press, 1997); Alexis Wright, *Tracker: Stories of Tracker Tilmouth* (Artarmon, NSW: Giramondo Publishing, 2017).

14  Jessica Hodgens, 'Colonisation, Violence and Ethics: Resisting Settler Colonial Erasure on Dja Dja Wurrung Country', PhD thesis (Monash, 2017); Bain Attwood, *The Good Country: The Djadja Wurrung, the Settlers and the Protectors* (Clayton, Victoria: Monash University Publishing, 2017).

15  Bain Attwood, *A Life Together, a Life Apart: A History of Relations between Europeans and Aborigines* (Carlton, Vic.: Melbourne University Press, 1994), 215–18. See also Miranda Johnson's account of the productive potential of irreconcilable differences between individual histories recalled through oral histories and the universal histories of the archive. Miranda Johnson, 'Honest Acts and Dangerous Supplements: Indigenous Oral History and Historical Practice in Settler Societies', *Postcolonial Studies* 8, no. 3 (2005): 273; and Peter Read's use of oral histories to portray the central experience of dispossession for custodians of Darug Country, a custodianship whose primary evidence resides in oral accounts of family relationships and disruptions. Peter Read, 'Dispossession is a Legitimate Experience', in *Long History, Deep Time: Deepening Histories of Place*, ed. Ann McGrath and Mary Ann Jebb (Canberra: ANU Press, 2015), 121.

16  Maria Nugent, *Captain Cook Was Here* (Cambridge; Melbourne: Cambridge University Press, 2009); Deborah Bird Rose, 'The Saga of Captain Cook: Morality in Aboriginal and European Law', *Australian Aboriginal Studies* 2 (1984); Tim Rowse, *After Mabo: Interpreting Indigenous Traditions* (Carlton, Vic: Melbourne University Press, 1993), 1–4.

17  Rose also characterizes the 'Cook saga' as a 'moral tale'. Rose, 'The Saga of Captain Cook', 30.

18  Nugent repeatedly points to the historical inaccuracies of Aboriginal people's accounts of Captain Cook in the chapter 'Never Ending' of Nugent, *Captain Cook Was Here*, 105–36. Historical inaccuracies are also emphasized in Maria Nugent, '"The Queen Gave Us the Land": Aboriginal People, Queen Victoria and Historical Remembrance', *History Australia* 9, no. 2 (2012). Of course, attention to geographical accuracy has also been scant in non-Indigenous rhetoric about Cook's exploits – Prime Minister Scott Morrison's proposal in his announcement in January 2019 for a replica of the

ship *Endeavour* to circumnavigate Australia was to be a re-enactment of history, though Cook never circumnavigated the continent. Jade Macmillan, '*Endeavour* Replica to Sail around Australia to Mark 250 Years Since Captain Cook's Arrival', ABC News, 22 January 2019. www.abc.net.au/news/2019-01-22/endeavour-replica-to-sail-around-australia/10734998, accessed 24 January 2019.

19 Nugent, *Captain Cook Was Here*, 125. See also Bain Attwood's characterization of Aboriginal narratives that are oriented by 'a sense of place rather than time'. Bain Attwood, 'Aboriginal History, Minority Histories and Historical Wounds: The Postcolonial Condition, Historical Knowledge and the Public Life of History in Australia', *Postcolonial Studies* 14, no. 2 (2011): 177.

20 At Kurnell on Sydney's coastline, commemorations of Cook's landing occurred at least annually from 1901 onwards, with fully staged re-enactments in significant years, always involving initial resistance to and eventual retreat from the visitors by Aboriginal people. 'James Cook M Ephemera – Box 1 – (1900–)', SLNSW.

21 See Miranda Johnson's discussion of Aboriginal advocacy tracing back to the 1870s, but marked by highly visible campaigns like the 1963 Yolngu bark petitions, 1966 Wave Hill walk-off and campaign around the 1967 referendum. Miranda C. L. Johnson, *The Land Is Our History: Indigeneity, Law, and the Settler State* (New York: Oxford University Press, 2016), 22–6; W. E. H. Stanner, *After the Dreaming: Black and White Australians – an Anthropologist's View*, ed. Australian Broadcasting Commission, The Boyer Lectures, 1968 (Sydney: Australian Broadcasting Commission, 1969).

22 Smith, *Decolonizing Methodologies*, 124. See the interrogative work of historians such as Henry Reynolds and Peter Read: Henry Reynolds, *The Other Side of the Frontier: Aboriginal Resistance to the European Invasion of Australia* (Sydney: UNSW Press, 2006); Peter Read, '"A Rape of the Soul So Profound": Some Reflections on the Dispersal Policy in New South Wales', *Aboriginal History* 7, no. 1/2 (1983).

23 Anna Clark, 'The History Wars', in *Australian History Now*, ed. Anna Clark and Paul Ashton (Sydney: NewSouth, 2013); Carla Wahlquist, '"History is Messy": Twin Art Shows that Could Aid Australia's Reconciliation', *The Guardian*, 15 March 2018. www.theguardian.com/australia-news/2018/mar/15/history-is-messy-twin-art-shows-that-could-aid-australias-reconciliation, accessed 24 January 2020.

24 This builds on other recent work aiming to understand the importance of music and music-making outside of aesthetic frameworks, see Kate Bowan and Paul A. Pickering, *Sounds of Liberty: Music, Radicalism and Reform in the Anglophone World, 1790–1914*, Studies in Imperialism (Manchester: Manchester University Press, 2017), 5.

25 The eighteen pages devoted to Aboriginal music in Covell's *Australia's Music* (1967, new edn 2016) are not typical of histories of Australian art music. Roger Covell, *Australia's Music: Themes of a New Society*. Melbourne: Sun Books, 1967.

26 But even Antill has suffered from subsequent assessments of his oeuvre as characterized by a single significant work, see David Symons, '*Corroboree* and After: John Antill as a "One-Work Composer"?', *Musicology Australia* 34, no. 1 (2012).

27 Anna Haebich, *Spinning the Dream: Assimilation in Australia 1950–1970* (North Fremantle: Fremantle Press, 2007), 302; Russell McGregor, *Indifferent Inclusion: Aboriginal People and the Australian Nation* (Canberra: Aboriginal Studies Press, 2011), 93–6.

28 In Victoria, the Act for Protection and Management of Aborigines was introduced in 1869, in NSW, the Aborigines Protection Board was formed in 1883.

29  Namatjira was granted citizenship in 1957. This entitled him, among other things, to purchase alcohol. However, this 'right' was wielded to charge him with supplying alcohol to a ward of the state, the artist Henoch Raberaba. Namatjira was detained for two months and died within months of completion of the sentence.
30  J. J. Fletcher, *Documents in the History of Aboriginal Education in New South Wales* (Carlton, NSW: J. Fletcher, 1989), 95.
31  Quoted in Tim Rowse, *White Flour, White Power: From Rations to Citizenship in Central Australia* (Melbourne: Cambridge University Press, 1998), 112.
32  Ngarigo woman Tabatha interviewed by Christine Hansen is one such person who recalls the inspections on the Mission where 'Blankets were lifted to examine the condition of the sheets, a gloved finger run across surfaces to check for dust and cupboards opened to check for food … if the mission manager felt you were not up to scratch, an unfavourable report could be made to the "welfare" and a review of whether your children might need to be taken into care could ensue'. Christine Frances Hansen, 'Telling Absence: Aboriginal Social History and the National Museum of Australia', PhD thesis, Australian National University, 2009, 135. See also Victoria Haskins, '"Could You See to the Return of My Daughter": Fathers and Daughters under the New South Wales Aborigines Protection Board Child Removal Policy', *Australian Historical Studies* 34, no. 121 (2003).
33  Sianan Healy, 'Shaking Hands with the Governor-General: Aboriginal Participation in White Celebrations of History and Heritage in 1930s Victoria', in *Historicising Whiteness: Transnational Perspectives on the Construction of an Identity*, ed. Leigh Boucher, Jane Carey and Katherine Ellinghouse (Melbourne: University of Melbourne, 2007), 291–7.
34  Sianan Healy, '"Years Ago Some Lived Here": Aboriginal Australians and the Production of Popular Culture, History and Identity in 1930s Victoria', *Australian Historical Studies* 37, no. 128 (2006): 18.
35  Renato Rosaldo, 'Imperialist Nostalgia', *Representations*, no. 26 (1989): 107–8.
36  Stephen Gapps, '"Blacking up" for the Explorers of 1951', in *Settler and Creole Reenactment*, ed. Vanessa Agnew, Jonathan Lamb and Daniel Spoth (London: Palgrave Macmillan UK, 2009), 211.
37  McKay and Memmott, 'Staged Savagery'.
38  There are examples of this throughout NSW Aborigines Protection Board records, for example the request 12 January 1933 'by a Mr Sam Feldman to take half caste Alby Roberts, boxer to Phillipine Islands' and on 3 August 1938 by Mr G. L. Fox Mapotic Cinema Auckland, NZ 'requesting that three male Aborigines be made available for a tour of theatres in New Zealand'. Both applications were denied. APB Minute Books, closed records of the NSW Aborigines Welfare Board (formerly Aborigines Protection Board), accessed with permission of AANSW.
39  See, for example, the concert programmes of Beth Dean and Victor Carell, discussed in Chapter 4.
40  Fred McCarthy, 'Aboriginal Tribes and Customs' excerpted in printed programme for 'Out of the Dark: An Aboriginal Moomba', Melbourne 1951.
41  Quoted in David Symons, *Before and after Corroboree: The Music of John Antill* (Farmham: Ashgate, 2015), 45.
42  Richard Waterhouse, 'Empire and Nation: Australian Popular Ideology and the Outbreak of the Pacific War', *History Australia* 12, no. 3 (2015): 53.

43 Examples of this are (American) Beth Dean who turned to Aboriginal culture for inspiration before she had even visited Australia, Australian Elizabethan Theatre Trust Director (Austrian) Stefan Haag and (Austrian) choreographer Gertrude Bodenwieser whose choreography was widely influential on Australian dance, and who was quick to look to Aboriginal dance and music for inspiration.

44 Patrick Wolfe, *Settler Colonialism and the Transformation of Anthropology: The Politics and Poetics of an Ethnographic Event* (London, New York: Cassell, 1999), 4. See also Chris Healy's discussion of self-referential 'Abo art'; Chris Healy, *Forgetting Aborigines* (Sydney: University of New South Wales Press, 2008), 83. And Lorenzo Veracini, *The Settler Colonial Present* (London: Palgrave Macmillan, 2015). I am also alert to Deborah Bird Rose's critique of Wolfe, in which she implies that Wolfe's focus on elite male theorists while ignoring his contemporaries also soliloquizes. Nevertheless the choreographers and composers I discuss also looked exclusively to the white male theorists that Wolfe centres in his analysis. Deborah Bird Rose, 'Review: Settler Colonialism and the Transformation of Anthropology', *Postcolonial Studies* 4, no. 2 (2001): 259–60.

45 Aileen Moreton-Robinson, *White Possessive: Property, Power, and Indigenous Sovereignty* (Minnesota: University of Minnesota Press, 2015), 10.

46 AIDT later became NAISDA and sparked the creation of Bangarra Dance Theatre.

47 H. O. Lethbridge and Arthur S. Loam, *Australian Aboriginal Songs: Melodies, Rhythm and Words Truly and Authentically Aboriginal* (Melbourne: Allan, 1937). See for example 'Aboriginal Songs' *Sunday Mail (Brisbane)*, 20 June 1937, 32. http://nla.gov.au/nla.news-article97889733; 'Australian Aboriginal Songs', *Sunday Times*, 20 June 1937: 23 (First Section). http://nla.gov.au/nla.news-article58782739.

48 The Australian National Dictionary defines 'corroboree' as 'An Aboriginal dance ceremony, of which song and rhythmical musical accompaniment are an integral part, and which may be sacred and ritualized or secular, occasional, and informal' likely derived from the Dharug language, and appearing in early written records of the Sydney language. www.australiannationaldictionary.com.au/oupnewindex1.php.

49 'Assimilation of Aborigines', *The Canberra Times*, 19 October 1951, 4. http://nla.gov.au/nla.news-article2840152.

50 Dancing as diplomacy has been explored by other scholars, see Clendinnen, *Dancing with Strangers*; Philip Jones, 'The Theatre of Contact: Aborigines and Exploring Expeditions', in *Expedition into Empire*, ed. Martin Thomas (New York: Routledge, 2014); Rachel Fensham, 'On Dancing with Strangers: Rechoreographing Indigenous and British Sovereignty in the Colonial Encounter', *Journal for the Anthropological Study of Human Movement* 14, no. 3 (2009).

51 Amanda Harris, 'Pan-Indigenous Encounter in the 1950s: "Ethnic Dancer" Beth Dean', *Australian Historical Studies* 48, no. 3 (2017); Bodenwieser Ballet – PROMPT file – Ephemera, NLA.

52 Amanda Harris, 'Representing Australia to the Commonwealth in 1965: Aborigiana and Indigenous Performance', *Twentieth Century Music* 17, no. 1 (February 2020): 3–22. https://doi.org/10.1017/S1478572219000331.

53 I capitalize 'Country' throughout to differentiate it as an Aboriginal concept that goes far beyond denoting just land, or nation. As Foster and Kinniburgh explain, 'it comprises ecologies of plants, animals, water, sky, air and every aspect of the "natural" environment'. Shannon Foster, Joanne Paterson Kinniburgh and Wann Country, 'There's No Place Like (Without) Country', in *Placemaking Fundamentals for the*

*Built Environment*, ed. Dominique Hes and Cristina Hernandez-Santin (Singapore: Palgrave Macmillan, 2020), 63–82.

54 On theatre and performance, see Maryrose Casey, 'Performing for Aboriginal Life and Culture: Aboriginal Theatre and Ngurrumilmarrmiriyu', *Australasian Drama Studies* 59 (2011); Maryrose Casey, *Telling Stories: Aboriginal Australian and Torres Strait Islander Performance* (North Melbourne, Vic.: Australian Scholarly, 2012); Helen Gilbert and Jacqueline Lo, *Performance and Cosmopolitics: Cross-Cultural Transactions in Australasia* (London: Palgrave Macmillan, 2009). On Western art music, see Steven Knopoff, 'Cross-Cultural Appropriation: A Musicologist's Perspective', *Sounds Australian* 67 (2006); Jonathan Paget, 'Has Sculthorpe Misappropriated Indigenous Melodies?', *Musicology Australia* 35, no. 1 (2013); Michael Hannan, 'Scoring *Essington*: Composition, Comprovisation, Collaboration', *Screen Sound* 2 (2011); Amanda Harris, 'Hearing Aboriginal Music Making in Non-Indigenous Accounts of the Bush from the Mid-20th Century', in *Circulating Cultures: Exchanges of Australian Indigenous Music, Dance and Media*, ed. Amanda Harris (Canberra: ANU Press, 2014).

55 Ian McLean, *How Aborigines Invented the Idea of Contemporary Art: An Anthology of Writing on Aboriginal Art 1980–2006* (Sydney: Power Publications, 2011), 18.

# Prelude

1 This song was written during a retreat made possible by the research project 'Reclaiming Performance Under Assimilation in Southeast Australia, 1935–75'. It describes the processes involved in the acquisition of Ancestral knowledges. It is a methodology and a practice, to sing up story and knowledges.
2 Bronwyn Carlson, *The Politics of Identity: Who Counts as Aboriginal Today?* (Canberra: Aboriginal Studies Press, 2016), vi.
3 Shannon Foster, 'White Bread Dreaming', in *Growing Up Aboriginal in Australia*, ed. Anita Heiss (Carlton, Vic: Black Inc., 2018).
4 For a more comprehensive understanding of 'Country', see Foster, Kinniburgh and Wann, 'There's No Place Like (Without) Country'.
5 Tom Foster, *My Thoughts, and I'm Happy To-day: Two Aboriginal Spirituals*, 1930, NLA. http://nla.gov.au/nla.obj-181580080.
6 Evelyn Araluen Corr, 'Silence and Resistance: Aboriginal Women Working Within and Against the Archive', *Continuum* 32, no. 4 (2018): 487–502.
7 Jacques Derrida, *Archive Fever: A Freudian Impression* (Chicago: University of Chicago Press, 1996).
8 Kirsten Thorpe, 'Indigenous Records: Connecting, Critiquing and Diversifying Collections', *Archives and Manuscripts* 42, no. 2 (2014): 211–14.
9 Due to the destructive forces of colonization, assimilation and genocide, vital connections to our Ancestors are often archivally based, for example, the story of my good friend, Michelle Locke, descendant of Bolongaia (Maria Locke) in Michelle Lea Locke, 'Wirrawi Bubuwul – Aboriginal Women Strong', *Australian Journal of Education* 62, no. 3 (2018): 299–310.
10 Evelyn Araluen, 'Resisting the Institution', *Overland*, Winter 227 (2017): 3.

11  26 January 1938 was the 150th anniversary of the invasion of British troops into Sydney Cove. This day is celebrated each year as 'Australia Day' by settler colonial populations of Australians but mourned by First Nations people and we refer to the day as 'Invasion Day' or 'Survival Day'.
12  Mark Rose and Kaye Price, 'The "Silent Apartheid" as the Practitioner's Blindspot', in *Aboriginal and Torres Strait Islander Education: An Introduction for the Teaching Profession*, 2nd edn (Cambridge: Cambridge University Press, 2015), 66–82.
13  'Our Historic Day of Mourning and Protest', *The Abo Call*, April 1938, 2. Accessed 31 October 2019, https://aiatsis.gov.au/sites/default/files/catalogue_resources/20373.pdf.
14  Gawaian Bodkin-Andrews and Bronwyn Carlson, 'The Legacy of Racism and Indigenous Australian Identity within Education', *Race Ethnicity and Education* 19, no. 4 (2016): 784–807.
15  Patrick D. Nunn and Nicholas J. Reid, 'Aboriginal Memories of Inundation of the Australian Coast Dating from More than 7000 Years Ago', *Australian Geographer*, 47 no. 1 (2016): 11–47.
16  'Vaucluse Pageant', *The Sydney Morning Herald*, 21 March 1932, 14. http://nla.gov.au/nla.news-article16849399.
17  Kirsten Thorpe, 'Speaking Back to Colonial Collections: Building Living Aboriginal Archives', *Artlink* 39, no. 2 (2019): 42.
18  'La Perouse Mission Church', NSW Office of Environment and Heritage. www.environment.nsw.gov.au/heritageapp/HeritageItemImage.aspx?ID=5061399#ad-image-10.
19  Eve Tuck, 'Rematriating Curriculum Studies', *Journal of Curriculum and Pedagogy* 8, no. 1 (2011): 34–7.
20  K. O'Dea, 'Preventable Chronic Diseases Among Indigenous Australians: The Need for a Comprehensive National Approach', *Heart, Lung and Circulation* 14, no. 3 (2005): 167–71.
21  Australian Institute of Aboriginal Studies, *La Perouse: The Place, The People and The Sea* (Canberra: Aboriginal Studies Press, 1988).
22  Moira G. Simpson, *Making Representations: Museums in the Post-Colonial Era* (London: Routledge, 1997).
23  Anne-Marie Willis and Tony Fry, 'Art as Ethnocide: The Case of Australia', *Third Text* 2, no. 5 (1988): 3–20.
24  Eve Tuck and K. Wayne Yang, 'R-words: Refusing Research', *Humanizing Research: Decolonizing Qualitative Inquiry with Youth and Communities*, ed. Django Paris and Maisha T. Winn (Los Angeles: Sage, 2014), 223–48.
25  Natalie Harkin, 'The Poetics of (Re) Mapping Archives: Memory in the Blood', *Journal of the Association for the Study of Australian Literature* 14, no. 3 (2014).
26  'Indigenous Music and Dance: Cultural Maintenance, Transmission and Transformation in the Twentieth Century', Sydney Conservatorium of Music, 13–14 December 2018. https://sydney.edu.au/music/our-research/research-events/indigenous-music-and-dance-conference.html.
27  Frances Bodkin and Lorraine Robertson, *D'harawal: Seasons and Climatic Cycles* (Sydney: Robertson, 2008).

# Chapter 2

1  Roslyn Poignant, *Professional Savages: Captive Lives and Western Spectacle* (Sydney: UNSW Press, 2004); Judith McKay and Paul Memmott, 'Staged Savagery: Archibald Meston and his Indigenous Exhibits', *Aboriginal History* 40 (2016): 182.

2  See also Maria Nugent's discussion of boomerang sellers at La Perouse, who accompanied sale of their crafted objects with stories of their grandparents' memories of Cook's landing, reminding listeners that Aboriginal people had been here then, and are still here. Maria Nugent, *Botany Bay: Where Histories Meet* (Sydney: Allen & Unwin, 2005), 85–6.
3  '"Warriors" on Relief Jobs', *The Sun*, 9 September 1937, 2 (Late Final Extra). http://nla.gov.au/nla.news-article229449751.
4  Undated list of Exhibitors including 'Abo Protection Board (Abos. and gunyah)' in Subject Files – Bushland Exhibition, 1935–1967, Box MLK1134/Item [5], Rangers League (Sydney, NSW) records, 1918–1976, MLMSS 3328, SLNSW.
5  Peter Read, '"A Rape of the Soul So Profound": Some Reflections on the Dispersal Policy in New South Wales', *Aboriginal History* 7, no. 1/2 (1983): 25–6; Tim Rowse, ed., *Contesting Assimilation* (Perth: API Network, 2005), 4.
6  Secretary to Mr T. Foster, 8 July 1936, 'Topics, Generally Useful' Box MLK1132, Rangers League (Sydney, NSW) records, 1918–1976, MLMSS 3328, SLNSW.
7  Subject Files – Bushland Exhibition, 1935–1967 Box MLK1134, Item [5], Rangers League (Sydney, NSW) records, 1918–1976, MLMSS 3328, SLNSW.
8  Nugent, *Botany Bay*, 72–3.
9  Charles Lloyd Jones describing the pageant in 'Sydney Harbour Bridge', *The Argus*, 14 January 1932, 9. http://nla.gov.au/nla.news-article4417296.
10  Lee Chittick and Terry Fox, *Travelling with Percy: A South Coast Journey* (Canberra: Aboriginal Studies Press, 1997), 54.
11  Personal communication 17 May 2019.
12  'Details of Bridge Pageant', *The Daily Telegraph*, 9 March 1932, 9. http://nla.gov.au/nla.news-article246547236. The APB had also been approached to arrange a corroboree in the Royal Agricultural Show coinciding with these events, but it declined to do so, suggesting the RAS could arrange something with Aborigines directly. Minutes 10 March 1932, APB minute books, closed records of the NSW Aborigines Welfare Board (formerly Aborigines Protection Board), accessed with permission of AANSW.
13  These are credited to Bob and Jack Simms based on 'anecdotal accounts', but Shannon Foster's account suggests Tom Foster was one of the artists. La Perouse Mission Church, Office of Environment & Heritage, NSW government. www.environment.nsw.gov.au/heritageapp/HeritageItemImage.aspx?ID=5061399#ad-image-10, accessed 30 October 2019.
14  'Vaucluse Pageant', *The Sydney Morning Herald*, 21 March 1932, 14. http://nla.gov.au/nla.news-article16849399.
15  Vaucluse Historical Celebrating Committee, *Vaucluse Historical Celebrations 1932* (Vaucluse, NSW: Vaucluse Historical Celebrating Committee, 1932).
16  'Disappointed', *The Sun*, 20 March 1932, 4. http://nla.gov.au/nla.news-article229894731.
17  Murray also commented that Aboriginal people had likely occupied the continent for 144,000 years. 'Our Very Oldest Families', *Queensland Times*, 5 March 1932, 7. http://nla.gov.au/nla.news-article113212220.
18  'Vaucluse Pageant', *The Sydney Morning Herald*, 21 March 1932: 14. http://nla.gov.au/nla.news-article16849399.
19  Keith Kennedy, *Wanderings in Many Lands: A Lecture-recital and Exhibition of Barbaric Musical Instruments, Weapons, and Implements of Sport, etc.* (Australasian Medical Publishing Co. (Australia) nd, NLA).
20  'In the Days of Captain Cook', Rockdale Council, 1930. Title no. 45395, NFSA.
21  A. P. Elkin, *Citizenship for the Aborigines – a National Aboriginal Policy* (Sydney: Australasian Publishing Co., 1944), 7, 11–12.

22  Russell McGregor, *Indifferent Inclusion: Aboriginal People and the Australian Nation* (Canberra: Aboriginal Studies Press, 2011), 68.
23  Commonwealth of Australia, 'Aboriginal Welfare: Initial Conference of Commonwealth and State Aboriginal Authorities', 21–3 April 1937.
24  Geoffrey Gray, 'From Nomadism to Citizenship: A. P. Elkin and Aboriginal Advancement', in *Citizenship and Indigenous Australians : Changing Conceptions and Possibilities*, ed. Nicolas Peterson and Will Sanders (Cambridge: Cambridge University Press, 1998).
25  Rowse, *Contesting Assimilation*, 1–24. I also note Catherine McConaghy's distinction, cited by Rowse, between 'assimilation' and 'assimilationism' – the latter being an ideology that has existed since the earliest colonial invasions. Catherine McConaghy, *Rethinking Indigenous Education: Culturalism, Colonialism and the Politics of Knowing* (Flaxton: Post Pressed, 2000), 151.
26  Gray, 'From Nomadism to Citizenship', 58.
27  'Aborigines' Display', *The Courier-Mail*, 4 December 1934, 3. http://nla.gov.au/nla.news-article35625968; 'Native Corroboree', *The Central Queensland Herald*, 6 December 1934, 37. http://nla.gov.au/nla.news-article70340211;'Brisbane Goes Native', *The Telegraph*, 8 December 1934, 7 (Sports Final). http://nla.gov.au/nla.news-article179667438.
28  'An Aboriginal Protest', *Westralian Worker*, 12 October 1934, 1. http://nla.gov.au/nla.news-article148384994. Quoted in Anna Haebich, *Dancing in Shadows: Histories of Nyungar Performance* (Crawley, Western Australia: UWA Publishing, 2018), 116.
29  'March to Nationhood', Committee Minutes 8 November 1937; 24 November 1937; and 15 December 1937, Australia's 150th anniversary celebrations – land pageant committee – march to nationhood [box 14], SP339/1, 39/8/92, NAA, Sydney.
30  Aimee Volkofsky, '"We thought they were going to be massacred": 80 Years since Forced First Fleet Re-enactment', *ABC News*, 25 January 2018, accessed 13 May 2019, www.abc.net.au/news/2018-01-25/eighty-years-since-forced-first-fleet-reenactment/9358854. It is no wonder that communities feared that men taken from their community would not return, given the widespread massacres of Aboriginal people that occurred after 1788 and continued into the twentieth century, and also the systematic displacement of people off Country onto reserves and settlements, and from one reserve to another with little notice – this had only recently occurred in Menindee as discussed in this chapter.
31  Personal communication.
32  'Aborigines Dance in Park', *The Sun*, 19 January 1938, 3. https://trove.nla.gov.au/newspaper/article/231113349.
33  'Aborigines for Pageant', *The Sun*, 17 January 1938, 7 (Late Final Extra). http://nla.gov.au/nla.news-article231118951.
34  '"Goes Close to Slavery"', *The Argus*, 3 December 1937, 1. http://nla.gov.au/nla.news-article11129390; '"Wicked Lie," Says Station Manager', *The Sun*, 6 January 1938, 2 (Late Final Extra). http://nla.gov.au/nla.news-article231109908.
35  'After Fifty Years', *Barrier Miner*, 19 December 1935, 3. http://nla.gov.au/nla.news-article46714857; 'Preparing City for Celebrations – Canadian Games Athletes in Training – New Customs Launch Tested', *The Sydney Morning Herald*, 18 January 1938, 14. http://nla.gov.au/nla.news-article17429138. See also Chris Sullivan, 'Non-Tribal Dance Music and Song: From First Contact to Citizen Rights', *Australian*

*Aboriginal Studies*, no. 1 (1988): 65. Hero and Gladys Black would also later travel to Broken Hill to see Queen Elizabeth II during her 1953 visit. 'Aboriginal King Dies', *Dawn* 4, no. 4 (April 1955): 6.

36 Jack Horner and Marcia Langton, 'The Day of Mourning', in *Australians 1938*, ed. Bill Gammage and Spearritt (Broadway: Fairfax, Syme & Weldon Associates, 1987), 13.

37 Discussed in Minutes 7 April 1937, APB Minute Books, closed records of the NSW AWB (formerly APB), accessed with permission of AANSW.

38 'Complaints About Treatment', *Barrier Miner*, 22 January 1938, 7 (Sports Edition). http://nla.gov.au/nla.news-article47962898; 'Chief Secretary on Aborigines Question', *Barrier Miner*, 25 January 1938, 1 (Home Edition). http://nla.gov.au/nla.news-article47963089.

39 Beverley P. Elphick and Don J. Elphick, *Menindee Mission Station: 1933–1949* (Canberra: B. and D. Elphick, 1996), 11. Milne and his wife were managers of several Aboriginal reserves in the 1930s including Cabbage Tree Island, Bellbrook and Angledool.

40 Minutes 3 August 1938, APB Minute Books, closed records of the NSW AWB (formerly Aborigines Protection Board), accessed with permission of AANSW.

41 Minutes 7 September 1938, ibid.

42 Minutes 15 July 1932, and 12 January 1933, ibid.

43 Minutes 12 September 1934, ibid.

44 Though discussed and planned in 1930 and 1931, it is not clear whether this exhibition ever eventuated. 'General News', *The Kadina and Wallaroo Times*, 20 August 1930, 2. http://nla.gov.au/nla.news-article110234693; the inclusion of Aboriginal people in this display was tabled at an APB meeting on 31 July 1930, ibid.

45 '"Back to the Bellinger" Aborigines to Play their Part', *The Gloucester Advocate*, 7 March 1933, 2. https://trove.nla.gov.au/newspaper/article/159651436. 'Back to the Bellinger', *The Wingham Chronicle and Manning River Observer*, 17 March 1933, 7. http://nla.gov.au/nla.news-article166499157; 'A Gay Day', *Coffs Harbour Advocate*, 24 March 1933, 4. http://nla.gov.au/nla.news-article187761754.

46 'Aborigine Village Novel Feature at Melbourne Centenary North Queensland Blacks Melbourne, November 22', *The Telegraph*, 23 November 1933, 11. https://trove.nla.gov.au/newspaper/article/181175052.

47 'Aborigines', *Cairns Post*, 25 November 1933, 6. http://nla.gov.au/nla.news-article41234526.

48 Healy notes that the BPA had initially posed no objections to Ted 'Chook' Mullett's performance in the events, but had later reported that he did not want to perform. Sianan Healy, '"Years Ago Some Lived Here": Aboriginal Australians and the Production of Popular Culture, History and Identity in 1930s Victoria', *Australian Historical Studies* 37, no. 128 (2006): 24–5; 'Shaking Hands with the Governor-General: Aboriginal Participation in White Celebrations of History and Heritage in 1930s Victoria', in *Historicising Whiteness: Transnational Perspectives on the Construction of an Identity*, ed. Leigh Boucher, Jane Carey and Katherine Ellinghouse (Melbourne: University of Melbourne, 2007), 293.

49 'Project Revived', *Cairns Post*, 8 March 1934, 4. http://nla.gov.au/nla.news-article41249934.

50 'Arts of the Stone Age', *The Herald*, 13 June 1934, 12. http://nla.gov.au/nla. news-article243174626; 'Display of Aboriginal Customs for Centenary', *News*, 29 August 1934, 5. http://nla.gov.au/nla.news-article128847874; Healy, 'Shaking Hands with the Governor-General', 293. Healy suggests that the import of performers from outside of Victoria was the direct result of the Victorian BPA refusing requests for participation of local performers, but she also notes that at least one performer from Lake Tyers Mission Station (Ted Foster) participated.

51 Healy, '"Years Ago Some Lived Here"', 25–6. 'Native Arts and Crafts', *The Herald*, 25 September 1934: 23. http://nla.gov.au/nla.news-article243107689; 'Blacks Astonished by the City', *Argus*, 26 September 1934, 8. http://nla.gov.au/nla.news-article10956595.

52 'Aborigines' Float', *Gilgandra Weekly and Castlereagh*, 24 January 1935, 1. http://nla.gov.au/nla.news-article113024440.

53 'Aboriginal Corroboree', *Wellington Times*, 11 January 1937, 3. http://nla.gov.au/nla.news-article143401299.

54 'For Women', *The Sydney Morning Herald*, 12 October 1935, 9. http://nla.gov.au/nla.news-article17226162; 'Aboriginal Leaf Band', *The Manaro Mercury, and Cooma and Bombala Advertiser*, 6 November 1931, 2v. http://nla.gov.au/nla.news-article119085218; 'Natives Stage Corroboree for Charity', *The Age*, 28 April 1934, 26. http://nla.gov.au/nla.news-article203839216; 'Music and Drama', *The Sydney Morning Herald*, 18 January 1936, 12. http://nla.gov.au/nla.news-article17222523; Greenhalgh and Meekin's Wild West Rodeo at the RAS Showground 23–6 December 1933 included a corroboree 'as done in Arnhem Land' and Aboriginal performers in 'war paint'. 'Advertising', *The Sydney Morning Herald*, 6 December 1933, 3. http://nla.gov.au/nla.news-article17029899; 'Wild West Rodeo', *The Sydney Morning Herald*, 26 December 1933, 2. http://nla.gov.au/nla.news-article17035367; 'Corroboree', *North West Champion*, 19 September 1932, 2. http://nla.gov.au/nla.news-article179128450.

55 Minutes 4 March 1932, APB Minute Books, closed records of the NSW AWB (formerly APB), accessed with permission of AANSW.

56 'Among Abos', *The Sun*, 26 February 1932, 9 (Final Extra). http://nla.gov.au/nla.news-article230524575.

57 (Misreported as Chief Eagle Hawk) 'Red Meets Black', *Sunday Times*, 25 January 1914, 22. http://nla.gov.au/nla.news-article120363890.

58 'Not an Alien', *Evening News*, 6 January 1914, 7. http://nla.gov.au/nla.news-article114488953.

59 Brumbie was secretary to activist for Aboriginal rights Charles Duguid at the time, 'Singer Meets Aboriginal', *News*, 5 July 1952, 10. http://nla.gov.au/nla.news-article130807881.

60 'Opportunity for Nancy Ellis Study to Continue in United States', *Great Southern Herald*, 11 July 1952: 2. http://nla.gov.au/nla.news-article147399594.

61 www.ausstage.edu.au/pages/event/25526; John Thomson. 'It's Australian – and It's Good!: The Australian Musical Collits' Inn', *National Library of Australia News* 14, no. 3 (2003): 8–9.

62 'The Princess "Collits' Inn" Revived', *The Argus*, 15 October 1934, 4. http://nla.gov.au/nla.news-article10988617.

63 'Collit's Inn', *The Central Queensland Herald*, 4 January 1934, 3. http://nla.gov.au/nla.news-article70311141. Elsewhere this was reported as the National Museum: 'Australian Musical Play Succeeds', *Weekly Times*, 30 December 1933, 10 (First Edition). http://nla.gov.au/nla.news-article223210414. The designer of the costumes,

Pierre Fornari later suggested (with corroboration from A. P. Elkin) that Aboriginal designs were ripe for take-up by Paris fashion houses. 'World's Women May Dress in Corroboree Designs', *The Daily Telegraph*, 12 June 1937, 7. http://nla.gov.au/nla.news-article247141018.

64  '"Collits' Inn" Breaks New Ground', *The Sydney Morning Herald*, 4 January 1934, 8 (Women's Supplement). http://nla.gov.au/nla.news-article17037585; 'Stage and Screen', *The Sydney Morning Herald*, 21 June 1934, 9 (Women's Supplement). http://nla.gov.au/nla.news-article17088508; 'Centenary of Illawarra', *The Sydney Morning Herald*, 16 March 1896, 5. http://nla.gov.au/nla.news-article14041563; PIC/15611/11087 LOC Cold store PIC/15611 Fairfax archive of glass plate negatives. http://nla.gov.au/nla.obj-162293978/view.

65  Quoted in Thomson, 'It's Australian – and It's Good!: The Australian Musical Collits' Inn', 9.

66  'Music, Drama & Films "Collits' Inn"', *The Argus*, 26 December 1933, 3. http://nla.gov.au/nla.news-article11724052. George H. Clutsam and Adrian Ross' reworking of Franz Schubert's music in *Lilac Time* had been toured in 1924, 1926 and 1928, and *Rose Marie* in 1926, 1927 and 1928 by J. C. Williamson. www.ausstage.edu.au/pages/work/840; www.ausstage.edu.au/pages/work/2223.

67  Roger Covell, *Australia's Music: Themes of a New Society* (Melbourne: Sun Books, 1967), 107.

68  *Australian Broadcasting Commission Act* 1932, Cth, s.24.

69  Kenneth Morgan, 'Cultural Advance: The Formation of Australia's Permanent Symphony Orchestras, 1944–1951', *Musicology Australia* 33, no. 1 (2011).

70  Kathleen E. Nelson, 'Percy Grainger's Work for the Australian Broadcasting Commission, 1934–1935: Background and Reception', *Australasian Music Research* 2–3 (1998): 99–100.

71  Kathleen E. Nelson, 'Grainger and the Australian Broadcasting Commission after 1935: Memories, Hopes and Frustrations', *Australasian Music Research* 5 (2000): 121.

72  The full text of the lectures is reproduced in John Blacking, *'A Common-Sense View of All Music': Reflections on Percy Grainger's Contribution to Ethnomusicology and Music Education* (Cambridge: Cambridge University Press, 1987), 154.

73  The Annual Report of the Australian Broadcasting Commission. Sydney: The Commission, 1933, quoted in Jennifer Hill, 'Clive Douglas and the ABC: Not a Favourite Aunt', in *One Hand on the Manuscript: Music in Australian Cultural History 1930–1960*, ed. Nicholas Brown et al. (Canberra: Humanities Research Centre, ANU, 1995), 239.

74  Douglas quoted in Rhoderick McNeill, 'Symphonies of the Bush: Indigenous Encounters in Australian Symphonies', in *Encounters: Meetings in Australian Music: Essays, Images, Interviews*, ed. Vincent Plush, Huib Schippers and Jocelyn Wolfe (Brisbane: Queensland Conservatorium Research Centre, 2005), 19.

75  Rhoderick McNeill, 'Clive Douglas and the Search for the Australian Symphony', *Legacies* conference (February 2009). https://eprints.usq.edu.au/7950/.

76  Harold Hort, 'Antill, John Henry (1904–1986)', *Australian Dictionary of Biography*, National Centre of Biography, Australian National University. http://adb.anu.edu.au/biography/antill-john-henry-12145/text21761, published first in hardcopy 2007.

77  Thorold Waters, 'Australia Tunes a Strange Lay', *The Listener In*, 6 February 1937. Also cited in David Symons, *Before and after Corroboree: The Music of John Antill* (Farnham: Ashgate, 2015), 47.

78 Belinda McKay, "'A Lovely Land ... By Shadows Dark Untainted?'": Whiteness and Early Queensland Women's Writing', in *Whitening Race: Essays in Social and Cultural Criticism*, ed. Aileen Moreton-Robinson (Canberra: Aboriginal Studies Press, 2004), 156.
79 Hill, 'Clive Douglas and the ABC', 238.
80 Clive Douglas, 'Folk Song and the Brown Man – Means to an Australian Expression in Symphonic Works', *Canon* 10, no. 3 (1956): 82.
81 Ibid., 83. This apparent slight to John Antill, whose ballet suite *Corroboree* was well known by the time this article was published, was possibly an attempt to differentiate Antill's symphonic ballet scores (which were nonetheless often performed and broadcast by symphony orchestras without the accompanying dance works) from pure symphonic music. Jennifer Hill has pointed to Douglas' bitterness about the extent to which Antill's success had overshadowed Douglas' own ambitions as a composer. Hill, 'Clive Douglas and the ABC', 240–1.
82 Amanda Harris, 'The Nature of Nordicism: Grainger's "Blue-Gold-Rosy-Race" and His Music', *Musicology Australia* 23 (2000).
83 Examples are Grainger's works *Colonial Song* (1913) and *Gumsuckers' March* (1916).
84 David Symons, 'Words and Music: Clive Douglas and the Jindyworobak Manifesto', in *The Soundscapes of Australia: Music, Place and Spirituality*, ed. Fiona Richards (Aldershot: Ashgate, 2007), 94.
85 Henry Tate, *Australian Musical Possibilities* (Melbourne: Edward A. Vidler, 1924), 16. Quoted in Rhoderick McNeill, *The Australian Symphony from Federation to 1960* (Farnham (UK): Ashgate, 2014), 117.
86 Graeme Skinner, 'Toward a General History of Australian Musical Composition: First National Music, 1788–c. 1860', PhD thesis, University of Sydney, 2011, 113.
87 Lhotsky's arrangement has recently been used by Ngarigu people in efforts at revitalization of cultural practice. In a workshop in May 2019 participants led by Jakelin Troy and Linda Barwick collaborated to reconstruct the language and meaning of the text and to strip away musical ornaments reflecting European conventions. On-Country Workshop, 15–18 May 2019, Thredbo NSW as part of the ARC Discovery Project 'Reclaiming Performance Under Assimilation in Southeast Australia, 1935–75'.
88 Isaac Nathan, *The Southern Euphrosyne and Australian Miscellany: Containing Oriental Moral Tales, Original Anecdote, Poetry and Music* (London, Sydney: Whittaker & Co., 1849).
89 Graeme Skinner, 'Australian Musical First Modernism', in *The Modernist World*, ed. Stephen Ross and Allana C. Lindgren (Abingdon: Routledge, 2015), 279. The impact of Roy Agnew's modernist works on Australian composition and the neglect of this by music historians such as Covell has been discussed by Catherine Bowan, 'Wild Men and Mystics: Rethinking Roy Agnew's Early Sydney Works', *Musicology Australia* 30 (2008).
90 See for example 'Aboriginal Songs', *Sunday Mail (Brisbane)*, 20 June 1937, 32. http://nla.gov.au/nla.news-article97889733; 'Australian Aboriginal Songs', *Sunday Times*, June 1937, 23 (First Section). http://nla.gov.au/nla.news-article58782739.
91 *Poor Fellow Me* was performed in 1950 by Raymond Beatty 'Farewell Broadcasts by Swing Club Band', *The Manning River Times and Advocate for the Northern Coast Districts of New South Wales*, 23 September 1950: 5. http://nla.gov.au/nla.news-article172829684, and 1955 by Norman Barnes Alfred Hill, 'The Grand Old Man of Australian Music', *Le Courrier Australien*, 11 February 1955, 6. http://trove.nla.gov.au/newspaper/article/225595938, while Loam's songs were included in some of the early performances by Carell, 'Outstanding Show By Beth Dean', *Camperdown Chronicle*, 22 September 1950, 7. http://nla.gov.au/nla.news-article23576459.

92  'The Beauties of Music', *The Murrumbidgee Irrigator*, 1 July 1938, 5. http://nla.gov.au/nla.news-article156146819.
93  Inga Clendinnen, *Dancing with Strangers* (Melbourne: Text Pub, 2003), 15; Steven Morris, 'First Australian Piano Comes Home to UK after 231 Years', *The Guardian*, 31 March 2019, accessed 3 April 2019, www.theguardian.com/australia-news/2019/mar/31/first-australian-piano-comes-home-to-uk-after-231-years.
94  Loam's songs were also recorded by Enid Conley-Williams in 1946, and Harold Blair in 1960, though he had been singing them since at least 1950, see NFSA title no. 245797 – unreleased recording of Blair singing *Maranoa Lullaby*; *Nananala Kututja*.
95  World Youth Festivals Prague 1947, Budapest 1949, Berlin 1951, Pieces 27–9 folder, Box 59 – 90-2-1 Unity Dance Group – Notices & Programmes, Margaret Walker papers MS 8495; Bodenwieser Ballet – PROMPT file – Ephemera, NLA.
96  David Salter, 'Goossens, Sir Eugene Aynsley (1893–1962)', *Australian Dictionary of Biography*, National Centre of Biography, Australian National University. http://adb.anu.edu.au/biography/goossens-sir-eugene-aynsley-10329/text18283, published first in hardcopy 1996.
97  Covell, *Australia's Music*, 152. See also James Murdoch, *Australia's Contemporary Composers* (Melbourne: Sun Books, 1972), 11.
98  Covell, *Australia's Music*, 153.
99  Watters-Cowan also cites James Murdoch's assessment of Sutherland's relationship with the ABC and its view of Sutherland as 'troublemaker and an agitator', he attributes this to the male chauvinism and conservatism of the editors of ABC music programmes. Personal communication from Murdoch quoted in Chérie Watters-Cowan, 'Reconstructing the Creative Life of Australian Composer Margaret Sutherland: The Evidence of Primary Source Documents' PhD thesis, (University of NSW, 2006), 303.
100 David Symons, *The Music of Margaret Sutherland* (Sydney: Currency Press, 1997), 19.

# Chapter 3

1  'Folk-dancing', *The West Australian*, 2 July 1947, 12. http://nla.gov.au/nla.news-article46322865; 'Plays and Players', *Western Mail*, 10 July 1947, 54. http://nla.gov.au/nla.news-article38580555; 'Shawn Sees Our "Great" Dancers', *The Mail*, 16 August 1947, 10. http://nla.gov.au/nla.news-article55891047.
2  'Polished Dancing by Ted Shawn', *The Sun*, 28 August 1947, 9 (Late Final Extra). http://nla.gov.au/nla.news-article229695822; 'Dance Artistry of Ted Shawn', *The Courier-Mail*, 8 September 1947, 8. http://nla.gov.au/nla.news-article49311342; 'Ted Shawn's Diverse Solo Dances', *The Sydney Morning Herald*, 1 September 1947, 9. http://nla.gov.au/nla.news-article18040946.
3  'Ted Shawn to "Sell Dancing for Men"', *The Sydney Morning Herald*, 24 April 1947, 6. http://nla.gov.au/nla.news-article18023070.
4  'The Abos Dance For A Famous Dancer', *News*, 5 August 1947, 2. http://nla.gov.au/nla.news-article127057604.
5  'Ted Shawn Hurts Knee', *The Daily News*, 2 August 1947, 22 (Late Sports). http://nla.gov.au/nla.news-article83747636.
6  'Abos are Sugar Dancers', *Gippsland Times*, 11 August 1947, 4. https://trove.nla.gov.au/newspaper/article/63260797.

7   John K. Ewers, 'Aboriginal Ballet', *Walkabout*, 1 December 1947, 33.
8   'Aboriginal Dancing "Discovered": We Can Learn from Corroborees', *The Argus*, 9 August 1947, 43. http://nla.gov.au/nla.news-article22447172.
9   Ewers, 'Aboriginal Ballet', 33.
10  Robert A. Hall, *The Black Diggers: Aborigines and Torres Strait Islanders in the Second World War* (Canberra: Aboriginal Studies Press, 1997), 18–20.
11  Alick Jackomos and Derek Fowell, *Living Aboriginal History of Victoria: Stories in the Oral Tradition* (Cambridge: Cambridge University Press, 1991), 34.
12  Robin Ryan dates the first public performances by the Wallaga Lakes gumleaf band to 1903 and suggests that the La Perouse gumleaf band might have been formed after gumleaf playing was popularized in that settlement by Wallaga Lakes men living there. Members of the Wallaga Lakes band were Thomas family members Whaler Billy, his brothers Max and Cecil, and sons Arthur, Ronald, Cecil and Ted 'Gubboo', John (Jacko) Campbell, Percy (Square) Davis, Ernie (Friday) and Ned Hoskins, Jimmy Little Senior and his brothers Jackie and Eddie, Percy and Frank Mumbulla, Charlie, Clem and Costin Parsons, and Albert Thomas. Robin Ryan, '"A Spiritual Sound, a Lonely Sound": Leaf Music of Southeastern Aboriginal Australians, 1890s–1990s', PhD thesis, Monash University, 1999, 117–20.
13  'Aboriginals of Wallaga Lake', *Sydney Mail*, 16 March 1921, 30. http://nla.gov.au/nla.news-article159038698; 'Bush Music Makers', *The Bombala Times*, 29 July 1927, 2. http://nla.gov.au/nla.news-article134555943; 'News of the Circuits', *The Methodist*, 17 February 1934, 15. http://nla.gov.au/nla.news-article155309651; 'Team of Abos', *Illawarra Mercury*, 21 August 1931, 8. http://nla.gov.au/nla.news-article132891654.
14  Ryan, '"A Spiritual Sound, a Lonely Sound"', chapter 3.
15  The young singer was likely Lucy Green, studying at the Melba Conservatorium at the time rather than Elizabeth Green as reported. 'Aboriginal Concert Party', *The Argus*, 18 March 1944: 10. http://nla.gov.au/nla.news-article11819781.
16  Margaret Tucker, *If Everyone Cared: Autobiography of Margaret Tucker M.B.E.* (London: Grosvenor, 1983), 163.
17  Karl Neuenfeldt, '"I Wouldn't Change Skins with Anybody": Dulcie Pitt/Georgia Lee, a Pioneering Indigenous Australian Jazz, Blues and Community Singer', *Jazz Research Journal* 8, no. 1–2 (2014): 206.
18  Ibid., 207–8.
19  The article (unusually) lists the names of all solo performers, including Rex Morris, Henry Russell, Reg Russell, Joan Hoskins, Charlie Edwards, Ron Marr, Elsie Russell, Priscillie Russell, Bill Turnbull, Bronk Morris, Arthur Russell, Joe Bungle, Allan Saunders, and sisters Flo and Kate [no surname given]. 'Entertainment at Wingham', *The Manning River Times and Advocate for the Northern Coast Districts of New South Wales*, 8 June 1940, 2. http://nla.gov.au/nla.news-article171230617.
20  'Native Artists', *The Gosford Times and Wyong District Advocate*, 15 November 1940, 1. http://nla.gov.au/nla.news-article166932492.
21  See Jackomos and Fowell, *Living Aboriginal History of Victoria*.
22  Ryan theorizes that gumleaf playing may have proliferated through inter-tribal travel and trade routes, possibly originating in NSW. Ryan, '"A Spiritual Sound, a Lonely Sound"', 64–7. It is not clear how hula dancing became so ubiquitous among Aboriginal performers from around the 1920s onwards, but the first touring hula show visited in 1911, with the show 'Bird of Paradise' featuring Canadian Muriel

Starr and Hawaiian ukulele musicians and dancers performing hula touring in 1918. "'The Bird of Paradise'", *Daily Herald*, 26 March 1918, 7. http://nla.gov.au/nla.news-article105461210; Robin Ryan, 'Ukuleles, Guitars or Gumleaves? Hula Dancing and Southeastern Australian Aboriginal Performers in the 1920s and 1930s', *Perfect Beat* 3, no. 2 (1997): 106; Jackey Coyle and Rebecca Coyle, 'Aloha Australia: Hawaiian Music in Australia (1920–55)', *Perfect Beat* 2, no. 2 (1995): 32–3.

23 Quoted in Ryan, "'A Spiritual Sound, a Lonely Sound'", 72.

24 Chris Illert, 'Early Ancestors of Illawarra's Wadi-Wadi People', *Bulletin of the Illawarra Aboriginal History Society* (November 2003): 10.

25 Ngunnawal, Ngambri and Ngarigu people alike also recall travels throughout the Canberra and Snowy Mountains region for festivals of bogong moth feasts. See Ngambri elder Jim 'Boza' Williams' painting *Kicked out of Parliament* and his assertion that Ngambri people have always been known as moth people, 'Community Stories: Canberra Region, Website of the National Museum of Australia', www.nma.gov.au/learn/encounters-education/community-stories/canberra, accessed 9 October 2019. Jakelin Troy discusses the Bogong moth feasts central to Ngarigu communities and their country across the Snowy Mountains. Personal communication. See also Mark McKenna, *Looking for Blackfellas' Point: An Australian History of Place* (Sydney: UNSW Press, 2002), 19.

26 (See Prelude) and 'Packed Hall', *Yass Tribune-Courier*, 13 February 1947, 1. http://nla.gov.au/nla.news-article248456226.

27 Clinton Walker, *Buried Country: The Story of Aboriginal Country Music* (Sydney: Pluto Press, 2000), 84.

28 The Aboriginal dancers included Harold Bux, Eric Onus, Winifred Onus, Joyce McKinnon, George McKinnon (the serviceman referred to), Edna Brown and Con Edwards. 'Amateur Theatre', *The Herald*, 13 August 1946, 8. http://nla.gov.au/nla.news-article245548755.

29 'Round Melbourne Shows', *The Argus*, 21 August 1946, 12 (Woman's Magazine). http://nla.gov.au/nla.news-article22322403.

30 Session 3, Margaret Walker interviewed by Barbara Blackman, ORAL TRC 1770, nla.obj-215449570, NLA.

31 'Aborigines Restore a Lost Culture', *The Herald*, 8 August 1946, 13. http://nla.gov.au/nla.news-article245546981.

32 Tiriki Onus and Alec Morgan, *Ablaze*. http://ablazethefilm.com/, accessed 9 October 2019.

33 Thanks to New Theatre archivist Lyn Collingwood for confirming this information 'From Club to Theatre'. http://newtheatrehistory.org.au/wiki/index.php/From_Club_to_Theatre, accessed 8 April 2019.

34 'Abo's views of bomb-site', *The Daily Telegraph*, 2 March 1947, 32. http://nla.gov.au/nla.news-article248359552.

35 'News of the Day', *The Age*, 8 March 1948, 2. http://nla.gov.au/nla.news-article206880854.

36 See also forthcoming article Amanda Harris, Tiriki Onus and Linda Barwick, 'Performing Aboriginal Workers' Rights in 1951: From the Top End to Australia's Southeast'.

37 Richard Broome and Corinne Manning, *A Man of All Tribes: The Life of Alick Jackomos* (Canberra: Aboriginal Studies Press, 2006), 119.

38  'Rifle Shooting', *Williamstown Chronicle*, 23 April 1948, 10. http://nla.gov.au/nla.news-article70723088.
39  'Reunions and Services', *The Argus*, 21 April 1949, 6. http://nla.gov.au/nla.news-article22723800.
40  'Seats Tangle at Corroboree', *The Age*, 26 April 1948, 3. http://nla.gov.au/nla.news-article206880443.
41  'Aborigines Prepare for Corroboree', *Daily Advertiser*, 23 April 1948, 1. http://nla.gov.au/nla.news-article144755228.
42  'Corroboree is Uneven', *The Age*, 18 April 1949, 3. http://nla.gov.au/nla.news-article206072359; 'New Shows: Australian Play Succeeds at the King's', *The Argus*, 18 April 1949, 2. http://nla.gov.au/nla.news-article22723043.
43  Lyn Collingwood, 'From Club to Theatre'. http://newtheatrehistory.org.au/wiki/index.php/From_Club_to_Theatre, accessed 8 April 2019.
44  Deborah Garland, 'Melbourne Theatres – Undergrads Will Go "On Tour"', *The Herald*, 17 December 1946, 12. http://nla.gov.au/nla.news-article245380244.
45  'Complaints Alleged by Aboriginal Harvesters', *The Herald*, 28 December 1942, 5. http://nla.gov.au/nla.news-article245129660; 'Protest by Aborigines', *The Herald*, 11 January 1946, 3. http://nla.gov.au/nla.news-article245949282.
46  'Pageant by Aborigines', *Sunday Times*, 25 April 1948, 3. http://nla.gov.au/nla.news-article59479822.
47  Minutes 19 August 1941; Minutes 28 October 1941, AWB Minute Books, closed records of the NSW AWB, accessed with permission of AANSW.
48  Dorothy and Nerida Blair confirmed to me that Harold and Dorothy were both proud of the account given of Harold's life in Harrison's biography, and that Harold was closely consulted on the content. Given this, I regard this biography as a version of Harold Blair's own account of his experiences. Kenneth Harrison, *Dark Man, White World: A Portrait of Tenor Harold Blair* (Melbourne: Novalt, 1975), 49–80.
49  Indeed, at least one media report in the 1930s of the discovery of Lawrence's talent for opera drew a line from the corroborees long practised in Australia to the drama of European operatic arts. 'Culture and the Centenary', *The Central Queensland Herald*, 21 June 1934, 13. http://nla.gov.au/nla.news-article70566442.
50  'Aborigine Sings for Marjorie Lawrence, is Highly Praised', *The Telegraph*, 29 September 1944, 3 (City Final Last Minute News). http://nla.gov.au/nla.news-article189850687.
51  Harrison, *Dark Man, White World*, 74–81.
52  Dorothy Helmrich, *The First Twenty-Five Years: A Study of the Arts Council of Australia* (Sydney: Southwood Press, 1968), 1; Phillip Deery and Lisa Milner, 'Political Theatre and the State Melbourne and Sydney, 1936–1953', *History Australia* 12, no. 3 (2015): 128.
53  Victoria, Royal Commission Inquiring into the Origins, Aims, Objects and Funds of the Communist Party in Victoria and Other Related Matters, *Report* (1950). www.parliament.vic.gov.au/papers/govpub/VPARL1950-51No12.pdf, accessed 3 February 2020.
54  The decision to travel to the United States under Duncan's mentorship has been cast as a key error in Blair's career, where he did not get the technical support he needed to progress as a singer, and plans to study at Juilliard never came to fruition, mainly for financial reasons. Margaret Sutherland had advised against the decision, but had

personally contributed funds to Blair's further expenses leading up to the travel when another benefactor pulled out. Harrison, *Dark Man, White World*, 90–1, 96.
55   'Better Education for Aborigines Sought', *Tribune*, 27 April 1949, clipping in ASIO file, Blair, Harold, 1917–1965, A6126, 292, NAA, Canberra.
56   At Northcote Town Hall, 21 November 1947. Folder 1. 1945–50, Papers of Harold Blair, 1924–1976, MS 8950, NLA.
57   Harrison, *Dark Man, White World*, 106–7.
58   Ibid., 116–17.
59   Stefan Haag (later to direct the Australian Elizabethan Theatre Trust) sang in this production as well, and became the National Theatre Opera's producer the following year. Frank Murphy, 'Theatre Music', *Advocate*, 2 December 1948, 18. http://nla.gov.au/nla.news-article172500602; 'Harold Blair's Operatic Debut', *The Age*, 29 November 1948, 2. http://nla.gov.au/nla.news-article205671966; Margaret Leask, 'Haag, Stefan Hermann (1925–1986)', Australian Dictionary of Biography, National Centre of Biography, Australian National University, http://adb.anu.edu.au/biography/haag-stefan-hermann-12577/text22647.
60   Public profiles of Blair commonly characterize his activism as beginning in the late 1950s, once he was well established as a singer, see for example, 'Harold Blair AO, 1924–1976', National Portrait Gallery, www.portrait.gov.au/people/harold-blair-1924, accessed 10 April 2019.
61   Blair made lengthy public speeches about the need for access to education and the poor state of Aboriginal settlements from as early as 1948. Reporting of these speeches caused Blair to be flagged to ASIO, who noted that many of Blair's associates and supporters were known communists. Journalist Frank Browne's 'Things I Hear' newsletter of 22 November 1948 is reproduced in Blair's ASIO file, reporting that in his interviews, Blair had 'nothing to say about singing, but plenty of screaming on the colour question and a few other Commo stalking horses'. Blair, Harold, 1917–1965, A6126, 292, NAA, Canberra.
62   Reports document the gifts of boomerangs, 'Aboriginal Singer Shows Gratitude', *The Courier-Mail*, 31 March 1945, 6. http://nla.gov.au/nla.news-article48943302; 'Aboriginal "Spell-Binder" Sings To Unionists', *The Herald*, 5 September 1947, 6. http://nla.gov.au/nla.news-article245086085.
63   Covell suggested that though Antill's *Corroboree* was the work to bring to the public's attention that music 'truly belonging to the twentieth century' was being composed in Australia, it was Sutherland who 'really naturalized the twentieth century in Australian music'. Roger Covell, *Australia's Music: Themes of a New Society* (Melbourne: Sun Books, 1967), 152.
64   Jennifer Hill, 'Clive Douglas and the ABC: Not a Favourite Aunt', in *One Hand on the Manuscript: Music in Australian Cultural History 1930–1960*, ed. Nicholas Brown et al. (Canberra: Humanities Research Centre, ANU, 1995), 240.
65   Eugene Goossens, 'Where Are the Scores?', *Canon* 2, no. 1 (1948): 5–6.
66   'Fund to Send Aust. Composer To London', *The Daily Telegraph*, 10 October 1946, 5. http://nla.gov.au/nla.news-article248403178; '£410 Subscribed To Antill Fund', *The Daily Telegraph*, 28 October 1946: 12. http://nla.gov.au/nla.news-article248408639; 'Your Radio', *The Daily Telegraph*, 20 October 1946, 6. http://nla.gov.au/nla.news-article248407019; 'Composer Leaves For London Today', *The Daily Telegraph*, 15 October 1946, 7. http://nla.gov.au/nla.news-article248407867; Beth Dean and Victor Carell, *Gentle Genius: A Life of John Antill* (Sydney: Akron Press, 1987), 91.

67   David Symons, 'The Jindyworobak Connection in Australian Music c.1940–1960', *Context* 23, Autumn (2002); 'Words and Music: Clive Douglas and the Jindyworobak Manifesto', in *The Soundscapes of Australia: Music, Place and Spirituality*, ed. Fiona Richards (Aldershot: Ashgate, 2007); Nicole St Ilan, 'Clive Douglas: When Is a Jindyworobak Not a Jindyworobak?', *Sounds Australian* 30 (1991); Anthony Linden Jones, 'The Circle of Songs: Traditional Song and the Musical Score to C.P. Mountford's Documentary Films', in *Circulating Cultures: Exchanges of Australian Indigenous Music, Dance and Media*, ed. Amanda Harris (Canberra: ANU Press, 2014).

68   'Euroka', *The Argus*, 17 September 1947, 3 (Woman's Magazine). http://nla.gov.au/nla.news-article22508040; 'Didgerydoos in Plenty for Musician', *The Argus*, 25 January 1949, 6. http://nla.gov.au/nla.news-article22699157; 'Aboriginal Ballet and Review', *The Argus*, 31 January 1949, 5. http://nla.gov.au/nla.news-article22711513. The Australian National Dictionary defines 'corroboree' as 'An Aboriginal dance ceremony, of which song and rhythmical musical accompaniment are an integral part, and which may be sacred and ritualized or secular, occasional, and informal' likely derived from the Dharug language, and appearing in early written records of the Sydney language. www.australiannationaldictionary.com.au/oupnewindex1.php.

69   Covell, *Australia's Music*, 65.

70   *Corroboree* holds a central place in Australian music history as the first major orchestral composition to enter the standard repertoire and as a work engaging with a unique Australian culture. See for example James Murdoch, *Australia's Contemporary Composers* (Melbourne: Sun Books, 1972), 11; Covell, *Australia's Music*, 70; Andrew McCredie, *Musical Composition in Australia: Including Select Bibliography and Discography* (Canberra: Advisory Board, Commonwealth Assistance to Australian Composers, 1969), 10; Joel Crotty, 'Towards an Australian Art-Music Canon', *Quadrant* 55, no. 10 (2011): 95.

71   The first three composers mentioned by Murdoch were ABC employees and the institutional support the ABC provided to emerging Australian music (discussed in Chapter 2) remained strong throughout the 1940s. Murdoch, *Australia's Contemporary Composers*, 10–11.

72   '1982 APRA Music Awards', http://apraamcos.com.au/awards/1980-1989/1982-music-awards/, accessed 3 May 2019.

73   Helmrich, *The First Twenty-Five Years*, 5.

74   Ibid., 6–7.

75   'Aust. Music Will Go to England by New Process', *The Daily Telegraph*, 17 June 1947, 7. http://nla.gov.au/nla.news-article248479584; Dean and Carell, *Gentle Genius*, 100.

76   'Negotiations for Ballet Break Down', *The Age*, 17 December 1949, 15 (The Age Literary Supplement). http://nla.gov.au/nla.news-article189481371; Dean and Carell, *Gentle Genius*, 106–7.

77   Mark St Leon, *The Wizard of the Wire* (Canberra: Aboriginal Studies Press, 1993), 193.

78   William Townsend ONUS Volume 1, 1951–53, A6119, 1063, NAA, Canberra.

79   Blair recalled the shock of observing 'Black men of distinction and prestige' working as lawyers, doctors, surgeons and architects in the United States after he had been warned about segregation and racism there. The experience highlighted the appalling segregation of Aboriginal people in Australia and consolidated his political position on the importance of Aboriginal rights, especially to education. Harrison, *Dark Man, White World*, 129–31.

Notes 173

80 'From Primitive to Ballet', *People*, 12 August 1953, 19, clipping in MLMSS 7804/24/2, Subject file: Research trip – Central Australia, 1949–1953, Beth Dean and Victor Carell papers, SLNSW. This story is also recounted in Dean and Carell, *Dust for the Dancers*, 1–2.

81 Victoria Haskins also discusses this encounter, pointing out that Mountford's diaries suggest that Dean and Carell already had a plan for an Aboriginal ballet in mind when they met with him in 1945: Victoria Haskins, 'Beth Dean and the Transnational Circulation of Aboriginal Dance Culture: Gender, Authority and C. P. Mountford', in *Circulating Cultures: Exchanges of Australian Indigenous Music, Dance and Media*, ed. Amanda Harris (Canberra: ANU Press, 2014), 30.

82 'From Primitive to Ballet', *People*, 12 August 1953, 17–19, clipping in Subject file: Research trip – Central Australia, 1949–1953, MLMSS 7804/24/2, Beth Dean and Victor Carell papers, SLNSW.

83 The Oenpelli songs were recorded by Colin Simpson and Ray Giles. Linda Barwick and Allan Marett, 'Aural Snapshots of Musical Life: The 1948 Recordings', in *Exploring the Legacy of the 1948 Arnhem Land Expedition*, ed. Martin Thomas and Margo Neale (Canberra: ANU E Press, 2011), 358.

84 'Three Aboriginal dances', arranged and composed by Mirrie Hill, Mirrie Hill Printed Music 1912–1978, Box 63, MLMSS 6357, Alfred and Mirrie Hill papers, music and pictorial material 1854–1984, SLNSW; Mirrie Hill, *Three Aboriginal Dances* (Sydney: Southern Music Publishing, 1950); Alfred Hill, *Poor Fellow Me: Wanderer's Song* (Sydney: Chappell, 1950); W. E. Harney and A. P. Elkin, *Songs of the Songmen: Aboriginal Myths Retold* (Melbourne: Cheshire, 1949). Alfred Hill had previously composed works based on musical material from New Zealand Maori traditions, where he had spent much of his life. For discussion of Alfred Hill's Maori compositions, see Melissa Cross, 'The Forgotten Soundtrack of Maoriland: Imagining the Nation through Alfred Hill's Songs for Rewi's Last Stand', Masters thesis, Massey University and Victoria University, 2015.

85 See copies of these works and press clippings in C. P. Mountford collection PRG 1218/86, SLSA.

86 See for example Patrick Brantlinger's discussion of the self-fulfilling prophecies of treating Aboriginal people as though their extinction was inevitable. Patrick Brantlinger, *Dark Vanishings: Discourse on the Extinction of Primitive Races, 1800–1930* (Ithaca, NY: Cornell University Press, 2003), Ch. 6.

87 Patrick Wolfe, *Settler Colonialism and the Transformation of Anthropology: The Politics and Poetics of an Ethnographic Event* (London, New York: Cassell, 1999), 4. See also Chris Healy's discussion of self-referential 'Abo art': Chris Healy, *Forgetting Aborigines* (Sydney: University of New South Wales Press, 2008), 83; Lorenzo Veracini, *The Settler Colonial Present* (London: Palgrave Macmillan, 2015).

88 Victor Carell to Ted Shawn, 27 September 1970, Subject File: Ted Shawn, 1947; 1968–84, Beth Dean and Victor Carell Papers, MLMSS 7804/25/2, SLNSW.

89 The shift in the international dynamics of empire can be seen from the 1950s, though Australia still strongly identified with Britain in the late 1940s, indicated by the fact that white Australian citizens in this era still identified their nationality/racial identification as 'British'. See census data for 1947 in *Official Year Book of the Commonwealth of Australia No. 39–1953*. Deaths of servicemen were also recorded as 'Heroes of Empire' in newspapers – e.g. in the *Adelaide Advertiser*, see 'Family Notices', during WWII, http://nla.gov.au/nla.news-title44. See also Haebich, *Spinning the Dream*, 37.

90  James Curran and Stuart Ward, *The Unknown Nation: Australia after Empire* (Melbourne: Melbourne University Press, 2010), 6-7, 14-16.
91  'Assimilation of Aborigines', *The Canberra Times*, 19 October 1951.
92  Russell McGregor has suggested that under Paul Hasluck's scenario of assimilation, 'the Aboriginal cultural heritage would not disappear, but rather would dissipate into folkloric remnants, and Aboriginal identity would not be erased but privatised, contracting to little more than an individual's sense of personal ancestry'. McGregor, *Indifferent Inclusion*, 93.

## Chapter 4

1  'No Corroboree', *Northern Standard*, 9 March 1951, 4. http://nla.gov.au/nla.news-article49476486.
2  *Waters Fred v. The Commonwealth and Others*, E72/DL1755, NAA, Darwin.
3  '"No Corroboree", Natives Say', *Northern Standard*, 16 February 1951, 3. Accessed 16 July 2019, from http://nla.gov.au/nla.news-article49482592; 'US Tourists' "Spending Spree" At Darwin', *The Advertiser*, 20 February 1951, 1. http://nla.gov.au/nla.news-article45689016.
4  'Waters Case Adjourned Protest Movement Mounts "Should Hear Promptly" — Judge', *Northern Standard*, 9 March 1951, 1. http://nla.gov.au/nla.news-article49476505.
5  (Emphasis in original) Review by 'Marg' of National Ballet Festival Programme, Unity Dance Group Bulletin – March 1951, Plastic sleeve marked as 'Pieces 18-19?', Box 59, Margaret Walker papers MS 8495, NLA.
6  'The Australian Elizabethan Theatre Trust', www.thetrust.org.au/, accessed 26 August 2019.
7  Anna Haebich, *Spinning the Dream: Assimilation in Australia 1950-1970* (North Fremantle: Fremantle Press, 2007), 29. See also Andrew Markus' discussion of the persistent racism that was a reaction to Japan's dominance of the war in the east, and that coexisted with international recognition that policy based on ideas of racial superiority was no longer acceptable. Andrew Markus, *Australian Race Relations 1788-1993* (Sydney: Allen & Unwin, 1994), 155. Dunham and Ailey were part of a tradition of African American dance initiated by Pearl Primus and Dunham. Ailey was later widely credited with mainstreaming modern dance. For more on African American modern dance, see Susan Manning, *Modern Dance, Negro Dance: Race in Motion* (Minneapolis: University of Minnesota Press, 2004).
8  'Dancer Opens Appeal', *The Argus*, 7 July 1956, 7. http://nla.gov.au/nla.news-article71644804. Dunham's intention to 'write about the Aborigines' in planning for the tour, appears to have taken a more political turn by the time she had arrived in Australia. Contact with Nicholls in his role in the Australian Aborigines' League may have played a part. 'A Dancer Will Write Aborigines' Story', *The Argus*, 16 February 1952, 7. http://nla.gov.au/nla.news-article23163436.
9  Dorothy Helmrich, *The First Twenty-Five Years: A Study of the Arts Council of Australia* (Sydney: Southwood Press, 1968).
10  Leslie Greener, 'Adult Education in Tasmania', *The Australian Highway*, December 1950, 83-4.

11  K. F. Brookes (Director), 'Adult Education in Tasmania', *The Australian Highway*, February 1957, 7.
12  Leslie Greener, 'Adult Education in Tasmania', *The Australian Highway*, December 1950, 83–4.
13  'State's Varied Jubilee Events', *The Sydney Morning Herald*, 9 May 1951, 4. http://nla.gov.au/nla.news-article18216962; '500,000 Line Streets to Watch Jubilee Parade through City', *The Sydney Morning Herald*, 30 January 1951, 4. http://nla.gov.au/nla.news-article18196935.
14  (Emphasis in original) Material collected by the general manager of ABC, as chairman of the Federal arts sub-committee for the Commonwealth Jubilee Celebrations 1951, Proposed Native Corroboree [box 13], SP497/1, 74, NAA, Sydney.
15  Ibid.
16  Director-general Berryman to C. A. Moses, convenor, arts sub-committee, Commonwealth Jubilee Celebrations, 6 October 1950; A. G. Mitchell, The University of Sydney to Miss Cook [Betty Cook, Charles Moses' PA] 1 October 1950; Memo: Miss Cook to GM, Proposed Native Corroboree [box 13], SP497/1, 74, NAA, Sydney.
17  Series of memos to and from Moses at the ABC with mix of typed and handwritten text, marked 'urgent', and 'SEEN', Proposed Native Corroboree [box 13], SP497/1, 74, NAA, Sydney.
18  These included performances by the ABC orchestras, nationwide tours of the Australian Ballet and Australia Opera, visits from international ensembles like the United Kingdom's Hallé Orchestra and Ballet Rambert as well as a visit by a major British composer (Ralph Vaughan Williams or Arthur Bliss were proposed), chamber music ensembles, children's choirs and competitions for new orchestral and song compositions. Pageants in capital cities and country centres across Australia would also be presented. At this stage a performance of Antill's *Corroboree* was already assured as a piece for a visiting orchestra to perform. Dorothy Helmrich continued to push for this in later meetings. Full list of proposed events in minutes 29 June 1950, Commonwealth Jubilee celebrations, arts sub-committee – minutes of meetings [box 3], SP497/1, 17, NAA, Sydney.
19  George Revill, 'Hiawatha and Pan-Africanism: Samuel Coleridge-Taylor (1875–1912), a Black Composer in Suburban London', *Cultural Geographies* 2, no. 3 (1995): 247.
20  'Music and Theatre is this the Kind of Jubilee Music we Want?' *The Sunday Herald*, 26 November 1950, 8 (Sunday Herald Features). http://nla.gov.au/nla.news-article18481984; Commonwealth of Australia, House of Representatives, *Debates*, 23 November 1950. http://historichansard.net/hofreps/1950/19501123_reps_19_210/, accessed 31 January 2020.
21  Minutes 14 February 1951, Commonwealth Jubilee celebrations, arts sub-committee – minutes of meetings [box 3], SP497/1, 17; Charles Moses, 19 July 1951, Hiawatha – part 1, SP497/1, 50, NAA, Sydney.
22  Antill was among the group invited onto the committee at its formation in 1950, but he does not seem to have remained a committee member. The committee included representatives of the major music institutions and other cultural institutions: Bernard Heinze, Eugene Goossens and Charles Lloyd Jones (who acted as convenor when Moses was absent overseas), in addition to those originally invited, J. Metcalfe (principal librarian of the public library of NSW), John Antill, Terence Hunt (supervisor of music, Department of Education), Arthur Davis (Musica Viva),

Eric Burnett (concert manager, ABC), Dorothy Helmrich (president, Arts Council of Australia), L. Harris, Hon. Mr Justice Nicholas (president, British Drama League), F. D. Clewlow, Miss P. Mander-Jones (Mitchell librarian), H. Missingham (director National Art Gallery), E. Langker (Royal Art Society), D. Dundas (Society of Artists), Mr A. Morris. Commonwealth Jubilee Celebrations, arts sub-committee – correspondence with state committees, New South Wales [box 3], SP487/1, 18, NAA, Sydney.

23  Report of the Theatre and Pageantry Committee at 22 August 1950, Commonwealth Jubilee celebrations, arts sub-committee – minutes of meetings [box 3], P497/1, 17, NAA, Sydney.

24  C. P. Mountford to Beth Dean and Victor Carell, 6 June 1951, Beth Dean and Victor Carell Papers, Subject file: Research trip – Central Australia, 1949–1953, MLMSS 7804/24/2, SLNSW.

25  Frank Doherty, 'We Discover "Old Australians' Aborigines Cynical about Jubilee"', *The Argus*, 30 January 1951, 2. http://nla.gov.au/nla.news-article23036858.

26  Stephen Gapps, '"Blacking up" for the Explorers of 1951', in *Settler and Creole Reenactment*, ed. Vanessa Agnew, Jonathan Lamb and Daniel Spoth (London: Palgrave Macmillan UK, 2009), 209–10, 17.

27  In correspondence with C. P. Mountford, Laurence Thomas indicated that he was borrowing paintings from the Melbourne Museum, from Elkin and would include photographs of rock art taken on one of Mountford's expeditions. Laurence Thomas to C. P. Mountford, 27 November 1950, The Aboriginal Works [box 14], SP497/1/10, 84, NAA, Sydney.

28  'Jubilee Tour of Queensland Is ... Something of Sentimental Journey for Harold Blair', *Queensland Times*, 4 August 1951, 2 (Daily). http://nla.gov.au/nla.news-article118221373.

29  'Uncle Tom (played by Aboriginal artist) Puts Clock Back', *The Herald*, 23 April 1962, Clipping in Papers of Harold Blair, 1924–1976, MS 8950, NLA.

30  Rex Ingamells, *Conditional Culture*, ed. Ian Tilbrook (Adelaide: F. W. Preece, 1938), 5. Also quoted in David Symons, *Before and after Corroboree: The Music of John Antill* (Farnham: Ashgate, 2015), 30.

31  Clipping (nd) from Folder 2 (1951–72), Papers of Harold Blair, 1924–1976, MS 8950, NLA.

32  'Music of Mirrabee', *The Herald*, 22 February 1952, 7. http://nla.gov.au/nla.news-article246053171; 'Didjeridoo trio', *The Herald*, 15 February 1952, 2. http://nla.gov.au/nla.news-article246046689.

33  Folder 4, Box 1, Papers of Harold Blair, 1924–1976, MS 8950, NLA.

34  Clipping 6 June 1951 in Papers of Harold Blair, 1924–1976, MS 8950, NLA; 'More Hymns May Be Set to Native Chants', *Chronicle*, 12 April 1951, 8. http://nla.gov.au/nla.news-article93921099.

35  'Natives and Whites in Novel Carols', *The Age*, 12 December 1953, 8. http://nla.gov.au/nla.news-article206909469; 'From Distant Ernabella', *Recorder*, 15 March 1954, 1. http://nla.gov.au/nla.news-article96184673; 'Outback Informality for Duke's Tour', *The Australian Women's Weekly*, 28 November 1956, 10. http://nla.gov.au/nla.news-article48072286; Carol Ann Pybus 'We Grew Up this Place': 'Ernabella Mission 1937–1974', PhD (University of Tasmania 2012). http://eprints.utas.edu.au/14683/2/whole-pybus-thesis-2012.pdf.

36  Dorothy Blair recalls that Tucker, the Greens and Briggs were part of the choir. Conversation with Nerida and Dorothy Blair, 7 October 2019, Terrigal, NSW; 'Jolly Swag Man', *The Argus*, 16 January 1957, 3. http://nla.gov.au/nla.news-article71776403.
37  See clippings in Papers of Harold Blair, 1924–1976, MS 8950, NLA.
38  'On Stage and Screen', *The Herald*, 5 October 1950, 23. http://nla.gov.au/nla.news-article244339447.
39  'Left out of Jubilee Ignored, Say Aborigines', *The Argus*, 8 January 1951, 3. http://nla.gov.au/nla.news-article23037389.
40  'Oldest Australians Mourn the Jubilee', *The Argus*, 16 January 1951, 5. http://nla.gov.au/nla.news-article23048214.
41  Conversation with Tiriki Onus, 20 June 2019, Melbourne.
42  'We Discover Old Australians' Aborigines Cynical about Jubilee', *Argus*, 30 January 1951, 2. http://nla.gov.au/nla.news-article23036858.
43  'Ballet Opens Arts Festival', *Weekly Times*, 7 February 1951, 38. http://nla.gov.au/nla.news-article225462617; Sylvia Kleinert, 'An Aboriginal Moomba: Remaking History', *Continuum* 13, no. 3 (1999): 351.
44  'Sundry Shows', *The Bulletin*, 72, no. 3725, 4 July 1951, 19. http://nla.gov.au/nla.obj-518251413.
45  Australian Aboriginal League, *An Aboriginal Moomba 'Out of the Dark'*, Princess Theatre.
46  The full list of performers was: Harold Blair, Georgia Lee (Dulcie Pitt), Margaret Tucker, Eric Onus, Foster Moffat, Fred Foster, Picanninny Pete, The Williams Brothers, Joan and Allan Saunders, Joyce McKinnon, Jacob Chirnside, Merle Davis, Melvina Cooper, Winnie Onus, Eileen Young, Winifred Douglas, Oscar Collins, Larry Leedy, Stanley Nerang, Dick Cobbo, Jack Cobbo, Reg Laurence, Harry Emerson, Tom Walters, George Daisy, Jack Gray, Pete Davis, Mervyn Williams, Lillian Nicholls, Ivy Bucks, Con Edwards, Charlie Williams, Tommy Lavett.
47  Peter Wyllie Johnston, '"Australian-Ness" in Musical Theatre: A Bran Nue Dae for Australia', *Australasian Drama Studies* 45 (2004): 163.
48  'Australian Musical is Good', *Weekly Times*, 22 November 1950, 44. http://nla.gov.au/nla.news-article224926473; Leslie Rees, 'Drama in Sydney', review of *Caroline Chisholm*, George Landen Dann; *The Highwayman*, Edmond Samuels; *Worm's Eye View*, R. Delderfield, *The Australian Quarterly* 23, no. 2 (1951): 126.
49  'Corroboree at Bondi Yulunga', *The Sun*, 18 January 1951, 28 (Late Final Extra). http://nla.gov.au/nla.news-article229190652; 'Hula-hula Bondi style', *The Daily Telegraph*, 27 February 1950, 5. http://nla.gov.au/nla.news-article249000688.
50  'Yulunga Natives Went Bush', *The Daily Telegraph*, 21 February 1950, 7. http://nla.gov.au/nla.news-article248991655.
51  'Champion in the Making', *The Daily Telegraph*, 15 January 1951, 7. http://nla.gov.au/nla.news-article248509588; 'Queen Excited at Boomerang Throwing', *Morning Bulletin*, 15 February 1954, 1. http://nla.gov.au/nla.news-article57283365.
52  'Boomerang Ace Organised Bondi Contests', *The Australian Women's Weekly*, 25 February 1950, 17. http://nla.gov.au/nla.news-article55480501.
53  On history of Palm Island tourist performances and their financial benefit for missions, see Toby Martin, '"Socialist Paradise" or "Inhospitable Island"? Visitor Responses to Palm Island in the 1920s and 1930s', *Aboriginal History* 38 (2014).
54  'Aborigines Might Play Before King', *The Argus*, 22 June 1951, 3. http://nla.gov.au/nla.news-article23066242.

55  'Moomba – Something to Rave About', *The Courier-Mail*, 29 June 1951, 2. http://nla.gov.au/nla.news-article50094479.
56  'Bagot Natives Corroboree', *Northern Standard*, 18 March 1954, 6. http://nla.gov.au/nla.news-article49483308; 'Queen Excited At Boomerang Throwing', *Morning Bulletin*, 15 February 1954, 1. http://nla.gov.au/nla.news-article57283365; 'Only Eleven Days to Go, then Starts', *The Courier-Mail*, 23 January 1954, 2. http://nla.gov.au/nla.news-article50580435; 'Aborigines Camping', *The Advertiser*, 20 March 1954, 12. http://nla.gov.au/nla.news-article47566367. See also Jane Holley Connors, 'The Glittering Thread: The 1954 Royal Tour of Australia' PhD thesis, (University of Technology, 1996).
57  Beth Dean to R. S. Leydin (Acting Administrator), 24 November 1953, Carell, Ruth Elizabeth (Beth Dean) – Research work on Aboriginal Culture – Northern Territory, A452, 1952/473, NAA, Canberra.
58  Proposed Visit of Aboriginal 'Nosepeg' to Sydney, Mrs Victor Carell, F1, 1953/827, NAA, Canberra.
59  'Aborigines Receive Only £3/10/of their £12 Salary', *The Argus*, 6 July 1951, 3. http://nla.gov.au/nla.news-article23070126. Indeed the Queensland government recently settled a class action over wages stolen between 1939 and 1972, 'Indigenous workers receive $190m stolen wages settlement from Queensland government', *The Guardian*, 9 July 2019. www.theguardian.com/australia-news/2019/jul/09/indigenous-workers-receive-190m-stolen-wages-settlement-from-queensland-government, accessed 24 October 2019.
60  Grace Millar, '"We Never Recovered": The Social Cost of the 1951 New Zealand Waterfront Dispute', *Labour History*, no. 108 (2015); Peter Turnbull and David Sapsford, 'Hitting the Bricks: An International Comparative Study of Conflict on the Waterfront', *Industrial Relations* 40, no. 2 (2001).
61  'Aborigines' Stand', *The West Australian*, 21 February 1951, 3. http://nla.gov.au/nla.news-article48184828.
62  Ibid.
63  Box 59 – 90-2-1 Unity Dance Group – Notices & Programmes, Margaret Walker papers MS 8495, NLA.
64  World Festival of Youth passport facilities Berlin Youth Festival, cancellation of passports, K1029, 1951/65/7421, NAA, Perth.
65  Session 2, Oral History, Ray Peckham interviewed by Rob Willis on 21 March and 30 April 2012 in Dubbo, NSW, ORAL TRC 6430, NLA. The role played by Bill Onus in organizing the strikes is attested to by Tiriki Onus, see Interlude, from conversation, 20 June 2019, Melbourne.
66  Session 2, Margaret Walker interviewed by Barbara Blackman, ORAL TRC 1770, nla.obj-215449570, NLA.
67  Box 59 – 90-2-1 Unity Dance Group – Notices & Programmes, Margaret Walker papers MS 8495, NLA.
68  Maryrose Casey, *Creating Frames: Contemporary Indigenous Theatre 1967–1990* (St Lucia: University of Queensland Press, 2004), 24.
69  Typed speech 'Dancing under slavery and feudalism', Box 13, Folder 7, Margaret Walker papers MS 8495, NLA.
70  Notes on the workings of the GDR are included in Walker's diaries from her visit in 1951, suggesting this was very much an education tour, not just a tour of her dance works. Box 11, and Box 13, Folder 6, Margaret Walker papers MS 8495, NLA.

71 Unity Dance Group Bulletin – March 1951, Plastic sleeve marked as 'Pieces 18–19?', Box 59, Margaret Walker papers MS 8495, NLA.
72 'Women Speakers at the Factories', *Tribune*, 13 March 1957, 9. http://nla.gov.au/nla.news-article236321951; 'Australian Artists in Peking', *Tribune*, 10 September 1958, 12. http://nla.gov.au/nla.news-article236323993.
73 See Amanda Harris, 'Pan-Indigenous Encounter in the 1950s: "Ethnic Dancer" Beth Dean', *Australian Historical Studies* 48, no. 3 (2017).
74 Programme for performance of Beth Dean, Victor Carell and Eric Mitchell with the Korumburra Choral Society for the Council of Adult Education, 10 October 1950. Beth Dean and Victor Carell Papers MLMSS 7804/8/3, SLNSW.
75 See, for example, Fidelio 'Dances and Songs', *The West Australian*, 10 January 1951, 4. http://nla.gov.au/nla.news-article48145606.
76 'US Couple took Australiana Overseas', *The Sun*, 6 May 1952. Clipping in Subject File: Overseas tour, 1951–1952, Beth Dean and Victor Carell Papers MLMSS 7804/22/4, SLNSW.
77 Invitations are contained in Beth Dean: correspondence concerning talks, lectures and tutorials, 1951–1988, Beth Dean and Victor Carell Papers MLMSS 7804/1/10, SLNSW.
78 Baldwin Spencer and F. J. Gillen, *The Native Tribes of Central Australia* (London: Macmillan and Co.), 1899.
79 The Oenpelli songs were recorded by Colin Simpson and Ray Giles, but claimed by Mountford. Linda Barwick and Allan Marett, 'Aural Snapshots of Musical Life: The 1948 Recordings', in *Exploring the Legacy of the 1948 Arnhem Land Expedition*, ed. Martin Thomas and Margo Neale (Canberra: ANU E Press, 2011), 358. Mirrie Hill, 'Three Aboriginal Dances', Sydney: Southern Music Publishing, 1950; W. E. Harney and A. P. Elkin, *Songs of the Songmen: Aboriginal Myths Retold* (Melbourne: Cheshire, 1949). On Mirrie Hill's use of Mountford's recordings in orchestral and piano works, see Anthony Linden Jones, 'The Circle of Songs: Traditional Song and the Musical Score to C.P. Mountford's Documentary Films', in *Circulating Cultures: Exchanges of Australian Indigenous Music, Dance and Media*, ed. Amanda Harris (Canberra: ANU Press, 2014). Elkin praised the songs in A. P. Elkin to Alfred Hill 21 September 1950. Elkin's co-author Bill Harney also wrote with praise of *Poor Fellow Me*, W. E. (Bill) Harney to Alfred Hill, 6 September 1950, Hill family – papers, music and pictorial material of Alfred Hill and Mirrie Hill, 1854–1984, MLMSS 6357/5, 531–76, SLNSW.
80 *Poor Fellow Me* was performed in 1950 by Raymond Beatty, 'Farewell Broadcasts by Swing Club Band', *The Manning River Times and Advocate for the Northern Coast Districts of New South Wales*, 23 September 1950, 5. http://nla.gov.au/nla.news-article172829684; and 1955 by Norman Barnes, 'Alfred Hill, The Grand Old Man of Australian Music', *Le Courrier Australien*, 11 February 1955, 6. http://trove.nla.gov.au/newspaper/article/225595938; while Loam's songs were included in some of the early performances by Carell, 'Outstanding Show By Beth Dean', *Camperdown*, 22 September 1950, 7. http://nla.gov.au/nla.news-article23576459; and later became standard items in Harold Blair's repertoire. See also Amanda Harris, 'Indigenising Australian Music: Authenticity and Representation in touring 1950s Art Songs', *Postcolonial Studies*, 23, no. 1 (2020).
81 *Poor Fellow Me* was recorded by baritones Alan Coad in 1951 (Columbia DO-3391) and Igor Gorin (HMV 7EBO-70001) (recordings in NFSA), and Loam's songs were recorded by Enid Conley-Williams in 1946, and Harold Blair in 1960, though he had been singing them since at least 1950, see NFSA title no. 245797 – unreleased recording of Blair singing *Maranoa Lullaby*; *Nananala Kututja*.

82  Victor Carell, Beth Dean and General Motors-Holden's Limited, 'Carrumbo: To Take a Long Journey' (General Motors Holden's Ltd, 1953); Victoria Haskins, 'Beth Dean and the Transnational Circulation of Aboriginal Dance Culture: Gender, Authority and C. P. Mountford', in *Circulating Cultures: Exchanges of Australian Indigenous Music, Dance and Media*, ed. Amanda Harris (Canberra: ANU Press, 2014), 34. Carrumbo contains footage of secret men's ceremony from 15 minutes 41 seconds until 19 minutes 34 seconds. The restricted material was identified in viewings by senior Warlpiri men from Yuendumu Harry Jagamara Nelson, Otto Jungarrayi Simms and Rex Japanangka Granites on 27 February 2018 in Canberra. In collaboration with PAW Media Community Media worker Simon Japangardi Fisher and with the permission of Kate Conti on behalf of the estate of Victor Carell, an edited (unrestricted) version of the film was made (with assistance of PARADISEC), and both restricted and unrestricted versions deposited with PAW Media in Yuendumu for use and viewing by the community.

83  Dean also explicitly stated in this article that she watched films of Mountford's that no woman is permitted to see. 'From Primitive to Ballet', *People*, 12 August 1953, 19. Clipping in Subject file: Research trip – Central Australia, 1949–1953, Beth Dean and Victor Carell Papers MLMSS 7804/24/2, SLNSW. In another article Mountford's films are described as being 'of inestimable value in revealing to the Carells dances which they would personally never have been able to see: sacred and secret dances forbidden to women and shown only to men who have been initiated into the tribe'. F. K. Manzie, 'World to See', *The Australasian Post*, 27 July 1950, 12–13. Subject File: Australian tour, 1950–1951, Beth Dean and Victor Carell Papers MLMSS 7804/8/5, SLNSW.

84  'Running order of programme for Beth Dean' [no event or date specified]. Beth Dean Literary Manuscripts: 'Lectures Beth', Beth Dean and Victor Carell Papers MLMSS 7804/47/2, SLNSW.

85  Beth Dean, *The Many Worlds of Dance* (Sydney: Murray, 1966), 8–9.

86  John Moses, 'Symbolism in Dancing of Beth Dean', *The Sun*, 30 October 1952.

87  'Beth Dean to Dance in Darwin', *Northern Standard*, 11 June 1953, 1. http://nla.gov.au/nla.news-article49483837.

88  See Lesley Head, *Second Nature: The History and Implications of Australia as Aboriginal Landscape* (Syracuse, NY: Syracuse University Press, 2000), 80.

89  The quote in the heading is from Margaret Sutherland's reflection on the context for her tone poem *Haunted Hills* (1950). Sutherland differentiated this work from the 'pastiche' of other contemporary Australianist works – 'this is what Antill did, you see, and that's the mess he made'. Margaret Sutherland interviewed by Mel Pratt for the Mel Pratt collection, 5 April 1972. http://nla.gov.au/nla.obj-214869222.

90  The 1954 staging is the one more commonly discussed by historians. Haebich, *Spinning the Dream*, 308–9, 324–5; Victoria Haskins, 'To Touch the Infinity of a Far Horizon: A Transnational History of Transcultural Appropriation in Beth Dean's Corroboree (1954)', *Australasian Drama Studies* 59 (2011): 24; Haskins, 'Dancing in the Dust: A Gendered History of Indigenising Australian Cultural Identity', in *Intersections: Gender, Race and Ethnicity in Australasian Studies*, ed. Margaret Allen and R. K. Dhawan (New Delhi: Prestige Books, 2007); Haskins, 'Beth Dean and the Transnational Circulation'; Amanda Card, 'From "Aboriginal Dance" to Aboriginals Dancing: The Appropriation of the "Primitive" in Australian Dance 1950–1963', in

*Heritage and Heresy: Green Mill Papers* (Braddon: Australia Dance Council, 1997); Suzanne Spunner, 'Corroboree Moderne', in *Modern Frontier: Aspects of the 1950s in Australia's Northern Territory*, ed. Julie T. Wells, Mickey Dewar and Suzanne Parry (Darwin: Charles Darwin University Press, 2005).
91 *Goorie* is an identifier usually used by Aboriginal people from northern NSW or southern Queensland, *Murri* collectively identifies Aboriginal people from southern Queensland.
92 Exemption Certificates are more commonly known as 'dog tags' among Aboriginal people.
93 Debra Bennet McLean, 'Right of Reply: An Indigenous Perspective of Encounters as a Source of Dialogue', in *Encounters: Meetings in Australian Music: Essays, Images, Interviews*, ed. Vincent Plush, Huib Schippers and Jocelyn Wolfe (South Brisbane: Queensland Conservatorium Research Centre, 2005), 7.
94 Margaret Sutherland interviewed by Mel Pratt for the Mel Pratt collection, 5 April 1972, ORAL TRC 121/31. http://nla.gov.au/nla.obj-214869222, NLA.
95 Penberthy alluded to commissions Antill and Scultorpe had received in James Penberthy to Stefan Haag, 25 September 1966, Divider – Commissioning Funds Contd. – Opera, Box 53 66/6, Records of Australian Elizabethan Theatre Trust, MS 5908, NLA.
96 James Penberthy to Robert Quentin, 10 October 1958, Correspondence 1955–66 with the Elizabethan Theatre Trust, Box 2, James Penberthy papers, MS 9748, NLA.
97 Correspondence 1955–66 with the Elizabethan Theatre Trust, Box 2, James Penberthy papers, MS 9748, NLA.
98 Robert Quentin to Penberthy, 30 May 1956, Correspondence 1955–66 with the Elizabethan Theatre Trust, Box 2, James Penberthy papers, MS 9748, NLA.
99 James Penberthy to Robert Quentin (general manager, Elizabethan Opera, Sydney), 10 October 1958, Correspondence 1955–66 with the Elizabethan Theatre Trust, Box 2, James Penberthy papers, MS 9748, NLA.
100 H. Drake-Brockman, 'Life and Letters', *The West Australian*, 29 November 1952, 17. http://nla.gov.au/nla.news-article49066252.
101 Ted Shawn to Keith [John Ewers] 4 March 1953, 5459A/405 Shawn, Ted, John Ewers Papers mn1870, SLWA.
102 'Aboriginal Theatricals', *The Lockhart Review and Oaklands Advertiser*, 3 February 1953, 3. http://nla.gov.au/nla.news-article138771084.
103 Note that 'Moomba' here is the annual Melbourne public festival that used the word Bill Onus suggested, but otherwise had no link to the *Aboriginal Moomba*. Harold Blair, 'They will appear in Moomba' [Likely presented at 3AR 18 February 1957], Papers of Harold Blair, 1924–1976 [manuscript] – MS 8950, NLA.

# Chapter 5

1 Programme of 'Aboriginal Theatre', Ephemera (PROMPT), NLA.
2 As reported by Allan Brissenden and Keith Glennon based on their memories of seeing the show. Alan Brissenden and Keith Glennon, *Australia Dances: Creating Australian Dance 1945–1965* (Kent Town: Wakefield Press, 2010), 236.

3   'Stars of their Dreaming', *Sun Herald*, 8 December 1963. Clipping in folder 'Aboriginal Art, 1948–1969' Group Exhibitions, Press Reviews, Conferences, Art Gallery of NSW Library, Sydney. I am indebted to Matt Poll for discussions that have fed into this research, also presented in our collaborative paper: Amanda Harris and Matt Poll (2018) 'Aboriginal Performances and Touring Art Works under Assimilation', *Australian Historical Association Conference*, Australian National University, Canberra, 3–6 July 2018.

4   The North Australian Eisteddfod began in 1957, but after its first few years of operation, added categories specifically for Aboriginal performance.

5   The inaugural meeting between the Australian Board of Missions and the Church Missionary Society occurred on 27 July 1956 with the first Aborigines Observance Day to follow on 12 July 1957. Jonathan Bollen and Anne Brewster, 'NADOC and the National Aborigines Day in Sydney, 1957–67', *Aboriginal History* 42, no. 3 (2018): 6.

6   Department of Territories and National Aborigines' Day Observance Committee, *Our Aborigines – Prepared under the Authority of the Minister for Territories with the Co-Operation of the Ministers Responsible for Aboriginal Welfare in the Australian States* (Canberra: Govt. Printer, 1957).

7   Bollen and Brewster, 'NADOC and the National Aborigines Day', 8.

8   Joyce Rogalsky 'National Aborigines Day Observance Committee: New South Wales Annual Report for 1961', *Dawn* 10, no. 11 (November 1961): 16.

9   The full membership of the talent quest committee was John Antill, Dr Keith Barry, William James, Godfrey Stirling, Ruth Ladd, Elizabeth Todd, Rev. T. D. Noffs, Rev. R. Warren, Mrs D. Rogalsky, Mrs L. Cocks, Mrs J. M. Moyle and Dr Ruth Fink. L. H. Cocks to Alice Moyle, 27 February 1962, Alice Moyle Collection, MS 3501, AIATSIS.

10  The photos of performers in the event accompanied an article in *Dawn* recounting Minister Kelly's address 'We cannot rush … Assimilation is Gradual', *Dawn* 10, no. 7 (July 1961): 1–4.

11  Ibid., 4.

12  Rogalsky, 'National Aborigines Day Observance Committee', 17.

13  'Aborigines Remembered', *Dawn* 9, no. 7 (July 1960): 1.

14  A. W. Grant papers relating to NADOC and Aboriginal Welfare, MLMSS 4265, SLNSW.

15  Featuring Jimmy Little, Dandy Devine, Betty Fisher, Claude (Candy) Williams, Freddie Little and Noel Stanley. Programme for the All Coloured Show, Mascot Town Hall, 23 August 1963, SLNSW.

16  Kerry Yates, 'Revue is Truly All-Australian', *The Australian Women's Weekly*, 17 July 1963, 12. http://nla.gov.au/nla.news-article51392997; Bollen and Brewster, 'NADOC and the National Aborigines Day', 20–1.

17  'Beulah Circuit Named in Honour of our Lorna', *Forbes Advocate*, 29 June 2015. www.forbesadvocate.com.au/story/3178157/beulah-circuit-named-in-honour-of-our-lorna, accessed 23 September 2019; 'Porgy and Bess', *The Australian Women's Weekly*, 1 December 1965, 3. http://nla.gov.au/nla.news-article48078237.

18  Clinton Walker, *Buried Country: The Story of Aboriginal Country Music* (Sydney: Pluto Press, 2000), 84.

19  'Nightingale Sang in Martin Place', *Dawn* 11, no. 8 (August 1962): 4.

20  Ibid., 3.

21  'She's a Cheerful, Singing Crusader', *Dawn* 12, no. 9 (September 1963): 8.

22  Pavilion of Australia, Expo 67 in Montreal, http://expo67.ncf.ca/expo_australia_p1.html, accessed 24 September 2019; The Australian Pavilion was called 'From Stone Age to Space Age', 'Australia on show at Expo 67', *The Australian Women's Weekly* 24 May 1967, 8. http://nla.gov.au/nla.news-article47591135; Clipping, Letter to the Editor: 'Boomerang Throwing for New Australians', 13 November 1967 [paper not recorded] in A. W. Grant papers relating to NADOC and Aboriginal Welfare, MLMSS 4265, SLNSW.
23  National Aborigines' Day Observance Committee (Australia) (1964), MS 3677, NLA; 'Aborigine for Montreal Plan', *The Canberra Times*, 9 July 1966, 26. http://nla.gov.au/nla.news-article107881079.
24  Bollen and Brewster, 'NADOC and the National Aborigines Day', 27.
25  'W.B. Entries for North Australian Eisteddfod – 1963', F1, 1962/3776, NAA, Darwin.
26  'A "new look" for Eisteddfod', *NT News*, 24 October 1971, Clipping in 'N.T. Darwin Eisteddfod', F941, 1971/261, NAA, Darwin.
27  Ted Evans noted that Aboriginal solo dances were 'by far the most popular with the audience' at the 1964 eisteddfod, Evans to Haag 15 July 1964, Divider – Aboriginal Theatre, Box 46, Folder 65/12, Records of Australian Elizabethan Theatre Trust MS 5908, NLA; A memo from the Welfare Branch to all Superintendents and District welfare officers in Darwin, Katherine, Tennant Creek and Alice Springs in 1963 noted that 'The success of the aboriginal contests at the last Eisteddfod was remarkable and it is hoped that at least that standard is maintained and even improved'. 'W.B. Entries for North Australian Eisteddfod – 1963', F1, 1962/3776, NAA, Darwin.
28  Thanks to Colin Worumbu Ferguson and Jordan Ashley for identifying Rusty Moreen in the film. Lee Robinson, *In Song and Dance*, Film Australia, 1964, courtesy of NFSA.
29  National Aborigines' Day Observance Committee (Australia) (1964), MS 3677, NLA.
30  'Education the Key: Slogan for National Aborigines' Day', *Dawn* 15, no. 8 (August 1966): 5.
31  Harry Giese remembers that the numbers became so large that the Welfare Board decided that kitchens had to be set up and people accommodated at the showgrounds. Harry Giese Oral History, NTRS 226 TS 755, NTA, Darwin, Tape 18, transcript p. 4.
32  C. C. Allom for L. N. Penhall, district welfare officer to the director 1968 eisteddfod, 27 May 1968, N.T. Darwin eisteddfod, F941, 1968/141, NAA, Darwin.
33  Ted Evans to Haag 6 October 1965, Divider – Aust. Aborigines, Box 58, Folder 66/18, Records of Australian Elizabethan Theatre Trust MS 5908, NLA; Tape 3, Side A, E. C. Evans Oral History, recorded in 1982, NTRS 219, NTA.
34  See also Dunbar-Hall and Gibson's discussion (following Ellis) of hymns as a continuation of the sacred function of music in the cultural practice of many Aboriginal people. Peter Dunbar-Hall and Chris Gibson, *Deadly Sounds, Deadly Places: Contemporary Aboriginal Music in Australia* (Sydney: UNSW Press, 2004), 42.
35  Interview with Jacinta Tipungwuti and others on 16 March 2019, Sydney while watching and listening to film, Lee Robinson, *In Song and Dance*, Film Australia, 1964, courtesy NFSA.
36  A 1963 letter from Harry Giese to Stefan Haag suggests he is writing to follow up on the latter's discussions with Coombs about the possibility of touring some dancers from the NT. H. C. Giese to Haag n.d. (1963), Folder 63/11 Correspondence A-B, Records of Australian Elizabethan Theatre Trust, MS 5908, NLA. Late in life Harry Giese's account of this had been revised to suggest he had lobbied Coombs before

any approach was made, his daughter Diana Giese's account reinforces this. Harry Giese, 'Planning a Program for Aborigines in the 1950s', in *Occasional Papers No. 16* (Darwin: Northern Territory Library Service 1990); Diana Giese, 'One Fabulous Night Only: Entertaining the Territory', in *Occasional Paper* (Darwin: Northern Territory Library, 2008). Harry Giese's account in his oral history recorded between 1987 and 1994 is more circumspect, claiming 'it was decided' that a performing group might be sent on tour outside of the Northern Territory to 'get the people in the rest of Australia to get some understanding of what Aboriginal culture was all about'. Giese also asserted that when first appointed as director of welfare for the Northern Territory Administration in 1954, he did not know much about Aboriginal people and so was guided by Ted Evans. Harry Giese Oral History, NTRS 226 TS 755, NTA, Darwin, Tape 18, transcript p. 4 and Tape 10, transcript p. 11.

37  Executive Director's Progress Report, 12 August 1963 [Stephan Haag], Box 48 1965/17 Correspondence Administration Executive Directors reports 1957–60, Records of Australian Elizabethan Theatre Trust, MS 5908, NLA.

38  The songmakers, musicians and dancers in this ensemble included: (from Daly River) Frank Artu Dumoo, Barney Munggin, Skipper Anggilidji, Sugar Garbat, Margaret Didji, (from Yirrkala) Narritjan, Mau, Deimbalibu, Warrini, Darqual, Dungala, Mungalili, Barngil, Yangarin, Junmal Djergujergu, Mulun, Dulainga, Bokara, Garmali, Riki, Roy Dadayna, Wadaymu, Dundiwoi, Jayila, (from Bathurst Island) Christopher Tipungwuti, Bennie Tipungwuti, Valentine Pauitjimi, Daniel Pauitjimi, Barry Puruntatameri, Noel Pauntalura, Declan Napuatimi, Conrad Paul Tipungwuti, Freddie Puruntatameri, Matthew Woneamini, Eddie Puruntatameri, Walter Kerinaiua, Hector Tipungwuti, Felix Kantilla, Raphael Napuatimi, Justin Puruntatameri, Timothy Polipuamini. Press Release: '45 Aborigines to arrive on Sunday for Sydney Presentation', 28 November 1963, Box 51, Folder 66/1 (Administration) Aboriginal Theatre & Exhibition, Records of the Australian Elizabethan Theatre Trust, MS 5908, NLA. Discussion of the choice to include firemakers and women is on Tape 3, Side A, E. C. Evans Oral History, recorded in 1982, NTRS 219, NTA.

39  Sam Passi to Stefan Haag, 11 October 1964, Divider – Aboriginal Theatre, Box 46, Folder 65/12, Records of Australian Elizabethan Theatre Trust MS 5908, NLA. Passi's grandfather had contributed a substantial manuscript to the records of the 1898 Cambridge Expedition led by Haddon, Passi would later collaborate with Eddie Mabo and others to initiate proceedings in the High Court that would eventually overturn the *terra nullius* doctrine in *Mabo v. Queensland* (though Passi had withdrawn from the claim by the time of the decision).

40  Indeed, Haag seems to have been even less inclined to consider Passi's proposal than the proposal of Wolfgang Laade (of the Native Affairs Branch in Thursday Island) who had proposed a group of Torres Strait Islanders to Haag in May 1964; Stefan Haag to Sam Passi, 12 January 1965, and Stefan Haag to Wolfgang Larde, 23 July 1964, ibid.

41  Minutes of the meeting of the board of directors of the AETT 20 January 1964, folder 'Central Administration Meetings', Box 91, Records of Australian Elizabethan Theatre Trust MS 5908, NLA.

42  In part the financial failure seems to have been the lack of international interest in a film made of the *Aboriginal Theatre*, which left the AETT unable to recoup their

investment. Stefan Haag to Harry Giese, 1 March 1965, Divider – Aboriginal Theatre, Box 46, Folder 65/12, Records of Australian Elizabethan Theatre Trust MS 5908, NLA.

43   In a review of the *Aboriginal Theatre* but also criticism of the AETT's late withdrawal of *Henry V* from Perth Festival, A. K. Stout wrote, 'An organisation like the Trust should have one administrative boss and one only. Its Executive Director should be able to give his whole time to forming and supervising the broad policies of the Trust and not get caught up in theatrical production'. A. K. Stout, 'Australian Theatre', *The Australian Quarterly* 36, no. 1 (1964): 122.

44   Interview with Jacinta Tipungwuti and others on 16 March 2019, Sydney while listening to audio recordings 'Songs and dances from Bathurst Island, Yirrkala and Daly River performed at the Aboriginal Theatre in Sydney in 1963', ELIZABETHAN_01, AIATSIS. Quoted with permission. The performers' agency over the music and dance performed is also reinforced by former patrol officer Bill Gray who was present at rehearsals of the Yolngu performers in Yirrkala and later rehearsals in Bagot Community in Darwin before the performers travelled south. Interview with Bill Gray on 1 December 2016, Canberra. Phillippa Deveson's discussion of Narritjin and others as the driving force behind films made with Ian Dunlop through the Yirrkala Film Project also demonstrate Yolngu performers' motivation to document, perform and share culture through diverse media. Philippa Deveson, 'The Agency of the Subject: Yolngu Involvement in the Yirrkala Film Project', *Journal of Australian Studies* 35, no. 2 (2011).

45   Review R. C. [Roger Covell], 'Aboriginal Theatre', *Sydney Morning Herald*, 6 December 1963, clipping in Aboriginal Theatre Foundation 1963–1983, Harry Christian Giese Collection, 15-036-005, ARA.

46   Beth Dean, 'Aboriginal Theatre: An Insight into Native World', *Daily Telegraph*, 6 December 1963. Clipping in Aboriginal Theatre Foundation 1963–1983, Harry Christian Giese Collection, 15-036-005, ARA. For further discussion of how Beth Dean positioned herself as an expert on the authenticity of Aboriginal dance, see Amanda Harris, 'Pan-Indigenous Encounter in the 1950s: "Ethnic Dancer" Beth Dean', *Australian Historical Studies* 48, no. 3 (2017); and 'Indigenising Australian Music: Authenticity and Appropriation in touring 1950s Art Songs', *Postcolonial Studies* (special issue: 'New Directions in Settler Colonial Studies', editors Jane Carey and Ben Silverstein) 23, no. 1 (2020).

47   Philip Gissing, 'Stout, Alan Ker (1900–1983)', Australian Dictionary of Biography, National Centre of Biography, Australian National University. http://adb.anu.edu.au/biography/stout-alan-ker-15921/text27122, accessed 22 February 2019.

48   Stout, 'Australian Theatre', 122.

49   Only some names of performers are printed in the 1966 Darwin Festival programme, but these indicate that at least some of the same people who had travelled to Sydney and Melbourne in 1963 performed there, including Christopher Tipungwuti, Bennie Tipungwuti and Hector Tipungwuti. The fourth performer listed by name was Dermot Tipungwuti, who was not present in 1963. Souvenir programme for Darwin Festival, 23 July–1 August 1966, NT Library, Darwin. In Perth there were only thirty performers from Yirrkala, Bathurst Island and Port Keats (Wadeye) at the Kings Park Tennis Club between 3–11 February 1967, see 'States on the Nation', *Tribune*, 8 February 1967, 4. http://nla.gov.au/nla.news-article237360748.

50  Indeed, they managed a range of events in which Aboriginal people travelled from the NT to southern events to represent Aboriginal culture at agricultural shows and other similar events. See Aborigines Attending Southern Shows – (1963–69), F941/0, 1971/456, NAA, Darwin.
51  Stefan Haag to Ted Evans, 24 September 1965 and Ted Evans to Stefan Haag, 1 October 1965, Divider – Aust. Aborigines, Box 58 66/18, Records of Australian Elizabethan Theatre Trust MS 5908, NLA.
52  Ted Evans to Stefan Haag, 12 November 1964, Divider – Aboriginal Theatre, Box 46, Folder 65/12, Records of Australian Elizabethan Theatre Trust MS 5908, NLA.
53  Minutes of the meeting of the board of directors of the AETT 20 January 1964, folder 'Central Administration Meetings', Box 91, Records of Australian Elizabethan Theatre Trust MS 5908, NLA.
54  John Birman (executive officer, Festival of Perth) to Stefan Haag, 28 November 1966, Box 65 66/35, Divider – Western Australia, Records of Australian Elizabethan Theatre Trust MS 5908, NLA.
55  In collections of Harry Giese's papers in Darwin, the 'Aboriginal Theatre' and 'Aboriginal Theatre Foundation' are collated in a way that supports his conception of the organizations as different phases of the same company, though administratively the two organizations had little in common. Aboriginal Theatre Foundation 1963–83, Harry Christian Giese Collection, 15-036-005, ARA.
56  H. Neil Truscott (for the secretary, Department of External Affairs, Canberra) to Stefan Haag, 4 August 1965, Divider – Aust. Aborigines, Box 58 66/18, Records of Australian Elizabethan Theatre Trust MS 5908, NLA.
57  Stefan Haag to H. C. Giese, 17 June 1965, Divider – Aboriginal Theatre, Box 46, Folder 65/12, Records of Australian Elizabethan Theatre Trust MS 5908, NLA.
58  The full list of performers was Djoli Laiwanga, Paddy Pamagore, Les Merikula, Williw Maljina, Jimmy Balk Balk, David Blanasi, Tommy Wuki Wuki, William Kulangoo, Jimmy Yupawanga, Dick Lingabani, Mick Yiribuma, Billy Lukanau, Jackie Lidju-Unga, John Yeinidi-Wanga, Roger Madaingu, Silver Laiwanga, George Manyita, Peter Manaberu, Johnny Wurungu and Allan Maralung. Programme: 'Pageant of Asia Spectacular', Sydney 1965, NLA.
59  Beth Dean to H. C. Coombs (chairman, Australian Council for the Arts, Sydney), 3 June 1969, Subject file: Ballet of the South Pacific – Correspondence, 1968–1969, Beth Dean and Victor Carell Papers, MLMSS 7804/10/2, SLNSW.
60  Stefan Haag to J. S. Baker (FCAA Preservation of Culture Sub-Committee) 4 April 1966, Divider – Aust. Aborigines, Box 58 66/18, Records of Australian Elizabethan Theatre Trust MS 5908, NLA.
61  Stefan Haag to Ted Evans, 22 September 1964, Box 46, Folder 65/12, Records of Australian Elizabethan Theatre Trust MS 5908, NLA.
62  Ted Evans to Stefan Haag, 15 July 1964, Divider – Aboriginal Theatre, Box 46, Folder 65/12, Records of Australian Elizabethan Theatre Trust MS 5908, NLA.
63  Radhika Natarajan, 'Performing Multiculturalism: The Commonwealth Arts Festival of 1965', *Journal of British Studies* 53, no. 3 (2014): 723.
64  Ian Hunter, 'The Commonwealth Arts Festival'. Journal of the Royal Society of Arts 113/5108 (1965): 608–9.
65  Natarajan has also pointed to the choice of classical (in genres already known outside of India), rather than contemporary traditions to represent India as attempts to minimize the politics of the past. Natarajan, 'Performing Multiculturalism', 706, 717.

66 In a tribute at the recent memorial for Roger Covell, composer Barry Conyngham recalled the significance of this seminar as a landmark moment in Australian composition. Speech to Roger Covell Memorial, 10 September 2019 at Sir John Clancy Auditorium, University of New South Wales. The composers present at the 1963 seminar included Gethen, Ian Harris, Sculthorpe, Sutherland, Hughes, Douglas, Noel Nickson, Werder, Helen Gifford, Antill, Dulcie Holland, Miriam Hyde, Mirrie Hill, Larry Sitsky, George English, Donald Peart, John Hemming, James Penberthy and Roger Covell. Graeme Skinner notes that Richard Meale and Nigel Butterley were notable omissions (Butterley being unable to remember being invited) and Dreyfus and Le Gallienne were unable to make it. Graeme Skinner, *Peter Sculthorpe: The Making of an Australian Composer* (Sydney: UNSW Press, 2015), 284.

67 In the case of the AETT, both kinds of production were supported, while the AETT were producing the *Aboriginal Theatre*, they were also bringing together Peter Sculthorpe and Patrick White with the aim of commissioning an opera on the story of Eliza Fraser and her time spent with Aboriginal people after surviving a shipwreck. Correspondence administration executive directors reports 1957–60, Box 48 1965/17, Records of Australian Elizabethan Theatre Trust MS 5908, NLA.

68 Reviews of the concerts do not mention *Corroboree*, but it was named in the AETT's published *Trust News* in the month of the festival as one of the Australian works on the programme for concerts in London, Cardiff, Glasgow and Liverpool. 'Commonwealth Arts Festival – 1965', *Trust News*, September (1965), 2. www.thetrust.org.au/pdf/trust-news/TN_1965_09_010.pdf.

69 Low has shown how the Commonwealth Arts Festival coincided with Britain's disinvestment from its former empire and turn towards Europe and the United States. It could be argued that it was this turn that Australia sought to be part of, to distinguish itself as not just another colony. See Gail Low, 'At Home? Discoursing on the Commonwealth at the 1965 Commonwealth Arts Festival', *The Journal of Commonwealth Literature* 48, no. 1 (2013): 108.

70 In the printed account of this lecture, Glass was prompted by the chair to comment whether Aboriginal music was being preserved, and conceded that 'musical aborigines' like Harold Blair 'might be a new hope for the aborigine music … It is very primitive, as you heard, but it has its own interest, and it may be among the aborigines themselves there will be enthusiasts, singers and instrumentalists, who will give the world the music of their bull-roarers and didjeridoos and their tribal chants. So we must not despair of the loss of this aborigine music yet'. Dudley Glass, 'Australia's Contribution to Music', *Journal of the Royal Society of Arts* 111, no. 5080 (1963): 307, 311.

71 H. C. Giese to Mr W. A. Judges (Reserve Bank of Australia), 9 July 1964, Box 46, Folder 65/12, Divider – Aboriginal Theatre, Records of Australian Elizabethan Theatre Trust MS 5908, NLA.

72 See Chapter 7 for further theorization of replacement as articulated by Lorenzo Veracini, *The Settler Colonial Present* (London: Palgrave Macmillan, 2015).

73 The broadcast also included another of their collaborative ballets *G'day Digger*. NFSA item number 371018, research copy obtained from ABC Archives: Accession number 165621.

74 Beth Dean and Victor Carell, *Gentle Genius: A Life of John Antill* (Sydney: Akron Press, 1987), 160.

75  Subject File: 'Pageant of Nationhood' 1963–1964, Beth Dean and Victor Carell Papers, MLMSS 7804/22/5, SLNSW.
76  'This Valley Must Die!', *Dawn*, August 1953, 16–17.
77  Jim Smith, 'Aboriginal Voters in the Burragorang Valley, NSW, 1869–1953', *Journal of the Royal Australian Historical Society* 98, no. 2 (2012): 189; 'Doomed Valley', *The Sun-Herald*, 19 December 1954, 24. http://nla.gov.au/nla.news-article12639597; see also Fox Movietone, '36 Million PDS Dam Goes into Service Warragamba', 20 October 1961, title no. 129646, NFSA.
78  Programme for this performance at the Royal Agricultural Society Showground in Sydney held in John Antill EPHEMERA Prompt, NLA.
79  Fifteen performers from Arnhem Bay and Caledon Bay performed a corroboree for the Queen during her visit to Darwin. 'Queen Calls On "Leper Hunter"', *The Canberra Times*, 19 March 1963, 3. http://nla.gov.au/nla.news-article104591325.
80  Initial comments in review: Roger Covell, 'Aboriginal Theatre', *Sydney Morning Herald*, 4 March 1963; 'diffuse and pointless' comes from: Roger Covell, *Australia's Music: Themes of a New Society* (Melbourne: Sun Books, 1967), 57. Also quoted in David Symons, '*Corroboree* and After: John Antill as a "One-Work Composer"?', *Musicology Australia* 34, no. 1 (2012).
81  See also Maryrose Casey, *Creating Frames: Contemporary Indigenous Theatre 1967–1990* (St Lucia: University of Queensland Press, 2004).
82  Covell, *Australia's Music*, 155. Antill was commissioned to compose the soundtrack for another commemorative piece in 1963 – a film *The Land that Waited*, broadcast on the ABC on 26 January 1963, which tells a story of British dominance of the Australian landscape. Drought Productions 'The Land that Waited', 1963, title no. 43839, NFSA. See also 'Settlement of Australia', *The Canberra Times*, 26 January 1963. http://nla.gov.au/nla.news-article104257317; and Dean and Carell, *Gentle Genius*, 159–60.
83  Dean and Carell, *Gentle Genius*, 163. Also quoted in David Symons, *Before and after Corroboree: The Music of John Antill* (Farmham: Ashgate, 2015), 127.
84  Symons, *Before and after Corroboree*, 108. Though, in 1973 Antill composed the fanfare *Jubugalee* (name of the site at Bennelong Point on which the Opera House is situated) for the opening of Sydney Opera House.
85  Dean and Carell, *Gentle Genius*, 162.
86  Alice Moyle to Peter Sculthorpe, 26 June 1963, Alice Moyle Collection, MS 3501, AIATSIS.
87  David Horton, ed., *The Encyclopaedia of Aboriginal Australia: Aboriginal and Torres Strait Islander History, Society and Culture* (Canberra: Aboriginal Studies Press, 1994). The Australian National Dictionary defines 'corroboree' as 'An Aboriginal dance ceremony, of which song and rhythmical musical accompaniment are an integral part, and which may be sacred and ritualized or secular, occasional, and informal' likely derived from the Dharug language, and appearing in early written records of the Sydney language. www.australiannationaldictionary.com.au/oupnewindex1.php, accessed 22 February 2019.
88  Paul Carter, *The Sound in Between: Voice, Space, Performance* (Kensington, NSW: NSW University Press, 1992), 169.

## Chapter 6

1. Among Asher Joel's (director of the Bicentenary Celebrations) papers in the Mitchell library are two folders of newspaper clippings of equal thickness. One is labelled 'Re-enactment of Cook's Landing Kurnell' (with at least half the articles featuring a stunt by University of Sydney students whose 'Captain Chook' managed to stage the landing ahead of the official party), the other is a folder entitled 'Aboriginal Protest'. II. Files of photocopies of news cuttings concerning the Bicentenary, 1970, MLK 376, Sir Asher Joel – papers, 1953–1970, MLMSS 3284, MLOH 3, SLNSW.
2. Slogan of Federal Council for the Advancement of Aborigines and Torres Strait Islanders (FCAATSI) on campaign posters for the referendum on 27 May 1967. SLSA. *Right Wrongs: Marking the 50th anniversary of the 1967 Referendum.* Online exhibition, 21 August 2017, SLSA. https://digital.collections.slsa.sa.gov.au/nodes/view/2743, accessed 21 May 2019.
3. Gary Williams speaking about the 1967 referendum on 27 May 2007 for *Al Jazeera*, YouTube. www.youtube.com/watch?v=V-vX5kNpyLU, accessed 11 September 2019.
4. Rodney Hall, interview, 'The Fair Go: Winning the 1967 Referendum', ABC Television, 1999, quoted in Bain Attwood and Andrew Markus, *The 1967 Referendum: Race, Power and the Australian Constitution* (Canberra: Aboriginal Studies Press, 2007), 57.
5. Maryrose Casey, *Creating Frames: Contemporary Indigenous Theatre 1967–1990* (St Lucia: University of Queensland Press, 2004).
6. Interestingly, though Peart and Sitsky agreed that the emerging Australian 'school' could be characterized as post-Webernian, Peart also saw John Cage as a major influence (especially on Richard Meale), while Sitsky asserted that contemporary American music, including Cage, had made little impact on the Australian school. Donald Peart, 'The Australian Avant-Garde', *Proceedings of the Royal Musical Association* 93, no. 1 (1966); Larry Sitsky, 'Australia: Emergence of the New Music in Australia', *Perspectives of New Music* 4, no. 1 (1965); James Murdoch, *Australia's Contemporary Composers* (Melbourne: Sun Books, 1972).
7. See, for example, compelling reframings of composers working in modern idioms: Catherine Bowan, 'Wild Men and Mystics: Rethinking Roy Agnew's Early Sydney Works', *Musicology Australia* 30 (2008); Graeme Skinner, 'Australian Musical First Modernism', in *The Modernist World*, ed. Stephen Ross and Allana C. Lindgren (Abingdon: Routledge, 2015).
8. Roger Covell, *Australia's Music: Themes of a New Society* (Melbourne: Sun Books, 1967), 33–63, 71–87.
9. The Australian Music Centre's tribute commemorates Covell as author of 'the first major study of the history, development and performance of Western classical music in Australia'. Australian Music Centre 'Roger Covell, 1931–2019', 4 June 2019. www.australianmusiccentre.com.au/article/roger-covell-1931-2019, accessed 7 June 2019. This account was echoed by Liz Bradtke's 'Vale: Roger Covell', email circulated to Fellows of the Academy of Humanities, 5 June 2019. Roger was professor of music at the University of New South Wales during the first years of my own undergraduate music studies there from 1995 to 1996.

10  John Blacking, 'A Common-Sense View of All Music': Reflections on Percy Grainger's Contribution to Ethnomusicology and Music Education (Cambridge: Cambridge University Press, 1987), 152.
11  See Vincent Plush, 'Roger Covell: The Go-Between', *Context* 41 (2016).
12  Covell, *Australia's Music*, 193, 203.
13  Ibid., 72.
14  Ibid., 201.
15  The melody, part of Maraian ceremonies in central Arnhem Land, was called *djilili* and recorded by Elkin at Mainoru in 1949, although Sculthorpe later stated that it was *djilile* recorded in the late 1950s. The spelling is restored by Michael Hannan who transcribed the melody used by Sculthorpe. A. P. Elkin, 'Arnhem Land Music (Part 3)', *Oceania* 25, no. 4 (1955): 331; 'Maraian at Mainoru, 1949: I. Description', *Oceania* 31, no. 4 (1961): 284; Michael Hannan, 'Scoring *Essington*: Composition, Comprovisation, Collaboration', *Screen Sound* 2 (2011): 51.
16  W. L. Hoffmann, 'Life Style', *The Canberra Times*, 5 October 1971, 15. http://nla.gov.au/nla.news-article110680425.
17  Reuben Brown et al., 'Dialogues with the Archives: Arrarrkpi Responses to Recordings as Part of the Living Song Tradition of Manyardi', in *Preservation, Digital Technology & Culture* (2018), 104.
18  Tim Rowse, *Indigenous and Other Australians since 1901* (Sydney: UNSW Press, 2017), 142.
19  Recent travelling performances include *11th Symposium on Indigenous Music and Dance*, Australian National University, Canberra, 1–2 December 2012, at the Wilin Centre, University of Melbourne, 26–9 November 2018, 17th Symposium on Indigenous Music and Dance, Edith Cowan University, Perth, 6–9 December 2018, International Council for Traditional Music, Bangkok, 11–17 July 2019.
20  Covell, *Australia's Music*, 290.
21  Beth Dean to Lloyd Edmonds, 14 October 1967, Subject file: 'Kukaitcha. Technical Papers, Letters etc.', 1967–1969 correspondence, Beth Dean and Victor Carell Papers, MLMSS 7804/19/5, SLNSW.
22  Dean to His Excellency Eugenie de Anzorena, Ambassador of Mexico, 4 November 1967, Subject file: 'Kukaitcha. Technical Papers, Letters etc.', 1967–1969 correspondence, Beth Dean and Victor Carell Papers, MLMSS 7804/19/5, SLNSW.
23  'NT Aborigine for London TV', *The Canberra Times*, 29 March 1967, 12. http://nla.gov.au/nla.news-article107034135; 'Spears Fly at TV Viewers', *The Canberra Times*, 3 April 1967, 6. http://nla.gov.au/nla.news-article131647361.
24  Beth Dean, 'Aboriginal Theatre: An Insight Into Native World', *Daily Telegraph*, 6 December 1963. Transcript of review retained in Divider – Aboriginal Theatre, Box 46 Folder 65–12, Records of Australian Elizabethan Theatre Trust MS 5908, NLA. Photos of Yangarin, Nalakan and Mungali performing for school children accompany those of Yangarin numbered AR00019.012.084 and AR00019.012.104 in the Beth Dean Carell collection no. 1, NMA. http://collectionsearch.nma.gov.au/object/178950.
25  Beth Dean to Alice Moyle, 1 March 1968, Subject file: 'Kukaitcha. Technical Papers, Letters etc.', 1967–1969 Correspondence, Beth Dean and Victor Carell Papers, MLMSS 7804/19/5, SLNSW.
26  Beth Dean to His Excellency Dudley McCarthy, Ambassador to Mexico, 26 February 1968, Subject file: 'Kukaitcha. Technical Papers, Letters etc.', 1967–1969 Correspondence, Beth Dean and Victor Carell Papers, MLMSS 7804/19/5, SLNSW.

27  Victor Carell, *Naked We Are Born* (Sydney: Ure Smith, 1960).
28  Baldwin Spencer and F. J. Gillen, *The Native Tribes of Central Australia* (London: Macmillan and Co., 1899).
29  Notebook in Subject file: 'Kukaitcha. Technical Papers, Letters etc.', 1967–1969, MLMSS 7804/19/6, SLNSW.
30  Stefan Haag to H. C. Giese, 27 May 1968, 'International Exhibition Expo 70 Osaka Japan – Aboriginal Dance Ensemble F1', 1968/3396, NAA, Darwin.
31  B. G. Dexter for director (Prime Minister's Department of Aboriginal Affairs, Canberra) to F. D. McCarthy (AIAS), 19 August 1968, International Exhibition Expo 70 Osaka Japan – Aboriginal Dance Ensemble F1, 1968/3396, NAA, Darwin.
32  B. G. Dexter, to the Commissioner-General (Australian Exhibit Organisation for Expo 70, Canberra), 16 September 1968, International Exhibition Expo 70 Osaka Japan – Aboriginal Dance Ensemble F1, 1968/3396, NAA, Darwin.
33  Marjorie Oakes (Mrs W. F. Oakes) to Rear Admiral T. K. Morrison, 6 August 1969, International Exhibition Expo 70 Osaka Japan – Aboriginal Dance Ensemble F1, 1968/3396, NAA, Darwin.
34  Linda Barwick and Allan Marett, 'Aural Snapshots of Musical Life: The 1948 Recordings', in *Exploring the Legacy of the 1948 Arnhem Land Expedition*, ed. Martin Thomas and Margo Neale (Canberra: ANU E Press, 2011); Sally Treloyn, 'Cross and Square: Variegation in the Transmission of Songs and Musical Styles between the Kimberley and Daly Regions of Northern Australia', in *Circulating Cultures: Exchanges of Australian Indigenous Music, Dance and Media*, ed. Amanda Harris (Canberra: ANU Press, 2014); Myfany Turpin, 'Return of a Travelling Song: Wanji-wanji in the Pintupi Region of Central Australia', in *Archival Returns: Central Australia and Beyond*, ed. Linda Barwick, Jennifer Green and Petronella Vaarzon-Morel (Sydney: Sydney University Press, 2020), 239–62.
35  Father M. Sims to E. C. Evans, 24 November 1969, 'International Exhibition Expo 70 Osaka Japan – Aboriginal Dance Ensemble F1', 1968/3396, NAA, Darwin.
36  E. C. Evans to Father M. Sims, 12 November 1969, 'International Exhibition Expo 70 Osaka Japan – Aboriginal Dance Ensemble F1', 1968/3396, NAA, Darwin.
37  The full list of performers named in the NAA (Darwin) records are Dhambuljawa Burarrwanga, Rrikin Burarrwanga, Mulun Yunupingu, Wulurrk Mununggurr, Banambi Wunungmurra, Justin Purantatamiri, Max Kerinaiua, Henry Kerinaiua, David Gulpilil, Dick Budalil, Talbert Jalkarara, Djoli Laiwanga, David Blanasi, Felix Wambunyi, Lawrence Biellum.
38  'Expo dancers Will Continue', *News*, 18 May 1970, clipping in International Exhibition Expo 70 Osaka Japan – Aboriginal Dance Ensemble F1, 1968/3396, NAA, Darwin.
39  President's Report 1969–1971, p. 6, 'Aboriginal Theatre Foundation 1963–1983', Harry Christian Giese Collection, 15-036-005, ARA.
40  Aboriginal Theatre Foundation 1963–1983, Harry Christian Giese Collection, 15-036-005, ARA. Giese recalled that Coombs had pushed for the foundation to be Aboriginal run, though he (Giese) had believed there would be benefits in retaining the expertise of the non-Indigenous members, Side A, Tape Eighteen, Harry Giese Oral History, NTRS 226 TS 755, NTA.
41  Sally Treloyn has documented the transfer of *balga* song traditions between the Kimberley and Daly region in which songs have been traded over hundreds of kilometres (since at least the 1940s, but likely earlier), Treloyn, 'Cross and Square'. On *wangga* and *lirrga* transmission, see also Allan Marett, *Songs, Dreamings, and Ghosts: The Wangga of North Australia* (Middletown, Conn.: Wesleyan University Press, 2005), 230–1.

42  Rosita Henry, 'Engaging with History by Performing Tradition: The Poetic Politics of Indigenous Australian Festivals', in *The State and the Arts: Articulating Power and Subversion*, ed. Judith Kapferer (New York: Berghahn Books, 2008), 57.
43  Other cultural festivals begun in the most recent two decades have developed into more pedagogical models that aim to educate settler Australians like Garma (Yolngu lands near Nhulunbuy) see Lisa Slater, *Anxieties of Belonging in Settler Colonialism: Australia, Race and Place*, 1st edn, Routledge Studies in Cultural History (Boca Raton: Routledge, 2018), 88; Peter Phipps, 'Globalization, Indigeneity and Performing Culture', *Local-Global: Identity, Security, Community* 6 (2009): 39), or those strongly oriented in the culture of the host community like Milpirri (Warlpiri lands in Lajamanu) or Mowanjum (Worrorra, Ngarinyin and Wunambal lands in Derby).
44  President's Report 1969–1971, 'Aboriginal Theatre Foundation 1963–1983', Harry Christian Giese Collection, 15-036-005, ARA.
45  Mary Durack, 'The Aboriginal Theatre Foundation Gets to Work: No Longer Just a Dream', *Identity*, October (1971): 18.
46  Rowse, *Indigenous and Other Australians since 1901*, 142.
47  List compiled by Lance Bennett, Aboriginal Theatre Foundation 1963–1983, Harry Christian Giese Collection, 15-036-005, ARA.
48  Victor Carell to W. C. Wentworth, Minister for Social Services and Aboriginal Affairs 26 May 1969, Carell, Victor – Proposed ballet of the South Pacific, A2354 1969/289, NAA, Canberra.
49  H. C. Coombs, Chairman to W. C. Wentworth 4 June 1969, Carell, Victor – Proposed ballet of the South Pacific, A2354 1969/289, NAA. Funding of $20,000 to establish the Aboriginal Theatre Foundation was matched by the Council for Aboriginal Affairs. Aboriginal Theatre Foundation 1963–1983, Harry Christian Giese Collection, 15-036-005, ARA.
50  Beth Dean to H. C. Coombs, 3 June 1969, Subject file: Ballet of the South Pacific – Correspondence, 1968–1969, Beth Dean and Victor Carell Papers, MLMSS 7804/10/2, SLNSW.
51  H. C. Coombs to Admiral Oldham (director Commonwealth Bi-Centenary Cook Celebrations), 25 July 1969, Carell, Victor – Proposed ballet of the South Pacific, A2354 1969/289, NAA, Canberra.
52  Beth Dean to F. McCarthy, 10 June (1969?), Subject file: Ballet of the South Pacific – Correspondence, 1968–1969, Beth Dean and Victor Carell Papers, MLMSS 7804/10/2, SLNSW.
53  Beth Dean Carell to W. C. Wentworth, 23 September 1969 and H. C. Coombs to Beth Dean, 10 September 1969, Carell, Victor – Proposed ballet of the South Pacific, A2354 1969/289, NAA, Canberra.
54  'NT Theatre Foundation Shuns Cook Celebrations', *Northern Territory News*, 14 February 1970, clipping in Carell, Victor – Proposed ballet of the South Pacific A2354 1969/289, NAA, Canberra.
55  Leslie Greener to Beth Dean and Victor Carell, 28 February 1970, Letters received from Leslie Greener Beth Dean and Victor Carell Papers, 1953–1970, MLMSS 7804/3/2, SLNSW.
56  'Aborigines' Ban Won't Stop Cook Ceremony', *Daily Telegraph*, 7 February 1970; 'They Won't Dance for Captain Cook', *Sydney Morning Herald*, 19 February 1970. Clippings in Folder 'Aboriginal Protest', II. Files of photocopies of news cuttings concerning

the Bicentenary, 1970, MLK 376, Sir Asher Joel – papers, 1953–1970, MLMSS 3284, MLOH 3, SLNSW. 'Land Rights Vigil', *The Canberra Times*, 25 April 1970, 2. http://nla.gov.au/nla.news-article107921778. Multiple articles about the protests appeared in the *Tribune* and *Woroni*.

57 'Ballet of the South Pacific', *The Australian Women's Weekly*, 1 April 1970, 25. http://nla.gov.au/nla.news-article47814074. *Ballet of the South Pacific* also toured to Canberra Theatre 24–5 April 1970, see Canberra Theatre Centre Ephemera at the ACT Heritage Library. Maori performers had originally been included, but had to pull out due to lack of government support. Report Australian Tour of the Ballet of the South Pacific April/May 1970, Subject file: Ballet of the South Pacific – Reports, Statements of Account and related papers, Beth Dean and Victor Carell Papers, MLMSS 7804/10/4, SLNSW.

58 Kalissa Alexeyeff, *Dancing from the Heart: Movement, Gender, and Sociality in the Cook Islands* (Honolulu: University of Hawaii Press, 2009), 52; Aboriginal Theatre Foundation 1963–1983, Harry Christian Giese Collection, 15-036-005, ARA.

59 The full cast of Australian performers was Irene Babui, Regina Portaminni, Simon Tipungwuti, Mathew Wonaeamirri, Edward Puruntatameri, Leon Puruntatameri, Frederick Nanganarralil, William Calder Nalagandi, Jackson Jacob, Larry Lanley, Gordon Watt, Arthur Roughsey, Yangarin Kumana, Nalakan Wanambi, Munguli Monangurr, Cyril Ninnal. Programme for Ballet of South Pacific, Subject file: Ballet of the South Pacific – Programs and Posters, Beth Dean and Victor Carell Papers, MLMSS 7804/10/7, SLNSW.

60 Victor Carell to Ted Shawn, 27 September 1970, Subject File: Ted Shawn, 1947; 1968–84, Beth Dean and Victor Carell Papers, MLMSS 7804/25/2, SLNSW.

61 The women were Tiwi in 1970, not the Daly Region women of 1963. Regina Portaminni and Irene Babui danced a medley of women's dances, Programme of *Ballet of the South Pacific* in James Cook M Ephemera – Box 2 – (1900–), SLNSW; and Richard Beattie, 'Aboriginal Girls to Dance in Sydney', *Sydney Morning Herald*, 21 March 1970, clipping in Carell, Victor – Proposed ballet of the South Pacific, A2354 1969/289, NAA, Canberra.

62 Frank Harris, 'Native Drummers Stir the Crowd', *Daily Mirror*, 7 April 1970, clipping in Carell, Victor – Proposed ballet of the South Pacific, A2354 1969/289, NAA, Canberra.

63 Sir Asher Joel, producer of the 1970 Cook bicentenary re-enactment events also became chairman of the citizens official opening committee for the Opera House. Much earlier in his career he had been involved with staging the 1938 First Fleet re-enactments. Joel and the general manager of the Sydney Opera House, S. L. Bacon, had also travelled to Fiji for the South Pacific Festival of Arts in 1972. Statement on Sydney Opera House Opening Night and Festival Fortnight, September 1972, Sydney Opera House – Official Opening – Festival Fortnight – Commonwealth assistance, A3753, 1972/1679, NAA, Canberra.

64 Programme for Royal Concert; Captain Cook Bi-Centenary Citizens Committee Report 26 May 1969, Box 2, James Cook M Ephemera, SLNSW.

65 Stephen Alomes, *When London Calls: The Expatriation of Australian Creative Artists to Britain* (Cambridge: Cambridge University Press, 1999), 146.

66 Peggy van Praagh to Beth Dean, 6 June 1969, 'Notes & letters re early efforts to get Ballet into National repertoire', 1954, Beth Dean and Victor Carell: correspondence: Corroboree, MLMSS 7804/3/6, SLNSW.

67 Victor Carell to van Praagh, 24 June 1969, 'Notes & letters re early efforts to get Ballet into National repertoire', 1954, Beth Dean and Victor Carell: correspondence: Corroboree, MLMSS 7804/3/6, SLNSW, Sydney.
68 Elkin to Dorothy Helmrich, 10 February 1969, Carell, Victor – Proposed ballet of the South Pacific A2354 1969/289, NAA, Canberra.
69 'Ballet in Open-air Theatre', *The Australian Women's Weekly*, 11 March 1970, 5. http://nla.gov.au/nla.news-article52621687.
70 Victor Carell to W. C. Wentworth, 25 February 1969, Carell, Victor – Proposed ballet of the South Pacific A2354 1969/289, NAA, Canberra. Correspondence in this collection and in the Mitchell Library shows the extent of their lobbying for inclusion in these events – first by proposing that Dean's ballet *Kukaitcha* be staged, then attempting to convince that their input was essential to any performance involving Aboriginal dancers from the Top End and asking to work with Stefan Haag on a production, and finally working with Helmrich on *Corroboree*. Carell again proposed that *Corroboree* be staged for the 1988 bicentenary, a proposal that was considered by the general manager of the Sydney Opera House and passed on to Sydney Dance Company artistic director Graeme Murphy, but ultimately rejected. Victor Carell to Lloyd Martin, 5 May 1985, Beth Dean and Victor Carell: correspondence: Corroboree; 'Notes & letters re early efforts to get Ballet into National repertoire', 1954, Beth Dean and Victor Carell papers, MLMSS 7804/3/6, SLNSW.
71 Three years later, though, Maori and Cook Islands groups accompanied the Queen's Royal Inspection of the Sydney Opera House. Programme for Official Opening by Her Majesty the Queen, 20 October 1973; Programme for Royal Concert, 20 October 1973, Sydney Opera House Archives, Sydney.
72 '"Captain Cook" Raises Cheer', *The Canberra Times*, 30 April 1970, 16. http://nla.gov.au/nla.news-article107922800.
73 'Royal Tour 1970 – Re-Enactment of Captain Cook Landing', C475, 1088331, NAA, Sydney. Research copy of film courtesy of ABC Archives.
74 Programme 'The Landing at Kurnell of Captain James Cook, 29th April 1770', James Cook M Ephemera – Box 2 – (1900–), SLNSW.
75 The full list of Aboriginal performers (adults and children) was Ken Gordon, Jim Madden, Steve Dodd, Deborah Lonsdale, Peter Cruse, Anthony Lonsdale, Fred Beale Jnr, Bryan Beale, Peter Lonsdale, Robert Ridgeway, Kerrie Cruse, Donna Beale, Greg Beale, Joan Beale, Betty Colbung, Vera Roach, Vince Sullivan, Ben Blakeney, Ken Colbung, Fred Beale, Stan Roach, Albert Brown, Rex McLenaghan, Camden Lonsdale, John Roddick, Kim Beale. 'The Landing at Kurnell of Captain James Cook on 29th April, 1770'. James Cook M Ephemera – Box 2 – (1900–), SLNSW.
76 Ben Blakeney interviewed by Terry Colhoun, 5–12 October 1994 in Canberra. ORAL TRC 3132, NLA.
77 'The Landing at Kurnell of Captain James Cook on 29th April, 1770', James Cook M Ephemera – Box 2 – (1900–), SLNSW.
78 The original plan had also been reported in some media: 'Aboriginal to be "shot"', *Broken Hill Truth*, 15 December 1969, clipping in Folder 'Re-enactment of Cook's Landing Kurnell', II. Files of photocopies of news cuttings concerning the Bicentenary, 1970, MLK 376, Sir Asher Joel – papers, 1953–1970, MLMSS 3284, MLOH 3, SLNSW, Sydney. Asher Joel memorandum to A. M. Lake executive officer of citizens

committee, 2 June 1969 NRS 12165 Special bundle: correspondence re royal visit 1970, 13/9317 Premier's Protocol Division Royal Visit Files 1951–73, SRNSW.

79  'Those fearsome islanders', *Sydney Telegraph*, 23 April 1970; 'Re-enactment of Cook's landing', *Canberra Times*, 23 April 1970; Alan Underwood, 'Queen Votes Cooktown as Greatest Day', *Brisbane Courier Mail*, 23 April 1970, clippings in Folder 'Aboriginal Protest', II. Files of photocopies of news cuttings concerning the Bicentenary, 1970, MLK 376, Sir Asher Joel – papers, 1953–1970, MLMSS 3284, MLOH 3, SLNSW.

80  Campbelltown City Sesqui-Centenary 1820–1970 Souvenir Programme of Events and Festivities 10–19 April 1970. James Cook M Ephemera – Box 2 – (1900–), SLNSW.

81  'Too Many Cooks?' *Tamworth Leader*, 30 April 1970, clipping in Folder 'Re-enactment of Cook's Landing Kurnell', II. Files of photocopies of news cuttings concerning the Bicentenary, 1970, MLK 376, Sir Asher Joel – papers, 1953–1970, MLMSS 3284, MLOH 3, SLNSW.

82  'Bad News Day at La Perouse', *Tribune*, 6 May 1970, 4. http://nla.gov.au/nla.news-article237506973.

83  Earlier that month, Aboriginal people living in the southwest Queensland town of Cunnamulla had invited Princess Anne to have a cup of tea with them at their home on the town rubbish dump. Katrina Schlunke, 'Entertaining Possession: Re-Enacting Cook's Arrival for the Queen', in *Conciliation on Colonial Frontiers: Conflict, Performance, and Commemoration in Australia and the Pacific Rim*, ed. Kate Darian-Smith and Penelope Edmonds (New York: Routledge, 2015), 229. 'Plain Australian', *Tribune*, 1 April 1970, 2. http://nla.gov.au/nla.news-article237503832; 'Aborigines and the Bicentenary', *Woroni*, 22 April 1970, 11. http://nla.gov.au/nla.news-page16010215.

84  Aileen Moreton-Robinson, *White Possessive: Property, Power, and Indigenous Sovereignty* (Minnesota: University of Minnesota Press, 2015), 16.

85  See especially Casey, *Creating Frames*.

# Chapter 7

1  Wainburranga contributed to the translations of his words into English from Rembarrnga and Kriol that I quote here. Wainburranga's Captain Cook saga relates modern 'Captain Cooks' to an ancestor Captain Cook, who fought Satan and won, earning him ownership of Sydney Harbour. As a result, he was speared and killed by his own relatives. But though this original Captain Cook ancestor never made war, subsequent people have tried to become new versions of him, vying for ownership of Sydney Harbour and leading to the decimation of Aboriginal people. Penny McDonald, 'Too Many Captain Cooks' (Ronin Films, 1989).

2  'Songs and dances from Bathurst Island, Yirrkala and Daly River performed at the Aboriginal Theatre in Sydney in 1963', ELIZABETHAN_01, AIATSIS.

3  Amanda Harris, 'Hearing Aboriginal Music Making in Non-Indigenous Accounts of the Bush from the Mid-20th Century', in *Circulating Cultures: Exchanges of Australian Indigenous Music, Dance and Media*, ed. Amanda Harris (Canberra: ANU Press, 2014).

4  Clive Douglas, 'Folk Song and the Brown Man – Means to an Australian Expression in Symphonic Works', *Canon* 10, no. 3 (1956): 82.

5  Patrick Wolfe, *Settler Colonialism and the Transformation of Anthropology: The Politics and Poetics of an Ethnographic Event* (London, New York: Cassell, 1999),

Chapter 1. While I present here Wolfe's assertion of this violence to relativism, I also acknowledge critiques of Wolfe's wholescale demolition of Spencer and Gillen by Philip Batty who reminds us that 'the descendants of the Aboriginal groups Spencer and Gillen documented are perhaps the most avid excavators of their ethnography'. Philip Batty, 'Assembling the Ethnographic Field: The 1901–02 Expedition of Baldwin Spencer and Francis Gillen', in *Expeditionary Anthropology: Teamwork, Travel and the 'Science of Man'*, ed. Martin Thomas and Amanda Harris (New York: Berghahn Books, 2018), 58.

6   Wolfe, *Settler Colonialism and the Transformation of Anthropology*, 22.
7   Ian McLean, *Rattling Spears: A History of Indigenous Australian Art* (London: Reaktion Books Ltd, 2016), 10–11. See also Mark McKenna, *Looking for Blackfellas' Point: An Australian History of Place* (Sydney: UNSW Press, 2002), 26–35.
8   Payi Linda Ford, Linda Barwick and Allan Marett, 'Mirrwana and Wurrkama: Applying an Indigenous Knowledge Framework to Collaborative Research on Ceremonies', in *Collaborative Ethnomusicology*, ed. Katelyn Barney (Melbourne: Lyrebird Press, 2014), 43–4.
9   Gayatri Chakravorty Spivak, 'Can the Subaltern Speak?', in *Marxism and the Interpretation of Culture*, ed, Cary Nelson and Lawrence Grossberg. (London: Macmillan, 1988), 271–313.
10  John Antill music manuscript for his ballet suite 'Corroboree' [1940s], together with list of performances, 1950–1970 (Safe 1/249), MLMSS 7072, SLNSW; Baldwin Spencer and Francis James Gillen, *The Arunta: A Study of a Stone Age People* (London: Macmillan, 1927); Baldwin Spencer, *Wanderings in Wild Australia* (London: Macmillan, 1928).
11  Olga Sedneva, 'Corroboree: White Fella Vision' Master's thesis, (State Library of NSW, 2013), 16–24.
12  Dean and Carell's acquisition of the *tjurungas* is inconsistently recounted in published and unpublished sources. In unpublished notebooks, Dean recorded the date on which Mr Wilson gave them honey ant *tjurungas*. In the published book, Dean and Carell reported that a *tjurunga* was given to them by Bullfrog, a man who, as ceremony-owner, was one of the few people who 'could have given us' the sacred gift. This may have been Bullfrog (Japanangka), the acknowledged killer of pastoralist Frederick Brooks in 1928. In retaliation, a reprisal party led by Constable George Murray murdered dozens of Warlpiri people – an event known as the Coniston massacre. Beth Dean: research notes and working papers – Aboriginal Australians 'Book IIIA', Beth Dean and Victor Carell Papers, MLMSS 7804/33/6, State Library of NSW; Beth Dean and Victor Carell, *Dust for the Dancers* (Sydney: Ure Smith, 1956), Preface.
13  Beth Dean Literary Manuscripts: 'Lectures Beth', Beth Dean and Victor Carell Papers, MLMSS 7804/47/2, SLNSW.
14  'Candid Comment', *The Sun-Herald*, 15 November 1953: 16. http://nla.gov.au/nla.news-article28656683; Beth Dean and Victor Carell, 'A Dancer in Our Stone-Age Land', *Pix*, 14 November 1953. A fuller report had appeared some weeks previously: 'Tragedy Comes Out of the Stone Age', *The Sun-Herald*, 18 October 1953, 65. http://nla.gov.au/nla.news-article28655142.
15  In music, the restricted bullroarer instrument held a similar allure. In the events discussed in this book, we might recall Keith Kennedy's incorporation of rock shelves to hold the Aborigines sacred *tjurunga* in his contribution to designs of

a performative Aboriginal village in the 1930s (Chapter 2), John Antill's use of a bullroarer in *Corroboree*'s score in the 1940s (Chapter 3), Peter Sculthorpe's attempts to acquire the same for film scores in the 1960s (Chapter 5) and the 1963 television series *Alcheringa* depicting Central Australian Aboriginal people and narrated by Bill Onus.
16  Folio Box 28, John Antill papers, MS 437, NLA.
17  J. Kēhaulani Kauanui, '"A Structure, Not an Event": Settler Colonialism and Enduring Indigeneity', *Lateral* 5, no. 1 (2016).
18  Patrick Wolfe, 'Settler Colonialism and the Elimination of the Native', *Journal of Genocide Research* 8, no. 4 (2006): 387.
19  Lorenzo Veracini, *The Settler Colonial Present* (London: Palgrave Macmillan, 2015), 70.
20  Wolfe, 'Settler Colonialism and the Elimination of the Native', 390.
21  For a useful discussion of the slippery defining features of musical modernism, see Catherine Bowan, 'Wild Men and Mystics: Rethinking Roy Agnew's Early Sydney Works', *Musicology Australia* 30 (2008). Graeme Skinner's assessment of Australian musical modernism places a variety of the contemporary composers discussed in this book on an arc of Australian modernism. Graeme Skinner, 'Australian Musical First Modernism', in *The Modernist World*, ed. Stephen Ross and Allana C. Lindgren (Abingdon: Routledge, 2015). Michael Hooper's recent book also takes a broad view of what can be constituted as modernist (though he ignores the earlier developments discussed by Bowan altogether, seeing modernism as contained within the period 1960–75). Michael Hooper, *Australian Music and Modernism, 1960–1975* (New York: Bloomsbury Academic, 2019).
22  For discussion of the fixation on Aboriginal culture in the remotest parts of Australia, see Lesley Head, *Second Nature: The History and Implications of Australia as Aboriginal Landscape* (Syracuse, NY: Syracuse University Press, 2000).
23  John Antill music manuscript for his ballet suite 'Corroboree', [1940s], together with list of performances, 1950–1970 (Safe 1/249), MLMSS 7072, SLNSW.
24  'The Procession', *The Sydney Morning Herald*, 27 March 1896. http://nla.gov.au/nla.news-article14043231; 'Centenary of Illawarra', *The Sydney Morning Herald*, 16 March 1896. http://nla.gov.au/nla.news-article14041563; 'Near and Far', *The Sydney Morning Herald*, 13 August 1923. http://nla.gov.au/nla.news-article16087100.
25  Sianan Healy, '"Years Ago Some Lived Here": Aboriginal Australians and the Production of Popular Culture, History and Identity in 1930s Victoria', *Australian Historical Studies* 37, no. 128 (2006): 24–5.
26  Sylvia Kleinert, 'Aboriginality in the City: Re-Reading Koorie Photography', *Aboriginal History* 30 (2006): 69–94.
27  Aileen Moreton-Robinson, *White Possessive: Property, Power, and Indigenous Sovereignty* (Minnesota: University of Minnesota Press, 2015), 10.
28  See Interlude, Tiriki Onus in conversation with me, recorded 20 June 2019 at the Wilin Centre, University of Melbourne.
29  Guboo Ted Thomas and Anne Thomas interviewed in the Chris Sullivan folklore collection, 21 January 1987, TRC 2750/378, NLA. Quoted with the permission of Lynne Thomas and Chris Sullivan. See also Sullivan's assertion that performance of popular folk music (or 'non-tribal music') 'quickly declined after citizen rights were obtained in the late 1960s', Chris Sullivan, 'Non-Tribal Dance Music and Song: From First Contact to Citizen Rights', *Australian Aboriginal Studies*, no. 1 (1988): 65.

30 Malcolm Quekett, 'Australia's First Aboriginal Ballerina Has Life of Wonder', *The West Australian*, 3 July 2016. https://thewest.com.au/news/australia/australias-first-aboriginal-ballerina-has-life-of-wonder-ng-ya-111800, accessed 12 August 2019.
31 'Minister for Territories (Mr Hasluck) Describes Government's "new deal" for Australia's Colored Minority', *The Daily Telegraph*, 19 March 1953. http://nla.gov.au/nla.news-article248862562; 'Nancy Ellis For Sydney', *Sunday Times*, 19 April 1953, 10. http://nla.gov.au/nla.news-article59552688.
32 Shino Konishi, 'First Nations Scholars, Settler Colonial Studies, and Indigenous History', *Australian Historical Studies* 50, no. 3 (2019): 20.
33 'Aborigines Restore a Lost Culture', *The Herald*, 8 August 1946, 13. http://nla.gov.au/nla.news-article245546981.
34 Leanne Betasamosake Simpson, *As We Have Always Done: Indigenous Freedom through Radical Resistance* (Minneapolis: University of Minnesota Press, 2017), 231.
35 Peter Maxwell Davies, 'Foreword', in *Australia's Contemporary Composers*, by James Murdoch (Melbourne: Sun Books, 1972), x.
36 Nicholas Jones, 'Peter Maxwell Davies in the 1950s: A Conversation with the Composer', *Tempo* 64, no. 254 (2010): 19.
37 Peter Maxwell Davies, 'Influence of Aboriginal Music', in *Peter Maxwell Davies: Selected Writings*, ed. Nicholas Jones (Cambridge: Cambridge University Press, 2017), 177.
38 Draft of unpublished autobiography, Box 12, Papers of James Penberthy, MS9748/18/2, NLA. Parts of this manuscript have recently been self-published by Penberthy's son, as David Reid, *James Penberthy: Music and Memories* (Tablo Publishing, 2019) https://tablo.io/david-reid-1/192e51523e4a.
39 James Penberthy, 'The Aboriginal Influence', *Sounds Australian* 30 (1991): 23–4.
40 James Penberthy interviewed by Laine Langridge in the Esso Performing Arts collection, Session 1, 29–30 December 1988, ORAL TRC 2377, NLA.
41 James Penberthy interviewed by Hazel de Berg for the Hazel de Berg collection, Session 1, 30 May 1965, ORAL TRC 1/98-99, NLA.
42 Leanne Betasamosake Simpson, 'Indigenous Resurgence and Co-Resistance', *Critical Ethnic Studies* 2, no. 2 (2016).
43 'News and Notes', *The West Australian*, 14 September 1954, 3. http://nla.gov.au/nla.news-article49880283. Thanks to Rachel Campbell for alerting me to this source.
44 'The 1964 Tour Kira Bousloff as Told to Val Green', *Brolga* 16 (1 June 2002), accessed 13 August 2019, https://ausdance.org.au/articles/details/the-1964-tour.
45 H. Drake-Brockman, 'Sundry Shows: Opera with a Difference', *The Bulletin* 80, no. 4153 (16 September 1959): 24. http://nla.gov.au/nla.obj–681525015. Vincent Plush also claims that Harold Blair performed in the 1959 performance, but I have found nothing to verify this. Vincent Plush, 'Black Unlike Me', *Griffith Review* 8 (Winter 2005): 167.
46 H. Drake-Brockman, 'Stage and Music', *The Bulletin* 81, no. 4193 (22 June 1960): 60. http://nla.gov.au/nla.obj–684074752; 'This Week on ABC-3', *The Canberra Times*, 4 February 1963, 16. http://nla.gov.au/nla.news-article104258165.
47 In earlier stagings of the work, non-Indigenous singers had performed all roles, though Penberthy had flagged the possibility of engaging Blair from the earliest performances. Penberthy to Robert Quentin, 10 October 1958, Correspondence 1955–66 with the Elizabethan Theatre Trust, Box 2, James Penberthy papers, MS 9748, NLA.

48 See, for example, H. Drake-Brockman, 'New Ballet in Perth', *The Bulletin* 80, no. 4148 (12 August 1959). http://nla.gov.au/nla.obj-681524652 and H. Drake-Brockman, 'Sundry Shows: Opera with a Difference', *The Bulletin* 80, no. 4153 (16 September 1959). http://nla.gov.au/nla.obj-681525015.
49 Elizabeth Silsbury, *State of Opera: An Intimate New History of the State Opera of South Australia 1957–2000* (Kent Town, South Australia: Wakefield Press, 2001), 35–6.
50 Liner notes to *Anthology of Australian Music on Disc 4th Series. Csm:31-Csm:36* (Canberra: Canberra School of Music, Institute of the Arts, Australian National University, 1999).
51 Blakeney asserted the importance of this role in representing Aboriginal people and as formational for his career, in spite of criticism from what he describes as black power groups or radicals. Ben Blakeney interviewed by Terry Colhoun, Recorded between 5–12 October 1994 in Canberra, Session 3, ORAL TRC 3132, NLA.
52 'Didjeridoo Work has Premiere', *The Canberra Times*, 4 October 1971, 9. http://nla.gov.au/nla.news-article110680395.
53 'Musica Viva's Third Spring Festival', *The Canberra Times*, 18 September 1971, 19. http://nla.gov.au/nla.news-article110678101.
54 W. L. Hoffmann, 'Life Style', *The Canberra Times*, 5 October 1971, 15. http://nla.gov.au/nla.news-article110680425.
55 George Winungudj, 'The Sound of the Didgeridu Overseas', *Dhawu* 1, no. 2 (1973).
56 Carmelo Musca, 'Didgeridoo in Deutschland' (Milsons Point, NSW: SBS-TV, 1988).
57 Roger Covell, 'Didjeridu Co-exists in Dreyfus Work', *The Sydney Morning Herald*, 1 August 1972. Reproduced in George Dreyfus, 'George Dreyfus: A Music Education Kit for Senior Students: Sextet for Didjeridu and Wind Instruments, Larino, Safe Haven', in *Music Education Kit for Senior Students* (Melbourne: Allans, 1991). Thanks to George Dreyfus for referring me to this source.
58 According to records of Australian performances maintained by the Australian Music Centre, www.australianmusiccentre.com.au/work/sculthorpe-peter-stars-turn, accessed 22 October 2019.
59 Hazel Reader, 'Malcolm Williamson in Australia', *The Canberra Times*, 27 October 1967, 2. http://nla.gov.au/nla.news-article106994731.
60 Much more recently singer and composer Katie Noonan commissioned ten new works to create a song cycle based on Oodgeroo's poetry for 'The Glad Tomorrow' with the Australian String Quartet (2019). The new works have been composed by Carl Vine, Elena Kats Chernin, Richard Tognetti, Iain Grandage, David Hirschfelder, Thomas Green, Robert Davidson, Connor D'Netto, William Barton and Katie Noonan. https://www.katienoonan.com/katie-and-asq.
61 C. J. Ellis, 'Creating with Traditions', *Sounds Australian* 30 (1991). See also my (2020) 'Indigenising Australian Music'. Many popular musicians have also evoked an Indigenous sound without the involvement of Aboriginal and Torres Strait Islander people as Clint Bracknell has shown. 'Identity, Language and Collaboration in Indigenous Music', in *The Difference Identity Makes*, edited by Lawrence Bamblett, Fred Myers and Tim Rowse (Canberra: Aboriginal Studies Press, 2019), 107.
62 Sara Ahmed, 'Declarations of Whiteness: The Non-Performativity of Anti-Racism', *Borderlands* 3, no. 2 (2004).
63 Indeed, the self-referential nature of Sculthorpe's approach to composition possibly had its zenith in his musings on his use of the *djilile* melody in an interview published in 2005, in which (in the face of considerable criticism for his appropriation of a

secret/sacred melody) Sculthorpe revised his previous defence that he had never directly quoted a melody, now realizing that actually he liked that melody because it was the same as one he had composed himself some twenty-five years earlier: 'The moment I heard *Djilile*, that was it. I didn't want to hear anything else. I didn't remember that it was a melody that I had written some 25 years earlier in *String Quartet No.4* ... Therefore, in a way, *Djilile* has become my melody, my very own song'. Vincent Plush and Peter Sculthorpe, 'Peter Sculthorpe in Conversation', in *Encounters: Meetings in Australian Music: Essays, Images, Interviews*, ed. Vincent Plush, Huib Schippers and Jocelyn Wolfe (South Brisbane: Queensland Conservatorium Research Centre, 2005), 37. Wolfe, *Settler Colonialism and the Transformation of Anthropology*, 4.

64 Penberthy suggested Harold Blair for the role of Mungit and 'a coloured Australian girl' for Noala, conceding that Leontyne Price would be right for the role of Dalgerie 'despite her race'. James Penberthy to Robert Quentin (general manager, Elizabethan Opera, Sydney), 10 October 1958, Correspondence 1955–66 with the Elizabethan Theatre Trust, Box 2, Papers of James Penberthy, MS 9748, NLA.

65 'Life and Letters', *The West Australian*, 29 November 1952, 17. http://nla.gov.au/nla.news-article49066252. This and several other articles are discussed in correspondence between journalist Keith Ewers and American dancer Ted Shawn, who were outraged by the lack of representation of Aboriginal arts at Perth Festival, Ted Shawn to Keith (John) Ewers, 4 March 1953, 5459A/405 Shawn, Ted, John Ewers Papers mn1870, SLWA, Perth.

66 'Council Grants to Arts', *The Canberra Times*, 12 December 1968, 33. http://nla.gov.au/nla.news-article136960737.

67 'Aboriginal Arts in Perth '83', *Filmnews*, 1 June 1983, 1. http://nla.gov.au/nla.news-article213734717.

68 Mickey Dewar, 'A Festival Event: Aspects of the Changing Nature and Content of Some Community Celebrations in Darwin in the Twentieth Century', *Journal of Northern Territory History* 19 (2008): 35–6.

69 Note that in the Darwin Festival's own account of its history, it records the start of the festival as the post-cyclone Tracy era: Darwin Festival: History, www.darwinfestival.org.au/about-us/darwin-festival/, accessed 6 August 2019; Dewar, 'A Festival Event', 41–2.

70 '$25,617 for Music 50 Arts Grants for $91,218 Announced', *The Canberra Times*, 1 May 1972, 9. http://nla.gov.au/nla.news-article102018868.

71 Maryrose Casey, *Creating Frames: Contemporary Indigenous Theatre 1967–1990* (St Lucia: University of Queensland Press, 2004), 21–2.

72 '$25,617 for Music 50 Arts Grants for $91,218 Announced', *The Canberra Times*, 1 May 1972, 9. http://nla.gov.au/nla.news-article102018868.

73 Johnson also received continued funding in subsequent rounds, see 'PM's Approval $256,412 in Grants to Aboriginal Arts', *The Canberra Times*, 11 May 1974, 3. http://nla.gov.au/nla.news-article110777819. Carole Johnson is now working on a doctoral thesis about the founding years of the Aboriginal dance movement in Australia at the University of Newcastle.

74 Kim Walker, Oral History interview with Lee Christofis, 11 January 2011, Session 1, ORAL TRC 6259, NLA.

75 Ibid.

76 Steven Knopoff, 'Indigenous and Non-Indigenous Collaboration in New Orchestral Music: Two Notable Successes from the Adelaide Festival of Arts', in *Encounters:*

*Meetings in Australian Music: Essays, Images, Interviews*, ed. Vincent Plush, Huib Schippers and Jocelyn Wolfe (South Brisbane: Queensland Conservatorium Research Centre, 2005), 45.

77 Gordon Kalton Williams, 'Utulura Inkantjaku (Let's Get Together and Sing): Australian Aboriginal Music and the Classical Music Strand', in *Encounters: Meetings in Australian Music, Essays, Images, Interviews*, ed. Vincent Plush, Huib Schippers and Jocelyn Wolfe (South Brisbane: Queensland Conservatorium Research Centre, 2005), 11; Iain Grandage, 'Journeys with Spinifex', *Sounds Australian* 68 (2006). Grandage, in his new role as artistic director of Perth Festival, has now dedicated the first week of his inaugural programme exclusively to First Nations work emphasizing that the festival is in and of this place. Richard Watts, 'Perth Festival Dedicates First Week Exclusively to First Nations', *Arts Hub*, 1 November 2019. www.artshub.com.au/festival/news-article/news/festivals/richard-watts/perth-festival-dedicates-first-week-exclusively-to-first-nations-259144, accessed 18 January 2020.

78 Harriet Cunningham, 'A Breath of Fresh Air for the Classical Tradition', *Sydney Morning Herald*, 2 April 2008, 14.

79 Paul Stanhope, 'Jandamarra – Sing for the Country', Sydney Symphony Orchestra (Sydney: Sydney Symphony Orchestra, 2014).

80 Paul Stanhope, 'Jandamarra: Sing for the Country', in *About Music Public Lecture Series* (Sydney Conservatorium of Music, 2015).

81 'David Page', Australian Music Centre, www.australianmusiccentre.com.au/artist/page-david, accessed 8 August 2019.

82 Aaron Corn, 'Nations of Song', *Humanities Research* 19, no. 3 (2013): 154.

83 Ngarukuruwala, *Ngiya awungarra: I am here, now (audio disc)* (Sydney: Rouseabout Records (RRR75), 2016). See http://www.undercovermusic.com.au/ngarukuruwala.htm Genevieve Campbell, 'Singing with the Ancestors: Musical Conversations with Archived Ethnographic Recordings', in *Recirculating Songs: Revitalising the Singing Practices of Indigenous Australia*, ed. Jim Wafer and Myfany Turpin (Canberra: Asia-Pacific Linguistics, 2017).

84 Nicholas Cook, 'We Are All (Ethno)Musicologists Now', in *The New (Ethno) Musicologies*, ed. Henry Stobart (Lanham, Maryland; Toronto; Plymouth, UK: Scarecrow Press, 2008).

85 Christopher Sainsbury, *Ngarra-Burria: New Music and the Search for an Australian Sound*, Platform Paper 59 (Currency Press, 2019), 12.

86 Deborah Cheetham, Daniel Browning, and Pamela Karantonis, '*Pecan Summer*: The Process of Making New Indigenous Opera in Australia', in *Opera Indigene: Re/Presenting First Nations and Indigenous Cultures*, ed. Pamela Karantonis and Dylan Robinson (Surrey: Ashgate, 2011), 333.

87 Christopher Sainsbury, *Ngarra-Burria*; Sydney Living Museums, Exhibition: Songs of Home, 10 August–17 November 2019, Museum of Sydney. https://sydneylivingmuseums.com.au/exhibitions/songs-home, accessed 17 October 2019. Sainsbury reported on approaches from other major organizations in a presentation to the symposium *Narrating Music and Social Change*, 10 October 2019, Sydney Conservatorium of Music, convenors Christopher Coady and Amanda Harris.

# Bibliography

'$25,617 for Music 50 Arts Grants for $91,218 Announced'. *The Canberra Times*, 1 May 1972, 9. http://nla.gov.au/nla.news-article102018868.

'£410 Subscribed to Antill Fund'. *The Daily Telegraph*, 28 October 1946, 12. http://nla.gov.au/nla.news-article248408639.

'500,000 Line Streets to Watch Jubilee Parade through City'. *The Sydney Morning Herald*, 30 January 1951, 4. http://nla.gov.au/nla.news-article18196935.

'A Dancer Will Write Aborigines' Story'. *The Argus*, 16 February 1952, 7. http://nla.gov.au/nla.news-article23163436.

'Aboriginal Arts in Perth '83'. *Filmnews*, 1 June 1983, 1. http://nla.gov.au/nla.news-article213734717.

'Aboriginal Ballet and Review'. *The Argus*, 31 January 1949, 5. http://nla.gov.au/nla.news-article22711513.

'Aboriginal Concert Party'. *The Argus*, 18 March 1944, 10. http://nla.gov.au/nla.news-article11819781.

'Aboriginal Corroboree'. *Wellington Times*, 11 January 1937, 3. http://nla.gov.au/nla.news-article143401299.

'Aboriginal Dancing "Discovered": We Can Learn from Corroborees'. *The Argus*, 9 August 1947, 43. http://nla.gov.au/nla.news-article22447172.

'Aboriginal Girls to Dance in Sydney'. *Sydney Morning Herald*, 21 March 1970, clipping in Carell, Victor – Proposed ballet of the South Pacific, A2354 1969/289, NAA.

'Aboriginal Leaf Band'. *The Manaro Mercury, and Cooma and Bombala Advertiser*, 6 November 1931, 2. http://nla.gov.au/nla.news-article119085218.

'Aboriginals of Wallaga Lake'. *Sydney Mail*, 16 March 1921, 30. http://nla.gov.au/nla.news-article159038698.

'Aboriginal Singer Shows Gratitude'. *The Courier-Mail*, 31 March 1945, 6. http://nla.gov.au/nla.news-article48943302.

'Aboriginal Songs', *Sunday Mail (Brisbane)*, 20 June 1937, 32. http://nla.gov.au/nla.news-article97889733.

'Aboriginal "Spell-Binder" Sings to Unionists'. *The Herald*, 5 September 1947, 6. http://nla.gov.au/nla.news-article245086085.

'Aboriginal Theatricals'. *The Lockhart Review and Oaklands Advertiser*, 3 February 1953, 3. http://nla.gov.au/nla.news-article138771084.

'Aborigine for Montreal Plan'. *The Canberra Times*, 9 July 1966, 26. http://nla.gov.au/nla.news-article107881079.

'Aborigine Sings for Marjorie Lawrence, is Highly Praised'. *The Telegraph*, 29 September 1944, 3 (City Final Last Minute News). http://nla.gov.au/nla.news-article189850687.

'Aborigine Village Novel Feature at Melbourne Centenary North Queensland Blacks Melbourne, November 22'. *The Telegraph*, 23 November 1933, 11.

'Aborigines and the Bicentenary'. *Woroni*, 22 April 1970, 11. http://nla.gov.au/nla.news-page16010215.

'Aborigines'. *Cairns Post*, 25 November 1933, 6. http://nla.gov.au/nla.news-article41234526.

'Aborigines Camping'. *The Advertiser*, 20 March 1954, 12. http://nla.gov.au/nla.news-article47566367.
'Aborigines' Display'. *The Courier-Mail*, 4 December 1934, 3. http://nla.gov.au/nla.news-article35625968.
'Aborigines' Float'. *Gilgandra Weekly and Castlereagh*, 24 January 1935, 1. http://nla.gov.au/nla.news-article113024440.
'Aborigines for Pageant'. *The Sun*, 17 January 1938, 7 (Late Final Extra). http://nla.gov.au/nla.news-article231118951.
'Aborigines Might Play Before King'. *The Argus*, 22 June 1951, 3. http://nla.gov.au/nla.news-article23066242.
'Aborigines Prepare for Corroboree'. *Daily Advertiser*, 23 April 1948, 1. http://nla.gov.au/nla.news-article144755228.
'Aborigines Receive Only £3/10/ of their £12 Salary'. *The Argus*, 6 July 1951, 3. http://nla.gov.au/nla.news-article23070126.
'Aborigines Remembered'. *Dawn* 9, no. 7 (July 1960): 1.
'Aborigines Restore a Lost Culture'. *The Herald*, 8 August 1946, 13. http://nla.gov.au/nla.news-article245546981.
'Aborigines' Stand'. *The West Australian*, 21 February 1951, 3. http://nla.gov.au/nla.news-article48184828.
'Abos are Sugar Dancers'. *Gippsland Times*, 11 August 1947, 4. https://trove.nla.gov.au/newspaper/article/63260797.
'Abo's Views of Bomb-site'. *The Daily Telegraph*, 2 March 1947, 32. http://nla.gov.au/nla.news-article248359552.
'Advertising'. *The Sydney Morning Herald*, 6 December 1933, 3. http://nla.gov.au/nla.news-article17029899.
'After Fifty Years'. *Barrier Miner*, 19 December 1935, 3. http://nla.gov.au/nla.news-article46714857.
'A Gay Day'. *Coffs Harbour Advocate*, 24 March 1933, 4. http://nla.gov.au/nla.news-article187761754.
Ahmed, Sara. 'Declarations of Whiteness: The Non-Performativity of Anti-Racism'. *Borderlands* 3, no. 2 (2004).
Alexeyeff, Kalissa. *Dancing from the Heart: Movement, Gender, and Sociality in the Cook Islands*. Honolulu: University of Hawaii Press, 2009.
Alomes, Stephen. *When London Calls: The Expatriation of Australian Creative Artists to Britain*. Cambridge: Cambridge University Press, 1999.
'Amateur Theatre'. *The Herald*, 13 August 1946, 8. http://nla.gov.au/nla.news-article245548755.
'Among Abos'. *The Sun*, 26 February 1932, 9 (Final Extra). http://nla.gov.au/nla.news-article230524575.
'An Aboriginal Protest'. *Westralian Worker*, 12 October 1934, 1. http://nla.gov.au/nla.news-article148384994.
*Anthology of Australian Music on Disc 4th Series*. Csm:31-Csm:36. Canberra: Canberra School of Music, Institute of the Arts, Australian National University, 1999.
Araluen Corr, Evelyn. 'Silence and Resistance: Aboriginal Women Working Within and Against the Archive'. *Continuum* 32, no. 4 (2018): 487–502.
Araluen, Evelyn. 'Resisting the Institution'. *Overland* Winter, no. 227 (2017): 3–10.
'Arts of the Stone Age'. *The Herald*, 13 June 1934, 12. http://nla.gov.au/nla.news-article243174626.

'Assimilation of Aborigines'. *The Canberra Times*, 19 October 1951, 4.
Attwood, Bain. 'Aboriginal History, Minority Histories and Historical Wounds: The Postcolonial Condition, Historical Knowledge and the Public Life of History in Australia'. *Postcolonial Studies* 14, no. 2 (2011): 171–86.
Attwood, Bain. *A Life Together, a Life Apart: A History of Relations between Europeans and Aborigines*. Carlton: Melbourne University Press, 1994.
Attwood, Bain. *The Good Country: The Djadja Wurrung, the Settlers and the Protectors*. Clayton, Victoria: Monash University Publishing, 2017.
Attwood, Bain, and Andrew Markus. *The 1967 Referendum: Race, Power and the Australian Constitution*. Canberra: Aboriginal Studies Press, 2007.
'Aust. Music Will Go to England by New Process'. *The Daily Telegraph*, 17 June 1947, 7. http://nla.gov.au/nla.news-article248479584.
'Australian Aboriginal Songs'. *Sunday Times*, 20 June 1937, 23 (First Section). http://nla.gov.au/nla.news-article58782739.
'Australian Artists in Peking', *Tribune*, 10 September 1958, 12. http://nla.gov.au/nla.news-article236323993.
Australian Institute of Aboriginal Studies. *La Perouse: The Place, the People and the Sea*. Canberra: Aboriginal Studies Press, 1988.
Australian Music Centre. 'Roger Covell, 1931–2019'. 4 June 2019. www.australianmusiccentre.com.au/article/roger-covell-1931-2019, accessed 7 June 2019.
'Australian Musical is Good'. *Weekly Times*, 22 November 1950, 44. http://nla.gov.au/nla.news-article224926473.
'Australian Musical Play Succeeds'. *Weekly Times*, 30 December 1933, 10 (First Edition). http://nla.gov.au/nla.news-article223210414.
'Back to the Bellinger'. *The Wingham Chronicle and Manning River Observer*, 17 March 1933, 7. http://nla.gov.au/nla.news-article166499157.
'"Back to the Bellinger". Aborigines to Play their Part'. *The Gloucester Advocate*, 7 March 1933, 2. https://trove.nla.gov.au/newspaper/article/159651436.
'Bad News Day at La Perouse'. *Tribune*, 6 May 1970, 4. http://nla.gov.au/nla.news-article237506973.
'Bagot Natives Corroboree'. *Northern Standard*, 18 March 1954, 6. http://nla.gov.au/nla.news-article49483308.
'Ballet in Open-air Theatre'. *The Australian Women's Weekly*, 11 March 1970, 5. http://nla.gov.au/nla.news-article52621687.
'Ballet of the South Pacific'. *The Australian Women's Weekly*, 1 April 1970, 25. http://nla.gov.au/nla.news-article47814074.
'Ballet Opens Arts Festival'. *Weekly Times*, 7 February 1951, 38. http://nla.gov.au/nla.news-article225462617.
Barwick, Linda, and Allan Marett. 'Aural Snapshots of Musical Life: The 1948 Recordings'. In *Exploring the Legacy of the 1948 Arnhem Land Expedition*, edited by Martin Thomas and Margo Neale, 355–76. Canberra: ANU E Press, 2011.
Batty, Philip. 'Assembling the Ethnographic Field: The 1901–02 Expedition of Baldwin Spencer and Francis Gillen'. In *Expeditionary Anthropology: Teamwork, Travel and the 'Science of Man'*, edited by Martin Thomas and Amanda Harris, 37–63. New York: Berghahn Books, 2018.
Bennet McLean, Debra. 'Right of Reply: An Indigenous Perspective of Encounters as a Source of Dialogue'. In *Encounters: Meetings in Australian Music: Essays, Images, Interviews*, edited by Vincent Plush, Huib Schippers and Jocelyn Wolfe, 6–7. South Brisbane: Queensland Conservatorium Research Centre, 2005.

'Beth Dean to Dance in Darwin'. *Northern Standard*, 11 June 1953, 1. http://nla.gov.au/nla. news-article49483837.
'Better Education for Aborigines Sought'. *Tribune*, 27 April 1949.
'Beulah Circuit Named in Honour of Our Lorna'. *Forbes Advocate*, 29 June 2015. www. forbesadvocate.com.au/story/3178157/beulah-circuit-named-in-honour-of-our-lorna, accessed 23 September 2019.
Bharucha, Rustom. *Theatre and the World: Performance and the Politics of Culture*. London: Routledge, 2003.
Bird Rose, Deborah. 'Review: Settler Colonialism and the Transformation of Anthropology'. *Postcolonial Studies* 4, no. 2 (2001): 251–61.
Blacking, John. *'A Common-Sense View of All Music': Reflections on Percy Grainger's Contribution to Ethnomusicology and Music Education*. Cambridge: Cambridge University Press, 1987.
'Blacks Astonished by the City'. *Argus*, 26 September 1934, 8. http://nla.gov.au/nla. news-article10956595.
Bodkin, Frances, and Lorraine Robertson. *D'harawal: Seasons and Climatic Cycles*. Sydney: F. Bodkin & L. Robertson, 2008.
Bodkin-Andrews, Gawaian, and Bronwyn Carlson. 'The Legacy of Racism and Indigenous Australian Identity within Education'. *Race Ethnicity and Education* 19, no. 4 (2016): 784–807.
Bollen, Jonathan, and Anne Brewster. 'NADOC and the National Aborigines Day in Sydney, 1957–67'. *Aboriginal History* 42, no. 3 (2018): 3–30.
'Boomerang Ace Organised Bondi Contests'. *The Australian Women's Weekly*, 25 February 1950, 17. http://nla.gov.au/nla.news-article55480501.
Bowan, Catherine. 'Wild Men and Mystics: Rethinking Roy Agnew's Early Sydney Works'. *Musicology Australia* 30 (2008): 1–28.
Bowan, Kate, and Paul A. Pickering. *Sounds of Liberty: Music, Radicalism and Reform in the Anglophone World, 1790–1914*. Studies in Imperialism. Manchester: Manchester University Press, 2017.
Bracknell, Clint. 'Identity, Language and Collaboration in Indigenous Music'. In *The Difference Identity Makes*, ed. Lawrence Bamblett, Fred Myers and Tim Rowse, 99–123 (Canberra: Aboriginal Studies Press, 2019).
Brantlinger, Patrick. *Dark Vanishings: Discourse on the Extinction of Primitive Races, 1800–1930*. Ithaca, NY: Cornell University Press, 2003.
'Brisbane Goes Native'. *The Telegraph*, 8 December 1934, 7 (Sports Final). http://nla.gov. au/nla.news-article179667438.
Brissenden, Alan, and Keith Glennon. *Australia Dances: Creating Australian Dance 1945–1965*. Kent Town: Wakefield Press, 2010.
Brookes, K. F. 'Adult Education in Tasmania'. *The Australian Highway*, February 1957, 7.
Broome, Richard, and Corinne Manning. *A Man of All Tribes: The Life of Alick Jackomos*. Canberra: Aboriginal Studies Press, 2006.
Brown, Reuben, David Manmurulu, Jenny Manmurulu and Isabel O'Keeffe. 'Dialogues with the Archives: Arrarrkpi Responses to Recordings as Part of the Living Song Tradition of Manyardi'. *Preservation, Digital Technology & Culture* 47, no. 3–4 (2018): 102–14.
'Bush Music Makers'. *The Bombala Times*, 29 July 1927, 2. http://nla.gov.au/nla. news-article134555943.
Campbell, Genevieve. 'Singing with the Ancestors: Musical Conversations with Archived Ethnographic Recordings'. In *Recirculating Songs: Revitalising the Singing Practices of*

*Indigenous Australia*, edited by Jim Wafer and Myfany Turpin, 289–304. Canberra: Asia-Pacific Linguistics, 2017.
'Candid Comment'. *The Sun-Herald*, 15 November 1953, 16. http://nla.gov.au/nla.news-article28656683.
'"Captain Cook" Raises Cheer'. *The Canberra Times*, 30 April 1970, 16. http://nla.gov.au/nla.news-article107922800.
Card, Amanda. 'From "Aboriginal Dance" to Aboriginals Dancing: The Appropriation of the "Primitive" in Australian Dance 1950–1963'. In *Heritage and Heresy: Green Mill Papers*, 40–6. Braddon: Australia Dance Council, 1997.
Carell, Victor. *Naked We Are Born*. Sydney: Ure Smith, 1960.
Carell, Victor, and Beth Dean. 'Carrumbo: To Take a Long Journey'. General Motors Holden Ltd, 1953.
Carlson, Bronwyn. *The Politics of Identity: Who Counts as Aboriginal Today?* Canberra: Aboriginal Studies Press, 2016.
Carter, Paul. *The Sound in Between: Voice, Space, Performance*. Kensington, NSW: NSW University Press, 1992.
Casey, Maryrose. 'Performing for Aboriginal Life and Culture: Aboriginal Theatre and Ngurrumilmarrmiriyu'. *Australasian Drama Studies* 59 (2011): 53–68.
Casey, Maryrose. *Creating Frames: Contemporary Indigenous Theatre 1967–1990*. St Lucia: University of Queensland Press, 2004.
'Centenary of Illawarra'. *The Sydney Morning Herald*, 16 March 1896, 5. http://nla.gov.au/nla.news-article14041563.
'Champion in the Making'. *The Daily Telegraph*, 15 January 1951, 7. http://nla.gov.au/nla.news-article248509588.
Cheetham, Deborah, Daniel Browning and Pamela Karantonis. '*Pecan Summer*: The Process of Making New Indigenous Opera in Australia'. In *Opera Indigene: Re/Presenting First Nations and Indigenous Cultures*, edited by Pamela Karantonis and Dylan Robinson. Surrey: Ashgate, 2011.
'Chief Secretary on Aborigines Question'. *Barrier Miner*, 25 January 1938, 1 (Home Edition). http://nla.gov.au/nla.news-article47963089.
Chittick, Lee, and Terry Fox. *Travelling with Percy: A South Coast Journey*. Canberra: Aboriginal Studies Press, 1997.
Clark, Anna. 'The History Wars'. In *Australian History Now*, edited by Anna Clark and Paul Ashton, 151–66. Sydney: NewSouth, 2013.
Clendinnen, Inga. *Dancing with Strangers*. Melbourne: Text Pub, 2003.
Cole, Malcolm. 'Tropical Sounds: A Cultural History of Music Education in Cairns and Yarrabah: 1930–1970'. PhD thesis, James Cook University, Cairns, 2014.
'Collit's Inn'. *The Central Queensland Herald*, 4 January 1934, 3. http://nla.gov.au/nla.news-article70311141.
'"Collits' Inn" Breaks New Ground'. *The Sydney Morning Herald*, 4 January 1934, 8 (Women's Supplement). http://nla.gov.au/nla.news-article17037585.
'Commonwealth Arts Festival – 1965'. *Trust News*, September 1965, 2. www.thetrust.org.au/pdf/trust-news/TN_1965_09_010.pdf.
'Complaints about Treatment'. *Barrier Miner*, 22 January 1938, 7 (Sports Edition). http://nla.gov.au/nla.news-article47962898.
'Complaints Alleged by Aboriginal Harvesters'. *The Herald*, 28 December 1942, 5. http://nla.gov.au/nla.news-article245129660.

'Composer Leaves for London Today'. *The Daily Telegraph*, 15 October 1946, 7. http://nla.gov.au/nla.news-article248407867.

Cook, Nicholas. 'We Are All (Ethno)Musicologists Now'. In *The New (Ethno)Musicologies*, edited by Henry Stobart. Lanham, Maryland; Toronto: Scarecrow Press, 2008.

Corn, Aaron. 'Nations of Song'. *Humanities Research* 19, no. 3 (2013): 145–60.

'Corroboree'. *North West Champion*, 19 September 1932, 2. http://nla.gov.au/nla.news-article179128450.

'Corroboree at Bondi Yulunga'. *The Sun*, 18 January 1951, 28 (Late Final Extra). http://nla.gov.au/nla.news-article229190652.

'Corroboree Is Uneven'. *The Age*, 18 April 1949, 3. http://nla.gov.au/nla.news-article206072359.

'Council Grants to Arts'. *The Canberra Times*, 12 December 1968, 33. http://nla.gov.au/nla.news-article136960737.

Covell, Roger. *Australia's Music: Themes of a New Society*. Melbourne: Sun Books, 1967.

Covell, Roger. 'Didjeridu Co-exists in Dreyfus Work'. *The Sydney Morning Herald*, 1 August 1972.

Coyle, Jackey, and Rebecca Coyle. 'Aloha Australia: Hawaiian Music in Australia (1920–55)'. *Perfect Beat* 2, no. 2 (January 1995): 31–63.

Cross, Melissa. 'The Forgotten Soundtrack of Maoriland: Imagining the Nation through Alfred Hill's Songs for Rewi's Last Stand'. Master's thesis, Massey University and Victoria University, 2015.

Crotty, Joel. 'Towards an Australian Art-Music Canon'. *Quadrant* 55, no. 10 (October 2011): 91–7.

'Culture and the Centenary'. *The Central Queensland Herald*, 21 June 1934, 13. http://nla.gov.au/nla.news-article70566442.

Cunningham, Harriet. 'A Breath of Fresh Air for the Classical Tradition'. *Sydney Morning Herald*, 2 (April 2008): 14.

Curran, James, and Stuart Ward. *The Unknown Nation: Australia after Empire*. Melbourne: Melbourne University Press, 2010.

Damousi, Joy, and Desley Deacon, eds. *Talking and Listening in the Age of Modernity: Essays on the History of Sound*. Canberra: ANU E Press, 2007.

'Dance Artistry of Ted Shawn'. *The Courier-Mail*, 8 September 1947, 8. http://nla.gov.au/nla.news-article49311342.

'Dancer Opens Appeal'. *The Argus*, 7 July 1956, 7. http://nla.gov.au/nla.news-article71644804.

'Dances and Songs'. *The West Australian*, 10 January 1951, 4. http://nla.gov.au/nla.news-article48145606.

Dean, Beth. 'Aboriginal Theatre: An Insight into Native World'. *Daily Telegraph*, 6 December 1963.

Dean, Beth. *The Many Worlds of Dance*. Sydney: Murray, 1966.

Dean, Beth, and Victor Carell. 'A Dancer in Our Stone-Age Land'. *Pix*, 14 November 1953, 17–21.

Dean, Beth, and Victor Carell. *Dust for the Dancers*. Sydney: Ure Smith, 1956.

Dean, Beth, and Victor Carell. *Gentle Genius: A Life of John Antill*. Sydney: Akron Press, 1987.

Deery, Phillip, and Lisa Milner. 'Political Theatre and the State Melbourne and Sydney, 1936–1953'. *History Australia* 12, no. 3 (December 2015): 113–36.

Deloria, Philip J. *Playing Indian*. New Haven: Yale University Press, 1999.

Department of Territories, and National Aborigines' Day Observance Committee. *Our Aborigines* – Prepared under the Authority of the Minister for Territories with the Co-Operation of the Ministers Responsible for Aboriginal Welfare in the Australian States. Canberra: Govt. Printer, 1957.

Derrida, Jacques. *Archive Fever: A Freudian Impression*. Chicago: University of Chicago Press, 1996.

'Details of Bridge Pageant'. *The Daily Telegraph*, 9 March 1932, 9. http://nla.gov.au/nla.news-article246547236.

Deveson, Philippa. 'The Agency of the Subject: Yolngu Involvement in the Yirrkala Film Project'. *Journal of Australian Studies* 35, no. 2 (2011): 153–64.

Dewar, Mickey. 'A Festival Event: Aspects of the Changing Nature and Content of Some Community Celebrations in Darwin in the Twentieth Century'. *Journal of Northern Territory History* 19 (2008): 33–49.

'Didjeridoo Trio'. *The Herald*, 15 February 1952, 2. http://nla.gov.au/nla.news-article246046689.

'Didjeridoo Work Has Premiere'. *The Canberra Times*, 4 October 1971, 9. http://nla.gov.au/nla.news-article110680395.

'Didgerydoos in Plenty for Musician'. *The Argus*, 25 January 1949, 6. http://nla.gov.au/nla.news-article22699157.

'Disappointed'. *The Sun*, 20 March 1932, 4. http://nla.gov.au/nla.news-article229894731

'Display of Aboriginal Customs for Centenary'. *News*, 29 August 1934, 5. http://nla.gov.au/nla.news-article128847874.

Doherty, Frank. 'We Discover "Old Australians" Aborigines Cynical about Jubilee'. *The Argus*, 30 January 1951, 2. http://nla.gov.au/nla.news-article23036858.

Douglas, Clive. 'Folk Song and the Brown Man – Means to an Australian Expression in Symphonic Works'. *Canon* 10, no. 3 (October 1956): 80–3.

Drake-Brockman, H. 'Life and Letters'. *The West Australian*, 29 November 1952, 17. http://nla.gov.au/nla.news-article49066252.

Drake-Brockman, H. 'New Ballet in Perth'. *The Bulletin* 80, no. 4148 (12 August 1959): 25, 49. http://nla.gov.au/nla.obj-681524652.

Drake-Brockman, H. 'Stage and Music'. *The Bulletin* 81, no. 4193 (22 June 1960): 60. http://nla.gov.au/nla.obj-684074752.

Drake-Brockman, H. 'Sundry Shows: Opera with a Difference'. *The Bulletin* 80, no. 4153 (16 September 1959): 24. http://nla.gov.au/nla.obj-681525015.

Dreyfus, George. 'George Dreyfus: A Music Education Kit for Senior Students: Sextet for Didjeridu and Wind Instruments, Larino, Safe Haven'. In *Music Education Kit for Senior Students*. Melbourne: Allans, 1991.

Dunbar-Hall, Peter, and Chris Gibson. *Deadly Sounds, Deadly Places: Contemporary Aboriginal Music in Australia*. Sydney: UNSW Press, 2004.

Durack, Mary. 'The Aboriginal Theatre Foundation Gets to Work: No Longer Just a Dream'. *Identity* (October 1971): 17–18.

'Education the Key: Slogan for National Aborigines' Day'. *Dawn* 15, no. 8 (August 1966): 5.

Elkin, A. P. 'Arnhem Land Music (Part 3)'. *Oceania* 25, no. 4 (1955): 292–342.

Elkin, A. P. *Citizenship for the Aborigines – A National Aboriginal Policy*. Sydney: Australasian Publishing Co., 1944.

Elkin, A. P. 'Maraian at Mainoru, 1949: I. Description'. *Oceania* 31, no. 4 (June 1961): 259–93.

Ellis, C. J. 'Creating with Traditions'. *Sounds Australian* 30 (1991): 13–15.

Elphick, Beverley P. and Don J. Elphick. *Menindee Mission Station: 1933–1949*. Canberra: B. and D. Elphick, 1996.
'Entertainment at Wingham'. *The Manning River Times and Advocate for the Northern Coast Districts of New South Wales*, 8 June 1940, 2. http://nla.gov.au/nla.news-article171230617.
'Euroka'. *The Argus*, 17 September 1947, 3 (Woman's Magazine). http://nla.gov.au/nla.news-article22508040.
Ewers, John K. 'Aboriginal Ballet'. *Walkabout*, 1 December 1947, 29–34.
'Farewell Broadcasts by Swing Club Band'. *The Manning River Times and Advocate for the Northern Coast Districts of New South Wales*, 23 September 1950, 5. http://nla.gov.au/nla.news-article172829684.
Fensham, Rachel. 'On Dancing with Strangers: Rechoreographing Indigenous and British Sovereignty in the Colonial Encounter'. *Journal for the Anthropological Study of Human Movement* 14, no. 3 (2009).
Fletcher, Jim J. *Documents in the History of Aboriginal Education in New South Wales*. Carlton, NSW: J. Fletcher, 1989.
'Folk-dancing'. *The West Australian*, 2 July 1947, 12. http://nla.gov.au/nla.news-article46322865.
'For Women', *The Sydney Morning Herald*, 12 October 1935, 9. http://nla.gov.au/nla.news-article17226162.
Ford, Payi Linda, Linda Barwick and Allan Marett. 'Mirrwana and Wurrkama: Applying an Indigenous Knowledge Framework to Collaborative Research on Ceremonies'. In *Collaborative Ethnomusicology*, edited by Katelyn Barney, 43–62. Melbourne: Lyrebird Press, 2014.
Foster, Shannon. 'White Bread Dreaming'. In *Growing Up Aboriginal in Australia*, edited by Anita Heiss. Carlton, Vic: Black Inc., 2018.
Foster, Shannon, Joanne Paterson Kinniburgh and Wann. 'There's No Place Like (Without) Country'. In *Placemaking Fundamentals for the Built Environment*, edited by Dominique Hes and Cristina Hernandez-Santin, 63–82. Sydney: Palgrave Macmillan, 2020.
Foster, Tom. *My Thoughts, and I'm Happy To-day: Two Aboriginal Spirituals*, 1930, National Library of Australia. http://nla.gov.au/nla.obj-181580080.
'From Distant Ernabella'. *Recorder*, 15 March 1954, 1. http://nla.gov.au/nla.news-article96184673.
'Fund to Send Aust. Composer to London'. *The Daily Telegraph*, 10 October 1946, 5. http://nla.gov.au/nla.news-article248403178.
Gapps, Stephen. '"Blacking up" for the Explorers of 1951'. In *Settler and Creole Reenactment*, edited by Vanessa Agnew, Jonathan Lamb and Daniel Spoth, 208–20. London: Palgrave Macmillan UK, 2009.
Garland, Deborah 'Melbourne Theatres – Undergrads Will Go "On Tour"'. *The Herald*, 17 December 1946, 12. http://nla.gov.au/nla.news-article245380244.
'General News'. *The Kadina and Wallaroo Times*, 20 August 1930, 2. http://nla.gov.au/nla.news-article110234693.
Giese, Diana. 'One Fabulous Night Only: Entertaining the Territory'. *Occasional Paper* no. 63, 2–30. Darwin: Northern Territory Library, 2008.
Giese, Harry. 'Planning a Program for Aborigines in the 1950s'. *Occasional Papers* no. 16, 1–13. Darwin: Northern Territory Library Service 1990.

Gilbert, Helen, and Jacqueline Lo. *Performance and Cosmopolitics: Cross-Cultural Transactions in Australasia*. London: Palgrave Macmillan, 2009.
Gissing, Philip. 'Stout, Alan Ker (1900–1983)'. *Australian Dictionary of Biography*, National Centre of Biography, Australian National University. http://adb.anu.edu.au/biography/stout-alan-ker-15921/text27122, accessed 22 February 2019.
Glass, Dudley. 'Australia's Contribution to Music'. *Journal of the Royal Society of Arts* 111, no. 5080 (1963): 302–11.
'"Goes Close to Slavery"'. *The Argus*, 3 December 1937, 1. http://nla.gov.au/nla.news-article11129390.
Goossens, Eugene. 'Where Are the Scores?'. *Canon* 2, no. 1 (August 1948): 5–6.
Grandage, Iain. 'Journeys with Spinifex'. *Sounds Australian* 68 (2006): 10–15.
Gray, Geoffrey. 'From Nomadism to Citizenship: A. P. Elkin and Aboriginal Advancement'. In *Citizenship and Indigenous Australians: Changing Conceptions and Possibilities*, edited by Nicolas Peterson and Will Sanders, 55–76. Cambridge: Cambridge University Press, 1998.
Greener, Leslie. 'Adult Education in Tasmania'. *The Australian Highway* (December 1950), 83–4.
Haebich, Anna. *Dancing in Shadows: Histories of Nyungar Performance*. Crawley, Western Australia: UWA Publishing, 2018.
Haebich, Anna. *Spinning the Dream: Assimilation in Australia 1950–1970*. North Fremantle: Fremantle Press, 2007.
Hall, Robert A. *The Black Diggers: Aborigines and Torres Strait Islanders in the Second World War*. Canberra: Aboriginal Studies Press, 1997.
Hannan, Michael. 'Scoring *Essington*: Composition, Comprovisation, Collaboration'. *Screen Sound* 2 (2011): 48–63.
Hansen, Christine Frances. 'Telling Absence: Aboriginal Social History and the National Museum of Australia'. PhD thesis, Australian National University, 2009.
Harkin, Natalie. 'The Poetics of (Re) Mapping Archives: Memory in the Blood'. *Journal of the Association for the Study of Australian Literature* 14, no. 3 (2014): 1–14.
Harney, W. E., and A. P. Elkin. *Songs of the Songmen: Aboriginal Myths Retold*. Melbourne: Cheshire, 1949.
'Harold Blair's Operatic Debut'. *The Age*, 29 November 1948, 2. http://nla.gov.au/nla.news-article205671966.
Harris, Amanda. 'Hearing Aboriginal Music Making in Non-Indigenous Accounts of the Bush from the Mid-20th Century'. In *Circulating Cultures: Exchanges of Australian Indigenous Music, Dance and Media*, edited by Amanda Harris, 73–97. Canberra: ANU Press, 2014.
Harris, Amanda. 'Indigenising Australian Music: Authenticity and Representation in Touring 1950s Art Songs'. *Postcolonial Studies* (special issue: 'New Directions in Settler Colonial Studies', edited by Jane Carey and Ben Silverstein) 23, no. 1 (2020): 132–52.
Harris, Amanda. 'Pan-Indigenous Encounter in the 1950s: "Ethnic Dancer" Beth Dean'. *Australian Historical Studies* 48, no. 3 (2017): 328–45.
Harris, Amanda. 'Representing Australia to the Commonwealth in 1965: Aborigiana and Indigenous Performance'. *Twentieth Century Music* 17, no. 1 (February 2020): 3–22. https://doi.org/10.1017/S1478572219000331.
Harris, Amanda. 'The Nature of Nordicism: Grainger's "Blue-Gold-Rosy-Race" and His Music'. *Musicology Australia* 23 (2000): 19–48.

Harris, Frank. 'Native Drummers Stir the Crowd'. *Daily Mirror*, 7 April 1970.
Harrison, Kenneth. *Dark Man, White World: A Portrait of Tenor Harold Blair*. Melbourne: Novalt, 1975.
Haskins, Victoria. 'Beth Dean and the Transnational Circulation of Aboriginal Dance Culture: Gender, Authority and C. P. Mountford'. In *Circulating Cultures: Exchanges of Australian Indigenous Music, Dance and Media*, edited by Amanda Harris, 19–44. Canberra: ANU Press, 2014.
Haskins, Victoria. '"Could You See to the Return of My Daughter": Fathers and Daughters under the New South Wales Aborigines Protection Board Child Removal Policy'. *Australian Historical Studies* 34, no. 121 (2003): 106–21.
Haskins, Victoria. 'Dancing in the Dust: A Gendered History of Indigenising Australian Cultural Identity'. In *Intersections: Gender, Race and Ethnicity in Australasian Studies*, edited by Margaret Allen and R. K. Dhawan, 55–75. New Delhi: Prestige Books, 2007.
Haskins, Victoria. 'To Touch the Infinity of a Far Horizon: A Transnational History of Transcultural Appropriation in Beth Dean's Corroboree (1954)'. *Australasian Drama Studies* 59 (2011): 23–38.
Head, Lesley. *Second Nature: The History and Implications of Australia as Aboriginal Landscape*. Syracuse, NY: Syracuse University Press, 2000.
Healy, Chris. *Forgetting Aborigines*. Sydney: University of New South Wales Press, 2008.
Healy, Sianan. 'Shaking Hands with the Governor-General: Aboriginal Participation in White Celebrations of History and Heritage in 1930s Victoria'. In *Historicising Whiteness: Transnational Perspectives on the Construction of an Identity*, edited by Leigh Boucher, Jane Carey and Katherine Ellinghouse, 291–7. Melbourne: University of Melbourne, 2007.
Healy, Sianan. '"Years Ago Some Lived Here": Aboriginal Australians and the Production of Popular Culture, History and Identity in 1930s Victoria'. *Australian Historical Studies* 37, no. 128 (2006): 18–34.
Helmrich, Dorothy. *The First Twenty-Five Years: A Study of the Arts Council of Australia*. Sydney: Southwood Press, 1968.
Henry, Rosita. 'Engaging with History by Performing Tradition: The Poetic Politics of Indigenous Australian Festivals'. In *The State and the Arts: Articulating Power and Subversion*, edited by Judith Kapferer, 52–69. New York: Berghahn Books, 2008.
Hill, Alfred. *Poor Fellow Me: Wanderer's Song*. Sydney: Chappell, 1950.
Hill, Jennifer. 'Clive Douglas and the ABC: Not a Favourite Aunt'. In *One Hand on the Manuscript: Music in Australian Cultural History 1930–1960*, edited by Nicholas Brown, Peter Campbell, Robyn Holmes, Peter Read and Larry Sitsky, 229–42. Canberra: Humanities Research Centre, ANU, 1995.
Hodgens, Jessica. 'Colonisation, Violence and Ethics: Resisting Settler Colonial Erasure on Dja Dja Wurrung Country'. PhD thesis, Monash University, 2017.
Hoffmann, W. L. 'Life Style'. *The Canberra Times*, 5 October 1971, 15. http://nla.gov.au/nla.news-article110680425.
Holley Connors, Jane. 'The Glittering Thread: The 1954 Royal Tour of Australia'. PhD thesis, University of Technology, Sydney, 1996.
Hooper, Michael. *Australian Music and Modernism, 1960–1975*. New York: Bloomsbury Academic, 2019.
Horner, Jack, and Marcia Langton. 'The Day of Mourning'. In *Australians 1938*, edited by Bill Gammage and Spearritt Broadway, 28–35. Broadway, NSW: Fairfax, Syme & Weldon Associates, 1987.

Horton, David, ed. *The Encyclopaedia of Aboriginal Australia: Aboriginal and Torres Strait Islander History, Society and Culture*. Canberra: Aboriginal Studies Press for the Australian Institute of Aboriginal Torres Strait Islander Studies, 1994.

'Hula-hula Bondi Style'. *The Daily Telegraph*, 27 February 1950, 5. http://nla.gov.au/nla.news-article249000688.

Hunter, Ian. 'The Commonwealth Arts Festival'. Journal of the Royal Society of Arts 113/5108 (1965), 605–11.

Illert, Chris. 'Early Ancestors of Illawarra's Wadi-Wadi People'. *Bulletin of the Illawarra Aboriginal History Society* (2003).

'Indigenous Workers Receive $190m Stolen Wages Settlement from Queensland Government'. *The Guardian*, 9 July 2019. Accessed 24 October 2019. www.theguardian.com/australia-news/2019/jul/09/indigenous-workers-receive-190m-stolen-wages-settlement-from-queensland-government.

Ingamells, Rex. *Conditional Culture*. Adelaide: F. W. Preece, 1938.

Jackomos, Alick, and Derek Fowell. *Living Aboriginal History of Victoria: Stories in the Oral Tradition*. Cambridge: Cambridge University Press, 1991.

Johnson, Miranda. 'Honest Acts and Dangerous Supplements: Indigenous Oral History and Historical Practice in Settler Societies'. *Postcolonial Studies* 8, no. 3 (2005): 261–76.

Johnson, Miranda C. L. *The Land is our History: Indigeneity, Law, and the Settler State*. New York: Oxford University Press, 2016.

Johnston, Peter Wyllie. '"Australian-Ness" in Musical Theatre: A Bran Nue Dae for Australia'. *Australasian Drama Studies* 45 (October 2004): 157–79.

'Jolly Swag Man'. *The Argus*, 16 January 1957, 3. http://nla.gov.au/nla.news-article71776403.

Jones, Anthony Linden. 'The Circle of Songs: Traditional Song and the Musical Score to C.P. Mountford's Documentary Films'. In *Circulating Cultures: Exchanges of Australian Indigenous Music, Dance and Media*, edited by Amanda Harris, 45–72. Canberra: ANU Press, 2014.

Jones, Nicholas. 'Peter Maxwell Davies in the 1950s: A Conversation with the Composer'. *Tempo* 64, no. 254 (2010): 11–19.

Jones, Philip. 'The Theatre of Contact: Aborigines and Exploring Expeditions'. In *Expedition into Empire*, edited by Martin Thomas, 88–107. New York: Routledge, 2014.

'Jubilee Tour of Queensland Is … Something of Sentimental Journey for Harold Blair'. *Queensland Times*, 4 August 1951, 2 (Daily). http://nla.gov.au/nla.news-article118221373.

Kalton Williams, Gordon. 'Utuḻura Inkantjaku (Let's Get Together and Sing): Australian Aboriginal Music and the Classical Music Strand'. In *Encounters: Meetings in Australian Music, Essays, Images, Interviews*, edited by Vincent Plush, Huib Schippers and Jocelyn Wolfe, 14. South Brisbane: Queensland Conservatorium Research Centre, 2005.

Kauanui, J. Kēhaulani. '"A Structure, Not an Event": Settler Colonialism and Enduring Indigeneity'. *Lateral* 5, no. 1 (2016).

Khatun, Samia. *Australianama: The South Asian Odyssey in Australia*. London: C. Hurst & Co., Publishers Ltd, 2018.

Kleinert, Sylvia. 'An Aboriginal Moomba: Remaking History'. *Continuum* 13, no. 3 (1999): 345–57.

Kleinert, Sylvia. 'Aboriginality in the City: Re-Reading Koorie Photography'. *Aboriginal History* 30 (2006): 69–94.

Knopoff, Steven. 'Cross-Cultural Appropriation: A Musicologist's Perspective'. *Sounds Australian* 67 (2006): 24–7.

Knopoff, Steven. 'Indigenous and Non-Indigenous Collaboration in New Orchestral Music: Two Notable Successes from the Adelaide Festival of Arts'. In *Encounters: Meetings in Australian Music: Essays, Images, Interviews*, edited by Vincent Plush, Huib Schippers and Jocelyn Wolfe, 44–6. South Brisbane: Queensland Conservatorium Research Centre, 2005.

Konishi, Shino. 'First Nations Scholars, Settler Colonial Studies, and Indigenous History'. *Australian Historical Studies* 50, no. 3 (2019): 285–304.

Lacey, Kate. *Listening Publics: The Politics and Experience of Listening in the Media Age*. Oxford: Polity Press, 2013.

'Land Rights Vigil'. *The Canberra Times*, 25 April 1970, 2. http://nla.gov.au/nla.news-article107921778.

Lea Locke, Michelle. 'Wirrawi Bubuwul–Aboriginal Women Strong'. *Australian Journal of Education* 62, no. 3 (2018): 299–310.

'Left Out of Jubilee Ignored, Say Aborigines'. *The Argus*, 8 January 1951, 3. http://nla.gov.au/nla.news-article23037389.

Lethbridge, H. O., and Arthur S. Loam. *Australian Aboriginal Songs: Melodies, Rhythm and Words Truly and Authentically Aboriginal*. Melbourne: Allan, 1937.

'Life and Letters'. *The West Australian*, 29 November 1952, 17. http://nla.gov.au/nla.news-article49066252.

Low, Gail. 'At Home? Discoursing on the Commonwealth at the 1965 Commonwealth Arts Festival'. *The Journal of Commonwealth Literature* 48, no. 1 (2013): 97–111.

Macmillan, Jade. 'Endeavour Replica to Sail around Australia to Mark 250 Years Since Captain Cook's Arrival'. ABC News, 22 January 2019. www.abc.net.au/news/2019-01-22/endeavour-replica-to-sail-around-australia/10734998, accessed 24 January 2019.

Manning, Susan. *Modern Dance, Negro Dance: Race in Motion*. Minneapolis: University of Minnesota Press, 2004.

Markus, Andrew. *Australian Race Relations 1788–1993*. Sydney: Allen & Unwin, 1994.

Marett, Allan. *Songs, Dreamings, and Ghosts: The Wangga of North Australia*. Middletown, Conn.: Wesleyan University Press, 2005.

Martin, Toby. '"Socialist Paradise" or "Inhospitable Island"? Visitor Responses to Palm Island in the 1920s and 1930s'. *Aboriginal History* 38 (2014): 131–53.

Maxwell Davies, Peter. 'Foreword'. In *Australia's Contemporary Composers*, by James Murdoch. Melbourne: Sun Books, 1972.

Maxwell Davies, Peter. 'Influence of Aboriginal Music'. In *Peter Maxwell Davies: Selected Writings*, edited by Nicholas Jones. Cambridge: Cambridge University Press, 2017.

Maynard, John. *Fight for Liberty and Freedom: The Origins of Australian Aboriginal Activism*. Canberra: Aboriginal Studies Press, 2007.

McConaghy, Catherine. *Rethinking Indigenous Education: Culturalism, Colonialism and the Politics of Knowing*. Flaxton: Post Pressed, 2000.

McCredie, Andrew. *Musical Composition in Australia: Including Select Bibliography and Discography*. Canberra: Advisory Board, Commonwealth Assistance to Australian Composers, 1969.

McDonald, Penny. 'Too Many Captain Cooks'. Ronin Films, 1989.

McGregor, Russell. *Indifferent Inclusion: Aboriginal People and the Australian Nation* Canberra: Aboriginal Studies Press, 2011.

McKay, Belinda. '"A Lovely Land … By Shadows Dark Untainted"?: Whiteness and Early Queensland Women's Writing'. In *Whitening Race: Essays in Social and Cultural*

*Criticism*, edited by Aileen Moreton-Robinson, 148–63. Canberra: Aboriginal Studies Press, 2004.

McKay, Judith, and Paul Memmott. 'Staged Savagery: Archibald Meston and His Indigenous Exhibits'. *Aboriginal History* 40 (2016): 181–203.

McKenna, Mark. *Looking for Blackfellas' Point: An Australian History of Place*. Sydney: UNSW Press, 2002.

McLean, Ian. *How Aborigines Invented the Idea of Contemporary Art: An Anthology of Writing on Aboriginal Art 1980–2006*. Sydney: Power Publications, 2011.

McLean, Ian. *Rattling Spears: A History of Indigenous Australian Art*. London: Reaktion Books Ltd, 2016.

McNeill, Rhoderick. 'Clive Douglas and the Search for the Australian Symphony'. *Legacies* conference (February 2009). https://eprints.usq.edu.au/7950/.

McNeill, Rhoderick. 'Symphonies of the Bush: Indigenous Encounters in Australian Symphonies'. In *Encounters: Meetings in Australian Music: Essays, Images, Interviews*, edited by Vincent Plush, Huib Schippers and Jocelyn Wolfe, 18–21. Brisbane: Queensland Conservatorium Research Centre, 2005.

McNeill, Rhoderick. *The Australian Symphony from Federation to 1960*. Farnham, UK: Ashgate, 2014.

Millar, Grace. '"We Never Recovered": The Social Cost of the 1951 New Zealand Waterfront Dispute'. *Labour History*, no. 108 (May 2015): 89–101.

'Minister for Territories (Mr Hasluck) Describes Government's "New Deal" for Australia's Colored Minority'. *The Daily Telegraph*, 19 March 1953. http://nla.gov.au/nla.news-article248862562.

'Moomba – Something to Rave About'. *The Courier-Mail*, 29 June 1951, 2. http://nla.gov.au/nla.news-article50094479.

'More Hymns May Be Set to Native Chants', *Chronicle*, 12 April 1951: 8. http://nla.gov.au/nla.news-article93921099.

Moreton-Robinson, Aileen. *White Possessive: Property, Power, and Indigenous Sovereignty*. Minnesota: University of Minnesota Press, 2015.

Morgan, Kenneth. 'Cultural Advance: The Formation of Australia's Permanent Symphony Orchestras, 1944–1951'. *Musicology Australia* 33, no. 1 (2011): 69–93.

Morris, Steven. 'First Australian Piano Comes Home to UK After 231 Years'. *The Guardian*, 31 March 2019. www.theguardian.com/australia-news/2019/mar/31/first-australian-piano-comes-home-to-uk-after-231-years, accessed 3 April 2019.

Moses, John. 'Symbolism in Dancing of Beth Dean'. *The Sun*, 30 October 1952.

Murdoch, James. *Australia's Contemporary Composers*. Melbourne: Sun Books, 1972.

Murphy, Frank. 'Theatre Music'. *Advocate*, 2 December 1948, 18. http://nla.gov.au/nla.news-article172500602.

Musca, Carmelo. 'Didgeridoo in Deutschland'. Milsons Point, NSW: SBS-TV, 1988.

'Musica Viva's Third Spring Festival'. *The Canberra Times*, 18 September 1971, 19. http://nla.gov.au/nla.news-article110678101.

'Music and Drama'. *The Sydney Morning Herald*, 18 January 1936, 12. http://nla.gov.au/nla.news-article17222523.

'Music and Theatre Is this the Kind of Jubilee Music we Want?'. *The Sunday Herald*, 26 November 1950, 8 (Sunday Herald Features). http://nla.gov.au/nla.news-article18481984.

'Music, Drama & Films "Collits' Inn"', *The Argus*, 26 December 1933, 3. http://nla.gov.au/nla.news-article11724052.

'Music of Mirrabee'. *The Herald*, 22 February 1952, 7. http://nla.gov.au/nla. news-article246053171.
Naepels, Michel. 'Introduction – Anthropology and History: Through the Disciplinary Looking Glass'. *Annales. Histoire, Sciences Sociales* 4 (2010): 873–4.
Nakata, Martin. 'Australian Indigenous Studies: A Question of Discipline'. In 'Delimiting Indigenous Cultures: Conceptual and Spatial Boundaries', special issue, *The Australian Journal of Anthropology* 17, no. 3 (2006): 265–75.
'Nancy Ellis For Sydney'. *Sunday Times*, 19 April 1953, 10. http://nla.gov.au/nla. news-article59552688.
Natarajan, Radhika. 'Performing Multiculturalism: The Commonwealth Arts Festival of 1965'. *Journal of British Studies* 53, no. 3 (2014): 705–33.
Nathan, Isaac. *The Southern Euphrosyne and Australian Miscellany: Containing Oriental Moral Tales, Original Anecdote, Poetry and Music*. London, Sydney: Whittaker & Co., 1849.
'Native Artists'. *The Gosford Times and Wyong District Advocate*, 15 November 1940, 1. http://nla.gov.au/nla.news-article166932492.
'Native Arts and Crafts'. *The Herald*, 25 September 1934, 23. http://nla.gov.au/nla.news-article243107689.
'Native Corroboree'. *The Central Queensland Herald*, 6 December 1934, 37. http://nla.gov.au/nla.news-article70340211.
'Natives and Whites in Novel Carols'. *The Age*, 12 December 1953, 8. http://nla.gov.au/nla.news-article206909469.
'Natives Stage Corroboree for Charity'. *The Age*, 28 April 1934, 26. http://nla.gov.au/nla.news-article203839216.
'Near and Far'. *The Sydney Morning Herald*, 23 August 1923. http://nla.gov.au/nla.news-article16087100.
'Negotiations for Ballet Break Down'. *The Age*, 17 December 1949, 15 (The Age Literary Supplement). http://nla.gov.au/nla.news-article189481371.
Nelson, Kathleen E. 'Grainger and the Australian Broadcasting Commission after 1935: Memories, Hopes and Frustrations'. *Australasian Music Research* 5 (2000): 113–24.
Nelson, Kathleen E. 'Percy Grainger's Work for the Australian Broadcasting Commission, 1934–1935: Background and Reception'. *Australasian Music Research* 2–3 (1998): 99–110.
Neuenfeldt, Karl. '"I Wouldn't Change Skins with Anybody": Dulcie Pitt/Georgia Lee, a Pioneering Indigenous Australian Jazz, Blues and Community Singer'. *Jazz Research Journal* 8, no. 1–2 (2014): 202–22.
'News and Notes'. *The West Australian*, 14 September 1954, 3. http://nla.gov.au/nla.news-article49880283.
'New Shows: Australian Play Succeeds at the King's'. *The Argus*, 18 April 1949, 2. http://nla.gov.au/nla.news-article22723043.
'News of the Circuits'. *The Methodist*, 17 February 1934, 15. http://nla.gov.au/nla.news-article155309651.
'News of the Day'. *The Age*, 8 March 1948, 2. http://nla.gov.au/nla.news-article206880854.
'Nightingale Sang in Martin Place'. *Dawn* 11, no. 8 (August 1962): 3–4.
'No Corroboree'. *Northern Standard*, 9 March 1951, 4. http://nla.gov.au/nla.news-article 49476486.
'"No Corroboree", Natives Say'. *Northern Standard*, 16 February 1951, 3. http://nla.gov.au/nla.news-article49482592.

'Not an Alien'. *Evening News*, 6 January 1914, 7. http://nla.gov.au/nla.news-article114488953.
'NT Aborigine for London TV'. *The Canberra Times*, 29 March 1967, 12. http://nla.gov.au/nla.news-article107034135.
Nugent, Maria. *Botany Bay: Where Histories Meet*. Crows Nest, NSW: Allen & Unwin, 2005.
Nugent, Maria. *Captain Cook Was Here*. Cambridge: Cambridge University Press, 2009.
Nugent, Maria. '"The Queen Gave Us the Land": Aboriginal People, Queen Victoria and Historical Remembrance'. *History Australia* 9, no. 2 (2012): 182–200.
Nunn, Patrick D., and Nicholas J. Reid. 'Aboriginal Memories of Inundation of the Australian Coast Dating from More than 7000 Years Ago'. *Australian Geographer* 47, no. 1 (2016): 11–47.
O'Dea, K. 'Preventable Chronic Diseases Among Indigenous Australians: The Need for a Comprehensive National Approach'. *Heart, Lung and Circulation* 14, no. 3 (2005): 167–71.
'Oldest Australians Mourn the Jubilee'. *The Argus*, 16 January 1951, 5. http://nla.gov.au/nla.news-article23048214.
'Only Eleven Days to Go, then Starts'. *The Courier-Mail*, 23 January 1954, 2. http://nla.gov.au/nla.news-article50580435.
'On Stage and Screen'. *The Herald*, 5 October 1950, 23. http://nla.gov.au/nla.news-article244339447.
'Our Very Oldest Families'. *Queensland Times*, 5 March 1932, 7. http://nla.gov.au/nla.news-article113212220.
'Outback Informality for Duke's Tour'. *The Australian Women's Weekly*, 28 November 1956, 10. http://nla.gov.au/nla.news-article48072286.
'Outstanding Show by Beth Dean'. *Camperdown Chronicle*, 22 September 1950, 7. http://nla.gov.au/nla.news-article23576459.
'Packed Hall'. *Yass Tribune-Courier*, 13 February 1947, 1. http://nla.gov.au/nla.news-article248456226.
'Pageant by Aborigines'. *Sunday Times*, 25 April 1948, 3. http://nla.gov.au/nla.news-article59479822.
Paget, Jonathan. 'Has Sculthorpe Misappropriated Indigenous Melodies?'. *Musicology Australia* 35, no. 1 (2013): 86–111.
Peart, Donald. 'The Australian Avant-Garde'. *Proceedings of the Royal Musical Association* 93, no. 1 (1966): 1–9.
Penberthy, James. 'The Aboriginal Influence'. *Sounds Australian* 30 (1991): 23–4.
Phipps, Peter. 'Globalization, Indigeneity and Performing Culture'. *Local-Global: Identity, Security, Community* 6 (2009): 28–48.
'Plain Australian'. *Tribune*, 1 April 1970, 2. http://nla.gov.au/nla.news-article237503832.
'Plays and Players'. *Western Mail*, 10 July 1947, 54. http://nla.gov.au/nla.news-article38580555.
Plush, Vincent. 'Black Unlike Me'. *Griffith Review* 8 (Winter 2005).
Plush, Vincent. 'Roger Covell: The Go-Between'. *Context* 41 (2016): 45–58.
Plush, Vincent, and Peter Sculthorpe. 'Peter Sculthorpe in Conversation'. In *Encounters: Meetings in Australian Music: Essays, Images, Interviews*, edited by Vincent Plush, Huib Schippers and Jocelyn Wolfe, 26–30. South Brisbane: Queensland Conservatorium Research Centre, 2005.
'PM's Approval $256,412 in Grants to Aboriginal Arts'. *The Canberra Times*, 11 May 1974, 3. http://nla.gov.au/nla.news-article110777819.

Poignant, Roslyn. *Professional Savages: Captive Lives and Western Spectacle*. Sydney: UNSW Press, 2004.

'Polished Dancing by Ted Shawn'. *The Sun*, 28 August 1947, 9 (Late Final Extra). http://nla.gov.au/nla.news-article229695822.

'Porgy and Bess'. *The Australian Women's Weekly*, 1 December 1965, 3. http://nla.gov.au/nla.news-article48078237.

'Preparing City for Celebrations – Canadian Games Athletes in Training – New Customs Launch Tested'. *The Sydney Morning Herald*, 18 January 1938, 14. http://nla.gov.au/nla.news-article17429138.

'Project Revived'. *Cairns Post*, 8 March 1934, 4. http://nla.gov.au/nla.news-article41249934.

'Protest by Aborigines'. *The Herald*, 11 January 1946, 3. http://nla.gov.au/nla.news-article245949282.

'Queen Calls On "Leper Hunter"'. *The Canberra Times*, 19 March 1963, 3. http://nla.gov.au/nla.news-article104591325.

'Queen Excited at Boomerang Throwing'. *Morning Bulletin*, 15 February 1954, 1. http://nla.gov.au/nla.news-article57283365.

Quekett, Malcolm. 'Australia's First Aboriginal Ballerina Has Life of Wonder'. *The West Australian*, 3 July 2016. https://thewest.com.au/news/australia/australias-first-aboriginal-ballerina-has-life-of-wonder-ng-ya-111800, accessed 12 August 2019.

Read, Peter. '"A Rape of the Soul So Profound": Some Reflections on the Dispersal Policy in New South Wales'. *Aboriginal History* 7, no. 1/2 (1983): 23–33.

Read, Peter. 'Dispossession is a Legitimate Experience'. In *Long History, Deep Time: Deepening Histories of Place*, edited by Ann McGrath and Mary Ann Jebb, 119–32. Canberra: ANU Press, 2015.

Reader, Hazel. 'Malcolm Williamson in Australia'. *The Canberra Times*, 27 October 1967, 2. http://nla.gov.au/nla.news-article106994731.

'Red Meets Black'. *Sunday Times*, 25 January 1914, 22. http://nla.gov.au/nla.news-article120363890.

'Re-enactment of Cook's Landing', *Canberra Times*, 23 April 1970.

Rees, Leslie. '"Drama in Sydney". Review of Caroline Chisholm, George Landen Dann; The Highwayman, Edmond Samuels; Worm's Eye View, R. Delderfield'. *The Australian Quarterly* 23, no. 2 (June 1951): 125–7.

Reid, David. *James Penberthy: Music and Memories*. Tablo Publishing, 2019. https://tablo.io/david-reid-1/192e51523e4a.

'Reunions and Services'. *The Argus*, 21 April 1949, 6. http://nla.gov.au/nla.news-article22723800.

Revill, George. 'Hiawatha and Pan-Africanism: Samuel Coleridge-Taylor (1875–1912), a Black Composer in Suburban London'. *Cultural Geographies* 2, no. 3 (1995): 247–66.

Reynolds, Henry. *The Other Side of the Frontier: Aboriginal Resistance to the European Invasion of Australia*. Sydney: UNSW Press, 2006.

'Rifle Shooting'. *Williamstown Chronicle*, 23 April 1948, 10. http://nla.gov.au/nla.news-article70723088.

Robinson, Dylan. 'Listening to the Politics of Aesthetics: Contemporary Encounters Between First Nations/Inuit and Early Music Traditions'. In *Aboriginal Music in Contemporary Canada*, edited by Anna Hoefnagels and Beverley Diamond, 222–48. Montreal & Kingston: McGill's-Queen's University Press, 2012.

Rogalsky, Joyce. 'National Aborigines Day Observance Committee: New South Wales Annual Report for 1961'. *Dawn* 10, no. 11 (November 1961): 16–17.

Rosaldo, Renato. 'Imperialist Nostalgia'. *Representations*, no. 26 (1989): 107–22.
Rose, Deborah Bird. 'The Saga of Captain Cook: Morality in Aboriginal and European Law'. *Australian Aboriginal Studies* 2 (1984): 24–39.
Rose, Mark, and Kaye Price. 'The "Silent Apartheid" as the Practitioner's Blindspot'. In *Aboriginal and Torres Strait Islander Education: An Introduction for the Teaching Profession*, 2nd edn, 66–82. Cambridge: Cambridge University Press, 2015.
'Round Melbourne Shows'. *The Argus*, 21 August 1946, 12 (Woman's Magazine). http://nla.gov.au/nla.news-article22322403.
Rowse, Tim. *After Mabo: Interpreting Indigenous Traditions*. Carlton: Melbourne University Press, 1993.
Rowse, Tim, ed. *Contesting Assimilation*. Perth: API Network, 2005.
Rowse, Tim. *Indigenous and Other Australians Since 1901*. Sydney: UNSW Press, 2017.
Rowse, Tim. *White Flour, White Power: From Rations to Citizenship in Central Australia*. Melbourne: Cambridge University Press, 1998.
Ryan, Robin. '"A Spiritual Sound, a Lonely Sound": Leaf Music of Southeastern Aboriginal Australians, 1890s–1990s'. PhD thesis, Monash University, 1999.
Ryan, Robin. 'Ukuleles, Guitars or Gumleaves? Hula Dancing and Southeastern Australian Aboriginal Performers in the 1920s and 1930s'. *Perfect Beat* 3, no. 2 (1997).
Sainsbury, Christopher. *Ngarra-Burria: New Music and the Search for an Australian Sound*. Platform Paper 59. Currency Press, 2019.
Schlunke, Katrina. 'Entertaining Possession: Re-Enacting Cook's Arrival for the Queen'. In *Conciliation on Colonial Frontiers: Conflict, Performance, and Commemoration in Australia and the Pacific Rim*, edited by Kate Darian-Smith and Penelope Edmonds, 227–42. New York: Routledge, 2015.
Schultz, Marianne. *Performing Indigenous Culture on Stage and Screen*. Basingstoke: Palgrave Macmillan, 2016.
'Seats Tangle at Corroboree'. *The Age*, 26 April 1948, 3. http://nla.gov.au/nla.news-article206880443.
Sedneva, Olga. 'Corroboree: White Fella Vision'. Master's thesis, University of Sydney, 2013.
'Settlement of Australia'. *The Canberra Times*, 26 January 1963. http://nla.gov.au/nla.news-article104257317.
'Shawn Sees Our "Great" Dancers'. *The Mail*, 16 August 1947, 10. http://nla.gov.au/nla.news-article55891047.
Shea Murphy, Jacqueline. *The People Have Never Stopped Dancing: Native American Modern Dance Histories*. Minneapolis: University of Minnesota Press, 2007.
'She's a Cheerful, Singing Crusader'. *Dawn* 12, no. 9 (September 1963): 8.
Silsbury, Elizabeth. *State of Opera: An Intimate New History of the State Opera of South Australia 1957–2000*. Kent Town, South Australia: Wakefield Press, 2001.
Simpson, Leanne Betasamosake. *As We Have Always Done: Indigenous Freedom through Radical Resistance*. Minneapolis: University of Minnesota Press, 2017.
Simpson, Leanne Betasamosake. 'Indigenous Resurgence and Co-Resistance'. *Critical Ethnic Studies* 2, no. 2 (2016).
Simpson, Moira G. *Making Representations: Museums in the Post-Colonial Era*. London: Routledge, 1997.
'Singer Meets Aboriginal'. *News*, 5 July 1952, 10. http://nla.gov.au/nla.news-article130807881.
Sitsky, Larry. 'Australia: Emergence of the New Music in Australia'. *Perspectives of New Music* 4, no. 1 (1965): 176–9.

Skinner, Graeme. 'Australian Musical First Modernism'. In *The Modernist World*, edited by Stephen Ross and Allana C. Lindgren, 273–81. Abingdon: Routledge, 2015.
Skinner, Graeme. *Peter Sculthorpe: The Making of an Australian Composer*. Sydney: UNSW Press, 2015.
Skinner, Graeme. 'Toward a General History of Australian Musical Composition: First National Music, 1788-c. 1860'. PhD thesis, University of Sydney, 2011.
Slater, Lisa. *Anxieties of Belonging in Settler Colonialism: Australia, Race and Place*. Routledge Studies in Cultural History. Boca Raton, FL: Routledge, 2018.
Smith, Jim. 'Aboriginal Voters in the Burragorang Valley, NSW, 1869-1953'. *Journal of the Royal Australian Historical Society* 98, no. 2 (December 2012): 170–92.
Smith, Linda Tuhiwai. *Decolonizing Methodologies: Research and Indigenous Peoples*. London: Zed Books, 2013.
'Spears Fly at TV Viewers'. *The Canberra Times*, 3 April 1967, 6. http://nla.gov.au/nla.news-article131647361.
Spencer, Baldwin, and Francis James Gillen. *The Arunta: A Study of a Stone Age People*. London: Macmillan, 1927.
Spencer, Baldwin, and F. J. Gillen. *The Native Tribes of Central Australia*. London: Macmillan and Co., 1899.
Spencer, Baldwin. *Wanderings in Wild Australia*. London: Macmillan, 1928.
Spivak, Gayatri Chakravorty. 'Can the Subaltern Speak?'. In *Marxism and the Interpretation of Culture*, edited by Cary Nelson and Lawrence Grossberg, 271–313. London: Macmillan, 1988.
Spunner, Suzanne. 'Corroboree Moderne'. In *Modern Frontier: Aspects of the 1950s in Australia's Northern Territory*, edited by Julie T. Wells, Mickey Dewar and Suzanne Parry, 143–64. Darwin: Charles Darwin University Press, 2005.
St Ilan, Nicole. 'Clive Douglas: When Is a Jindyworobak Not a Jindyworobak?'. *Sounds Australian* 30 (1991): 32–38.
St Leon, Mark. *The Wizard of the Wire*. Canberra: Aboriginal Studies Press, 1993.
'Stage and Screen'. *The Sydney Morning Herald*, 21 June 1934, 9 (Women's Supplement). http://nla.gov.au/nla.news-article17088508
Stanhope, Paul. 'Jandamarra – Sing for the Country'. Sydney: Sydney Symphony Orchestra, 2014.
Stanhope, Paul. 'Jandamarra: Sing for the Country'. About Music Public Lecture Series. Sydney Conservatorium of Music, 2015.
Stanner, W. E. H. 'After the Dreaming: Black and White Australians – an Anthropologist's View'. In *The Boyer Lectures, 1968*, edited by Australian Broadcasting Commission Sydney: Australian Broadcasting Commission, 1969.
'States on the Nation'. *Tribune*, 8 February 1967, 4. http://nla.gov.au/nla.news-article237360748.
'State's Varied Jubilee Events'. *The Sydney Morning Herald*, 9 May 1951, 4. http://nla.gov.au/nla.news-article18216962.
Stout, A. K. 'Australian Theatre'. *The Australian Quarterly* 36, no. 1 (March 1964): 121–4.
Sullivan, Chris. 'Non-Tribal Dance Music and Song: From First Contact to Citizen Rights'. *Australian Aboriginal Studies*, no. 1 (1988): 64–7.
'Sundry Shows'. *The Bulletin*, 72, no. 3725, 4 July 1951, 19. http://nla.gov.au/nla.obj-518251413.
'Sydney Harbour Bridge', *The Argus*, 14 January 1932, 9. http://nla.gov.au/nla.news-article4417296.

Symons, David. *Before and After Corroboree: The Music of John Antill.* Farnham, UK: Ashgate, 2015.
Symons, David. '*Corroboree* and After: John Antill as a "One-Work Composer"?' *Musicology Australia* 34, no. 1 (July 2012): 53–80.
Symons, David. 'The Jindyworobak Connection in Australian Music c.1940–1960'. *Context* 23 (Autumn 2002): 33–47.
Symons, David. *The Music of Margaret Sutherland.* Sydney: Currency Press, 1997.
Symons, David. 'Words and Music: Clive Douglas and the Jindyworobak Manifesto'. In *The Soundscapes of Australia: Music, Place and Spirituality*, edited by Fiona Richards, 93–115. Aldershot: Ashgate, 2007.
Tate, Henry. *Australian Musical Possibilities.* Melbourne: Edward A. Vidler, 1924.
'Team of Abos', *Illawarra Mercury*, 21 August 1931, 8. http://nla.gov.au/nla.news-article132891654.
'Ted Shawn's Diverse Solo Dances'. *The Sydney Morning Herald*, 1 September 1947, 9. http://nla.gov.au/nla.news-article18040946.
'Ted Shawn Hurts Knee'. *The Daily News*, 2 August 1947, 22 (Late Sports). http://nla.gov.au/nla.news-article83747636.
'Ted Shawn to "Sell Dancing for Men"'. *The Sydney Morning Herald*, 24 April 1947, 6. http://nla.gov.au/nla.news-article18023070.
'The 1964 Tour Kira Bousloff as Told to Val Green'. *Brolga* 16 (1 June 2002). https://ausdance.org.au/articles/details/the-1964-tour, accessed 13 August 2019.
'The Abos Dance for A Famous Dancer'. *News*, 5 August 1947, 2. http://nla.gov.au/nla.news-article127057604.
'The Australian Elizabethan Theatre Trust'. www.thetrust.org.au/, accessed 26 August 2019.
'The Beauties of Music'. *The Murrumbidgee Irrigator*, 1 July 1938, 5. http://nla.gov.au/nla.news-article156146819.
'"The Bird of Paradise"'. *Daily Herald*, 26 March 1918, 7. http://nla.gov.au/nla.news-article105461210.
'The Grand Old Man of Australian Music'. *Le Courrier Australien*, 11 February 1955, 6. http://trove.nla.gov.au/newspaper/article/225595938.
'The Princess "Collits' Inn" Revived'. *The Argus*, 15 October 1934, 4. http://nla.gov.au/nla.news-article10988617.
'The Procession'. *The Sydney Morning Herald*, 27 March 1896. http://nla.gov.au/nla.news-article14043231.
'This Week on ABC-3'. *The Canberra Times*, 4 February 1963, 16. http://nla.gov.au/nla.news-article104258165.
Thomas, Martin. 'The Rush to Record: Transmitting the Sound of Aboriginal Culture'. *Journal of Australian Studies* 31, no. 90 (2007): 107–202.
Thomson, John. '"It's Australian – and It's Good!": The Australian Musical Collits' Inn'. *National Library of Australia News* 14, no. 3 (December 2003): 7–10.
Thorpe, Kirsten. 'Indigenous Records: Connecting, Critiquing and Diversifying Collections'. *Archives and Manuscripts* 42, no. 2 (2014): 211–14.
Thorpe, Kirsten. 'Speaking Back to Colonial Collections: Building Living Aboriginal Archives'. *Artlink* 39, no. 2 (2019).
'Those Fearsome Islanders'. *Sydney Telegraph*, 23 April 1970.
'Too Many Cooks?' *Tamworth Leader*, 30 April 1970.

'Tragedy Comes Out of the Stone Age'. *The Sun-Herald*, 18 October 1953, 65. http://nla.gov.au/nla.news-article28655142.

Treloyn, Sally. 'Cross and Square: Variegation in the Transmission of Songs and Musical Styles between the Kimberley and Daly Regions of Northern Australia'. In *Circulating Cultures: Exchanges of Australian Indigenous Music, Dance and Media*, edited by Amanda Harris, 203–38. Canberra: ANU Press, 2014.

Tuck, Eve. 'Rematriating Curriculum Studies'. *Journal of Curriculum and Pedagogy* 8, no. 1 (2011): 34–7.

Tuck, Eve, and K. Wayne Yang. 'R-words: Refusing Research'. In *Humanizing Research: Decolonizing Qualitative Inquiry with Youth and Communities*, edited by Django Paris and Maisha T. Winn, 223–48. Los Angeles: Sage, 2014.

Tucker, Margaret. *If Everyone Cared: Autobiography of Margaret Tucker MBE*. New edn. London: Grosvenor, 1983. First published in 1977 by Ure Smith (Sydney).

Turnbull, Peter, and David Sapsford. 'Hitting the Bricks: An International Comparative Study of Conflict on the Waterfront'. *Industrial Relations* 40, no. 2 (2001): 231–57.

Turpin, Myfany. 'Return of a Travelling Song: Wanji-wanji in the Pintupi Region of Central Australia'. In *Archival Returns: Central Australia and Beyond*, edited by Linda Barwick, Jennifer Green and Petronella Vaarzon-Morel, 239–63. Sydney: Sydney University Press, 2020.

Underwood, Alan. 'Queen Votes Cooktown as Greatest Day'. *Brisbane Courier Mail*, 23 April 1970.

'US Tourists' "Spending Spree" At Darwin'. *The Advertiser*, 20 February 1951, 1. http://nla.gov.au/nla.news-article45689016.

'Vaucluse Pageant'. *The Sydney Morning Herald*, 21 March 1932, 14. http://nla.gov.au/nla.news-article16849399.

Veracini, Lorenzo. *The Settler Colonial Present*. London: Palgrave Macmillan, 2015.

Volkofsky, Aimee. '"We thought they were going to be massacred": 80 Years Since Forced First Fleet Re-enactment'. *ABC News*, 25 January 2018. www.abc.net.au/news/2018-01-25/eighty-years-since-forced-first-fleet-reenactment/9358854, accessed 13 May 2019.

Wahlquist, Carla. '"History is Messy": Twin Art Shows that Could Aid Australia's Reconciliation'. *The Guardian*, 15 March 2018. www.theguardian.com/australia-news/2018/mar/15/history-is-messy-twin-art-shows-that-could-aid-australias-reconciliation, accessed 24 January 2020.

Wainburranga, Paddy Fordham. 'Too Many Captain Cooks' [artwork]. http://collections.anmm.gov.au/en/objects/details/31547/too-many-captain-cooks.

Walker, Clinton. *Buried Country: The Story of Aboriginal Country Music*. Sydney: Pluto Press, 2000.

'"Warriors" on Relief Jobs'. *The Sun*, 9 September 1937, 2 (Late Final Extra). http://nla.gov.au/nla.news-article229449751.

Waterhouse, Richard. 'Empire and Nation: Australian Popular Ideology and the Outbreak of the Pacific War'. *History Australia* 12, no. 3 (2015): 30–54.

'Waters Case Adjourned Protest Movement Mounts "Should Hear Promptly" — Judge'. *Northern Standard*, 9 March 1951, 1. http://nla.gov.au/nla.news-article49476505.

Waters, Thorold. 'Australia Tunes a Strange Lay'. *The Listener In*, 6 February 1937, 16.

Watters-Cowan, Chérie. 'Reconstructing the Creative Life of Australian Composer Margaret Sutherland: The Evidence of Primary Source Documents'. PhD thesis, University of NSW, 2006.

Watts, Richard. 'Perth Festival Dedicates First Week Exclusively to First Nations'. *Arts Hub*, 1 November 2019. www.artshub.com.au/festival/news-article/news/festivals/richard-watts/perth-festival-dedicates-first-week-exclusively-to-first-nations-259144, accessed 18 January 2020.

'We Cannot Rush ... Assimilation is Gradual'. *Dawn* 10, no. 7 (July 1961): 1–4.

'"We Discover Old Australians". Aborigines Cynical about Jubilee'. *Argus*, 30 January 1951, 2. http://nla.gov.au/nla.news-article23036858.

'"Wicked Lie," Says Station Manager'. *The Sun*, 6 January 1938, 2 (Late Final Extra). http://nla.gov.au/nla.news-article231109908.

'Wild West Rodeo'. *The Sydney Morning Herald*, 26 December 1933, 2. http://nla.gov.au/nla.news-article17035367.

Willis, Anne-Marie, and Tony Fry. 'Art as Ethnocide: The Case of Australia'. *Third Text* 2, no. 5 (1988): 3–20.

Winungudj, George. 'The Sound of the Didgeridu Overseas'. *Dhawu* 1, no. 2 (1973): 4.

Wolfe, Patrick. 'Settler Colonialism and the Elimination of the Native'. *Journal of Genocide Research* 8, no. 4 (2006): 387–409.

Wolfe, Patrick. *Settler Colonialism and the Transformation of Anthropology: The Politics and Poetics of an Ethnographic Event*. London, New York: Cassell, 1999.

'Women Speakers at the Factories'. *Tribune*, 13 March 1957, 9. http://nla.gov.au/nla.news-article236321951.

'World's Women May Dress in Corroboree Designs'. *The Daily Telegraph*, 12 June 1937, 7. http://nla.gov.au/nla.news-article247141018.

Wright, Alexis. *Tracker: Stories of Tracker Tilmouth*. Artarmon, NSW: Giramondo Publishing, 2017.

Yates, Kerry. 'Revue Is Truly All-Australian'. *The Australian Women's Weekly*, 17 July 1963, 12. http://nla.gov.au/nla.news-article51392997.

'Your Radio'. *The Daily Telegraph*, 20 October 1946, 6. http://nla.gov.au/nla.news-article248407019.

'Yulunga Natives Went Bush'. *The Daily Telegraph*, 21 February 1950, 7. http://nla.gov.au/nla.news-article248991655.

# Index

ABC, *see* Australian Broadcasting Commission
Aboriginal activism 6, 10, 12, 13, 14, 26, 33, 36, 37, 53, 56, 56, 72, 73, 97, 143, 145, 148, 171 n.60
Aboriginal Affairs, Department of 119, 124, 191 n.31, 192 n.48-9
Aboriginal and Torres Strait Islander dance 34-5, 45-7, 50-1, 53, 56, 65, 72, 98, 103-4, 121-2, 123, 128, 139, 144-5, 158 n.48, 158 n.50, 200 n.73
Aboriginal and Torres Strait Islander music 1-4, 6, 8, 10-14, 27, 40-2, 62, 110-11, 156 n.25, 158 n.48, 187 n.70; song, 2, 4, 6, 15-16, 17, 20, 22, 23, 38, 43, 48, 60, 61, 77, 93, 95, 98-101, 110, 116-18, 121, 125, 131, 132, 136, 137, 140, 143, 146, 147, 150, 173 n.83, 179 n.79, 199 n.60
Aboriginal Arts Board 11
Aboriginal Enterprises 86, 89
Aboriginal Islander Dance Theatre (AIDT) 10-11, 65, 114, 144, 158 n.46
*Aboriginal Moomba* 9, 13, 56, 71, 72, 73-4, 83, 86, 88-90
Aboriginal rights 10, 14, 15, 18, 33, 37, 39, 48, 52-4, 57, 64, 73, 74, 84, 85, 97, 138, 164 n.59, 172 n.79 ( *see also* citizenship, land rights, referendum for constitutional change, civil rights)
*Aboriginal Theatre* 13, 93-4, 100-3, 105, 107, 109-11, 114, 118-19, 121-3, 125, 131, 136, 141, 143, 144, 184 n.42, 185 n.43, 186 n.55
Aboriginal Theatre Foundation (Aboriginal Cultural Foundation) 11, 93, 103, 105, 109, 111, 114, 116, 119, 121, 122-3, 124, 144, 186 n.55, 192 n.49
Aborigines' Inland Mission of Australia 38, 95
Aborigines Progressive Association 36, 38, 86
Aborigines Protection Board (NSW) 7, 9, 10, 19, 20, 26, 27, 30, 31, 32-7, 39, 54, 67, 97, 108, 136, 156 n.28, 157 n.38
Aborigines Welfare Board, *see* Aborigines Protection Board
absorption 8, 32-3
Adelaide Wind Quintet 116, 141, 144
Adult Education Boards 61, 65, 77, 106
African American performers 13, 39, 45, 48, 56, 65-6, 77, 82, 97, 127, 129, 144-5, 174 n.7
Agnew, Roy 42, 166 n.89; *Dance of the Wild Men*, 42
Ahmed, Sara 142
Ailey, Alvin 39, 65, 144, 174 n.7
Aistone, George 38
*Alcheringa* (tv series) 86, 197 n.15 (*see also* Dreamtime)
Anggilidji, Skipper 93, 184 n.38
anthropology/anthropologists 4, 6, 9, 10, 30, 31, 60-1, 80, 101, 124-5, 133, 134, 155 n.12
Antill, John 1, 7, 11-13, 27, 41-2, 44, 46, 52, 57-9, 63-5, 68-74, 81-4, 87-8, 95-7, 106-7, 109, 131-48, 156 n.26, 166 n.81, 175 n.22, 180 n.89, 181 n.95, 182 n.9, 188 n.82; *Black Opal*, 109; *Burragorang Dreamtime*, 13, 94, 107, 108-9, 142; *Corroboree*, 1, 7, 12, 41, 44, 46, 52, 57-9, 61, 63-6, 68-74, 78, 81-4, 87-8, 106-7, 110, 117, 124, 126-7, 131-48; 166 n.81, 171 n.63, 172 n.70, 175 n.18, 194 n.70, 197 n.15; film music, 135, 188 n.82; *Jubugalee*, 126, 188 n.84

appropriation 4, 6, 9, 81, 106, 111, 124, 132, 136, 199 n.63
archives (as contested sources) 17–18, 20–2, 155 n.15
Arnhem Land 13, 61, 67, 78, 93, 102, 110, 116, 118, 140, 141, 164 n.54, 188 n.79, 190 n.15
Arnold, Amy Waylee 50
Arnold, Ronne 66, 124, 127, 144
Arrernte (Aranda, Arunta) 8, 41, 68, 118, 132–134
art (visual); Aboriginal, 14, 27, 60, 69, 83–4, 85, 86, 89, 93, 94, 101, 127, 129, 132, 137; bark painting, 38, 93, 94, 97, 107; exhibitions, 6, 25–8, 37, 38, 84, 89, 93, 122, 201 n.87; rock art, 25, 52, 60, 69, 176 n.27
art (music) 4, 6, 14, 40, 41, 43, 56, 59, 68, 71, 78, 101, 106, 110, 114, 115, 117, 129, 132, 136, 139, 140, 142, 146, 147, 156 n.25, 159
Arts Council of Australia 12, 59, 64, 65, 69, 70, 71, 78, 101, 107, 113, 126–7
ASIO, *see* Australian Security Intelligence Organisation
Assimilation era (assimilation policy) 1, 7–9, 11, 12, 14, 26, 32–3, 44, 54, 62, 89, 95, 97, 99, 107, 113, 119, 120, 122, 133, 138, 139, 159 n.9, 162 n.25, 174 n.92
assimilationist thinking 8, 9, 13, 16, 33, 62, 83, 162 n.25
Attwood, Bain 5
Australia Council for the Arts (*also* Australian Council for the Arts) 124, 143, 149
Australia Hall 18, 19, 20
Australian Aborigines' League 13, 51, 53, 57, 63, 71, 74, 83, 86–91, 143, 174 n.8
Australian Ballet 106, 113, 126, 175 n.18
Australian Broadcasting Commission (ABC) 10, 12, 27, 40–1, 56, 58, 64, 67–8, 69, 70, 71, 95, 106, 109, 110, 115, 135, 167 n.99, 172 n.71
Australian Elizabethan Theatre Trust 13, 64–5, 82, 93, 100, 102, 104–6, 118–19, 125, 131, 141, 143, 184 n.42
Australian Museum 30, 31

Australian Performing Rights Association (APRA) 59
Australian Security Intelligence Organisation (ASIO) 60, 75, 86, 90, 171 n.61
Australianist music 14, 41, 44, 57, 58, 137
authenticity 9, 21, 30, 54, 73, 77, 78, 101, 102, 116, 137, 185 n.46
Avery, Eric 147

Babui, Irene 125, 193 n.59, 193 n.61
Bagot Aboriginal Reserve 63, 74, 185 n.44
Balk Balk, Jimmy 186 n.58
ballet, *see* dance
Baluka, Michel 99
Bandler, Faith 64, 75, 87, 90
Bangarra Dance Theatre 76, 129, 144, 146, 158 n.46
Banks, Don 126
Bargo, Bill 52
Barngil 184 n.38
Barr, Margaret 135
Barton, William 141, 145–6, 199 n.60
Barunga, Albert 116, 122
Barwick, Linda 15, 17, 133
Bates, Daisy 141
Beale, Bryan 194 n.75
Beale, Donna 194 n.75
Beale, Fred 194 n.75
Beale, Greg 194 n.75
Beale, Joan 194 n.75
Beale, Kim 194 n.75
Beale Jr., Fred 194 n.75
Beeanamu (Bianomu) 46, 125
Bell, Eva, *see* Mumbler, Eva
Bennet Maclean, Debra 81, 83
Bennett, Dorothy 93–4, 107, 122
Bennett, Lance 122
Berlin, Irving, 60–1; *Annie Get Your Gun*, 61, 78
Beswick Aboriginal Settlement 103, 123
Beulah, Lorna 71, 97, 182 n.17
Bharucha, Rustom 1
Biellum, Lawrence 121, 191 n.37
Bilayna, Larry 99
Black Theatre 76, 88, 114, 144
Black, Gladys 163 n.35

Black, Hero 36, 163 n.35; *The Menindee Waltz*, 36
blackface (blacking up) 53, 69, 70, 76, 81, 87, 107, 141
Blair, Harold 43, 47, 52, 54–7, 59, 70–2, 78, 82–3, 90, 94, 97, 138–9, 141, 144, 167 n.94, 170 n.48, 170–1 n.54, 171 n.60–1, 172 n.79, 177 n.46, 179 n.80–1, 187 n.70, 198 n.45, 198 n.47, 200 n.64
Blakeney, Ben 128, 141, 194 n.75, 199 n.51
Blanasi, David 104, 118, 121, 122, 141, 144, 186 n.58, 191 n.37
Board for the Protection of Aborigines (Victoria) 7, 10, 27, 32, 38, 163 n.48, 164 n.50
Bodenwieser, Gertrud 13, 43, 59, 66, 158 n.43, 167 n.95; *The Kunkarunkara Woman*, 13, 43
Bokara 184 n.38
Boney, Archie 36
boomerang 12, 15, 20, 21, 22, 28, 32, 38, 53, 57, 67, 70, 73, 83, 85, 87, 89, 97, 108, 128, 139, 161 n.2
Borovansky, Eduard 59
Botany Bay (Kamay) 9, 16, 31, 113
Bousloff, Kira 82, 139, 141
BPA, *see* Board for the Protection of Aborigines
Briggs, Evelyn 71, 83, 177 n.36
Briggs, Geraldine 71, 83, 177 n.36
Brown, Albert 194 n.75
Brown, Edna 169 n.28
Brumbie, Nancy 39, 164 n.59
Bucks, Ivy 177 n.46
Bullfrog (Japanangka) 196 n.12
bullroarer 110, 187 n.70, 196–7 n.15
Bundilil (Budalil), Dick 121, 141, 191 n.37
Bundjalung 120, 128
Bungle, Joe 168 n.19
Burarrwanga, Dhambuljawa 121, 191 n.37
Burarrwanga, Rrikin 121, 191 n.37
Butterley, Nigel 126, 187 n.66
Bux, Edgar 52
Bux, Harold 169 n.28

Calder Nalagandi, William 193 n.59
Campbell, John (Jacko) 168 n.12
Capell, Arthur 101

Carell, Victor 11, 60–1, 65, 74, 77–81, 109, 118, 124–7, 134, 157 n.39, 166 n.91, 173 n.81, 179 n.80, 194 n.70, 196 n.12; *Carrumbo*, 79, 180 n.82
Carey, Bundathunoo Fred 50
Carmichael, Aunty Beryl Philp 34–5
Carowra Tank Aboriginal Reserve 36
Carrodus, J. A. 33
Carter, Paul 111
CEMA, *see* Council for the Encouragement of Music and the Arts
ceremony 8, 23, 93, 107, 124, 125, 131, 133, 158 n.48, 172 n.68, 180 n.82, 188 n.87, 196 n.12
Chan, Harry 99
Charles, Herbert 120
Charles, Jack 76, 88, 144
Chauvel, Charles; *Uncivilised*, 34
Cheetham, Deborah 147
Cherbourg Mission 54
child removal 8, 27, 120, 133, 139, 157 n.32
Chirnside, Jacob 72, 177 n.46
churinga, *see* tjuringa
citizenship 6, 8, 32, 33, 37, 54, 57, 62, 98, 113–14, 157 n.29
civil rights 18, 44, 60, 68, 71, 88
clapsticks 29, 88, 94, 127–8, 131–2
Clark, Manning 142
Clem, Charlie 168 n.12
Close, Rory 120
Clutsam and Ross; *Lilac Time*, 40, 165 n.66
Coad, Alan 43, 78, 179 n.81
Cobbo, Dick 177 n.46
Cobbo, Jack 177 n.46
Colbung, Betty 194 n.75
Colbung, Ken (Nundjan Djiridjarkan) 128, 194 n.75
Coleridge, Samuel Taylor 68; *Hiawatha*, 68, 69
collaboration 17
Colleano, Con 60
Collins, Oscar 177 n.46
commemoration 3, 8, 9, 12, 14, 31, 37–8, 48, 109, 113, 135, 137, 156 n.20, 160 n.11

Commonwealth Festival of Arts (London 1965) 13, 105–7, 110
Commonwealth Film Unit, *see* Film Australia
Communist Party 52, 54, 55, 60, 75, 77, 88, 171 n.61
Conference of Commonwealth and State Aboriginal Authorities (1937) 32
Constable, William 134
Conyngham, Barry 126, 187 n.66
Cook, Captain James 3, 5, 9, 14, 28–9, 31, 38, 43, 49, 73, 113, 127, 129, 131, 156 n.20, 161 n.2; bicentenary, 14, 113, 123–7, 189 n.1, 193 n.63
Cook, Dr C. E. 8
Cook Islands National Arts Theatre 125–6
Cook, Nicholas 147
Cook saga 5, 155 n.17, 195 n.1
Cooktown 5, 128, 195 n.79
Coombs, H. C. (Nugget) 100, 124–5, 183 n.36, 191 n.40
Cooper, Melvina 177 n.46
Cooper, William 19, 33
Corn, Aaron 146
Corner, Sadie 50
corroboree 1, 19–20, 26, 28, 29–30, 34, 38–9, 40, 50, 52, 53–4, 56, 58, 63–4, 66–75, 83, 86–9, 99, 109, 111, 120, 141, 158 n.48, 161 n.12, 164 n.54, 170 n.49, 172 n.68, 188 n.79
Council for the Encouragement of Music and the Arts (CEMA) 55, 59, 65, 138
Country (Aboriginal) 14, 15, 21, 30, 32, 74, 87, 99, 102, 135, 137, 138, 139, 140, 149, 158 n.53, 159 n.4, 162 n.30
Covell, Roger 40, 44, 58, 101–2, 109, 114–17, 141, 156 n.25, 166 n.89, 171 n.63, 187 n.66, 189 n.9
Crawford, Jim 51–2, 76
cross-cultural interaction 1, 5, 54, 57, 98, 111, 132, 154 n.8
Cruse, Kerrie 194 n.75
Cruse, Peter 194 n.75
Cugley, Ian 126, 141
Cummeragunja 37, 48, 54, 88
Curran, James 62

Cutmore, Clive 95
Cutmore, Max 95

Dadayna, Roy 184 n.38
Daisy, George 177 n.46
Daly River Region 13, 45, 63, 93, 100, 103, 121, 125, 131, 184 n.38, 185 n.44, 191 n.41, 193 n.61, 195 n.2
Danaiyarri, Hobbles 5
dance: 'ethnic dance', 61, 65, 77, 79; Aboriginal (*see* Aboriginal and Torres Strait Islander dance); ballet, 1, 7, 12–14, 40, 49–52, 58–9, 63–5, 68–79, 81, 94, 98, 106–9, 117, 120, 124–6, 194 n.67, 194 n.70; Cuban, 45; folk, 75, 76; hula, 12, 48–9, 52, 56, 73, 168 n.22; Indian, 45, 65–6, 106; Japanese, 45; modern, 65, 81; Native American, 45; Osage-Pawnee, 45; Spanish, 45; Syrian Sufi dervish, 45
Darqual 184 n.38
Darwin Festival 98, 103, 143–4, 185 n.49, 200 n.69
Darwin Symphony Orchestra 145
Davis, Merle 177 n.46
Davis, Percy (Square) 168 n.12
Davis, Pete 177 n.46
*Dawn* magazine 96–7, 108, 182 n.10
Day of Mourning 9, 12, 15, 18–19, 33–6, 71, 113, 137, 160 n.13
Dean, Beth 11, 13–14, 60–1, 65–6, 74, 77–83, 101–2, 104, 107–10, 117–19, 124–7, 134, 157 n.39, 158 n.43, 173 n.81, 180 n.83, 194 n.70, 196 n.12; *Ballet of the South Pacific*, 118, 124–7; *Burragorang Dreamtime* (*see* Antill, John: *Burragorang Dreamtime*); *Corroboree* (*see* Antill, John: *Corroboree*); *Dreaming Time Legends*, 107; *Kukaitcha*, 14, 118, 134, 194 n.70
Deimbalibu, 184 n.38
Delissaville (Belyuen) 45–6, 61, 99, 125
Deloria, Philip J. 2–3
Department of Territories 44
Devine, Dandy 182 n.15

Dewar, Micky 144
Dharawal (D'harawal) 11, 12, 15, 16, 23, 25, 40, 49, 72, 111, 136
Dharug 12, 58, 111, 147, 158 n.48, 172 n.68, 188 n.87
didjeridu 1, 43, 70, 93–4, 97–9, 110, 116–18, 125, 128, 134, 141–2, 144–5, 155 n.15, 187 n.70, 199 n.57
Didji, Margaret 184 n.38
displacement 72, 108–9, 162 n.30
Dixon, Chicka 145
Dixon, Dean 106
Dja Dja Warrung 5, 11
Djergujergu, Junmal 184 n.38
Dodd, Steve 194 n.75
Donnellan, Frank 97
Doolan, Peter 95
Douglas, Clive 27, 41–2, 44–5, 57–9, 132, 166 n.81, 187 n.66; *Bush Legend (Kaditcha)*, 41; *Carwoola*, 41; *Corroboree*, 41, 44, 58; *Namatjira*, 59, 70
Douglas, Winifred 177 n.46
Drake Brockman, Henrietta 83
Dreamtime (Alcheringa, Tjukurrpa) 133, 142
Dreyfus, George 115–17, 141–3, 145, 187 n.66, 199 n.57; *Sextet for didjeridu and wind instruments*, 116, 141
Drysdale, Russell 101
Duguid, Charles 164 n.59
Duke, Steve 95
Dulainga 184 n.38
Dumoo, Frank Artu 93, 184 n.38
Duncan, Todd 56, 60, 170 n.54
Dundiwoi 184 n.38
Dungala 184 n.38
Dunham, Katherine 39, 65, 174 n.7–8
Durack, Mary 82, 122–3, 140, 143
'dying race' discourse 6, 61, 95, 173 n.86

Eagle Horse, Chief 39
Earle, Bitha Joy 50
Edwards, Charlie 168 n.19
Edwards, Con 169 n.28
Edwards, Ross 14, 126, 134, 142; *Missa Alchera*, 134, 142
Elcho Island Dancer 145
Eleo Pomare Dance Company 65, 144

Elizabeth II, Queen 13, 61, 64–5, 71, 73–4, 81, 97, 107, 109, 113, 127, 154 n.9, 163 n.35, 188 n.79, 194 n.71
Elkin, A. P. 9, 32–3, 38, 54, 61, 67, 69, 78, 101, 110, 116, 126, 165 n.63, 176 n.27, 179 n.79, 190 n.15
Ellis, Catherine 140, 142, 183 n.34
Ellis, Nancy 39, 77, 139, 164 n.60, 198 n.31
Embu Drummers 106
Emerson, Harry 177 n.46
entrepreneurs; cultural 11, 12, 138
Ernabella Choir 71
Evans, Stanley 50
Evans, Ted 99, 100, 103, 105, 119, 121, 122, 124, 183 n.27
Ewers, John (Keith) 45, 83, 200 n.65
exemption certificates 7, 33, 54, 81, 181 n.92
expeditions 60, 61, 78, 176 n.27, 184 n.39

Federal Council for the Advancement of Aborigines and Torres Strait Islanders (FCAATSI) 105, 189 n.2
Federation 1, 64, 66, 68, 70
Ferguson, Duncan 36
Ferguson, William 33, 36, 38, 54
festivals 123, 125, 137, 143, 144, 167 n.95, 169 n.25, 192 n.43 (*see also* Musica Viva: festival)
Film Australia 44, 135
First Fleet 3, 5, 9, 12, 29–30, 33, 43, 107, 137, 162 n.30, 193 n.63
Fisher, Betty 97, 182 n.15
Flemming, Claude 34
Foley, Gary 145
folk music, *see* song: folk
Ford, Payi Linda 133
Fordham, Paddy Wainburranga 131, 195 n.1
Fosbery, MP Edmund 8
Foster, Eliza 34
Foster, Fred 16–17, 72, 73, 177 n.46
Foster, Shannon 11, 15, 26, 29
Foster, Stephen 48
Foster, Ted 164 n.50
Foster, Tom (La Perouse) 11, 12, 15–17, 16–23, 25–9, 33–4, 161 n.13; *I'm Happy Today*, 16, 23, 49; *My Thoughts*, 16, 23

Foster, Tom (Lake Tyers) 52
Friml, Rudolf 39, 40; *Rose-Marie*, 39, 40, 165 n.66

Gadigal 15
Galpu Wilderness Dancers 145
Gapps, Stephen 69
Garbat, Sugar 184 n.38
Garmali 184 n.38
Geddes, William 101
Gershwin, George; *Porgy and Bess*, 97, 105
Giese, Harry 100, 107, 122, 183 n.31, 183–4 n.36, 186 n.55, 191 n.40
Gifford, Brenda 147
Gillen, Francis 61, 78, 118, 133–5, 143, 196 n.5
Gloucester, Duke of 34
Goldner, Richard 59
Goorie 81, 181 n.91
Goossens, Eugene 44, 57, 58, 167 n.95, 175 n.22
Gordon, Ken 128, 194 n.75
Gorton, Prime Minister John 127
Goulburn Island (Warruwi) 116, 117, 122
Grabowsky, Paul 146
Grainger, Percy 40–2, 115, 166 n.83; *Colonial Song*, 166 n.83; *Gumsuckers' March*, 166 n.83; *The Warriors*, 42
Grandage, Iain 145, 199 n.60, 201 n.77
Gray, Bill 122, 185 n.44
Gray, Geoffrey 33
Gray, Jack 177 n.46
Gray, Tim 147
Green, Harry 54–6
Green, Lucy 48, 56, 71, 168 n.15, 177 n.36
Grosvenor, Helen 33, 36
Gulpilil, David 121, 122, 141, 191 n.37
gumleaf bands 12, 15, 20, 28, 29, 30, 38, 39, 48, 49, 52, 73, 95–6, 128, 138, 168 n.12, 168 n.22
Gundungarra 108–9
gunya(h) 1, 26, 30, 127 (*see also* mia mia)
Gweagal people 107, 113, 127, 148

Haag, Stefan 82, 100–5, 118, 119, 122, 124, 125, 158 n.43, 171 n.59, 183 n.36, 184 n.40, 194 n.70

Haasts Bluff (Ikuntji) 63–4, 134
Haebich, Anna 7
Hardy, Col 97
Harney, Bill 45, 61, 179 n.79
Harold Davies, E. 41
Harris, Dan 50
Harris, Rolf 117, 122
Hasluck, Paul 8, 13, 62, 77, 97, 103, 139, 174 n.92
Hawke, Prime Minister Bob 123
Hawke, Steve 146
Heinze, Sir Bernard 101, 106, 175 n.22
Helmrich, Dorothy 56, 59, 65, 78, 101, 126, 127, 175 n.18, 175 n.22, 176 n.22, 194 n.70
Helpmann, (Sir) Robert 59, 126
Hill, Alfred 41, 60–1, 69, 78, 142, 173 n.84; *Auster*, 41; *Poor Fellow Me*, 166 n.91, 179 n.79, 179 n.81
Hill, Mirrie 60–1, 69, 77, 78, 179 n.79, 187 n.66
Hindson, Matthew 145–6
Hodgens, Jessica 5
Hoskins, Ernie (Friday) 168 n.12
Hoskins, Joan 168 n.19
Hoskins, Ned 168 n.12
Hughes, Robert 27, 187 n.66; *Sinfonietta*, 59
hula, *see* dance
Hunt, Kevin 23
hybrid performances 6–7, 14, 99, 107, 138, 144

identity 1, 7, 10, 12, 14, 16, 18, 21, 44, 45, 58, 59–62, 64, 88, 105, 110, 116, 123, 137, 144, 174 n.92
Ingamells, Rex 58, 70
international tours 47, 60, 77, 94, 102–4, 107, 109, 111, 117–19, 122, 123, 131, 144

Jackomos, Alick 48
Jacob, Jackson 193 n.59
Jalkarara, Talbert 121, 191 n.37
Japan 119, 121, 174 n.7
Jayila 184 n.38
jindyworobak 58, 70, 115, 116

## Index

Johnson, Carole 65, 129, 144, 200 n.73
Johnson, King Mickie (Mickey) 40, 136
Johnson, Peter 36
Johnston, Laurel Nganyun (Cooper) 50
Jones, Jessie 50
Josephson, Joshua 42
Jubilee (of Federation – 1951) 1, 12, 63–75, 77, 79, 81, 83, 85, 89, 90, 137, 143, 154 n.2

Kaberry, Phyllis 79, 82
Kalton Williams, Gordon 145
Kantilla, Felix 184 n.38
Kauanui, J. Kēhaulani 155 n.11
Kelly, A. C. 96, 101, 182 n.10
Kennedy, Keith 30–1, 196 n.15
Kerinaiua, Henry 121, 191 n.37
Kerinaiua, Max 121, 191 n.37
Kerinaiua, Walter 184 n.38
Khattak Dancers 106
Kinchela, Jack 33
King Jr, Martin Luther 18
kinship networks 11, 37, 133
Kiwat, Jardine 95
Knopoff, Stephen 145
Kolumboort, Harry 122
Konishi, Shino 139
Koori 4, 5
Kulangoo, William 186 n.58
Kurnell 9, 31, 32, 49, 127, 156 n.20, 189 n.1

La Perouse (Guriwal) 16, 21, 26, 28, 56, 72, 73, 88, 113, 128, 129, 161 n.2, 168 n.12
La Perouse Aboriginal Reserve 9, 12, 15, 16, 21, 25, 26, 28, 29, 31, 32, 34, 39, 49, 56, 73, 128, 136, 161 n.2, 168 n.12
Laiwanga, Djoli 104, 121, 122, 186 n.58, 191 n.37
Laiwanga, Silver 186 n.58
Lake Tyers Concert Party 38, 136
Lake Tyers Mission Station 12, 38, 48, 52, 72, 90, 136, 164 n.50, 191 n.37
land rights 6, 129, 138, 193 n.56
Lanley, Larry 193 n.59

Laurence, Reg 177 n.46
Lavett, Tommy 177 n.46
Lawrence, Marjorie 54, 170 n.50
Lee, Georgia, *see* Pitt, Dulcie
Lee, Sara, 56
Leedy, Larry 177 n.46
Leslie, Michael 144
Lethbridge, Dr H. O. 2, 12, 43
Lhotsky, John 42, 43, 166 n.87; *A Song of the Women of the Menero Tribe*, 42
Lidju-Unga, Jackie 186 n.58
Lim, Liza 145
Lingabani, Dick 186 n.58
Little, Eddie 168 n.12
Little, Freddie 97, 182 n.15
Little, Jackie 168 n.12
Little, Jimmy 96, 97, 128, 150, 182 n.15
Little, Jimmy Sr. 96, 168 n.12
Loam, Alfred S.; *Aboriginal Songs* 2, 12, 13, 42, 43, 70, 75, 77, 78, 116, 128, 166 n.91, 167 n.94, 179 n.80, 179 n.81
Lockwood, Douglas 45
Longfellow, Henry Wadsworth 68
Lonsdale, Anthony 194 n.75
Lonsdale, Camden 194 n.75
Lonsdale, Deborah 194 n.75
Lonsdale, Peter 194 n.75
Lovejoy, Robin 134
Lovett, John 4
Lovett, May 52
Lukanau, Billy 186 n.58

Mabo, Eddie 184 n.39
Madaingu, Roger 186 n.58
Madden, Jim 128, 194 n.75
Maljina, Williw 186 n.58
Manaberu, Johnny 186 n.58
Manaberu, Peter 186 n.58
Mandela, Nelson 18
Manunggurr, Wulurrk 121, 191 n.37
Manyita, George 186 n.58
Maori music and dance 77, 78, 80, 81, 97, 105, 125, 173 n.84, 193 n.57, 194 n.71
Mapotic Cinema Auckland 37, 157 n.38
Maralung, Alan 186 n.58

Marett, Allan 133
Marr, Ron 168 n.19
Mason, Ben 50
Mau 184 n.38
Mawng 117, 141, 142
Maxwell Davies, Peter 140, 142, 143
Maymuru, Narritjin 93, 184 n.38, 185 n.44
Maynor, Dorothy 39, 77
Maza, Bob 76, 144
McCarthy, Fred 9, 101, 124
McCredie, Andrew 115
McDonald, Ningan Malcolm 50
McEwan, John 33
McGregor, Russell 7
McGuiness, Olive 97
McKay, Judith 25
McKenzie, Kerry 95
McKinnon, George 169 n.28, 177 n.46
McKinnon, Joyce 52, 169 n.28
McLean, Ian 14, 133
McLenaghan, Rex 194 n.75
Meale, Richard 187 n.66, 189 n.6
Melba Conservatorium of Music 54–6, 70, 168 n.15
Memmott, Paul 25
Menindee Aboriginal Reserve 9, 29, 34–6, 162 n.30
Menuhin, Yehudi 106
Menzies, Prime Minister Robert 63, 68
Merikula, Les 186 n.58
Meston, Archibald 9, 154 n.3
mia mia 38 (*see also* gunya)
Mickie, King, *see* Johnson, King Mickie
Miller, May (O'Brien) 50
Miller, Mary (Pearson) 139, 141
Mills, Richard 145
Milne, J. R. (Jock) 36, 38, 48, 163 n.39
missions 35, 63, 68, 88, 79, 135, 150, 164, 157 n.32
modernist music 69, 131–2, 135, 147, 197 n.21
Moffat, Foster 177 n.46
Monk, Varney 39, 40, 128, 136; *Collits' Inn*, 39, 40, 128, 136
Moomba Festival (Melbourne) 83, 181 n.103 (*see also* Aboriginal Moomba)

Moreen, Rusty 99, 183 n.28
Moreton-Robinson, Aileen 10, 137
Morris, Bronk 168 n.19
Morris, Rex 168 n.19
Morrison, Prime Minister Scott 155 n.18
Moses, Charles 67–8, 175 n.22
Mosik (Mosek, Mosec) 46, 47, 61, 125
Mountford, C. P. 9, 52, 60, 61, 69, 77–9, 173 n.81, 176 n.27, 179 n.79, 180 n.83; *Walkabout*, 52
Moyle, Alice 95, 101, 110, 118, 182 n.9
Mt Margaret Native Minstrels 49
Mudburra 5
Mullett, Ted (Chook) 52, 72, 136, 137, 163 n.48
multiculturalism 98, 106
Mulun 184 n.38
Mumbler (Mumbulla), Percy 29–30, 168 n.12
Mumbler, Eva 97
Mumbulla, Frank 168 n.12
Mungalili, *see* Mununggurr, Munguli
Munggin, Barney 93, 131, 184 n.38
Mununggurr (Monangurr), Munguli 184 n.38, 190 n.24, 193 n.59
Murdoch, James 58, 115, 140, 167 n.99, 172 n.71
Murri 81, 181
Musica Viva 59, 69, 116, 126, 141, 142, 175 n.22, 199 n.53; Festivals, 116, 126, 141, 142, 199 n.53

NADOC, *see* National Aborigines Day Observance Committee
Naepels, Michel 4
NAIDOC, *see* National Aborigines Day Observance Committee
NAISDA, *see* National Aboriginal Islander Skills Development Association
Nakata, Martin 3
Nalakan, *see* Wanambi, Nalakan
Namatjira, Albert 8, 70, 87, 90, 157 n.29
Nanganarralil, Frederick 193 n.59
Napuatimi, Declan 184 n.38
Napuatimi, Raphael 184 n.38
Natarajan, Radhika 106

Nathan, Isaac 8, 42, 43
National Aboriginal Islander Skills Development Association (NAISDA) 66, 76, 114, 129, 144, 158 n.46
National Aborigines Day Observance Committee (NADOC) 13, 94–9, 111, 120, 182 n.5, 183 n.22
national anthem 127–8
national style 27, 40–1, 44, 58, 64, 110
National Theatre Opera and Ballet 1, 171 n.59
nationalism 42, 62, 106
Nerang, Stanley 177 n.46
New Deal (NT) 8, 32–3, 139
New Theatre 46, 49, 59, 88, 89; *Coming Our Way*, 49, 88; *Fountains Beyond*, 53; Melbourne, 50, 52, 72, 75, 87, 88, 144; Sydney, 52, 63, 76; *White Justice*, 50–3, 87, 88
Ngarigu (Ngarigo) 12, 15, 42, 157 n.32, 166 n.87, 169 n.25
Ngarra Burria; First Peoples Composers Initiative 147–8, 152–3
Ngiyampaa 12, 35, 37, 69
Nicholls, Lillian 177 n.46
Nicholls, Pastor Douglas (Doug) 11, 13, 19, 33, 35, 38, 56, 65, 70–4, 89, 90, 139, 174 n.8
Nicol, Wayne 144
Nindethana Theatre 76, 88, 114, 144
Ninnal, Cyril 193 n.59
noble savage 25
Noonuccal, Oodgeroo (Kath Walker) 142, 143, 199 n.60
North Australian Eisteddfod 13, 94, 95, 98, 105, 111, 123, 144, 182 n.4, 183 n.27
Northern Territory Welfare Office 94, 99, 103, 119, 121, 125, 183 n.31
nostalgia 8–9, 106
NSW Conservatorium of Music (Sydney Conservatorium of Music) 15, 44, 58, 69, 77, 97, 101, 105, 139
Nugent, Maria 5, 28, 155 n.18, 161 n.2
Nyungar (Noongar) 34

Olympics 82, 83, 117–19
Onus, Cissy 73

Onus, Eric 50–4, 83, 87, 90, 139, 144, 169 n.28, 177 n.46
Onus, Tiriki 11, 51, 71, 85–91, 137, 177 n.41, 178 n.65, 197 n.28
Onus, William (Bill) 9, 11, 13, 33, 49, 51, 52, 54, 56, 60, 71–5, 83, 137, 138, 139, 178 n.65, 181 n.103, 197 n.15
Onus, Winnie (Winifred) 83, 177 n.46, 169 n.28
oral history 3–6, 11, 20–1, 49, 82, 140, 144, 155 n.15
Outback Australia Exhibition 38

Paakantji 36, 37, 69
Pageant of Nationhood 107–10, 188 n.75
Palm Island Aboriginal Settlement 34, 73, 74, 177 n.53
Pamagore, Paddy 186 n.58
Park, Agnes May 36
Parks, Rosa 18
Parsons, Charlie 168 n.12
Parsons, Clem 168 n.12
Parsons, Costin 168 n.12
Passi, Sam 100, 184 n.39–40
Patten, Jack 18, 33
Patten, Selina 33
Pauitjimi, Daniel 184 n.38
Pauntalura, Noel 184 n.38
Pearson, James 42
Peart, Donald 114, 187 n.66, 189 n.6
Peckham, Ray 64, 75, 87, 90
Penberthy, James 58, 82, 122, 140–3, 181 n.95, 187 n.66, 198 n.47, 200 n.64; *Brolga*, 82, 140, 141; *Dalgerie*, 82, 122, 140, 141, 143; *Euroka*, 58
performative cultures 4, 6, 7, 15, 27, 30, 37, 51, 52, 54, 57, 62, 70, 73, 86, 93, 94, 111, 123, 131, 185 n.44
Perkins, Charles 97
Perth Festival 103, 141, 143, 185 n.43, 185 n.49, 200 n.65, 201 n.77
Peters, Doug 97
Pettitt, C. E. 30
Phillip, Captain Arthur 35, 37, 107–8
Picanniny Pete 177 n.46
Pintubi 134

Pitjantjatjara 52, 71, 74, 134
Pitt, Dulcie (Georgia Lee) 48, 72, 90, 168 n.17, 177 n.46
Pittman, Eileen 29
*Pix* magazine 54, 74, 134
Poignant, Roslyn 25
Polipuamini, Timothy 184 n.38
Portaminni, Regina (now Kantilla) 125, 193 n.59, 193 n.61
Porter, John 38
Post, Joseph 106
postcolonizing 10, 132, 135, 137, 138
Price, Leontyne 82, 200 n.64
Prichard, Katharine Susannah 82, 140
primitivism 43, 57, 73, 132
Protection era 7–8, 25–7, 32–3, 156 n.28
protectionist thinking 7–8, 33, 36–7, 67, 119
protest 3, 12, 18, 19, 22, 34, 36, 37, 53, 54, 63, 64, 85, 99, 113, 125, 127–9, 137, 144, 156 n.21, 192–3 n.56
Purantatameri, Leon 193 n.59
Purfleet Aboriginal Station 48
Purga Mission 54
Puruntatameri, Barry 184 n.38
Puruntatameri, Eddie 184 n.38, 193 n.59
Puruntatameri, Freddie 184 n.38
Puruntatameri, Justin 121, 184 n.38, 191 n.37
Puruntatameri, Leon 193 n.59
Puruntatameri, Timothy 184 n.38

Queensland Chief Protector of Aborigines (also Native Affairs) 34–5, 38, 54, 74

Racial Discrimination Act 10, 129
Randall, Bob 145
Randall, Dorothea 144
Rangers' League 12, 25, 27
re-enactment 9, 14, 30, 33–8, 48, 69, 107–8, 113, 127–9, 155–6 n.18, 162 n.30, 189 n.1, 193 n.63, 194 n.73, 194 n.78
referendum for constitutional change (1967) 10, 14, 81, 84, 86, 95, 98, 111, 113–14, 117–18, 119, 123, 129, 143, 156 n.21, 189 n.2-3

Reid, Rex 1, 59, 63, 64, 72, 81, 87; *Corroboree* (*see* Antill, John: *Corroboree*)
Rembarrnga 1, 103, 131, 195 n.1
replacement (erasure) 4, 17, 19, 21–2, 32, 62, 107–9, 132, 135, 137, 139, 155 n.11, 174 n.92, 187 n.72
representation 2, 3, 6–12, 14, 27, 29, 31, 33, 34, 38, 39, 40, 43, 46, 47, 54, 57, 65–6, 69, 73, 74, 77, 78, 81–4, 87, 93–5, 97, 102, 105–7, 109, 113, 114, 117–20, 123, 129, 131–9, 142–5, 186 n.50, 200 n.65; self-representation, 8, 69–70, 73, 87, 93, 94, 105, 111, 113, 127, 143
Ridgeway, Robert 194 n.75
Riki 184 n.38
Roach, Stan 128, 194 n.75
Roach, Vera 128, 194 n.75
Roberts, Alby 37, 157 n.38
Robeson, Paul 39
Roddick, John 194 n.75
rodeos 38
Rosaldo, Renato 9
Rose, Deborah Bird 5, 158 n.44
Rosenwax, Nathalie 39
Rosie, Queen 40, 49, 136, 137
Rotumah, Grayson 95
Roughsey, Arthur 193 n.59
Rowse, Tim 5, 33
Russell, Arthur 168 n.19
Russell, Elsie 168 n.19
Russell, Henry 168 n.19
Russell, Priscillie 168 n.19
Russell, Reg 168 n.19

Sahlins, Marshall 4
Sainsbury, Chris 147, 152, 201 n.87
Samuels, Edmond; *The Highwayman*, 72, 136
Saunders, Allan 168 n.19, 177 n.46
Saunders, Joan 177 n.46
Scath, Jamesy 52
Schultz, Chester 95
Scott, James 83
Sculthorpe, Peter 14, 43, 58, 59, 82, 106–7, 110, 115, 116, 131, 141–3, 145, 159 n.54, 181 n.95, 187 n.66-7, 188

n.86, 190 n.15, 197 n.15, 199–200 n.63; *Djilile*, 116, 142; *Dua Chant*, 116, 142; *Into the Dreaming/For Cello Alone*, 43, 116; *Kakadu*, 116, 142; *Lullaby*, 116; *Maranoa Lullaby*, 43; *Port Essington*, 116, 142; *Requiem*, 43, 116, 145; *Sun Music I*, 59, 110; *The Fifth Continent*, 110; *The Stars Turn*, 141–2; *Two Aboriginal Songs*, 43
segregation 60, 71, 81, 98, 172 n.79
self-determination 7, 10, 14, 76, 91, 103, 114, 122, 143, 144
settler colonialism 2, 27, 47, 105, 107, 109, 132–4, 137, 139, 155 n.11
Shankar, Ravi 106
Shawn, Ted 45, 46, 61, 83, 125, 200 n.65
Sheppard, Elizabeth 147
Shivaram 65
Short, Johnny 122
Simms, Wesley 12, 25–6, 28
Simpson, Leanne Betasamosake 139, 140
Simpson, Nardi 11, 147–53
Sims, Wesley 25
Sippe, George 42
Sitsky, Larry 115, 187 n.66, 189 n.6
Smith, Linda Tuhiwai 3
social Darwinism 79
songs: Aboriginal (*see* Aboriginal and Torres Strait Islander music: songs); folk, 12, 41, 94, 115, 128, 129, 128, 138, 145; hymns, 15, 16, 23, 48, 100, 183 n.34; minstrel, 48, 49, 81; piano accompanied, 23, 43, 77, 98; spirituals, 49, 87, 159 n.5; trade, 121, 123, 191 n.41; *Waltzing Matilda*, 99, 128
South Pacific Festival of Arts 125, 193 n.63
souvenirs 83, 86, 89–91
Spencer, Baldwin 61, 78, 118, 133–5, 143, 196 n.5
Spinifex Lands, Elders of the 145
St Denis, Ruth 61
Stanhope, Paul 146
Stanley, Noel 182 n.15
stolen wages 74, 178 n.59
Stone, Cheryl 144

Strehlow, T. G. H. 9, 61, 78
strikes 23, 63, 75, 88, 178 n.65
Sullivan, Vince 194 n.75
Sutherland, Margaret 44, 47, 55–8, 82, 126, 141, 167 n.99, 170–1 n.54, 171 n.63, 180 n.89, 181 n.94, 187 n.66; *Haunted Hills*, 44, 57, 82, 180 n.89; *Land of Ours*, 44; *The Bush*, 56, 57; *The Young Kabbarli*, 44, 141
Sydney Conservatorium of Music, *see* NSW Conservatorium of Music
Sydney Harbour Bridge 9, 12, 19, 20, 21, 28, 29, 34, 36, 48, 161 n.9
Sydney Opera House 126, 128, 141, 188 n.84, 193 n.63, 194 n.70–1
Sydney Symphony Orchestra 12, 44, 58, 106, 110, 117, 126

Talonga, Richard 144
Tasmanian Symphony Orchestra 41
Tate, Henry 42
Taylor, Cecil 120
Thomas, Albert 168 n.12
Thomas, Anne (Wirrimah) 138
Thomas, Arthur 168 n.12
Thomas, Cecil Jnr. 168 n.12
Thomas, Lois 50
Thomas, Max 168 n.12
Thomas, Ronald 168 n.12
Thomas, Ted (Guboo) 29, 138, 168 n.12
Thomas, Whaler Billy 168 n.12
Thorpe, Kirsten 20
Timbery, Emma 39
Timbery, Joe 73, 74, 97, 128
Tipungwuti, Bennie 184 n.38, 185 n.49
Tipungwuti, Christopher 184 n.38, 185 n.49
Tipungwuti, Conrad Paul 184 n.38
Tipungwuti, Dermot 185 n.49
Tipungwuti, Hector 184 n.38, 185 n.49
Tipungwuti, Jacinta 100, 101, 183 n.35
Tipungwuti, Simon 193 n.59
Tiwi 63, 76, 93, 100, 101, 146, 147, 193 n.61
Tiwi Islands 13, 93, 100, 103, 125, 184 n.38, 185 n.49
Tiwi Strong Women's Group 147

Tjupurrula, Nosepeg Junkata 74
tjurunga (also tjuringa, churinga) 30, 79, 118, 132–4, 196 n.12, 196 n.15
Torres Strait Islanders 48, 72, 74, 90, 100, 128
Troy, Jakelin 15, 166 n.87, 169 n.25
Trudinger, Ronald M. 71; *Nananala Kututja*, 71
Tucker, Margaret (Lilardia) 33, 48, 52, 56, 71, 83, 177 n.36, 177 n.46
Tuhiwai Smith, Linda 3
Turnbull, Bill 168 n.19

Uluru 2, 52
Unaipon, David 38
unions 55, 60, 87, 138; Actors Equity, 58, 74, 113; North Australian Workers' Union (NAWU), 63, 64, 75
United States of America (United States) 2, 39, 42, 45, 47, 54, 56, 59, 60, 62, 70, 71, 77, 78, 90, 103, 116, 123, 164 n.60, 170 n.54, 172 n.79, 187 n.69
Unity Dance Group 43, 63, 75, 76, 87, 145

van Praagh, Peggy 126
Vaucluse House 30, 34
vaudeville 48, 52, 54, 78, 81, 86, 89, 137, 138
Veracini, Lorenzo 135
Vētra, Vija 66

Wadeye 121, 122, 185 n.49
Wadaymu 184 n.38
Wainburranga, *see* Fordham, Paddy Wainburranga
Wake, Tom 45
Walford, Arch 95
Walker, Kath, *see* Noonuccal, Oodgeroo
Walker, Kim 76, 144, 200 n.74
Walker, Margaret 43, 51, 63, 75, 76, 79, 80, 88, 144, 145, 178 n.70
Wallaga Lakes 48, 168 n.12
Walley, Richard 141
Walters, Tom 177 n.46
Wambunyi, Felix 121, 191 n.37
Wanambi, Nalakan 190 n.24, 193 n.59
Wangkangurru (Wonkonguru) 38

Ward, Stuart 62
Warlpiri 74, 79, 98, 134, 150, 180 n.82, 192 n.43, 196 n.12
Warrini 184 n.38
Warusam, Jensen 95
Waterhouse, Richard 10
Waters, Fred (Nadpur) 63–4, 75, 76
Waters, Thorold 41, 44
Watt, Gordon 193 n.59
Wave Hill walk-off 156 n.21
West Australian Symphony Orchestra 145
White Australia policy 39, 65
White Cliffs Aboriginal Settlement 73
Wikmunea, Horace 122
Wild Australia Show 25
Wild West shows 38, 164 n.54
Wilfred, Benjamin 146
Williams, Anzac 36
Williams, Candy 49, 96, 97, 182 n.15
Williams, Charlie 71, 83, 177 n.46
Williams, Gary 113, 189 n.3
Williams, Margaret 96
Williams, Mervyn 177 n.46
Williamson, Malcolm 69, 106, 115, 142, 143
Wilson Hayes, Lola 56
Wilson, Les (L. G.) 134
Winunguj, George 116–17, 122, 141, 142, 144, 145
Wiradjuri 42, 64, 75
Wirth's Olympia 13, 52–4, 72, 83, 86–9, 138
Wolfe, Patrick 10, 61, 133, 135, 143, 155 n.11, 158 n.44, 196 n.5
Woneamini, Matthew 184 n.38, 193 n.59
Wongrem, Jimmy 36
Wooderbong Aboriginal Reserve 120
Worgan, George 43
World War II 10, 12, 46–7, 48, 62, 66, 139, 173 n.89
Wuki Wuki, Tommy 186 n.58
Wunungmurra (Kumana), Yangarin 118, 125, 184 n.38, 190 n.24, 193 n.59
Wunungmurra, Banambi 121, 191 n.37
Wurrpen, Lawrence (Urban) 63, 75, 76
Wurundjeri 85
Wurungu, Johnny 186 n.58

Yalata Mission 74
Yangarin, Joe, *see* Wunungmurra (Kumana), Yangarin
Yeinidi-Wanga, John 186 n.58
yidaki, *see* didjeridu
Yilimbirri Ensemble 146
Yiribuma, Mick 186 n.58
Yirrkala 93, 100, 103, 118, 123, 125, 141, 184 n.38, 185 n.44, 185 n.49
Yirrkala bark petition (Yolngu Bark petition) 156 n.21

Yolngu 99, 118, 125, 156 n.21, 185 n.44, 192 n.43
Yorta Yorta 11, 85, 88, 144, 147
Young Wagilak Group 146
Young, Eileen 177 n.46
Yuin 12
Yunupingu, Mulun 121, 191 n.37
Yupawanga, Jimmy 186 n.58
Yuwaalaraay 11, 148–52

www.ingramcontent.com/pod-product-compliance
Lightning Source LLC
Chambersburg PA
CBHW072145290426
44111CB00012B/1978